MODERNISM: *Challenges and Perspectives*

MODERNISM

Challenges and Perspectives

Edited by
Monique Chefdor
Ricardo Quinones
and
Albert Wachtel

UNIVERSITY OF ILLINOIS PRESS
Urbana and Chicago

"Secret Languages: The Roots of Musical Modernism," by
Robert P. Morgan, first appeared in *Critical Inquiry* 10:3
(1984). Reprinted with permission. © 1984 by the University of Chicago.

This book is printed on acid-free paper.

LIBRARY OF CONGRESS CATALOGING IN PUBLICATION DATA

Main entry under title:

Modernism : challenges and perspectives.

  Bibliography: p.
  Includes index.
  1. Modernism (Art)—Addresses, essays, lectures.
2. Arts, Modern—19th century—Addresses, essays, lectures.
3. Arts, Modern—20th century—Addresses, essays, lectures. I. Chefdor, Monique. II. Quinones, Ricardo.
III. Wachtel, Albert.
NX454.5.M63M6 1986   700'.9'04   84-21932
ISBN 0-252-01207-0

Contents

Section 3. The Far Side of Modernism
Presented by Albert Wachtel

Preface

The collection of essays presented in this volume constitutes a selection from papers given at the Comparative Literature
Conference on Modernism recently held at the Claremont Colleges and
the Claremont Colleges comparative literature lecture series on Modernism
that followed. Organized by Professors Monique Chefdor and Ricardo
Quinones with a committee of ten other colleagues from the Claremont
Colleges representing five disciplines (literature, history of art, music,
dramatic arts, and history), the conference brought together guest speakers
from four foreign countries and several major American universities,
with 253 registered participants coming from Canada and ten states in
various regions of the United States. Not only did the speakers represent
different national cultures and disciplines, they also reflected a broad
range of scholarly approaches; younger scholars who had not yet achieved
international reputation were invited as well as leading authorities in
the field.

The realization of this project was made possible by a grant from
the Rockefeller Foundation, contributions from each of the five Claremont
Colleges and the Claremont Graduate School, the Mellon funds for the
Claremont Colleges, a Scripps College Professor Emerita, and travel
grants to foreign speakers from the French government through the
French Cultural Services in Los Angeles and the Fundaçao de Amparo
a Pesquisa do Estado de São Paulo.

The purpose of the conference was not to compile yet another survey
of Modernism in literature and the arts nor to propose a synopsis of
Modernism in a "state of the arts" fashion. Nor was it to draw the
definitive chart of the distinctions between Modernism and its successor,
usurper, or illegitimate progeny, postmodernism. All these tasks have
already been undertaken repeatedly without ever bringing debates to a
close or reducing the vigor and abundance of scholarly discourse on

Preface

Modernism. A mere glance at bibliographical entries during the last two decades gives evidence of the intensified interest in issues raised by Modernism in all its varieties and this interest shows no sign of abating. The urge to take the measure of the Modernist achievement in this fourth quarter of the century appears to be increasingly pressing. The goal of this conference, therefore, was to bring into focus some of the directions taken by this recently growing corpus of Modernist scholarship, and to do so by drawing together a variety of viewpoints within international and interdisciplinary perspectives.

The array of national literatures and arts discussed was vast enough to satisfy the most exacting comparatist. The intent, however, was not to present an exhaustive panorama but rather, in true comparative spirit, to concentrate on significant areas of exchange and convergence, whether these were cultural, stylistic, or ideological. Thus survey-like considerations of independent national Modernisms have been avoided and the input from disciplines other than literature purposely centered on points of convergence. It should also be noted, perhaps, that, in the same spirit, no particular mode of criticism was imposed as a predominant approach. For the sake of ternary balance, to "international" and "interdisciplinary" one might add "interdenominational." These have also been the guiding principles in making the further selections for this publication.

Two introductory essays by the conference organizers outline the overall direction and significance of the volume. The articles presented here have been grouped into three sections, an overview of the origins and ideologies of modernism, analyses of its practice, and finally far-ranging discussions of its current manifestations. A bibliographical appendix offers a selected list of titles of particular interest in recent studies of Modernism. Whereas the selection made for this volume could not be all-inclusive, the bibliography extends beyond the geographical limits represented in the present essays. For instance, entries on Brazilian Modernism include several publications in Portuguese and in French by one of the conference participants.

The PMLA editorial policy of giving quotations in their original languages followed by translations in English has been generally adopted. Exceptions to this rule have only been made in three instances: once when quotations are only given in the original out of respect for the author's commitment to make meaning clear without resorting to "inevitably inadequate translations," and twice when only English translations are given because the insertion of the original language would break the flow of ideas without offering the reader any nuance which is not adequately supplied in the translation. Unless otherwise indicated in the notes, quotations are translated by the editors. Deliberately no attempt has been made by the editors to adopt a unified policy of capitalizing "Modernism" or not throughout the book. The very discrepancy of spelling itself reflects a deeper discrepancy among various national interpretations. Consistency, however, has been observed within each individual paper and to avoid any possible ambiguity the French *modernité* has been kept as such throughout the volume.

The editors would like to express their deep gratitude to the Rockefeller Foundation, to the presidents of Scripps College, Claremont McKenna College, Claremont Graduate School, Harvey Mudd College, Pitzer College, Pomona College, and to all other previously mentioned donors for supporting a project without which this volume could not have appeared. Nor would this conference have taken place without the two-year-long collaboration of the entire organizing committee whose members are listed at the end of this volume. From among them, Thomas Flaherty, Henry Jerome Gibbons, A. Kent Gravett, and Arthur D. Stevens should be singled out for their contributions to the program in the fields of music, history, drama, and art, respectively. Michael F. Harper, Arden Reed, and Howard T. Young deserve a special word of thanks for their advisory role in the initial stages of the editorial work.

For the preparation of this volume more particularly, the editors first wish to thank all of the contributors for their prompt and understanding collaboration. For the manuscript preparation and other related secretarial tasks they are greatly indebted to two Scripps College comparative literature honors students: Esther Allen, whose reliability and dedication throughout the academic year has been invaluable, and Drucilla James, who devoted several weeks of her summer to the completion of the manuscript. Drucilla James also deserves the editorial committee's appreciation for her assistance in preparing the bibliographical appendix. Last but not least, Esther Allen must also be credited for her translations into English of Michel Décaudin's and Claude Leroy's articles, originally written in French. Although the editors ultimately accept responsibility for the versions given, only relatively minor revisions were made.

The Editors
M.C., R.Q., A.W.

Organizing Committee

MONIQUE CHEFDOR, Professor of French and Comparative Literature, Chairman, Comparative Literature, Scripps College. Conference Organizer.

THOMAS FLAHERTY, Assistant Professor of Music, Scripps College.

HENRY JEROME GIBBONS, Assistant Professor of History, Claremont Graduate School.

A. KENT GRAVETT, Assistant Professor of Theater, Pomona College.

MICHAEL F. HARPER, Assistant Professor of British and American Literature, Scripps College.

ROBERTA JOHNSON, Associate Professor of Spanish. Chairman, Department of Hispanic Studies, Scripps College.

RICARDO J. QUINONES, Professor of Comparative Literature, Claremont McKenna College. Conference Co-organizer.

ARDEN REED, Assistant Professor of English, Pomona College.

J'NAN SELLERY, Professor of English, Harvey Mudd College.

ARTHUR D. STEVENS, Associate Professor of Art History. Convener, Departments of Art, Music, and Dance, Scripps College.

ALBERT WACHTEL, Professor of English, Pitzer College.

HOWARD T. YOUNG, Edwin Sexton and Edna Patrick Smith Professor of Romance Languages. Chairman, Modern Languages and Literatures, Pomona College.

Student Assistants to the Editorial Committee

ESTHER ALLEN, 1983 Scripps graduate with Honors in Comparative Literature. Presently, graduate student at New York University, Department of Comparative Literature.

DRUCILLA JAMES, 1983 Scripps graduate with Honors in Comparative Literature. Presently, graduate student at the University of Chicago, Department of Comparative Literature.

Monique Chefdor

Modernism: Babel Revisited?

This is certainly not the first nor will it be the last attempt to map out the Modernist territory to be made by critics of various nations, creeds, and allegiances. The mercurial character of Modernism makes it an ever-renewed cause for debates and discoveries. It may indeed be a "featherbed for critics and professors," as one character quipped in the short story written by Roger Shattuck for the conference.[1] It is, nevertheless, also strongly dominated by what Shattuck perceptively recognizes as a tendency toward the "metaphysical picaresque" as a unifying genre. When confronted with the variety of conflicting interpretations it continues to evoke one might prefer, however, to share with Claude Leroy the feeling that Modernism is a tantalizing, never-surrendering virginal "tease" which, like Madame Récamier, has "distributed dividends without touching its capital."

One of the major obstacles encountered by critics of Modernism, particularly by comparatists, is the semantic confusion generated by the term itself. No one would take exception to Malcolm Bradbury and James McFarlane's statement in their preface to the 1976 Pelican guide to Modernism that "one of the defining features of Modernism has been the breaking down of traditional frontiers in matters of literary and cultural concern."[2] The international character of Modernism is taken for granted and yet no international agreement has ever been reached on the use and significance of the term. The present collection of essays constitutes no exception to the rule. Representatives of Anglo-American schools of criticism capitalize the word since to them it represents a historically and conceptually defined movement in literature and the arts. Their continental European counterparts do not since they conceive it mostly as a concept encompassing the endless variety of "isms" that have mushroomed in the Western world since the late 1880s. Moreover, they tend to question the fundamental validity of the term and prefer to use "modern," "avant-garde," and *"modernité"* instead. To make matters even simpler *modernité* simply cannot be translated in English since its cognate actually means what the French understand by "modernism"! Only the Hispanic and Luso-Brazilian traditions are saved from such ambiguities, since in their case *modernismo* designates clearly delineated movements. One cannot, however, escape the irony that the same name in Spain and Hispanic Latin America applies to a movement akin to symbolism whereas in Brazil it refers to a radically avant-garde reaction against the symbolist influence.

Our purpose, nevertheless, is not to establish a new taxonomy of the Modern. These dilemmas have been signaled several times. In the introduction to their volume, Bradbury and McFarlane themselves proceeded with a review of these "international connotations." A year before, in a *Clio* article, Matei Calinescu (who, in this volume, presents his views on Modernism and ideology) had cautioned his readers against the excessively wide meaning of modernism in contemporary American criticism.[3] Another European scholar in America, the late Harvard professor Renato Poggioli, in his landmark study *The Theory of the Avant-Garde* uses the term to designate a broad cultural trend that he perceives as degenerative and denounces as an "unconscious parody of modernity," as "the honest-to-goodness nemesis of modernity."[4] The very existence, in Anglo-American critical vocabulary, of the expression "High Modernism" to distinguish a more lofty, aristocratic form of early Modernism (Mann, Proust, Woolf, Rilke, etc.) from the variety of iconoclastic experiments of the avant-gardes, is in itself indicative of a certain degree of uneasiness with the expanded use of the word as an umbrella term.

Paradoxically enough, although the cultural innovations it is meant to identify are as polymorphous and protean as those of its matrix, the derivative term "postmodernism" has not encountered the same difficulties. As Ihab Hassan points out in his contribution to this volume, it suffers from as much "semantic instability," since no "clear consensus about its meaning exists among scholars." Yet it seems to cross lexical boundaries with less reticence. Of somewhat parochial character in its first North American literary usage, postmodernism is becoming part and parcel of the international vocabulary of criticism. Some in Germany (Bürger, Habermas) tend to prefer the alternate "post-avant-gardes," and for a while the French cautiously spoke about the "post-modern" (e.g., Lyotard), judiciously avoiding falling back into the snares of the ity/ism ambiguity; but now postmodernism-e-ismo or -ismus is of current usage in France, Italy, and Germany. Hassan refers us to Köhler's history of the term in the German *Amerikastudien* and, in the spring of 1983, for instance, the Parisian literary journal *Babylone* devoted its second issue to a full dossier on "le post-modernisme." There is still some margin of dissent, though, since to the option of capitalization or not is added that of hyphenation!

The posthumous implicit acceptance of the root element "modernism" as a common denominator makes a reexamination of the Modernist achievement in an international context even more pressing. In a friendly parody of another one of our contributors (Mary Ann Caws) one might say that this POST-erity calls for a remembering and RE-membering of the parts of the body of the fostering corpus. To judge by the number of discussion sessions recently organized on diverse aspects of Modernism at the MLA and other professional organizations here and abroad, the urge is felt widely. In March of 1983, for instance, (almost a year after our own California international gathering) the Collège de France in Paris invited Jürgen Habermas for a series of four lectures on "concepts de la modernité." From a hermeneutic standpoint, indeed, an endless series of questions arises from the initial paradox inherent in the semi-universal adoption of a term built on what some still view as conceptual shifting sands.

The overtly temporal implications of this popular qualifier of cultural change seem to indicate a general agreement to declare a radical rupture, to record (condone?) the end of an era. Thus Barthelme's *Dead Father* is received as an appropriate emblem for the Modernist past, a past, says Alan Wilde ironically in *Horizons of Assent* (1981), "alive enough . . . to remain a provocation to different factions of the postmodern camp, an incitement to sometimes irascible, sometimes querulous literary and academic violence."[5] The same year, across the Atlantic, the more nostalgic but no less ironic voice of Michel Leiris, musing in *Le ruban au cou d'Olympia* about the various styles of modernities as so many forms of a new *mal du siècle,* wonders whether "cette modernité . . . n'est pas . . . une préoccupation de dilettante qu'il vaudrait mieux ranger au magasin des accessoires" (this *modernité . . .* is not . . . a dilettante's concern which one would be well advised to relegate to the junk shop).[6]

The vitality of the ongoing critical discourse on Modernism suffices to allay those fears. The roots of the issue, however, do not lie in a matter of periodization, as Hassan's brief recapitulation of the history of the term at the beginning of his essay usefully recalls.

Postmodernism does not succeed Modernism. It "evokes what it wishes to surpass or suppress" says Hassan, hence its inevitable affinities with the "irreverent spirit of the avant-garde." The analysts of post-modernism all recognize similar symptoms in earlier manifestations of the Modern. Joyce, Duchamp, and Dada are recurrently cited as examples. William Carlos Williams is rediscovered in the light of postmodernism (Ridell's *The Inverted Bell*) in opposition to the paragon of Modernism, T. S. Eliot. The coexistence of both canons is noted in the works of major Modernists. Alan Wilde's convincing demonstration in *Horizons of Assent* of the postmodern elements in Virginia Woolf's later novels is but one recent example. A similar case could easily be made for many other writers and artists, such as Italo Calvino, Borges, Blaise Cendrars, Günter Grass, Garcia Marquez, Picasso, and Picabia, among others. Is Alexander Blok's *The Twelve* postmodern and *To a Stranger* Modern? The answer ultimately depends on the reader's angle. The apocalyptic mode that Bensimon rightly perceives in today's creative trends was already pervasive in symbolism, in German expressionism, and in several later representatives of Modernism. Albert Aurier's 1889 eccentric of *Le Moderniste Illustré,* presented by Michel Décaudin, would not be out of place in Los Angeles or New York's postmodern haunts. The list could be endless.

Is not the "irreverence" which postmodernism shares with the avant-gardes part of the typically Modernist subversion of established modes? Here lurks one of the major paradoxes inherent in the concept of post-modernism, which evokes the shadow of Modernism's "major paradox" as identified by Anna Balakian. In view of her theory of bifurcation, would not postmodernism fall within the broader Modernist enterprise, as a prolongation of one of its directions? As Claude Leroy suggests, postmodernism's intended parricide of Modernism implies its own vam-pirization. Ironically—and is not irony a Modernist mode *par excellence?*—postmodernism can legitimately claim autonomous status only if all the more exacerbated expressions of Modernist sensibility are categorized separately as "avant-gardes" (i.e., antimodernist manifestations) and Modernism reduced to its more Olympian High or early Modernist version. Yet, if one agrees with Clement Greenberg that "Modernism has meant . . . the devolution of a tradition" one can without hesitation incorporate postmodernism in the Modernist enterprise. Ihab Hassan's advice not to choose between the One and the Many is certainly a most appropriate conclusion to this volume.

In this last quarter of the century more than ever the international recognition of postmodernism calls for new explorations of the Modernist edifice. As Marcelin Pleynet said only a few years ago in the introduction to a contemporary exhibit on the theme of art and the history of art: "Cette réévaluation de l'ensemble des problèmes que pose la 'modernité' ne fait que s'amorcer" (The process of an overall reevaluation of the problems raised by 'modernity' is barely starting).[7] The point, however, he added, is not to "confondre Histoire et Théorie, Théorie et Système" (confuse History and Theory, Theory and System). This has, unequivocally, been the spirit which brought together the scholars whose present "challenges and perspectives" constitute a major contribution to this ongoing "reevaluation" of Modernism.

Notes

1. Roger Shattuck's short story "The Poverty of Modernism" was published in the 14 Mar. 1983 issue of *The New Republic;* reprinted in *The Innocent Eye* (Farrar, Straus & Giroux, 1985).

2. Malcolm Bradbury and James McFarlane, eds., *Modernism: 1890–1930* (New York: Penguin, 1976), 14.

3. Matei Calinescu, "The Benevolent Monster: Reflections on *Kitsch* as an Aesthetic Concept," *Clio* 6, no. 1 (Fall 1976): 3–21.

4. Renato Poggioli, *The Theory of the Avant-Garde,* trans. Gerald Fitzgerald (Cambridge: Harvard Univ. Press, 1968), 218.

5. Alan Wilde, *Horizons of Assent: Modernism, Postmodernism and the Ironic Imagination* (Baltimore, Md.: Johns Hopkins Univ. Press, 1981), 19.

6. Michel Leiris, *Le Ruban au cou d'Olympia* (Paris: Gallimard, 1981).

7. Marcelin Pleynet, *Documents Sur* 6.7.8. (Sept. 1980): 6.

Ricardo Quinones

From Resistance to Reassessment

It is almost natural that a wide disparity of approaches
and attitudes should exist in a collective enterprise of this sort, and even
more particularly should this be the case with a subject as volatile as
Modernism, which not only nominally but also substantively appears
determined to resist crystallization. Indeed, the surprising point is that
there should emerge any consensus at all. Yet, undeniably, throughout
all these papers, independently conceived (and defended with equal independence), clear common purposes do appear. All are in agreement
that there was a thing, or series of things, with sufficient family resemblance
to bear the surname Modernism (even with all the nuances of distinction
between the more continental "modernité" and the Anglo-American
"Modernism"); that this event (or series of events) was (and is) of
fundamental importance for the cultural life of the twentieth century;
that this event, Modernism, in all of its family affiliations, is pan-European,
even extending to the Americas, North and South; and that this movement
was both independently achieved and reciprocally active in all forms of
art and literature, as well as in the other intellectual disciplines (philosophy,
physics, psychology, for example).

Obviously what we are dealing with is a movement, or series of
related movements, that has acquired such extensive and pervasive cultural
force that it may be said to characterize an epoch. This means that
Modernism needs to be discussed with the same unifying wholeness,
with the same sense of cultural completeness and the same atomistic

discriminations we are accustomed to employ in discussing other such periods, most notably romanticism. In fact, as romanticism dominated the nineteenth century, Modernism has come to dominate the twentieth. This means that while the term "modern" in its various cognative forms has had a long history,[1] it has acquired historical specificity (to borrow Clement Greenberg's phrase from his essay in section one) in our epoch. Its center of intellectual gravity is weightiest in the period extending from the decade prior to World War I into the early years of World War II, and even its dissident heirs (postmodernism) continue to manifest family resemblances somewhat in the way that realism is obviously a derivation of romanticism.

Given the accelerating pace of cultural change in our time, Modernism has moved, in the briefest period, from resistance, to acceptance (even co-optation), and finally to critical reassessment in the public response. While we can set aside those whose instantaneous reaction was one of uncomprehending indignation, we must recognize that not all resistance was similarly uninformed. The more sophisticated complaints are of two sorts: either that Modernism was a mere derivation of romanticism or that Modernism failed to evolve its own positive character and typology. It was either derivative or marred by negativity. Northrop Frye in "The Drunken Boat" has maintained that Modernism had no resources for becoming anything but post-romanticism, and critics like Harold Bloom and George Bornstein continue to follow that argument.[2] Graham Hough in "Reflections on a Literary Revolution," while granting its stylistic difference from romanticism, has argued that Modernism represented no equivalent spiritual shift in values; and Georg Lukács, in "The Ideology of Modernism," seems to be saying something similar when he declares that Modernism has failed to evolve a stable typology.[3]

On the other hand, all of the essays in this volume are in agreement that Modernism (whatever its roots in nineteenth-century culture—and they are extensive) was something special in itself, that in fact the moment of sustained creativity by which Modernist artists and writers became recognizably themselves was marked by a rupture either with the social forces around them or with the cultural traditions of their particular art form. In most instances, this moment of creative self-definition, in which their ways and their means were being determined, may be characterized as counter-romantic. The list of the new concerns could go on, and they will be presented in the various essays throughout this volume. Here let me simply indicate the more salient ones: a determination to look at events from radically shifting points of view, the close juxtaposition of references from different areas of experience (the lofty as well as the banal, the Dionysian as well as the Apollonian), the evolution of character types whose register is complex enough to contain these rapidly shifting emotional, imagistic, and lexical changes, and finally the location of this complex of emotional interrelations in a setting that is decidedly cosmopolitan (and polyglot), urban, industrial, and even technological.

Although this most generalized list of concerns would seem to answer both types of criticism, I would like to linger over the second, the charge of essential Modernist "negativity," because it brings us to the current stage of reassessment and points up the essential contribution of this volume. It seems we have gone beyond resistance to but also beyond uncritical acceptance of Modernism. Painters I know no longer think all Picasso's work great, or even good. We have absorbed the notes to *The Waste Land*—they are no longer deemed essential to the poem either in a negative or positive way. Rather we are in a position to consider Modernism and Modernists from the point of view of their achieved performances. That is, we are in a position to demythologize Modernism. In some ways history has done this for us, in that it has through time intruded other interests upon our attention, so that the cultural force of Modernism no longer seems so prepossessing. One could indicate the movements to counterculture and Pop culture, the simple moral fire of the sixties and its revolutionary reaction to the ambivalences and studied complexities of the fifties, the revival of forms of Marxism, and finally postmodernism itself. All have meant that when we look at Modernism again we are forced to go beyond explication, beyond an understanding of theoretical intentions, into the more difficult, more challenging, and ultimately more satisfying realm of critical evaluation; we are called upon to take the measure of Modernism, to gauge its achievements. I do not say that we are up to the challenge; I merely say this is the order of the day.

It is a difficult order for several reasons. For one, we must begin separating ourselves from the movement in whose aura we acquired literary, artistic, and cultural consciousness. Second, we are being asked to confer on a movement, which, as Ortega has shown, was always marked by a need for youthfulness, a historical identity, to weigh its accomplishments, to submit it to judgment. This seems particularly hard when the subject is Modernism, one of whose resolutions, in the complexity of its consciousness, seems to have been a fierce determination to avoid all resolutions, to devour in its consuming reflexiveness all points of view, including its own.

What is significant about this volume is that more and more one senses in its contributors a willingness to meet this order of the day. And this is significant because the response is coming from defenders of Modernism. Clement Greenberg has called Modernism a "creative devolution." Robert Morgan has questioned whether Modernism evolved a truly sustaining technique—and both see the situation of the arts as existing in what Leonard B. Meyer in *Music, the Arts, and Ideas* has called aesthetic stasis, with a number of competing styles and moments and without any stylistic hegemony. Martin Esslin wonders whether the dissolution of the thin veil separating actor and spectator does not mean the end of drama. "Are we not reaching an area of total negation, total anarchy?" The doctrine of compulsory accelerated change seems to have done away with all bases for change: what does the landscape look like from the window of a bullet train? This seems also to be Claude Leroy's position, that the extreme reflexivity of Modernism appears destined for ultimate self-cannibalism. At the original Clarement conference Roger Shattuck certainly showed up much of the foolishness in Modernist criticism (although not in Modernism itself) in a paper which attracted much critical attention and was immediately published in the *New Republic,* and Ihab Hassan, in the most compelling synthesis of the postmodernist position, has shown the limits of Modernism. This particular strain of reassessment in a volume whose contributors rank among the leading defenders of Modernism is a singular accomplishment.

Notes

1. For the history of the term "modern" or its variants see Franco Lombardi, *Nascità del Mondo Moderno* (Asti: Casa editrice arethusa, 1953), 316–20; Herbert Anton, "Modernität als Aporie und Ereignis" in *Aspekte der Modernität,* ed. Hans Steffen (Göttingen: Vandenhoeck und Ruprecht, 1965), 7–13. See also Matei Calinescu, *Faces of Modernity: Avant-garde, Decadence, Kitsch* (Bloomington: Indiana Univ. Press, 1979), 14–58, for a literary survey. Most recently see Jaroslav Pelikan, *The Growth of Medieval Theology (600–1300),* vol. 3 of *The Christian Tradition: A History of the Development of Doctrine* (Chicago: Univ. of Chicago Press, 1978), 1–2.

2. Northrop Frye, "The Drunken Boat," in *Romanticism Reconsidered,* ed. Northrop Frye (New York: Columbia Univ. Press, 1963), 24; also see Harold

Bloom, *The Ringers in the Tower: Studies in Romantic Tradition* (Chicago: Univ. of Chicago Press, 1971) and *Wallace Stevens: The Poems of Our Climate* (Ithaca: Cornell Univ. Press, 1976); and for Bornstein's views see, among several works dealing with romanticism and Modernism, *Transformations of Romanticism in Yeats, Eliot, and Stevens* (Chicago: Univ. of Chicago Press, 1976).

3. Graham Hough, "Reflections on a Literary Revolution," in *Image and Experience* (Lincoln: Univ. of Nebraska Press, 1960), 74–78; and Georg Lukács, "The Ideology of Modernism," in *Realism in Our Time,* trans. John Mander and Necke Mander (New York: Harper & Row, 1964).

SECTION 1

Purviews and Provocations

presented by
Ricardo Quinones

This first section is marked by large purviews that seem to call forth provocative answers to substantial questions. Their range is historical and societal, establishing relationships with the traditions inherent in an art form and with the social pressures of the time.

While it may be safely stated that the center of intellectual gravity for the Modernist movement was located roughly in the period 1900–1940, there will always be a strong impulse to push back the initiating boundaries of Modernism. Given the plurality of arts considered here, there is obviously and quite reasonably a plurality of responses. But what all of the contributors are clear about is that they are referring not merely to chronological beginnings but to an experience of breakthrough or rupture, which established a kind of defining pattern, a new departure that sustained itself and would become characteristic of Modernism. There were of course "discoverers" of "America" before Columbus, but, in the immortal words of Jimmy Durante (if they were his words), with Columbus it *stayed* discovered—and, moreover, received its name. Clement Greenberg, in his almost casual but quite thoughtful essay, discerns the arrival of Modernism in Manet's paintings of the early 1860s. What is significant is not chronology but the new problem: the aesthetic disorientation produced by the new art. Indeed, in considerations of Modernism its reception is what must be regarded as a capital critical fact, the outrage to be found among those who were normally comprehending. The new way of looking, not the new subject matter, caused the scandal. But this perception causes a further leap of Greenberg's historical imagination: if Modernism is a period of "creative devolution" why is it that a possibly parallel period of "devolution," the early Middle Ages, when Byzantine art replaced Greco-Roman naturalism, did not arouse similar resistance? The possible answers throng to present themselves to such an enormous question.

Michel Décaudin sights a particularly poignant and decadent anticipation of Modernism in 1885, and even earlier, in the vision of that isolated precursor, Charles Baudelaire, with his remarkable need to bring together in an urban setting the random meeting of the temporal and the eternal, the spectral and the pedestrian. And although Décaudin does not acknowledge the linkage between his *modernité* and Modernism, realizations of the aims of Baudelaire in more modern style can certainly be seen in Eliot's poems (even as early as "The Love Song of J. Alfred Prufrock" and "Preludes"). Similar parallels can be made with Joyce's *Ulysses,* not to mention Eliot's extremely important review of that work, in which he calls attention to Joyce's use of myth for giving order to the anarchy of urban life.

From the vantage point of drama, Martin Esslin locates in naturalism a precursor of Modernism, particularly in its break with traditionalist values. He makes frequent reference to Nietzsche, that prophet and prototype of Modernism, whose great task was to make clear that the so-called traditional values were not that traditional at all, but historically derived. Robert Morgan, in his very full essay on Modernist music, supports our contention that the beginning of a period is more than a chronological matter—it involves a decisive break that leads to a sustained period of creativity—particularly in regard to Schoenberg, whose "final break initiated the most productive period of his life." Interestingly enough, as I mentioned in my introductory essay, both Morgan and Esslin express reservations about Modernism, reservations that should be taken with the greatest seriousness.

Rupture with the traditions of a particular form is paralleled by rupture with the directions of society. Décaudin sees the rupture between the artist and the bourgeois ("the representative of the world founded on production and profit") as originating with romanticism but taking on a "particular flavor" in the 1880s. Robert Wohl's definition of Modernism might indeed be the most comprehensive: he regards it "as a response by clusters of intellectuals and artists to the converging processes of industrialization." Of course, two political responses to the same conditions were communism and fascism. And just as Modernism was involved unavoidably with economic processes, so too it was forced to confront these giant "isms."

Martin Esslin finds Modernism to be antipathetic to both political systems, primarily because they are "closed." Indeed, one of the most stirring moments in the conference occurred when he rose to accuse Russell Berman of a political sin of omission. By concentrating on the relationship of Modernism to fascism and ignoring Marxism, was Berman not, Esslin queried with cogency and force, implying that fascism was the more serious problem, whereas they are both totalitarian and hence opposed to Modernism? Berman's response justified the need to isolate a "fascist aesthetics." Indeed, it does seem that the question of Modernism and fascism is of particular interest, certainly so if Modernism is seen as a negative critique of nineteenth-century social and ethical values. Then the intellectual danger confronting many writers, including Mann, Yeats, Eliot, Lawrence, and Pound, was that they would find the fascist aestheticization of politics too appealing. While Berman's essay does not always use the most representative works of Eliot or Lawrence (they are hardly to be identified with *After Strange Gods* or *Lady Chatterley's Lover*), nevertheless the terms of his analysis are highly useful.

Matei Calinescu, with his usual critical acumen, takes the issue one step further by pointing out that the "reactionary" charge is largely of Anglo-American derivation, primarily because those writers had so little real experience with fascism, and that on the continent, where the avant-garde was most in force, the charge against Modernism was that it was too "left-wing." This is a useful dichotomy since it registers once again the kind of distinctions that may be made between Anglo-American and continental Modernism. Following Bakhtin, Calinescu proposes a dialogic, constitutive solution to the problems of politics and great art.

Throughout this section—one devoted to the larger issues of periodicity and society—the reader will be visited by the strong sense of an ending, a sense, made more acute by the growing number of attacks on Modernism's "negativity," its self-replicating mode of infinite regress, that this extreme self-reflexiveness, as particularly shown in its later manifestations, is a sign of its own undoing. In this sense, critical deconstructionism, although not represented in this section, nevertheless bears on it, since it is only an extreme expression of this end of an era as well as, perhaps, of the greater need to prepare for a new age. But even it is not so sad nor so desperate and terminal as co-optation. What are we to do now that corporate institutions (those royal houses of today) have Picasso rooms—in which only "top management" is permitted to dine?

Clement Greenberg

Beginnings of Modernism

The term "Modernism" points to a historical fact, an episode, in Western culture, just as classicism and romanticism do. But there are extra-historical ways of applying the adjectives "classical" and "romantic"; they can be used to characterize phenomena of any time or place. "Modernist" cannot be used with the same freedom; it remains time-bound, more historically specific.

But for all its historical specificity, it is not easy to say when Modernism actually began. It used to be viewed as a prolongation of romanticism, of its temper and mood if not of the romantic period as such. This may be partly true, though not true enough to be useful. But I do not propose to try here to extricate the beginnings of Modernism from the after-life of romanticism. That cannot be done any more conclusively than extricating the beginnings of romanticism itself from eighteenth-century classicism, let alone neoclassicism (where it is more a matter of differentiation than of extrication).

My subject gets me into a question of classification, which makes me uncomfortable. But how am I to talk about beginnings without distinguishing between what was there in the first place and what came after, and how am I to do this without classification? And then, how is classification possible without definition? Yet the last thing I want to do is attempt a definition of Modernism. I must proceed with "Modernism" as I would proceed with "art." Art has not been and probably never will be defined acceptably, yet that does not prevent us from telling the difference by and large between art and everything else. We do that by intuition, and I would say that the same must be true, or at least for the time being, with Modernism. We identify Modernism too without help of a definition, by intuition. How else settle an argument about whether or not Puvis de Chavannes, say, or Thomas Hardy was a Modernist?

Like romanticism, like almost any other broad cultural tendency, Modernism emerged at different times in the different arts—but not for the most part in different places. Except for architecture and dance, where Modernism came latest, it appeared first in France, and from there its creative impulse was exported to other countries. In this Modernism is like Gothic architecture and the *roman courtois* and much else. Even in the case of music, where Modernism came relatively late, it still originated with a Frenchman, Debussy.[1] It came even later— curiously enough—in sculpture: if not with Rodin or even Degas, then with Maillol and Despiau; if not quite with them, then most definitely with Brancusi and Picasso, who, though foreigners, could not have done what they did when they did without having lived in Paris.

The notion of Modernism comes up first in French literature, "historically" if not conclusively. Gustave Lanson, in his monumental and wonderful history of French literature, writes that "it is on Gautier somehow that our literature pivots in order to turn from Romanticism towards Naturalism." In his equally absorbing history of French literature after 1789, Albert Thibaudet writes that "the term Modernism [*modernisme*] [was] introduced by the Goncourts to give expression to a form of literary art." At first glance I do not see Gautier as tending toward naturalism any more than I see the Goncourts as tending toward what I would recognize as Modernism. But then I realize that my focus is too narrow. Widening it, I see that naturalism, a more detached, more impassive realism, did lie somehow at the origins of Modernism in French fiction. Flaubert is there to tell me that: the first Modernist in whatever art or medium, Flaubert is the key, as much the first "art-for-art's-sake"–ist as Gautier, and far more the first naturalist, Lanson's pivot or hinge.

A contradiction seems to be under way here, but it is resolved even before its start. Art for art's sake and naturalism do not have to be in opposition, and as it turns out were not. This is most readily apparent in painting. (Henry Zirner and Charles Rosen, in the *New York Review of Books*, 4 March 1982, are enlightening here, up to a point.) If any poet, moreover, was a naturalist it was Baudelaire, who was at the same time an "art-for-art's-sake"–ist before he was anything else, along with Flaubert. But I must not be unjust to Gautier: both Flaubert and Baudelaire

occupies that sphere, and I suspect that today's music, looked back on in future years, will be seen to be the art form in which those issues will have been most clearly revealed, if not decided. (Modernist music's very lack of a sufficient public seems to me to make its case exemplary and most significant.)

After this brief digressive tour of the arts, I repeat that Manet's compulsion to innovate, like Flaubert's and Baudelaire's, had behind it the same (if more urgent) need to be "modern." And art for art's sake was a natural product of modernity's heightened, rationalizing awareness of the relation between means and ends: as with well-being, happiness, the soul's salvation, art finally became recognized as an end in itself. Modern-ness meant at bottom this impulse to establish the means for better art. And better art—not life for the sake of art—is all that art for art's sake meant to begin with. (Flaubert to Baudelaire in 1857: "What I like most of all about your book is that art comes first.")

The question remains why Modernism, together with its art-for-art's-sake doctrine, should have compelled innovation in a way that it had never, apparently, been compelled before: disturbingly, shockingly, provocatively. There had always been innovation in the arts. But before Modernism innovation had never been so startling (not only in Western but in any other tradition). Originality had always been essential to the vitality of art, to its quality and effectiveness, but only with Modernism did artistic innovation begin to be so disruptive to taste, so shocking, and so disorienting. Why? The case has been with us for a hundred-odd years, but still hardly any real attention has been paid to the questions it raises.

Every successive move of Modernism proved shocking at first to cultivated, "elite" taste, not only to that of philistines. True, after a generation or so what was new and shocking became assimilated, accepted; ironically, Modernist art, after its initial shock, in almost every medium came to be regarded as art had been regarded before. Despite all talk about "breaks," revolutions, and so on, continuity persisted. And, yes, innovation in the arts had been resisted before Modernism; still, neither the shock nor the outcry was the same. What was most surprising, more of an indication that something new was being done, was the depth of the reactions to Modernism's innovations. Never before, as far as we can tell, had there been such a blocking off of aesthetic reaction, such an initial blindness, deafness, or incomprehension.

The urgency of Modernist innovation and the resistance to it are basic questions that involve one another, as do their answers. Modernism has meant, among other things, the devolution of a tradition. The continued production of superior aesthetic value after the mid–nineteenth century began, turn by turn in most of the arts, to require the devolution, the gradual unravelling—not so much the dismantling—of the Renaissance tradition of common-sense rationality, conformity to ostensible Nature (from which even tonality in music was held to be derived), and conformity, too, to the way things in general seemed to happen. Modernist architecture, which began late, may be an exception: it turned against the Renaissance and historicist revivals precisely because of their "irrationality." And Modernist architecture did not so much devolve a tradition as start, suddenly, a new one. The same might be said about Modernist dance. But these exceptions do not make it any the less true that devolution is the general rule in Modernism, not revolution.

The very fact of devolution might seem to account for the resistance to Modernist innovation. Taste and habits had been disoriented, just as disturbingly as if there had been revolution instead of devolution. Maybe devolution can be more disturbing and disorienting than outright revolution, and maybe devolution can also generate a greater momentum of innovation, a greater urgency. I find it easy to envisage that.

But accounting for the resistance to Modernist innovation by the fact of devolution alone does not answer the question adequately, if only because the past offers one very clear precedent for creative devolution, at least in the visual arts, that did not meet resistance. Between the fourth and sixth centuries of our era Greco-Roman pictorial art underwent a creative devolution that turned it into Byzantine art. Then, too, painting flattened itself out as under Modernism, after having been the first and only pictorial art before the Western European to create sculptural, three-dimensional illusion by means of shading-modelling. Then, too, what had been the subordinately decorative infiltrated and finally identified itself with the autonomously pictorial. Sculpture in the round declined and finally disappeared (being prohibited anyway by the Eastern church because it was reminiscent of pagan idols). But sculpture did persist as bas-relief, usually small in scale and shallow-cut, and it did so under the guidance of the pictorial—just as Western sculpture got its new lease on life in the twentieth century from the bas-relief constructions that emerged from cubist painting at the hands of Picasso. But the parallels between the two creative devolutions stop with their respective receptions.

The late Greco-Roman and then Byzantine devolution was accepted from the first, its products installed straightway in church, palace, and other official places. With architecture, which likewise underwent a creative devolution, the situation was the same. I would like to think that this acceptance came about because the devolution was so gradual, and because it so soon became an evolution, one of a largely new tradition of visual art and architecture. In contrast, the Modernist devolution constantly accelerated; instead of two or three centuries or more, it took place, in effect, within a matter of fifty years, between the 1850s and the 1910s (though it is not finished yet). Never had innovation in the arts proceeded nearly so fast. This speed explains in part the resistance to Modernism—but only in part.

The Byzantine devolution-evolution expressed a general, radical change in sensibility, and not only among the upper classes. Has Modernism expressed a similar change in the West? Yes and no. The change may not have been so widespread in its effects, and maybe it still is not. Obviously, we are too close to it in time to be able to tell. Whether the Modernist devolution means the start of the evolution of a new tradition, as did the Byzantine devolution, at least in visual art, remains debatable (despite Modernist architecture and maybe dance).

Another sharp difference between the two devolutions is that Byzantine art had no competitor or alternative. The production and practice of anything that looked like classical Hellenic or Greco-Roman art had fallen off and finally become extinct. Renaissance-adherent art, on the other hand, continued and still continues in the presence of Modernism. I mean "faithfully" representational art, which still produces work of at least minor significance. There is an analogous situation in literature and in music, too. This coexistence of Renaissance-adherent art as a living, productive, even creative alternative has had much to do with the resistance to Modernism.

The question stays open. Such attempts to answer it as I have made do not satisfy even me. The case is too historically unusual. There has been *creative* devolution in all the arts under Modernism, as there was not in Byzantium, where, for instance, Hellenic literary tradition did not only devolve, it declined and failed for the most part. The parallels with Western Modernism are valid in visual art and architecture alone. A fully adequate explanation of the resistance to Modernism, as well as of the urgency and dynamism of Modernist innovation, has still to be sought.

That over the last two decades the art-interested public, along with officialdom, has turned around and now embraces the *idea* of Modernist innovation—but without being aware of its point, the maintaining of

Greenberg

aesthetic value—hardly affects the matter. This turnaround, mass co-optation, is a problem all by itself, but only within the larger one with which I have been wrestling.

Note

1. See the essay by Robert P. Morgan, pp. 33–53. —Ed.

Michel Décaudin

Being Modern in 1885
or
Variations on "Modern,"
"Modernism," "Modernité"

Aesop said that language is the best and the worst of things. What superlatives would he not have employed had he known our critical, or even historical, vocabulary! Where one had the right to expect a universal code, a Volapük of literary and artistic notions, there reigns a confusion worthy of Babel, with terms whose meanings vary from one language to the other, or even in the same language according to author or discipline.

Within the series *modern, modernism, modernité* which concerns us we certainly speak with good reason of a modern style, whose aesthetic and historic contours are easily recognizable and do not lend themselves to discussion, of a Latin-American "modernismo" that renews poetic inspiration at the end of the nineteenth century, of a religious modernism, which strives to reconcile theology, Biblical interpretation, and the teaching of the Church with the scientific discoveries and the necessities of the era. But if it is evident that there have always been writers and artists who call themselves modern by opposition to the past, to tradition, to academicism, we notice as well that neither "modern" nor "modernism"— leaving "*modernité*" aside for an instant—corresponds, in French usage, to a movement or a school that adopted in its title one of these words, nor does either correspond to a designation chosen later by critics.

Except in several vague and often unconsidered occurrences, our vocabulary ignores the concept of modernism, whether it is a question of periodization in literary and artistic history or the designation of a group. As to the use made of the term "modernism" in American criticism it seems to me too indeterminate and loosely circumscribed. It encompasses far too broad and diverse tendencies and approaches to be truly pertinent. To a globalizing criticism that aims at establishing broad categories and condemns itself to retaining only general traits (the tip of the iceberg, to use a classic image), I prefer a criticism of differences (to criticize means, etymologically, to distinguish) based on the study of individualities or micro-organizations, grasped in their creative originality, a criticism that would entail a more nuanced view, more faithful to all the variations and fluctuations of life. The fundamental question posed by the notion of modernism remains unanswered, namely the position of the artist in relation to tradition on the one hand and to environment on the other. This is where *modernité* comes in, particularly with the anticipatory example of Baudelaire. It is well-known that, in "Le Peintre de la vie moderne," the author of *L'Art romantique* outlined a theory of *modernité* that has lost none of its vigor or efficacy today. To rapidly resume its points of anchorage: In every work of art, Baudelaire tells us, we find two elements, one which is the "eternal," the "immutable," and another which is the "transitory," the "fugitive," the "contingent"; on one hand, values that do not involve time, on the other, all those that emerge from the moment, from *la mode*. By cultivating only the first of these elements, artists condemn themselves to academicism, to the "void of an abstract and undefinable beauty"; but the second by itself engenders nothing but works as ephemeral as the fashion that inspired them. The great artist is the one who, seeking "this thing we will be permitted to call '*modernité*,'" will succeed in joining the "poetic" and the "historic," in "eliciting the eternal from the transitory." *Modernité* is neither a doctrine nor a category of history, but the relation of the artist to his time and to tradition (in Baudelaire's terms to the "immutable" and to the "contingent"). The consciousness that he has of it can be a simple fact of existence (the artist is bound up with his era, he "speaks" it, even in his revolt), or it can be a prejudice chosen deliberately, even provocatively. The phenomenon is certainly not recent and was not invented by us. But the *querelle des anciens et des modernes* has become particularly acute for the last hundred and fifty years, possibly because during this period, the world, as Péguy said, has undergone greater transformation than it ever has since the time of Jesus Christ. Its stability has given way to a mobility ensured by speed, long-distance verbal and visual communication, movement reproduction, relativity of time and space, atomic theory, modern logic, and so on, in short everything that makes up the environment of our lives and the structures of our minds. How could we remain indifferent to such a mutation? Since romanticism there have been writers and artists who have refused it as the agent of the ruin of values, and who pretend that art, poetry, literature must resolutely turn their backs to it: these are the traditionalists of all kinds, those who demand a restoration of classicism, the "passé-ists." There are others who proclaim that the creator should be, according to the romantic image, the lookout who, at the prow of the ship, scans unknown horizons, or, in another metaphor, the soldier of the vanguard, the "avant-garde," who precedes the body of troops and explores the terrain. Between these two extremes, then, lies the domain of modernity, with all its nuances and modalities.

Three poets, of essentially the same age, illustrate these attitudes. For Jean-Marc Bernard, poetry is reduced to gallant or epicurean themes treated in traditional genres such as the elegy, the epistle, and the ode; he is a "Maurassian" in politics, a neoclassicist in literature. Marinetti wants to break all ties with the past; he projects the content and the form of art into an imagination of the future, retaining of the present only its dynamics and its promises: this is futurism in the strict sense of the word. Apollinaire, in all the manifestations of his thought, of his sensitivity, of his writing, assumes his time, that is, a present rich with a past there is no need to deny and laden with a fascinating future. "Passé-ism," avant-garde, modernity: naturally I schematize the positions. The "passé-ist" cannot remove himself completely from the exterior world (unless he isolates himself in an ivory tower). The avant-garde has its roots in modernity. *Modernité* maintains subtle relations with tradition as with the most audacious aesthetics. Rather than being separated by boundaries, they find multiple points of intersection in a combination of margins with variable degrees of flexibility and width.

This is truly saying that there is no abstract, general category of *modernité,* but several modernities experienced successively and simultaneously. A critique of *modernité,* therefore, will not consist in the identification of distinctive features that would enable us to constitute its concept, in order to submit later artists and works to it. It will rather disclose the particularities of groups or of individuals in their relationship with their time in order ultimately to characterize an era.

I return, here, to the year 1885 for an analysis that could have an

Décaudin

experimental value. It is not a year particularly rich in intellectual, literary, and artistic events. For these, I would rather have chosen 1884, the year of the publication of Huysmans' *À rebours,* Verlaine's *Les Poètes maudits,* Moréas's *Les Syrtes,* and the opening of the first Salon des Indépendants. Or 1886, with Rimbaud's *Illuminations,* Moréas's symbolist manifesto, Mallarmé's "Avant-dire," René Ghil's *Traité du Verbe,* the last impressionist exhibit, Fénéon's art criticism . . . But the relative banality of this year (which is, nonetheless, the year of *Germinal,* the *Prose pour des Esseintes,* Laforgue's *Complaintes*—and of the death of Victor Hugo) is all the more interesting if we undertake our inquiry with the perspectives defined above.

One characteristic must be noted at once: the presence and the frequency of the adjective "modern." One is "modern" in 1885 as one will be "new" in 1900 or "young" in 1930. This is a keyword, a password in which a community of thought and sensibility expresses itself. When attempting to define it, one notes with surprise that it does not refer to the developments of industrial civilization, nor to the mechanization which permeates daily life. In 1884, among other inventions or innovations, the steam turbine was first put to use, as was the linotype that was to revolutionize printing techniques, leading to the lowered price of newspapers; so too in 1884 were the first commercial electric trains, the first tests of the Marquis de Dion's steam-operated tricycle. In 1885, we find the first bicycle put on the market by Peugeot, the notation of movement by Marey with his chronophotograph . . . but none of that seems to have penetrated into the ideology, literature, or art of the time, contrary to what will happen twenty-five years later, for instance, with the interest shown by Apollinaire, Cendrars, and Marinetti in the "people of the machines."

Instead, urban reality is seized upon as the form *par excellence* of modern life. The experience of the city, of the street, the feeling of being part, willingly or not, of an overwhelming collectivity is the source of a double chain of reactions. The city is at the same time the place of collective life and that of solitude, of communication and of lack of communication, of freedom and of all forms of alienation. It is the source of new impressions just as intoxicating as physical or moral pollutions. Poetry illustrates this fact, with an abundance of short prose poems (the fashion for several years) that attempt to capture these impressions, and Laforgue's *Complaintes,* obsessed with the dreariness of life, the sadness of Sundays, a daily agitation that does not prevent the fact that "l'histoire va toujours dressant, raturant ses Tables criblées de piteux idem, ô Bilan, va quelconque! ô Bilan, va quelconque . . . "

(History goes on, forever erecting, forever erasing its Tables riddled with piteous *idem,* O Reckoning, nothing much! O Reckoning, nothing much . . .).

This confrontation with the conditions of urban existence provokes a feeling of marginality among many artists. We know very well that the divorce between the artist and the bourgeois—the representative of a world founded on production and profit—dates from romanticism, but this situation, which continues throughout the century, takes on, during the eighties, a particular color. It is no longer a kind of lover's quarrel with a society lacking understanding, or a splendid scornful isolation; rather it is the double and contradictory experience of a difference that is necessary and of a separation that is impossible to sustain, of the malaise that comes with considering oneself at the same time inside and outside the social group. One phenomenon of this era, the development of literary and artistic life in the cafés, taverns, and cabarets, perhaps finds its explanation here. Did these places, which have not all achieved the celebrity of the Chat Noir, but which were often comparable to it in importance, not in fact succeed in combining at the same time the complicity of the group, assembled around a table or in a back room, with a view on the outside world, represented by the comings and goings of the front room and the proximity of the street? That a Verlaine, a Villiers, or a Moréas should have used such a place as his headquarters should not surprise us: more than the attraction of the drink, which is too easily invoked, it is the very image of his social condition which holds him there.

The refusal, or the impossibility, of participation is expressed by the transgression of traditional values and the quest for an "elsewhere": drugs, loose manners, prostitution, male and female homosexuality pervade the literature and are clearly linked to modern life. More than one example is to be found in the daily chronicles, as well as in the naturalist novel, but we also find them in poems such as those published by Jean Lorrain during that year entitled *Modernités.* This quatrain sets the tone:

Modernité, Modernité!	Modernité, Modernité!
A travers les cris, les huées	Through cries, catcalls,
L'impudeur des prostituées	The shamelessness of prostitutes,
Resplendit dans l'éternité.	Shines into eternity.

The modern city is "Paris proxénète" ("Paris the pimp") with its women who are "voleuses" ("thieves"), "coquines" ("scamps"), "débutantes," "abandonnées," ("abandoned ones"), its sad "modernisants" ("modernisers"). Its universe is at the same time composed of novelty and decadence, thirst for life and mortal disappointment.

Je me suis brûlé dans la fête!	I got burnt in the festivity!
Clown ébloui tombé du faîte,	A dazzled clown fallen from the pinnacle,
J'ai voulu rire et j'ai pleuré	I wanted to laugh and I cried
Et, sous la gaîté qui me grise	And, beneath this intoxicating gaiety
Je sais au fond qui je méprise	I know at heart whom I scorn
Dans ce livre d'homme écoeuré!	In this book of a sickened man!
Modernité, Modernité	Modernité, Modernité
Sous le sarcasme et la huée	Under sarcasm and catcall
La nudité prostituée	Prostituted nudity
Saigne au fond de l'éternité.	Bleeds at the heart of eternity.

"Everyone," as Achille Segard wrote later, "wanted to create an artificial paradise for himself." Or, according to Stanislas de Gauita, intoxicated with esotericism as much as with narcotics,

Puis, que le Rêve instruise ou mente,	Then, let the dream instruct or lie
Et qu'importe au poète-doux?	What does it matter to the gentle poet?
Il fuit la Bêtise	He flees from degrading stupidity
Dans le Dormir clément aux fous.	Into sleep, a solace to the insane.

This recourse to transgression, which is not afraid to border on insanity, this alliance of the modern and the decadent, will reach its apex in 1885. Before 1880, just as after 1890, it is moral and social repression that has the upper hand (one need only think of the reprobation that weighed on the relationship of Verlaine and Rimbaud during the seventies or of the care with which, over many years, André Gide felt constrained to hide his true nature). From another angle, however, symbolism and idealism, which will develop after 1886, together with the crisis of naturalism, will soon subdue this feeling of a *modernité* which inscribes and realizes itself in decadence.

A year of latent crisis as far as the concept of modernity is concerned, 1885 is also the year of a crisis in writing. The triumph of Zola and of naturalism does not prevent a questioning of narrative forms. Works such as *À rebours* (Against the Grain) in 1884, and *Les Lauriers sont coupés* (The Laurels Are Cut) in 1886, by the originality of their conception and their composition, set the stage, so to speak, for a crisis of the novel as established by the realist tradition of the nineteenth century. The success of the short story in the style of Maupassant, with its brevity, its simplicity, its behaviorism, is not only due to technical reasons linked with publication in magazines; it constitutes a counterpart to the dominant narrative discourse. In poetry, even if Jean Lorrain's *Modernités* are cast in very traditional molds like the sonnet, new modalities are beginning to appear. First there is the prose poem, whose vogue precedes 1885 by several years, but will then rapidly taper off. Free verse also makes its appearance. "Whatever is thought of our technique and our poems," Gustave Kahn wrote in 1912, "everyone today agrees that in 1885 French poetry needed an emetic shock. It was asleep." Free verse was perhaps this revulsive, in any case free verse of the symbolist type, as Kahn himself, Régnier, and others invented it. Laforgue's verses in the *Complaintes* should be added to this with their altogether different structure heralding a form of verse that will delight the twentieth century. Everything thus takes place as if this year 1885 were the meeting place of diverse experimentations whose profound motive is a questioning of poetic expression.

This questioning, in fact, extends to include all manifestations of language. It is important that the first edition of the *Almanach Vermot,* a canonical collection of puns, was published in 1885. What humorists like Alphonse Allais and Sapack, and also Charles Cros in more than one monologue, introduce under the guise of a joke, a hoax, or a farce, is a questioning of the coherence and the operation of language, which opens the way to the logical inconsistency of the absurd.

Such could be the dominant features of the *modernité* of 1885. If I wanted to recapitulate them I could do it at the cost of a bit of cheating—for the text is from 6 April 1889, in the first edition of the *Moderniste Illustré*—by quoting this "Boniment initial" (initial claptrap) by Albert Aurier:

> Le *moderniste,* ce paradoxal élégant, que nous vous présentons, ce preste Pierrot, hilare, splénétique, fumiste, macabre, logiquement incohérent, dont le frac azur et les culottes lèvres-de-pucelles sont élaborées par le conjectural Tailleur de toutes les exquisités futures, le *moderniste,* cet enragé chercheur d'artisteries rares, ce passionné dilettante des joailleries néo-byzantine d'après-demain, ce féroce contempteur des habiles pasticheries, des académies, des écoles frigorifriques, des casques héroïques, des cnémides démodées, des moyenâgeux bric-à-brac, des moules (dans le sens qu'il vois plaira), des copies et des Coppées, des conventions, des traditions, de toutes les ambiantes banalités, ce railleur plus superfinement sceptique que Montaigne, plus précieusement détraqué que des Esseintes, le *moderniste*, cet inquiet astrologue des comètes du prochain siècle, condescendra jusqu'à obèir à l'USAGE, jusqu'à se placarder sur la poitrine le manifeste que voici:
>
> Candide Public,
> Ne t'avise point de contester mon utilité.
> Car je veux être, car je serai le représentant consciencieux,
> et incontestablement très utile, *de toutes les Inutilités Vitales.*

(The modernist, this paradoxical swell that we introduce to you, this agile Pierrot, hilarious, splenetic, carefree, macabre, logically incoherent, whose azure coat and "lèvres-de-pucelle" trousers are elaborated by the conjectural Tailor of all future exquisities, the modernist, this enraged searcher of rare artistries, this impassioned dilettante of the neo-byzantine jewelry of the day after tomorrow, this ferocious disdainer of clever imitations, academies, refrigerating schools, heroic helmets, outmoded armory, phony medieval bric-à-brac, mollusks (with whatever meaning you wish), copies and Coppées, convention, tradition, of all ambient banalities, this heckler more superfinely sceptical than Montaigne, more pretentiously deranged than des Esseintes, the *modernist,* this worried astrologer of the comets of the next century, will condescend even to obey USAGE, to placard on his chest the following manifesto:

> Candid Public,
> Do not venture to contest my utility.
> For I want to be, for I will be the conscientious
> and incontestably very useful representative
>   *of all the vital inutilities.)*

Vital inutilities which are art, poetry, "les indispensables superflus, les luxes vains, les bijouteries du corps et de l'âme, les subtiles élégances, les émaux miroitants des absurdes fantaisies, les modes inutiles, les délicates mondanités, toutes les futiles et savantes parisienneries, toutes les illusoires promenades dans la lune!" (The indispensable superfluities, the vain luxuries, the jewelries of the body and soul, the subtle elegances, the bevelled enamels of absurd fantasies, useless fashions, exquisite vanities, all the futile and knowing *parisienneries,* all the illusory outings in the moon!)

Modernité of 1885, which we have striven to capture in the inimitable and irreplaceable quality of its unique savor.

Robert P. Morgan

Secret Languages: The Roots of Musical Modernism

In der modernen Prosa sprechen wir eine Sprache, die wir mit dem Gefühle nicht verstehen. . . . Wir können nach unserer innersten Empfindung in dieser Sprache gewissermassen nicht mitsprechen, denn es ist uns unmöglich, nach dieser Empfindung in ihr zu *erfinden*; wir können unsere Empfindungen in *ihr* nur dem Verstande, nicht aber dem zuversichtlich verstehenden Gefühle mittheilen. . . . In der modernen Sprache kann nicht *gedichtet* werden, d.h. . . . eine dichterische Absicht kann in ihr verwirklicht, sondern eben nur *als solche* ausgesprochen werden.

(In modern prose we speak a language we do not understand with the feeling. . . . we cannot discourse in this language according to our innermost emotion, for it is impossible to *invent* in it according to that emotion; in *it,* we can only impart our emotions to the understanding, but not to the implicitly understood feeling. . . . In modern speech no *poesis* is possible, that is to say, poetic aim cannot be realized therein, but only spoken out *as such.*)

Seitdem nun die modernen europäischen Sprachen . . . mit immer ersichtlicherer Tendenz ihrer rein Konventionellen Ausbildung folgten, entwickelte sich andererseits die Musik zu einem bisher der Welt unbekannten Vermögen des Ausdruckes. Es ist, als ob das durch die Kompression seitens der konventionellen Civilization gesteigerte rein menschliche Gefühl sich

einen Ausweg zur Geltendmachung seiner ihm eigenthümlichen
Sprachgesetze gesucht hätte, durch welche es, frei vom Zwange
der logischen Denkgesetze, sich selbst verständlich sich aus-
drüken könnte.

(Now, ever since the modern European languages ... have
followed this conventional drift to a more and more obvious
tendency, music, on the other hand, has been developing a
power of expression unknown to the world before. It is as
though the purely human feeling, intensified by the pressure
of a conventional civilization, has been seeking an outlet for
the operation of its own peculiar laws of speech; an outlet
through which, unfettered by the laws of logical thought, it
might express itself intelligibly to itself.)[1]

In reading recent literature on the history and aesthetics
of Western music, one consistently encounters references to the "language"
of this music, especially with regard to the practice of eighteenth- and
nineteenth-century tonality. Although the word "language" is used met-
aphorically in such cases, the metaphor seems remarkably apt (and
convenient), and this no doubt accounts for its persistence. When applied
to twentieth-century music, however, the sense of the term—and thus
the nature of the metaphor—requires significant adjustment. For here,
unlike the case in earlier Western music, one is unable to find that most
characteristic feature of all natural languages, the universal acceptance
of an enduring set of formal conventions evident throughout a given
linguistic domain. Attempts, as in Donald Mitchell's *The Language of
Modern Music,* to define a twentieth-century musical mainstream (in
Mitchell's case, Schoenbergian dodecaphony), elevating its technical and
systematic foundation to the status of a uniquely "proper" language for
the age, appear seriously misguided and in flagrant opposition to the
actual course of twentieth-century musical developments.[2] Musical modernism is marked, above all, by its "linguistic plurality" and by the
failure of any one language to assume a dominant position.

This plurality and the significant transformations in musical structure,
expression, and intent it reflects form interesting parallels with characteristic
features of the modernist movement in general; and it is primarily these
connections that I wish to explore here. That such parallels exist is
hardly surprising, since music—or perhaps more accurately the *idea* of
music—is intimately tied to certain basic conceptions underlying the
modernist revolution. Indeed, musical developments of the critical years
around the turn of the century mirror with particular clarity the general
intellectual and artistic climate of the period as a whole.

Although considerable controversy persists concerning both the nature and chronology of modernism, there seems to be widespread agreement that it incorporated a wish to turn away from concrete, everyday reality, to break out of the routine of ordinary actions in the hope of attaining a more personal and idealized vision of reality. There were of course precedents for this attitude in romanticism, but its artistic manifestations began to take on uniquely modern colorations toward the end of the century. In particular, there is a prevalent move away from realism and naturalism toward a new and radical abstractionism, evident not only in a turn toward less representational modes in the visual arts but in new attitudes toward language in literature and, as we shall see, in music (by metaphorical extension) as well.

It is frequently noted that a "crisis in language" accompanied the profound changes in human consciousness everywhere evident near the turn of the century. As the nature of reality itself became problematic—or at least suspect, distrusted for its imposition of limits upon individual imagination—so necessarily did the relationship of language to reality. Thus the later nineteenth century increasingly questioned the adequacy of an essentially standardized form of "classical" writing—writing that, even though often in "elevated" form, bore a close connection to ordinary discourse—as an effective vehicle for artistic expression. Indeed, it was precisely the mutually shared, conventional aspects of language that came to be most deeply distrusted for their failure to mirror the more subjective, obscure, and improbable manifestations of a transcendent reality—or rather realities, the plural reflecting an insistence upon the optional and provisional nature of human experience. Language in its normal manifestations, with its conventionalized vocabulary and standardized rules for syntactical combination, proved inadequate for an artistic sensibility insisting upon, in Nietzsche's words, "a world of abnormally drawn perspectives."

This dissatisfaction with "normal" language received its classic statement through Hofmannsthal's Lord Chandos. Writing in 1902, Hofmannsthal conveys through the figure of the aristocratic Chandos the loss of an encompassing framework within which the various objects of external reality are connected with one another and integrated with the internal reality of human feelings. Chandos's world has become one of disparate, disconnected fragments, resistant to the abstractions of ordinary language. It is a world characterized by "a sort of feverish thought, but thought in a material that is more immediate, more fluid and more intense than that of language." Chandos longs for a new language in which "not a single word is known to me, a language in which mute objects speak to me and in which perhaps one day, in the grave, I will give account of myself before an unknown judge."[3] The content and forms of art thus shift away from exterior reality, which no longer provides a stable, "given" material, toward language itself— to "pure" language in a sense closely related to the symbolists' "pure" poetry. "No artist tolerates reality," Nietzsche proclaimed;[4] and, according to Flaubert, he should write "a book about nothing, a book without external attachments, which would hold itself together by itself through the internal force of its style."[5]

It is more than coincidental, I think, that both Nietzsche and Hofmannsthal were intensely musical and intimately involved with music. For both, music provided a sort of idealized model for the reformulation of art and language. Indeed, music acquired the status of a central symbolic image for many of the principal artistic concerns of the years immediately preceding and following the turn of the century. Walter Pater provided perhaps the strongest statement (certainly the most famous) in asserting (in 1873) that "all art constantly aspires towards the condition of music."[6] Removed from ordinary reality by its nonsubstantive and nondesignative nature, music offered the age an ideal embodiment of the notion that art is pure form, and thus pure language. Pater's is only one of a series of such pronouncements appearing in the aesthetic literature of the period, e.g., in Verlaine's "De la musique avant toute chose,"[7] or in Valéry's "Reprendre à la musique leur bien."[8] Music, with its apparent indifference to external reality, comes to be viewed as the purest manifestation of human thought—as a "language" capable of producing the sort of "immediacy, fluidity and intensity" that Hofmannsthal found missing in ordinary words.[9]

The tendency to propose music as a model for artistic intentions and aspirations is equally evident among painters. Delacroix, for example, stressed "the music of a picture"; and Gauguin, when questioned concerning the meaning of one of his paintings ("Where are we going . . . "), said that it should be understood as "music without a libretto." But perhaps the most fully developed argument for a musical "basis" for painting appeared in Kandinsky's writings from the early years of the present century, in which he calls for the creation of a "pure painting" independent of external reality. Kandinsky repeatedly evokes music as an ideal for a more abstract, "object-free" art: "After music, painting will be the second of the arts . . . [it] will attain to the higher level of pure art, upon which music has already stood for several centuries."[10] Similarly: "Music, which externally is completely emancipated from nature, does not need to borrow external forms from anywhere in order to create its language. Painting today is still almost entirely dependent upon natural forms, upon forms borrowed from nature. And its task today is to examine its forces and its materials, to become acquainted with them, as music has long since done, and to attempt to use these materials and forces in a purely painterly way for the purpose of creation."[11] Indeed, Kandinsky goes so far as to envision the eventual development of a *malerische Generalbass* and a *Harmonielehre der Malerei* (i.e., theories of figured bass and of harmony for painting).[12]

The idea of music as a uniquely privileged medium able to penetrate to the essence of reality and thus express things inaccessible to language as such has a history extending back at least to the turn of the nineteenth century. Its definitive philosophical statement was supplied by Schopenhauer, in whose formulation it became a cornerstone of the aesthetics of romanticism. Writing in 1819, in *The World as Will and Idea,*[13] he praises music above all other arts as a "universal language" capable of expressing, "in a homogeneous material, mere tone, and with the greatest determinateness and truth, the inner nature, the in-itself of the world." Unlike the other arts, it is not a "copy of the phenomenon, or more accurately, the adequate objectivity of will, but is the direct copy of the will itself, and therefore exhibits itself as the metaphysical to everything physical in the world." The composer thus becomes in Schopenhauer's eyes a sort of clairvoyant, privy to truths hidden from ordinary beings: he "reveals the inner nature of the world, and expresses the deepest wisdom in a language which his reason does not understand; as a person under the influence of mesmerism tells things of which he has no conception when he awakes."

This view reflects, and presupposes, a uniquely modern and Western conception of music as an autonomous art, freed from the verbal texts to which it had traditionally been attached and upon which its meaning and significance had always depended. Schopenhauer is explicit on the point that only *instrumental* music enjoys the special powers he ascribes to the art: "It is precisely this universality, which belongs exclusively to it, together with the greatest determinateness, that give music the high worth which it has as the panacea for all our woes. Thus, if music is too closely united with the words, and tries to form itself according to the events, it is striving to speak a language which is not its own." It was not until the eighteenth century, however, that instrumental music gradually began to emerge as an equal partner to vocal music; and thus only then could such a "pure" music be taken seriously, and questions arise as to what this textless music might be "saying."[14] Already by the early years of the nineteenth century the prevailing attitude toward instrumental music had completely changed. For many it had become the only true music, the only form in which music could attain its highest and purest expression. Wilhelm Wackenroder, writing at the end of the eighteenth century, praises music above all other arts, for "it speaks a language we do not know in ordinary life, which we have learned, we know not where or how, and which one can only take to be the language of angels."[15]

Yet though many thus viewed the insubstantiality of musical material—its "purity"—as sufficient to justify its role as a model for artistic regeneration, for the composer matters were by no means so simple. Indeed, by the end of the century a crisis had developed in musical language as shattering as that in the language of literature. To the composer, the idea that music offered a "pure material" must have seemed grotesquely naive. Far from supplying a sort of *tabula rasa* on which could be inscribed, free from all external interference, the "hidden hieroglyphics" of uninhibited fantasy, music in fact came tied to a remarkably fixed system of built-in conventions and constraints. Not by chance, this system began to be theoretically codified at just the time that instrumental music began to break away from its vocal-linguistic heritage. It was as if music, suddenly removed from the semantic and syntactic foundation previously supplied by language, had to discover its own grammar. With Rameau's *Traité de l'harmonie* of 1722 as the most conspicuous initiator, the history of modern Western music theory represents a concerted effort to map out the coordinates of a new and autonomous musical system capable of matching the logical coherence and expressive power of language itself. If music was to be a world removed from ordinary reality (in Wackenroder's phrase, *eine abgesonderte Welt*), it was nevertheless to be a world of reason, logic, and systemization.

This increasingly systematic conception of musical structure was bound to take its toll. As the nineteenth century progressed, a growing number of composers felt that musical language was becoming frozen in the conventions of an overly standardized harmonic vocabulary and a formal framework too heavily bound to empty symmetrical regularities. By the middle of the century, Wagner was already acutely conscious of the delimiting nature of the inherited style. His inclination to dissolve tonality through chromatic saturation of the triadic substructure, producing almost constant harmonic ambiguity, is one well-known symptom of this concern, as is his dissatisfaction with what he had come to view as the meaningless periodicities of "quadratic compositional construction." Wagner wanted music to become "endless melody," free to develop continuously according to its own inner impulses rather than to the "outward forms" of an imposed convention.

Intensifying the growing discontent with a musical language that, flattened out under the weight of its own habits, seemed to be rapidly losing its former expressive power was the dramatic growth of "lighter" music during this period. The nineteenth century gave birth to a veritable industry for the production of music for instruction and household entertainment—not popular music, but so-called "salon" music pretending to a degree of technical complexity and emotional depth designed to satisfy the cultural ambitions of a growing middle class. Such music was turned out in increasing volume throughout the nineteenth century as part of the burgeoning publishing and printing business. Compositions were often offered in periodic series on a subscription basis, and many of the better-known composers of the day provided songs, piano pieces, etc., for such purposes on commission. The degree of banality and sentimentality in these pieces, suitable for unsophisticated yet "aspiring" music lovers, was necessarily high. Hanslick, writing in the 1860s, commented on the phenomenon: "By far the largest portion of the music published here [in Vienna] consists of little dances, practice pieces, and the basest kind of brilliant piano music, which makes no secret of its spiritual and technical poverty."[16]

A sense of malaise thus developed in the musical world paralleling that found in the other arts of the period. For the composer committed to a similar quest for "spirituality," the inherited language of music seemed no "purer" than the languages of such "representational" artistic modes as painting and literature. It was equally burdened with a system of conventions that, trivialized through overuse and exploitation, had been rendered unresponsive to the more immediate and intuitive dimensions of human experience. Trapped under syntactical and formal constraints rooted in the past, the composer was as much the prisoner of an "external" reality as was the poet or painter. He might well have echoed Nietzsche's famous remark: "I fear we shall never be rid of God, so long as we still believe in grammar."[17]

Debussy, writing in the early years of the new century, expresses the dilemma in a typically witty, yet revealing, manner in ridiculing the ossified formal prescriptions of the classical-romantic symphony (a genre generally held to be the highest manifestation of absolute music):

> The first section is the customary presentation of a theme on which the composer proposes to work; then begins the necessary dismemberment; the second section seems to take place in an experimental laboratory; the third section cheers up a little in a quite childish way interspersed with deeply sentimental phrases during which the chant withdraws as is more seemly; but it reappears and the dismemberment goes on; the professional gentlemen, obviously interested, mop their brows and the audience calls for the composer. But the composer does not appear. He is engaged in listening modestly to the voice of tradition which prevents him, it seems to me, from hearing the voice that speaks within him.[18]

The inner voice has become the important one for Debussy, as well as for many others of his generation. One can already recognize the condition in Wagner, who praises Liszt's symphonic poems, for example, precisely for "those individual peculiarities of view that made their creation possible."[19] It is what is individual and unique, rather than general and conventional, that now matters.

Yet even Wagner, certainly among the most radical composers of the later nineteenth century, remained faithful to a latent foundation of traditional tonal and formal principles. The triad remains for him an always implicit, and usually explicit, structural norm, even when the underlying diatonic basis is obscured by his richly chromatic textures; and so does the dominant-to-tonic harmonic progression, the main key-defining agent in the classical canon. Moreover, the same is true of all of his contemporaries, and even of the earlier Debussy. Thus Ferruccio Busoni, writing in 1906, can look back over the entire nineteenth century (and specifically to late Beethoven, which he takes as representative of the extremes of musical freedom attained during the century) and comment (in his *New Aesthetic of Music,* perhaps the first conscious—or self-conscious—manifesto of musical modernism) on the ultimate failure of even its most progressive figures to achieve a radical break with the past:

> Such lust of liberation filled Beethoven, the romantic revolutionary, that he ascended one short step on the way leading music back to its loftier self: —a short step in the great task, a wide step in his own path. He did not quite reach absolute music, but in certain moments he divined it, as in the introduction to the fugue of the Sonata for Hammerklavier. Indeed, all composers have drawn nearest the true nature of music in preparatory and intermediate passages (preludes and transitions), where they felt at liberty to disregard symmetrical proportions, and unconsciously drew free breath.[20]

Busoni's words again recall Nietzsche's aphorism about God and grammar: the apparent order and logical precision of standardized language is distrusted as bearing false witness to an increasingly unstable world of "degrees and many refinements of relationships." As if in response to this view, which I take to be fundamental to all the main currents of modernism (for "grammar" can be replaced by "conventional tonal structure," by "traditional modes of visual representation," etc.), the major progressive composers of the first decade of the new century undertook a radical dismantling of the established syntax of Western music. This move "beyond tonality" was remarkably widespread (although it assumed very different forms in different composers). It profoundly altered the face of music and supplied the technical foundation for musical modernism.

Although the technical consequences of this musical revolution are, I believe, ultimately comprehensible only within the context of the broader cultural crisis I have focused upon up to now, they are themselves of considerable interest and significance. I will thus turn now to consider some of the more specialized developments in musical language that occurred during the first decade of the century. It will be useful to treat these in rather general terms, for they are thus applicable to a wide range of composers (including Debussy, Scriabin, Stravinsky, Schoenberg, and Bartók) who in other respects might seem to have relatively little in common. Of course these technical developments did not come about instantaneously; they had an extended history. But the final step was taken only after the turn of the century; and in this instance this step produced a difference in kind rather than simply another one of degree.

One way to view the revolution in musical language during these years is as a transformation in the relationship between compositional foreground and compositional background—that is, between the musical surface and its formal substructure.[21] (I have already made tacit use of this distinction in discussing the music of Wagner.) Music is above all an art of ornament and elaboration; and it must maintain a subtle, and often fragile, relationship between its variegated embellishments and the simpler, stricter, and more solid supporting framework that holds these embellishments together and supplies their foundation. Indeed, a striking feature of the foreground-background relation is the mutual dependence of the two. The underlying framework is often not sounded at all, but must be deduced from the implications of the foreground; while the foreground, though actually sounded, owes its "grammatical" meaning solely to its connection with a "virtual" background. The history of Western music theory can be read as an attempt to codify a set of rules for, on the one hand, approved background relationships and, on the other, permissible foreground divergences. To take a few relatively simple examples applying mainly to "local" levels of structure, such theoretical concepts as consonance, diatonicism, triad, and fundamental progression belong to background phenomena, while those of dissonance, chromaticism, and auxiliary tones belong to the foreground.

Since at any given moment the background elements are not necessarily present on the surface, their proper apperception must depend upon strong conventions concerning what is "normal" and thus structural, as opposed to what is "abnormal" and thus superficial and ornamental. All Western music, at least since the Renaissance, displays a more or less complex interaction between foreground and background structures. Although the degree to which these levels can depart from one another has varied considerably from style to style, it is characteristic of the post-Renaissance period as a whole that a sufficient balance is maintained to ensure that the underlying structure is never seriously threatened. During the nineteenth century, however, this balance begins noticeably to waver. Since the background represents what is essentially fixed and unchanging, while the foreground contains what is unique, individual, and characteristic in a composition, it is not surprising that an age of such marked individualism should produce a radical shift in the foreground-background dialectic, tilting the balance heavily toward the surface. The growth of chromaticism, an emphasis on novel dissonances, an ever-greater exploitation of motivic and thematic elements at the expense of architectural ones—all this reflects a significant structural realignment. By the latter part of the century such technical innovations often make it extremely difficult to hear an implied background at all through the heavy accumulations of wayward foreground detail. The latter becomes so complex, so laden with multiple, entangled, and often contradictory layers of implication that the underlying structure (to the extent that one can still be inferred) is brought to the edge of collapse.

The more adventurous composers of the nineteenth century countered the problem largely by structuring the foreground features of their compositions at the expense of background ones. The various techniques of thematic transformation evident in Liszt, Wagner, and other composers of the period serve to hold together through surface correspondences extended spans of music whose background structures have been seriously weakened. Similarly, lengthy symphonic movements are often organized according to shifting and opposed key areas that, according to conventional background criteria, form dissonant relationships applicable only to local formal contexts (e.g., the C/B dichotomy in Strauss's *Also Sprach Zarathustra*).

Yet even in such extreme instances, traditional background structures continue to exert a strong influence. Despite the often exotic surface peculiarities, the music maintains at least a latent reference to the standardized grammar of Western tonality. The triad still represents the sole harmonic norm (no matter how rarely a pure triad may appear); and the traditional dominant-to-tonic progression still retains its key-defining function (though it may now appear more by implication than by actual statement).

Nevertheless, the growing strain brought on by the conflicting claims of foreground and background in complex European music reached a crisis point by the end of the century. If, on the one hand, the substructure became too obscure, the "meaning" of the foreground was apt to seem unclear; whereas if the substructure was rendered too clearly audible, the luxurious surface detail so typical of fin-de-siècle textures tended to sound like nothing more than "junk"—i.e., decoration in the worst sense of the term. One notes the latter problem, it seems to me, to some degree in even the greatest composers of the turn of the century. It is especially evident in such figures as Reger and Franck, who attempted to reconcile a classicizing tendency with a penchant for the most progressive technical procedures of the day. Thus Reger's complex modulations and intensely chromatic voice-leading are contained within a highly regular phrase structure with cadential points defined by blatantly unambiguous dominant-tonic progressions. The heightened chromatic motion on the surface seems to have no influence upon the substructure, which sounds through with schematic clarity. Both surface and background take on the aspect of cliché: the surface, because it acquires the attributes of a momentary decoration without wider repercussions; the background, because it provides a too "easy" (because too obviously conventional) resolution for the entangled interrelationships suggested by the surface. But it is not only in Reger that one hears the problem: the specter of kitsch looms over even the greatest achievements of an age in which music threatened literally to become pure ornament.

A solution demanded a major restructuring of the received musical language. In the broadest terms, it involved a projection of musical phenomena previously considered to belong solely to the foreground—elements that are ephemeral, passing, structurally unessential, and thus, in a sense, accidental (the "chance" results of voice leading, etc.)—onto the structural background. I have already noted a tendency in this direction in nineteenth-century music, in the increasing emphasis on individual foreground features. Nevertheless, the moment when agreed-upon background relationships no longer supplied even an implicit matrix for controlling the confusion of surface detail marked a fundamental turn in the history of compositional thought. A fixed and conventional conception of musical structure gave way to one that was variable, contingent, and contextual—dependent upon the specific attributes of the particular composition. Those qualities of uniqueness and individuality, of the ephemeral and accidental, that had previously marked the foreground alone now characterized the background as well.

The final, conclusive break occurred in the first decade of the century, in Scriabin, Debussy, Schoenberg, and Stravinsky, as well as others. Significantly, the leaders in this musical revolution were themselves all nurtured within the tonal tradition and produced in their earlier careers compositions written according to more or less traditional tonal assumptions. The rift with the past led to different responses, but the particular solution of each composer can be largely understood as a direct outgrowth of the stylistic evolution of his earlier music and thus of a particular orientation toward tonality.

It will be helpful to consider briefly two composers who arrived at radically different solutions to this common problem: Scriabin and Schoenberg. Scriabin's early music seems remarkable mainly for its conservatism, its unequivocal harmonic relationships ordered within an essentially conventional larger tonal context. Yet as in much music of the later nineteenth century (Scriabin was born in 1872 and his first mature works began to appear in the 1890s), the harmonic structure is covered with a dense network of auxiliary tones that, although clearly subordinate (there is never any doubt about the triadic background), resolve only with the greatest reluctance. The obvious disparity between the rich accretions of surface detail and the all-too-apparent harmonic underpinnings produces formal-expressive problems similar to the ones noted in Reger. Only in Scriabin the dissonances are prolonged over such long spans that the whole structure seems to float precariously over the delicately maintained chordal foundation; and in the later 1890s and early 1900s, the complex surface sonorities are increasingly emphasized at the expense of their background supports. When triadic resolutions do occur, they sound more and more like perfunctory nods to tradition, dictated solely by protocol. The heart of the music has been displaced from the substructure to the surface, so that the resolutions sound like a breach of faith.

Scriabin's own particular development of extended chromaticism and delayed resolution is closely tied to his use of elaborate dominant-type sonorities. The dominant seventh is the one chordal type within the traditional vocabulary whose tonal function is, at least under normal circumstances, unambiguous, and which is thus able to define a key area entirely by itself. By focusing upon elaborations of such harmonies in his earlier music, Scriabin was able to preserve at least some degree of tonal definition; despite the increasing avoidance of resolution, one is usually able to infer what the resolution *should* be. Moreover, up until about 1907 tonal resolutions do ultimately occur, although they may be delayed right up to the final measure. The moment arrives in Scriabin's evolution, however, when the dominant-type sonorities completely lose their functional subordination to an inferred background tonic. The dominant, one might say, has moved deeper into the structural background to become an "absolute" sonority in its own right, with a meaning no longer dependent upon its relationship to a simpler, more stable structure. The dominant-type harmony, in fact, assumes the role of a center, or tonic, itself; but it is a new kind of unstable tonic, whose priority must be contextually defined within each composition.

Significantly, Scriabin referred to this new tonic sonority as the "mystic chord," for to him it was the source of previously unimagined musical power. Moreover, he conceived of it as built up of intervals of a fourth, thus distinguishing it from previous harmonic norms. Yet the chord can just as readily be viewed as a series of thirds, in which case it conforms to traditional conceptions of triadic extension. What was actually novel about the chord, then, was not so much its internal structure, or even the way it sounds in isolation, but its functional location in the background. There it shed its traditional grammatical meaning, acquiring a new and seemingly inscrutable one more in keeping with Scriabin's growing mystical orientation. Only through such drastic structural means could music become more responsive to those transcendent and visionary claims that increasingly occupied the composer from about 1908 to 1915, the final years of his brief life.

Schoenberg's development, though different in many ways, reveals significant parallels with Scriabin's. In his earlier works, too, the surface elaborations of a still basically tonal language are stressed to a point that eventually brings about the latter's dissolution. But Schoenberg's chromaticism is the product of rich webs of thematic and motivic development that bury the structural background under a complex, thickly woven contrapuntal overlay. Whereas in Scriabin the harmonic background moves slowly and projects its triadic nature with relative clarity, in

Schoenberg's music of the early 1900s the density and speed of the counterpoint produce a constantly shifting harmonic basis that at every moment appears ready to dissolve the argument into complete tonal uncertainty. Dominant-type harmonies, though still present, are increasingly de-emphasized as too suggestive of unwanted conventional resolutions. The stress is on highly varied dissonant complexes, which sound like opaque, heavily refracted distortions of the traditional harmonic functions that were fast becoming grammatical impossibilities, or at least embarrassments, to Schoenberg's ears. The final resolutions in the op. 8 orchestral songs, for example, or those of the Second String Quartet and *Kammersymphonie*, are still triadic; but they seem like reluctant tributes to a remote and distrusted authority.

Schoenberg's theoretical writings also reflect his new conception of foreground-background relationships. In a famous passage in his *Harmonielehre*, first published in 1911, he points to several momentary vertical structures cut out of compositions by Bach and Mozart, claiming to show that the sort of complex and highly differentiated dissonant harmonic structures found in his own work were already present in music of the eighteenth century.[22] What for Bach and Mozart were passing "accidents," the result of surface contrapuntal elaborations firmly tied to an unmistakably inferrable triadic background, have become for Schoenberg absolute entities warranting theoretical investigation and explanation in their own right.

In Schoenberg's music, as in Scriabin's, the moment at which the latent background completely receded, leaving virtually no trace, is approached gradually, almost imperceptibly; but sometime around 1907–8 a final margin was irreparably traversed. Despite this step-by-step evolution, the consequences were fundamental. Schoenberg's own awareness of having made a critical turn is apparent in the preface to his song cycle *Das Buch der hängenden Gärten* (generally considered to be the first major composition in the new style): "For the first time I have been successful in coming near an ideal of expression and form which I had had in mind for years. . . . Now that I have finally embarked upon this path I am conscious that I have broken all barriers of a past aesthetic."[23] And later he remarked of the last two movements of his Second String Quartet, a work briefly predating the cycle: "No longer could the great variety of dissonant sonorities be balanced out through occasional insertion of such tonal chords as one normally uses to express a tonality"; it was no longer "appropriate to force the motion into the Procrustean bed of tonality."[24]

Schoenberg thus sacrificed a traditional background in order to allow the compositional foreground to speak more freely, unencumbered by the constraints of a conventional syntax. Here, finally, was a music that could communicate directly, unmediated by external controls, and that was thus actually able to approach that "purity" of language so indiscriminately attributed to music in general by those working in the other arts. Yet the price to be paid was severe: Schoenberg's newly liberated foreground projected a "language" that no one, not even the composer himself, could understand, at least in the sense that one had always been able to "understand" traditional tonal music. As the composer himself remarked in his *Harmonielehre,* referring to the advanced harmonic constructions found in music of the century's first decade: "Why it is as it is, and why it is correct, I am at the moment unable to say."[25]

There can be no coincidence, certainly, in the fact that Schoenberg's final break with traditional tonality initiated the most productive period of his creative life. Within a two-year span from 1907 to 1909 he completed seven major compositions, including such extended works as the Second String Quartet, op. 10, *Das Buch der hängenden Gärten,* op. 15, the Five Orchestral Pieces, op. 16, and *Erwartung,* op. 17. The sense of a release, of a newly won freedom suddenly available beyond the "barriers of a past aesthetic," is evident in both the quantity and character of this music. Yet Schoenberg, working at the outer edges of what then seemed musically possible (at least to one committed to the notion of a continuously evolving tradition), increasingly felt the strain of operating at such disorienting heights, where only his unconscious, intuitive feeling for what was musically valid could serve him as guide. After the brief period of unprecedented productivity coinciding with the first explorations of the atonal terrain, Schoenberg's output decreased dramatically, coming to a virtual halt by 1916. For seven years thereafter no new compositions were published; and when new works began to appear again in 1923, they revealed a composer embarked upon a radically different course. In the intervening years Schoenberg had evolved a new musical system intended to replace tonality, one that—like tonality— would provide a method for consciously determining compositional choices.

This was the twelve-tone system, which Schoenberg envisioned as supplying the basis for a new "musical language," the *lingua franca* of a new stage in musical history. For despite the revolutionary character of many aspects of his thought, Schoenberg remained committed to the idea that this next stage would share with past ones a dependence upon a set of widely accepted compositional conventions, within whose terms all composers could shape their own personal statements. As a consequence, he came to view his own earlier atonal works as representatives of an essentially transitional phase of music history. Writing in 1932 on the historical necessity of the twelve-tone system, he commented upon his atonal work:

> The first compositions in this new style were written by me around 1908. . . . From the very beginnings such compositions differed from all preceding music, not only harmonically but also melodically, thematically, and motivically. But the foremost characteristic of these pieces in *statu nascendi* were their extreme expressiveness and their extraordinary brevity. . . . Thus, subconsciously, consequences were drawn from an innovation which, like every innovation, destroys while it produces. New colorful harmony was offered; but much was lost. . . . Fulfillment of all formal functions—comparable to the effect of punctuation in the construction of sentences, of subdivision into paragraphs, and of fusion into chapters—could scarcely be assured with chords whose constructive values had not as yet been explored. Hence it seemed at first impossible to compose pieces of complicated organization or of great length. . . . the conviction that these new sounds obey the laws of nature and of our manner of thinking—the conviction that order, logic, comprehensibility and form cannot be present without obedience to such laws—forces the composer along the road of exploration. He must find, if not laws or values, at least ways to justify the dissonant character of these harmonies and their successions.[26]

Schoenberg's change of attitude was by no means exceptional. Following World War I, Western composers generally tended to pull back from the heady, more experimental atmosphere of the prewar years. Manifestations of a new point of view were everywhere evident: e.g., in the simpler, more objective and more "everyday" type of music fostered by Satie and *Les Six,* and in the various moves toward a "new classicism" by such otherwise diverse figures as Stravinsky, Bartók, and Hindemith. Yet what seems in retrospect most telling about all of these developments was their failure to produce a new set of musical procedures even remotely comparable—in terms of commonality, of reflecting a consensus—to those of traditional tonality. Thus the twelve-tone system, though indisputably one of the most remarkable and influential technical achievements of twentieth-century music, has remained an essentially provisional method, occasionally employed by many composers but consistently used by relatively few. Nor did the widespread neoclassical turn of the between-the-war years produce an even marginally unified technical orientation; rather, it gave rise to a series of strongly personal and thus divergent and idiosyncratic reformulations of technical and stylistic traits drawn from virtually the entire range of Western music history. Cocteau's famous "call to order," which reverberated throughout the postwar period, remained in this respect largely unanswered.

From the present perspective, then, it would appear that the most important historical moment in defining the main coordinates of twentieth-century music was the widespread break from traditional tonality that occurred during the first decade of the century. From this moment springs the unprecedented stylistic, technical, and expressive variety of the music of the modern age—in short, what I have previously referred to as its linguistic plurality. Despite the numerous attempts that have been—and continue to be—made to offer a systematic account of Schoenberg's prewar music, the true force and significance of this music lies, it seems to me, precisely in its determination to speak in an unknown and enigmatic tongue that largely defies rational comprehension.[27]

This may help explain the unique position this music continues to occupy in our consciousness. Along with other composers of the time (one thinks also, inevitably, of the Stravinsky of the *Rite of Spring*), Schoenberg set the essential tone of music in the modern age. He attempted to transform musical language from a public vehicle, susceptible to comprehension by ordinary people (but thereby also limited to more or less ordinary statement), to a private one capable of speaking the unspeakable. Music became an incantation, a language of ritual that, just because of its inscrutability, revealed secrets hidden from normal understanding.

The fifteen songs of *Das Buch der hängenden Gärten* are settings of poems drawn from the volume of that title by Stefan George, who himself favored "a language inaccessible to the profane multitude." George's distinct elitism equally colors Schoenberg's aesthetic. (The composer once commented: "If it is art, it is not for all; and if it is for all, it is not art."[28]) But Schoenberg's elitism can be understood in part as an understandable reaction against a musical language that had lost its fundamental expressive core and thus its capacity to challenge, to illuminate, and to astonish. The composers of the first decade of the century undertook to revive musical language by reinventing it. They tried to disengage musical sounds from their inherited attachments, to set them free from conventional associations in pursuit of what Schoenberg (along with Kandinsky) called the "spiritual." In sober retrospect, they may seem to have failed; yet theirs was a brave and exhilarating effort that fundamentally altered the nature of musical discourse.

Notes

1. Richard Wagner, "Das Schauspiel und das Wesen der dramatischen Dichtkunst," *Oper und Drama*, vol. 4 of *Gesammelte Schriften und Dichtungen* (Leipzig: Giegel's Musikalienhandlung, 1907), 97–98; "Zukunftsmusik," ibid., 7:111. Translations of these passages are taken from Richard Wagner, *Prose Works*, ed. and trans. W. A. Ellis, 8 vols. (1892–99; reprint, London: Broude Brothers, 1966), 2:213 and 3:319. Italics are mine.

2. Donald Mitchell, *The Language of Modern Music* (London: Faber and Faber, 1963).

3. Hugo von Hofmannsthal, *Gesammelte Werke*, ed. Bernd Schoeller, 10 vols. (Frankfurt: Fischer-Taschenbuch-Verlag, 1979), 7:471–72.

4. Friedrich Nietzsche, *The Will to Power*, vol. 15 of *Complete Works*, trans. A. W. Ludovici, ed. Oscar Levy, 18 vols. (London: T. N. Foulis, 1909–15), 74.

5. *The Letters of Gustave Flaubert 1830–1857*, ed. Francis Steegmuller (Cambridge: Harvard Univ. Press, 1980), 154. The comment is made in a letter written in 1852 to Louise Colet. Other passages are equally remarkable for their "modernist" tone. Flaubert argues that from the standpoint of *l'Art pur*, "one might almost establish the axiom that there is no such thing as subject—style in itself being an absolute manner of seeing things." Further: "The finest works are those that contain the least matter; the closer expression comes to thought, the closer language comes to coinciding and merging with it, the finer the result. I believe the future of art lies in this direction. I see it, as it has developed from its beginnings, growing progressively more ethereal. Form, in becoming more skillful, becomes attenuated, it leaves behind all liturgy, rule, measure; the epic is discarded in favor of the novel, verse in favor of prose; there is no longer any orthodoxy, and form is as free as the will of its creator. The progressive shedding of the burden of tradition can be observed everywhere: governments have gone through similar evolution from oriental despotisms to the socialisms of the future."

6. Walter Pater, *Selected Works*, ed. Richard Aldington (London: W. Heinemann, 1948), 27. These words appear in Pater's article "The School of Giorgione," in an introductory section dealing with relationships among the arts, in which music is especially praised for its "abstract language." The passage continues in a vein closely resembling that of the Flaubert letter quoted above: "That the mere matter of a poem, its subject matter, namely, its given incidents or situation—that the mere matter of a picture, the actual circumstances of an event, the actual topography of a landscape—should be nothing without the form, the spirit of the handling, that this form, this mode of handling, should become an end in itself, should penetrate every part of the matter: this is what

all art constantly strives after, and achieves in different degrees. . . . Art, then, is thus always striving . . . to get rid of its responsibilities to its subject or material."

7. Paul Verlaine, *Oeuvres Poétiques,* ed. Yves-Gerard le Dantec, 5 vols. (Paris: Yves-Gerard le Dantec, 1900–1904), 2:21. These words form the opening line of the poem *Art poétique.*

8. Paul Valéry, *Oeuvres,* 11 vols. (Paris: Editions du saggitaire, 1931–38), 7:163–64. The complete passage, which appears in the essay "Situation de Baudelaire," reads: "Ce qui fut baptisé le Symbolisme se résume très simplement dans l'intention commune à plusieurs familles de poètes de reprendre à la musique leur bien." It follows a discussion of Poe's influence on Baudelaire, in which Valéry mentions the modern tendency to separate "the modes and the domains of activity" in order to achieve *l'état pur,* and thus *la poésie absolue.* Compare the following, from Valéry's lecture entitled "Aesthetic Invention": "Poetry, an art of language, is thus obliged to struggle against its practical uses. It will emphasize everything that distinguishes it from prose. Thus, quite unlike the musician and less fortunate, the poet is compelled, in each of his creations, to create . . . the psychological and emotional state in which language can fulfill a role free from that of signifying what is or was or will be." *Aesthetics,* vol. 13 of *The Collected Works of Paul Valéry,* trans. Paul Manheim, ed. Jackson Mathews, 15 vols. (New York: Pantheon, 1956–75), 68.

9. Again this recalls Nietzsche: "Compared with music, communication by means of words is a shameless mode of procedure; words reduce and stultify; words make impersonal; words make common that which is uncommon." *Complete Works,* 15:254. An article by Henri Peyre, "Poets against music in the age of symbolism," included in *Symbolism and Modern Literature: Studies in Honor of Wallace Fowlie,* ed. Marcel Tetel (Durham, N.C.: Duke Univ. Press, 1978), 179–92, perhaps deserves comment here, as it contends that the symbolists were on the whole not very interested in music and, frequently, were even vigorously opposed to it. Yet much of Peyre's argument turns out to rest on the fact that many of the symbolists *envied* music, which is not at all the same thing as being "against" it. A recurrent refrain is Peyre's claim that many of the symbolist poets were quite unmusical, had little if any technical or historical knowledge of music, and did not even enjoy it as an art form. Even if that is true, it in no way eliminates the possibility of these same poets' relying upon the *idea* of music as a sort of general aesthetic model. Moreover, one must doubt the reliability of a writer who refers to Webern's settings of "Baudelaire's hardly inspired poems on wine" (the reference is presumably to Alban Berg's cantata *Der Wein,* which is based on Stefan George's very free German translations of selections from Baudelaire's cycle *Le Vin*) as a judge of musical knowledge and musicality.

10. Wassily Kandinsky, *Complete Writings on Art,* ed. Kenneth C. Lindsay and Peter Vergo, 2 vols. (Boston: G. K. Hall, 1982), 1:107.

11. Ibid., 1:154–55.

12. Ibid., 1:196 and 209.

13. Arthur Schopenhauer, *The World as Will and Idea,* 4th ed., trans. R. B. Haldange and J. Kemp, 4 vols. (London: K. Paul, Trench, Trubner, 1896).

Schopenhauer's discussion of music, from which all quotations in this paragraph are taken, appears at the end of the third book of vol. 1, 330–46.

14. For a revealing discussion of this topic, see Carl Dahlhaus, *Die Idee der absoluten Musik* (Kassel: Deutscher Tasschenbuch-Verlag, 1978).

15. Wilhelm Heinrich Wackenroder, *Werke und Briefe*, ed. Friedrich von der Leyen, 2 vols. (Jena: E. Diederich, 1910), 1:168.

16. Quoted in George Knepler, *Musikgeschichte des 19. Jahrhunderts*, 2 vols. (Berlin: Henschelverlag, 1961), 2:684.

17. Friedrich Nietzsche, *The Twilight of the Idols*, vol. 16 of *Complete Works*, 22.

18. Claude Debussy, *Monsieur Croche the Dilettante Hater* (London: Noel Douglas, 1927), 32.

19. Richard Wagner, "On Liszt's Symphonic Poems," *Prose Works*, 3:253.

20. Ferruccio Busoni, *A New Aesthetic of Music* (New York: G. Schirmer, 1911), 7–8.

21. The terms "foreground" and "background" are derived from the Austrian musical theorist Heinrich Schenker, although I am using them here in a more general, and more informal, sense than Schenker does.

22. Arnold Schoenberg, *Harmonielehre*, 2d ed. (Vienna: Universal-edition, 1922), 392.

23. Arnold Schoenberg, *Lieder mit Klavierbegleitung, Sämtliche Werke*, ed. Joseph Rufer (Mainz: B. Schott's Sohne, 1966), ser. A, 1:xix.

24. Arnold Schoenberg, *Die Streichquartette der Wiener Schule: Eine Dokumentation*, ed. Ursula v. Rauchhaupt (München: H. Ellermann, 1971), 15.

25. Arnold Schoenberg, *Harmonielehre*, 504.

26. Arnold Schoenberg, *Style and Idea*, ed. Leonard Stein (New York: St. Martin's Press, 1975), 217–18.

27. Of course the question of comprehensibility is one of degree, and it is also subject to historical revision. I would not claim, certainly, that Schoenberg's atonal music makes no "rational" sense whatever. Even its most extreme manifestations (e.g., *Erwartung*) retain sufficient formal and expressive ties to the music of late German romanticism—including Schoenberg's own earlier tonal compositions—to ensure a degree of traditional comprehensibility. Indeed, the extraordinary expressive impact of Schoenberg's atonal work stems largely, in my view, precisely from the fact that it presents a radically distorted image of this earlier music; and any effective hearing must somehow trace the shadowy remains of the very musical conventions it purports to have overthrown. In addition, the music reveals purely internal consistencies, especially intervallic correspondences, that—no matter how tenuous—ensure some measure of coherence. And of course the more we hear and study the music, the more it will doubtless gain in clarity.

Thus the "privacy" or "secrecy" of the musical language of Schoenbergian atonality is relative. Nevertheless, it seems highly unlikely that this music will ever give up its "secrets" to anything like the extent that compositions of the eighteenth and nineteenth centuries have (or others of the twentieth century, for that matter). This is confirmed by the present state of theoretical knowledge: the very sophistication and methodological complexity required of the best current analyses of Schoenberg's atonal works to establish even the most rudimentary sorts of musical correspondences offer convincing, if ironic, evidence of the extraordinary resistance of this music to systematic technical clarification. And although it is always possible, at least in principle, that a convincing theoretical model will eventually be developed, providing analyses of this music with an explanatory power comparable to that of the best analyses of tonal music, the prospect strikes me as very doubtful. Moreover, it would undermine what seems to me the essential nature of this music and totally alter its historical and aesthetic meaning. More important, the music would thereby lose perhaps its most distinguishing expressive feature: its mystery.

28. Schoenberg, *Style and Idea*, 124.

Martin Esslin

Modernity and Drama

Concepts, it must be said at the outset, like modernity, modernism, and the avant-garde fill me with apprehension and doubt. They are, after all, concepts of relation rather than fact. To ask, "What is the avant-garde? What is modern?" is rather like asking: "How long is a piece of string?" In relation to yesterday's art, today's art is modern, or avant-garde. As the great illuminator Oderisi tells Dante in the eleventh canto of the *Purgatorio:*

> Credette Cimabue nella pittura
> tener lo campo, ed ora ha Giotto il grido,
> sì che la fama di colui è scura.
>
> Così ha tolto l'uno a l'altro Guido
> la gloria de la lingua; e forse è nato
> chi l'uno e l'altro caccerà del nido.

(Once Cimabue held sway in painting, but now does Giotto have the cry, so that the fame of the former is obscured. Similarly has the one Guido taken from the other the glory of the language, and perhaps one has been born who will chase both from the nest.)

"Modern," after all, only means "le dernier cri." In German it can even mean no more than "fashionable." The term, I suppose, entered discourse about art and literature with the Renaissance, when there were disputes as to the relative merit of works produced in Greek and Roman antiquity as against those of the period; Swift later dramatized this conflict in his *Battle of the Books.*

And yet, in the course of the nineteenth century the concept of modernity *did* acquire a special significance, at least for the people then experiencing what to them seemed a truly epochal change of lifestyle and thinking. With the coming of the industrial revolution, the introduction of the steam engine, powerlooms, railways, the telegraph, and photography, and the new uses of electricity, together with the rise of new ideologies (Darwinism, Marxism, positivism) and the decline of belief in revealed religions, it must have seemed to these people that an age had truly come to an end. As it happens—and this is particularly true of the drama—there had previously been a longish period during which academicism, i.e., a fairly rigid adherence to what seemed immutable standards of excellence and technique in the writing and performance of plays, was prevalent, so that it really seemed that these orthodoxies were destined to undergo the fate of all the others that were being swept away. In fact, of course, this was merely an optical illusion: the rigid standards of the French Academy or the English Augustans were themselves fairly recent phenomena and by no means immovably fixed as absolutes, as then appeared.

Seen from this angle, the beginnings of Modernism, in our present sense, in drama dates from the rise of the romantic movement, or, in Germany, from the *Sturm und Drang*. As such, initially, it was a revolt against *formal* restraints, the tyranny of the three unities, and the rigid rules of seemliness that governed the art of acting, the restraints on what could and what could not be shown on the stage.

When absolutes are dethroned, everything becomes *relative;* and the beginnings of Modernism in this sense are intimately linked with the growth of a sense of the differences between cultures synchronically and between historical epochs diachronically. Different standards of ethics, different values of beauty are suddenly perceived as possible. With the rapid technological changes of the nineteenth century the historical sense became dominant. As Nietzsche put it in *Jenseits von Gut und Böse* (1886):

> Der historische Sinn . . . auf welchen wir Europäer als auf unsre Besonderheit Anspruch machen, ist uns im Gefolge der bezaubernden und tollen Halb-barbarei gekommen, in welche Europa durch die demokratische Vermengung der Stände und Rassen gestürzt worden ist—erst das neunzehnte Jahrhundert kennt diesen Sinn, als seinen sechsten Sinn. Die Vergangenheit von jeder Form und Lebensweise, von Kulturen, die früher hart nebeneinander, über-einander lagen, strömt dank jener Mischung in uns "moderne Seelen" aus, unsre Instinkte laufen nunmehr überallhin zurück; wir selbst sind eine Art Chaos. . . . Durch unsre Halbbarbarei in Leib und Begierde haben wir geheime Zugänge überallhin.

(The historical sense ... which we Europeans claim as our specialty, has come to us as a consequence of the enchanting and mad semibarbarism into which Europe has been plunged by the democratic commingling of social classes and races—the nineteenth century is the first to know this sense, as its own sixth sense. The past of every form and way of life, of cultures, that previously had lain in hard distinction side by side, or one above the other, now, thanks to that commingling streams into us "modern" souls, our instincts now run back to everywhere; we, ourselves, are a kind of chaos. ... Through our semibarbarism, in body and in desire, we have secret access everywhere.)

And, significantly, among the examples Nietzsche quotes for this semi-barbarity, caused by the newly acquired historical sense, is the renewed vogue of Shakespeare, whose drama he calls an

erstaunliche spanisch-maurisch-sächsischen Geschmacks-Synthesis, über welchen sich ein Altathener aus der Freundschaft des Äschylos halbtot gelacht oder geärgert haben würde: aber wir—nehmen gerade diese wilde Buntheit, dies Durcheinander des Zartesten, Gröbsten und Küntstlichsten, mit einer geheimen Vertraulichkeit und Herzlichkeit an, wir geniessen ihn als das gerade uns aufgesparte Raffinement der Kunst und lassen uns dabei von den widrigen Dämpfen und der Nähe des englischen Pöbels, in welcher Shakespeares Kunst und Geschmack lebt, so wenig stören als etwas auf der Chiaja Neapels: wo wir mit allen unsren Sinnen, bezaubert und willig, unsres Wegs gehn, wie sehr auch die Kloaken der Pöbel-Quartiere in der Luft sind.

(astonishing Spanish-Moorish-Saxon synthesis of tastes, about which an ancient Athenian from among the friends of Aeschylus would have almost died of laughter or anger: but we—we accept this very wild proliferation of colors, this mixture of the most tender with the most coarse and artificial, with a secret connivance and heartiness, we savor him as the highest refinement of art that has been specially vouchsafed to *us;* and in doing so we are as little disturbed by the noxious exhalations, and the proximity, of the English mob, in which Shakespeare's art is at home, as we are when walking down the Chiaia in Naples: where we go on our way, enchanted and willing with all our senses, however much the cloacas of the slums are in the air.)

And to complete this analysis Nietzsche—who, while obviously deploring what he describes, yet must reckon himself one of the semibarbarians of the modern age, with its sense of history—adds:

Das *Mass* ist uns fremd, gestehn wir es uns; unser Kitzel ist gerade der Kitzel des Unendlichen, Ungemessnen. Gleich dem Reiter auf vorwärts-schnaubendem Rosse lassen wir vor dem Unendlichen die Zügel fallen, wir modernen Menschen, wir Halbbarbaren—und sind erst dort *in unsrer* Seligkeit, wo wir auch am meisten—*in Gefahr sind.*

(Let us admit it: we are strangers to the concept of *measure;* what tickles us is precisely the tickle of the infinite, the unmeasured. Like a rider on a horse that is bolting we drop our reins, confronted with the infinite, we modern human beings, we semibarbarians—and we are in our greatest ecstasy where we also are most—*in danger.*[1]

I have quoted this passage of Nietzsche's at such length because I believe that he more than anyone else was the true prophet of modernity, whose wild, extravagant thought perceived and penetrated the nature of the epochal change that the nineteenth century brought to human history, and predicted with astonishing insight many of the terrible and cataclysmic events that inevitably followed from that change of human destiny. It is ironic that Nietzsche is just now being discovered by the currently fashionable intellectual gurus in France, for already in his own time he was very much perceived, even by the popular imagination, as the embodiment of all that was dangerous in modernity. I remember how as a child I got hold of some pious piece of popular fiction—alas, I have forgotten its author and title—published in Germany around the turn of the century. When its heroine confessed to her parents that she had fallen in love with a young man, her father sternly said, "I hope he is not one of those who reads Ibsen and Nietzsche."

And indeed, Ibsen and Nietzsche have much in common. It is sometimes as though Ibsen, outwardly the sober, well-regulated bourgeois, embodied basic traits of Nietzsche in his characters; Nietzsche, for example, wrote the passages I have just quoted in the highest village of the Swiss Alps, Sils-Maria, at the foot of a glacier, shortly before madness engulfed him—as though he was living out the destiny that Ibsen had given Brand; and Ibsen's Stockmann rages against the rule of the mob as much as Nietzsche ever did. Above all, Ibsen, like Nietzsche, denounced the false morality of a dying world. This, to my mind, is the essence of Modernism in the sense in which we are discussing it here: the "revaluation of all values" of which Nietzsche spoke, the quest for a new morality beyond the old concepts of Good and Evil; and the rejection of the philosophical and religious, metaphysical, basis of those beliefs. If Ibsen, in *The Lady from the Sea,* created the first truly, and consciously, existential heroine in drama, who can make her choice only after she has been given total freedom to make it (and whether Ibsen got this existentialism from Kierkegaard or not is as yet a matter of dispute), Nietzsche also clearly prefigured the drama of existential choice:

Wenn ich den Vorgang zerlege, der in dem Satz "ich denke" ausgedrückt ist, so bekomme ich eine Reihe von verwegnen Behauptungen, deren Begründung schwer, vielleicht unmöglich ist,—zum Beispiel, dass *ich* es bin, der denkt, dass überhaupt ein Etwas es sein muss, das denkt, dass Denken eine Tätigkeit und Wirkung seitens eines Wesens ist, welches als Ursache gedacht wird, dass es ein "Ich" gibt, endlich, dass es bereits feststeht, was mit Denken zu bezeichnen ist—dass ich *weiss,* was Denken ist.

(If I dismantle [perhaps today we should translate "deconstruct"] what happens that is expressed in the phrase "I think," I'll get a series of daring assertions, that are difficult, perhaps impossible, to prove: for example that it is *I* who is thinking; that, indeed, it must be something that is thinking: that thinking is an activity and an effect on the part of an entity that can be regarded as a cause; that, finally, there is such a thing as I; and that it is already established what it is that can be called thinking—that I *know* what thinking is.[2]

Much of Beckett is prefigured in these ideas, as it is, even more clearly, in this passage in which Nietzsche deals with the concept of the soul:

Man muss zunächst auch jener andern und verhängnisvolleren Atomistik den Garaus machen, welche das Christentum am besten und längsten gelehrt hat, der *Seelen-Atomistik.* Mit diesem Wort sei es erlaubt, jenen Glauben zu bezeichnen, der die Seele als etwas Unvertilgbares, Ewiges, Unteilbares, als eine Monade, als ein *Atomon* nimmt: *diesen* Glauben soll man aus der Wissenschaft hinausschaffen! Es ist unter uns gesagt, ganz und gar nicht nötig, "die Seele" selbst dabei loszuwerden und auf eine der ältesten und ehrwürdigsten Hypothesen Verzicht zu leisten: wie es dem Ungeschick der Naturalisten zu begegnen pflegt, welche, kaum dass sie an "die Seele" rühren, sie auch verlieren. Aber der Weg zu neuen Fassungen und Verfein- erungen der Seelen-Hypothese steht offen: und Begriffe wie "sterbliche Seele" und "Seele als Subjekts-Vielheit" und "Seele als Gesellschaftsbau der Triebe und Affekte" wollen fürderhin in der Wissenschaft Bürgerrecht haben.

(We must give a *coup de grâce* to that other and even more fatal atomism that Christianity has been teaching best and longest, the *atomism of the soul.* Let us be permitted to use that term to denote the belief that regards the soul as something ineradicable, eternal, indivisible, as a monad, an *atomon:* that belief must be thrown out of science. It is, let it be said among ourselves, quite unnecessary to get rid of the soul itself in doing so . . . as happens through the clumsiness of those naturalists who, hardly have they touched the soul, immediately lose it altogether. But the way to new versions and refinements of the hypothesis of the soul is open: and concepts like "a mortal soul" or "the soul as the multiplicity of the subject" and "the soul as the social edifice of drives and emotions" should in future have their right of citizenship without science.)[3]

If the little play by Yevreinov, *The Theater of the Soul,* which was produced at the Claremont Colleges Comparative Literature Conference on Modernism, is almost a word-for-word translation of this passage from Nietzsche's *Jenseits von Gut und Böse* into theatrical terms, how much more so is the whole mighty *oeuvre* of Samuel Beckett, who never ceases to dismantle and deconstruct the Cartesian "cogito ergo sum." And, if we turn to another giant among the creators of Modernism in drama, Antonin Artaud, we find that he, too, in his own way, followed on a path that Nietzsche, as the first thinker to gain an insight into the meaning of what was happening in his time, had opened up and prescribed:

> Man soll über die Grausamkeit umlernen und die Augen aufmachen; man soll endlich Ungeduld lernen, damit nicht länger solche unbescheidne dicke Irrtümer tugendhaft und dreist herumwandeln, wie sie zum Beispiel in betreff der Tragödie von alten und neuen Philosophen aufgefüttert worden sind. Fast alles, was wir "höhere Kultur" nenne, beruht auf der Vergeistigung und Vertiefung der *Grausamkeit*—dies ist mein Satz; jenes "wilde Tier" ist gar nicht abgetötet worden, es lebt, es blüht, es hat sich nur—vergöttlicht. Was die schmerzliche Wollust der Tragödie ausmacht, ist Grausamkeit; was im sogenannten tragischen Mitleiden, im Grunde sogar in allem Erhabnen bis hinauf zu den höchsten und zartesten Schaudern der Metaphysik, angenehm wirkt, bekommt seine Süssigkeit allein von der eingemischten Ingredienz der Grausamkeit.

> (We have to revise our notions of cruelty and open our eyes; we should at last be eager to prevent such immodest and gross mistakes to run about virtuously and impertinently, as, for example, those that have been bred up by ancient and new philosophers about tragedy. Almost everything that we call "higher culture" is based on the spiritualization and deepening of *cruelty*—that is my verdict; that "wild beast" has not been deadened, it lives, it flourishes, it has even been made divine. What determines the sorrowful lust of tragedy is cruelty; what is felt as pleasurable in the so-called tragic pity and essentially even in everything sublime right up to the highest and most tender tremors of metaphysics, gets its sweetness solely from the ingredient of cruelty that is mixed up with it.)[4]

I apologize for quoting Nietzsche so copiously, but I feel that his diagnosis of the nature and consequences of the sea-change that European culture had undergone in his time is a profound help in understanding the quality of that change. And, of course, Nietzsche has an intimate connection with drama, not only because he started on his career as a brilliant and original interpreter of the nature of Greek tragedy, but also because he was intimately associated with another of the great creators of the modern theater, Richard Wagner. Wagner, I believe, is as important as Ibsen and Strindberg in the genesis of the Modernist drama. It is no coincidence that the man who did most to naturalize the concept of Modernist drama in the English-speaking world, George

Bernard Shaw, was an Ibsenite as well as a Wagnerian, and, of course, philosophically decidedly a Nietzschean. What is Shaw's life force but an English version of Nietzsche's vitalism, his will to power? Shaw's love of paradox is comparable to Nietzsche's revaluation of all values with the addition of an Anglo-Irish sense of humor. (If we wanted to bring Strindberg into the Nietzschean orbit we would only have to mention Nietzsche's insane anti-feminism, so religiously echoed by Strindberg. But, of course, Strindberg's de-atomization of the human soul and his take-off into introspective expressionism also echo Nietzsche's insights about the ultimate consequences of the abandonment of the Christian concept of the immortal soul, one and indivisible.)

But to go back to the beginnings: the revolt of the romantics and their precursors against the classical ideal and the tyranny of the unities and the Alexandrine was initially a revolt against worn-out forms. That the whole movement ultimately arose from an endeavor to reinstate Shakespeare as the model of great drama shows not only the modernity of Shakespeare but that ultimately the "Modernist" movement was a return to the roots of drama *before* the academicism of the seventeenth and eighteenth centuries seemed to have put a stop to all development by decreeing a perfect model to be followed (and in painting and sculpture as much as in drama).

But once the formal bounds had been broken, new subject matter, new substance, could stream into the drama. And it must not be forgotten that of all forms of art the drama is most closely linked with technology, back to the *deus ex machina,* the God who appeared by courtesy of a machine in ancient Greece. Throughout history drama has been highly technological. In fourteenth- and fifteenth-century Florence elaborate machines enabled the angels in mystery plays to fly high above the worshippers in some of the great churches of the city. The baroque age luxuriated in machinery for transformation scenes, flying clouds inhabited by Gods, and other spectacular effects. The coming of gas and then electric light, hydraulically operated stage machinery, and the cinema and other means for mechanically reproducing and electronically distributing drama have put drama into the very center of a whole series of industrial revolutions. And each of these innovations and technological advances has, in turn, opened the floodgates for the new contents, the new things that drama could say, that Nietzsche had so brilliantly discerned.

If romanticism was the initial revolt, naturalism seems to me the actual root of all our Modernist drama. As Otto Brahm, the German apostle of Ibsen, put it in one of the earliest manifestos of his *Freie Bühne:*

Der Bannerspruch der neuen Kunst, mit goldenen Lettern aufgezeichnet
... ist das eine Wort: Wahrheit; und Wahrheit, Wahrheit auf jedem Le-
benspfade ist es, die auch wir erstreben und fordern. Nicht die objektive
Wahrheit, die dem Kämpfenden entgeht, sondern die individuelle Wahrheit,
welche aus der innersten Überzeugung frei geschöpft ist und frei ausgesprochen: die Wahrheit des unabhängigen Geistes, der nichts zu beschönigen
und nichts zu vertuschen hat. Und der darum nur einen Gegner kennt,
seinen Erbfeind und Todfeind: die Lüge in jeglicher Gestalt. ...
    ... Die moderne Kunst, wo sie ihre lebensvollsten Triebe ansetzt, hat
auf dem Boden des Naturalismus Wurzel geschlagen. Sie hat, einem tiefinnern
Zuge dieser Zeit gehorchend, sich auf die Erkenntnis der natürlichen Das-
einsmächte gerichtet und zeigt uns mit rücksichtslosem Wahrheitstriebe die
Welt wie sie ist. Dem Naturalismus Freund, wollen wir eine gute Strecke
Weges mit ihm schreiten, allein es soll uns nicht erstaunen, wenn im Verlauf
der Wanderschaft, an einem Punkt, den wir heute noch nicht überschauen,
die Strasse plötzlich sich biegt und überraschende neue Blicke in Kunst
und Leben sich auftun. Denn an keine Formel, auch an die jüngste nicht,
ist die unendliche Entwickelung menschlicher Kultur gebunden; und in
dieser Zuversicht, im Glauben an das ewig Werdende, haben wir eine freie
Bühne aufgeschlagen, für das moderne Leben.

(The slogan that the new art carries in golden letters on its flag ... is one
word: truth; and truth, truth on every path of our life is what we strive
for and demand. Not objective truth, which escapes anyone engaged in a
fight, but individual truth, which is freely arrived at from deepest convictions
and freely uttered: the truth of the independent spirit who has nothing to
embellish or conceal. And who, therefore, has only one opponent: his
hereditary and mortal enemy: the lie in any form whatever. ...
    ... Modern art, where it is developing its most vital shoots, has put
its roots into the soil of naturalism. It has, obeying a deep inner feature
of our time, directed its attention to gaining knowledge of the powers of
nature and it shows us the world as it is, with ruthless truthfulness. Friends
as we are of naturalism we want to travel a good deal of the road with
it, but it should not surprise us if, in the course of our wanderings, at a
point we cannot as yet see, the road should suddenly bend and unexpectedly
disclose new vistas in art and life. For the infinite development of human
culture is not bound to any formula, not even the most recent; and in this
hope in continuous growth we have established a free stage for modern
life.)[5]

This openness of the naturalists, indeed, their eagerness to branch out
into an infinity of new, as yet undiscovered paths, is often overlooked
by those whose own ideas originated in a rejection of the original,
primitive forms of naturalism as a photographic reproduction of reality,
as life in a room without its fourth wall. In fact, just as, in the novel,
it was a consequent application of the desire for the truth, the whole
truth, and nothing but the truth that led Dujardin, Schnitzler, and Joyce

into the realms of the internal monologue, so in the case of Strindberg and the expressionists it was introspection and the desire to represent the world as it was perceived by an individual (this being the only verifiable experience of reality available to anyone) that led to the dramatization of dreams, hallucinations, fantasies, and nightmares.

"Der mittelpunkt den Welt ist in jedem ich" (The center of the world is inside each ego), said Theodor Däubler in one of the early manifestos of German expressionism, which contains what I find to be one of the pithiest definitions of that style:

> Der Volksmund sagt: wenn einer gehängt wird, so erlebt er im letzten Augenblick sein ganzes Leben nochmals. Das kann nur Expressionismus sein!
>
> (Popular belief has it: when someone is being hanged he relives his whole life in his last moment. And that can only be Expressionism!)[6]

That is how realism turned into surrealism; it was Apollinaire who coined the term in his preface to *Les Mamelles de Tirésias*. He felt that the reality, the truth, of walking was best expressed in the invention of the wheel, which did not look like walking legs but performed the same action more efficiently and therefore more truly. Yvan Goll, the bilingual French and German poet, formulated the same thought when he said, in his preface to one of his *Überdramen* (superdramas) in 1922:

> Überrealismus ist die stärkste Negierung des Realismus. Die Wirklichkeit des Scheins wird entlarvt, zugunsten der Wahrheit des Seins. "Masken," grob, grotesk, wie die Gefühle, deren Ausdruck sie sind. Nicht mehr "Helden," sondern Menschen, nicht Charaktere mehr, sondern die nackten Instinkte. Ganz nackt.
>
> Der Dramatiker ist ein Forscher, ein Politiker und ein Gesetzgeber. Als Überrealist statuiert er Dinge aus einem fernen Reich der Wahrheit, die er erhorchte, als er das Ohr an die verschlossenen Wände der Welt legte.
>
> Alogik ist heute der geistige Humor, also die beste Waffe gegen die Phrasen, die das ganze Leben beherrschen. Der Mensch redet in seinem. Alltag fast immer nur, um die Zunge, nicht um den Geist in Bewegung zu setzen. Wozu soviel reden, und das alles so ernst nehmen!
>
> (Surrealism is the strongest negation of realism. The reality of appearance is unmasked in favor of the truth of being. "Masks," coarse, grotesque, like the feelings of which they are the expression. No longer "heroes" but human beings, no longer "characters" but naked instincts. Totally naked.
>
> The playwright is an explorer, a politician and a legislator. As a surrealist he decrees things that come from a distant realm of truth, that he has overheard when he laid his ear against the closed walls of the world.
>
> Nonsense [Goll calls it "Alogik"] is today the humor of the spirit, and thus the best weapon against the clichés that rule all of our lives.

Human beings in their everyday existence almost always merely talk to move their tongues, not their intellects. Why should one talk so much and take everything seriously!)[7]

So here too the argument for surrealism, for what we later came to call "the absurd," is derived from the same search for the *truth* that animated the early naturalists, who had rejected the concept of *beauty,* or *seemliness, measure,* and *control.* Thus had the scientific spirit turned a somersault into the absurd.

How then does that other self-proclaimed scientific impulse, that of Marxism, which lies behind the work of Brecht and the Brechtians— another important sector of Modernist drama—fit into this picture? Well, surely Marxism, out of Hegel, is a blatant case of the historicism, that sense of history, that Nietzsche had diagnosed as the essential characteristic, the sixth sense, of the modern world. And what is more: Brecht's theory of epic theater and the *Verfremdungseffekt,* his rejection of introspective psychology in favor of a behavioristic model of man as the product of his social environment, is another variant of Nietzsche's rejection of the soul as a monad, of character as an indivisible whole. If the introspection of the expressionists, surrealists, and absurdists dissolves that unity of the soul from the *inside,* Brecht's insistence that all that matters is what is observable on the *outside* dissolves it from the opposite end of the spectrum. There is no such thing as one individual human character, Brecht claimed, there is only one human being in social contact with another; the same person will be utterly different when confronted with his boss from what he is when confronted with a social inferior. Human character, Brecht once said, is *not* like a grease stain that you can't get out of a garment however much you rub it.

The point I am trying to make is simply this: behind the vast diversity, the proliferation of forms and -isms, the seemingly diametrical opposition between the different strands of contemporary drama, there still lies that one single impulse, born of the nineteenth century's rejection of the traditional world system that had seemed to contain and explain the ways of the world and to justify the ways of God to Man. The impulse behind all this modernity to this day is thus essentially a negative one—a rejection of any closed worldviews, any closed world systems. Hence the curious paradox, for example, that totalitarian countries, whether Marxist or fascist, reject Modernist art, because they *need* to constitute a closed system, however simplistic and primitive it might be. Hence Brecht's Marxist dramatic theory and practice had to struggle against the totalitarian orthodoxies of the Stalinist aesthetics and prevailed in the end in that world only after it had been rigidified into a lifeless exhibit in a museum of prestigious artifacts.

The original negative impulse of Modernism, however, that rejection of formal rules that arose with the romantics and broke through with naturalism, has by no means exhausted itself: the contemporary avant-garde in drama, whether political or aesthetic, environmental or street-theatrical, whether in performance art or Grotowskian intensity, is still nourished by that impulse.

Where will it end? Have we not reached the limits, the point at which even the definition of what drama, what theater, *is* has been almost totally dissolved by the tearing down of the distinction between actor and spectator, audience and participant-in-the-action? Are we not reaching an area of total negation, total anarchy?

I must confess that I do not know the answer to these questions. What is undoubtedly the case, however, is that the proliferation of new forms and theories (that all, ultimately, go back to the same root concept) has not obliterated all previous forms; we still have classical drama, well performed today, perhaps better than at any previous time; and we still have, in the mass media, an almost obscene profusion of the most old-fashioned premodernist comedy and melodrama. All that is still drama, and indeed we have today more old-fashioned, premodernist drama than at any time in human history: it has become omnipresent. The revenge of the philistines, of the fathers who did not want their sons to find their own ways, is all around us. Perhaps in light of this fact, the cavortings of the heirs to the Modernist impulse, those knights in shining armor who see themselves as the advance guard of a new and better humanity, are reduced to their true proportion and their true function: to continue hammering at the fossilized rules of form and seemliness that spread a simplistic and primitive worldview and thus carry an obtuse and outmoded content into the consciousness of the people of a homogenized mass culture and an atomized society.

Or is it that it was the destruction of those old formal structures that has created the present state of affairs? It is at least possible that this is the case, and it *would* be the ultimate irony.

What, to my mind, is essential is that in the area of serious endeavor at the frontiers of the art of drama there should be a powerful desire to maintain the highest standards of quality. In fields where new soil is being broken, where rules have been overthrown and new conventions are being sought, it is inevitable that there should be much that is pretentious, silly, stupid, and untalented. That is inevitable and will always remain so; it lies in the very nature of things. All the more important then has the function of the critic become; all the more crucial is it that his or her endeavors should be pursued without pretentiousness, censoriousness, or pedantry, but with insight, humility, openness of mind, rejection of all prejudice, and above all with the maximum of intelligent self-awareness and self-criticism.

Notes

1. Friedrich Nietzsche, *Jenseits von Gut und Böse,* vol. 2 of *Werke in drei Bänden* (Munich: Hanser, 1955), 686–88. All translations are mine.

2. Ibid., 579–80.

3. Ibid., 577.

4. Ibid., 693–94.

5. Otto Brahm, from "Vorrede zu 'Freie Bühne' für modernes leben" (Frankfurt-am-Main: Fischer, 1890).

6. Theodor Däubler, "Expressionismus," in *Der Neue Standpunkt* (Dresden-Hellerau: Jacob Megin, 1916).

7. Ivan Goll, preface to *Methusalem* (Potsdam: G. Kiepheuer, 1922).

Robert Wohl

The Generation of 1914
and Modernism

Desde hace veinte años, los jóvenes más alertas de dos gen-
eraciones sucesivas—en Paris, en Berlín, en Londrés, Nueva
York, Roma, Madrid—se han encontrado sorprendidos por
el hecho ineluctable de que el arte tradicional no les interesaba;
más aún: les repugnaba. Con estos jóvenes cabe hacer una
de dos cosas: o fusilarlos o esforzarse en comprenderlos. Yo
he optado resueltamente por esta segunda operación.

(For twenty years the most alert young people of two successive
generations—in Paris, Berlin, London, New York, Rome,
Madrid—have found themselves surprised by the unavoidable
fact that traditional art holds no interest for them; even more,
that it disgusts them. With these young people one can do
one of two things: shoot them or try to understand them. I
have opted resolutely for this second operation.)[1]

The generation of 1914 and modernism—to talk about
the role played by the first in the second is to run the risk of explicating
one mystification by means of another. Both concepts share a fuzzy and
enticing ambiguity; still emanating waves of feeling generated by battles
fought long ago, they are capable of engaging our emotions and must
be used with the greatest care. Let me begin therefore by clarifying what
I mean by these terms before attempting to link them together.

Modernism is not a word that the historian ordinarily uses. Glancing
through the books in my library that deal with the cultural history of
Europe during the last century, I seldom find it on a title page, in the

text, or even in an index. One may feel that this is testimony to the intellectual bulkheads that separate the academic disciplines; but I suspect that it is also an indication that historians have found the term difficult to apply, irrelevant to their interests, or contrary to their intuitions.

Historians are more at home when speaking of modernity, a term they often employ to designate the period that followed the Middle Ages; or modernization, a concept they have lifted from the discourse of sociology to describe the process by which Europe, and later non-European peoples, became modern. Lately historians have become nervous about using both these terms because they have not been able to agree on a definition of modernity nor a chronology of modernization. Did modernization begin in the fifteenth century with secular humanism; in the sixteenth century with the breakup of medieval religious unity; in the seventeenth century with the development of modern science; in the eighteenth century with the attack on privilege and the desacralization of politics; in the nineteenth century with the spread of new technologies, new market relationships, and new methods of production and exchange; or in the twentieth century with the coming of an urban mass society? Since all these processes converged to create the society in which we presently live, and since they developed at different paces in different parts of the West, it is difficult to find the point of rupture between the old and the new. Moreover, recent studies indicate the extent to which premodern, or traditional, attitudes and cultural patterns have survived the so-called process of modernization. The modern does not replace the traditional; it joins with it to produce something new. Hence many historians have dropped the word "modernity" from their working vocabulary and others use it with circumspection, while waiting for a better concept to come along.[2]

There is another reason that the historian tends to view the concept of modernism with some caution, if not with outright skepticism. Modernism is often used loosely to denote the culture of the twentieth century. Yet by its very nature, this movement—or, more accurately, this series of movements—was confined to small groups of intellectuals and artists who proclaimed themselves to be avant-garde. To the historian, then, the relationship of modernism to twentieth-century Western culture is problematic and something that needs to be established through empirical study. Or, to put it in a slightly different way, the historian is likely to take at face value the modernist intellectuals' assertion that they are somehow divorced from and marginal to the society in which they live. Indeed, Theodore Zeldin, in his much-acclaimed history of modern France, went so far as to define the intellectual as someone unable to tolerate the contradictions of modern life, someone essentially abnormal in his or her attitudes. Intellectuals, he writes, "made an issue of the difficulties of living. They therefore confirmed themselves as outsiders, and that greatly limited their influence. They influenced each other most of all."[3]

As a historian, consequently—though as one who sees the history of French intellectuals differently than does Zeldin[4]—I approach modernism not as a single style or a dominant sensibility, but as the product of a many-layered culture in the process of disintegration and recomposition. On the one hand one sees popular cultures and an official hegemonic culture combining aristocratic and bourgeois values left over from earlier centuries and welded by the last third of the nineteenth century into some kind of synthesis that varies from country to country; on the other hand, as the century comes to an end, one begins to glimpse the outlines of a new consumption-oriented mass culture called into being by social and economic change. And in between that which is waning and that which is coming into existence is an avant-garde, numerically small but nonetheless important, which perceives this change in terms of both a threat and an opportunity and which attempts a daring reformulation of culture along radically new lines. I see modernism, therefore, as a response by clusters of intellectuals and artists to the converging processes of modernization as they presented themselves and were perceived at the end of the nineteenth and the beginning of the twentieth centuries, with the epicenter of modernism located in the decades just preceding and following the Great War, that is, between 1890 and 1933.[5]

One way to understand this many-faceted and stylistically heterogeneous response is to look at it from a generational perspective. The idea of historical generations is a heuristic device with an empirical basis in the facts of life and death. In all human societies, the population consists of a mix of people of different ages. There are always people entering and people leaving the population; and this means that people of different ages experience, and are active in, different segments of historical time. Such fundamental realities as the past, the future, and what is taken for granted as normal behavior are different for the person of twenty, the person of forty, and the person of sixty. Here we have the source of the dialectic of generations and one possible explanation for social and cultural change.[6]

The problem arises when one tries to move from the individual to the group. How can one establish with any precision the chronological boundaries of a historical generation when the process of birth and death is a relatively even and unceasing flow, more like a human river than the regular, interval-like products of a machine? The answer is that one cannot establish these limits with precision, and it has been in trying to do so that most generational thinkers have gone wrong and thrown themselves against an insuperable theoretical obstacle. For what matters about a generation—again, remember that I am using the term as a heuristic device—is not its limits but its center; and what constitutes the center of a generation and acts as a magnetic field, drawing its members together and giving them a sense of unity, is a series of experiences which is unique because these experiences are undergone collectively by large numbers of people at more or less the same stage of life.[7]

How does one discover and identify historical generations? This problem has tormented scientifically-minded generational theorists; but it need not trouble us, because during the period of modernism generations were quick to discover and identify themselves, seizing upon the circumstance that fresh talent usually gathers in like-minded clusters and announces its appearance with fanfare and extravagant promises of future achievement. Because of this clustering effect, some scholars prefer the notion of the decade to that of the generation. And clearly decades often have their own atmospheres, created in part by the emergence of new historical actors who claim to represent youth.[8] But the danger here is to jumble together people of different age groups, whose collaboration is usually only temporary, and to glide from the concept of coevality to that of contemporaneity, which is not the same thing. A generation consists of coevals, not of contemporaries.

Nonetheless, having said that, I would go on to argue that generations can best be identified by the date at which they enter and make their first impression on public life; and in the West during the last century this has usually occurred about thirty years after the generation's most representative and innovative figures were born.

If we apply these notions to the phenomenon of modernism during its period of greatest vitality, we find four generations separated by intervals of about fifteen years and increasingly conscious of themselves as constituting generational unities. First came the generation of 1875, with Paul Cézanne (1840),[9] Otto Wagner (1841), Stéphane Mallarmé (1842), Henry James (1843), Paul Verlaine (1844), Friedrich Nietzsche (1844), Joris-Karl Huysmans (1848), August Strindberg (1849), Vincent Van Gogh (1853), and Emile Verhaeren (1855). This was a generation of precursors who called into question many of the values, convictions, and conventions of the official high culture and who laid down paths that their successors would follow. Then in the next generation, the generation of 1890, one finds a real explosion of modernist creativity. Sigmund Freud (1856), George Bernard Shaw (1856), Hermann Bang (1857), Joseph Conrad (1857), Anton Chekhov (1860), Jules Laforgue (1860), Italo Svevo (1861), Maurice Maeterlinck (1862), Gustav Klimt (1862), Arthur Schnitzler (1862), Claude Debussy (1862), Maurice Barrès (1863), Gabriele D'Annunzio (1863), Richard Strauss (1864), Miguel de Unamuno (1864), Frank Wedekind (1864), W. B. Yeats (1865), Erik Satie (1866), Wassily Kandinsky (1866), Emile Nolde (1867), Luigi Pirandello (1867), Stefan George (1868), Maxim Gorky (1868), Paul Claudel (1868), Henri Matisse (1869), and André Gide (1869) all make their presence felt during the years just preceding or following the turn of the century. They break with accepted conventions of art, push to the forefront matters that had earlier been considered beyond the pale of good taste, redefine notions of time and space, reveal the irrational elements in the personality, and expose the relativity and subjective nature of all truths. They continue the work of the precursors, but they do so with greater authority, credibility, and *réclame*.[10]

Next comes the generation of 1905. Here 1880 seems to be the critical date around which important birthdates cluster. Karl Kraus (1874), Gertrude Stein (1874), Arnold Schoenberg (1874), Thomas Mann (1875), Maurice Ravel (1875), Rainer Maria Rilke (1875), F. T. Marinetti (1876), Kasimir Malevich (1878), Paul Klee (1879), E. M. Forster (1879), Guillaume Apollinaire (1880), Franz Marc (1880), Robert Musil (1880), Ernst Ludwig Kirchner (1880), Sean O'Casey (1880), Alexander Blok (1880), Andrei Biely (1880), Fernand Léger (1881), Pablo Picasso (1881), Virginia Woolf (1882), James Joyce (1882), Igor Stravinsky (1882), Umberto Boccioni (1882), Walter Gropius (1883), Franz Kafka (1883), Wyndham Lewis (1884), Ezra Pound (1885), Alban Berg (1885), D. H. Lawrence (1885), and Robert Delaunay (1885) all belong to this generation, as does Marcel Proust (1871), who made his impact felt relatively late. A mere glance at these names reveals that it was this generation that launched the avant-garde movements of the period between 1905 and 1914, when modernist enthusiasm and élan reached their peak. Die Brücke, Der Blaue Reiter, expressionism, cubism, futurism, orphism, constructivism, and vorticism were all conceived and dominated by members of the generation of 1905. It was also members of this generation who realized the great modernist masterpieces in literature, music, and the visual arts: *À la recherche du temps perdu; Der Prozess; Ulysses; Der Zauberberg; The Rite of Spring; Les Demoiselles d'Avignon.*

Here then are three modernist generations. For purposes of classification, let me call them the generation of precursors, the generation of founders, and the generation of realizers. A fourth modernist generation may be identified as the generation of 1914.[11] Though some of its members had been active before the outbreak of the war, the collective impact of this generation was not felt until the conflict had ended. Its central figures were born in the late 1880s and early 1890s and included among others Oscar Kokoschka (1886), Hermann Broch (1886), Mies van der Rohe (1886), Marc Chagall (1887), Marcel Duchamp (1887), Le Corbusier (1887), Blaise Cendrars (1887), Georg Trakl (1887), Edith Sitwell (1887), T. S. Eliot (1888), Giorgio de Chirico (1888), Eugene O'Neill (1888), Jean Cocteau (1889), Martin Heidegger (1889), Charlie Chaplin (1889), Abel Gance (1889), Boris Pasternak (1890), Fritz Lang (1890), Pier Luigi Nervi (1891), Otto Dix (1891), Sergei Prokofiev (1891), Darius Milhaud (1892), Arthur Honegger (1892), Richard Neutra (1892), Osbert Sitwell (1892), Vladimir Mayakovsky (1893), Vsevolod Pudovkin (1893), Ernst Toller (1893), Erwin Piscator (1893), Georg Grosz (1893), Joan Miró (1893), Joseph Roth (1894), Louis-Ferdinand Céline (1894), Jean Renoir (1894), Paul Hindemith (1895), László Moholy-Nagy (1895), Tristan Tzara (1896), Eugenio Montale (1896), John Dos Passos (1896), William Faulkner (1897), Ernest Hemingway (1898), Bertolt Brecht (1898), Alvar Aalto (1898), Aldous Huxley (1898), Sergei Eisenstein (1898), and Vladimir Nabokov (1899). We are now ready to ask what role this fourth generation, the generation of 1914, played in the modernist movement.

To answer this question we must reconstruct the distinctive experience that the intellectuals and artists of the generation of 1914 brought to modernism. Those members of the generation who survived into the postwar period always perceived their lives as being divided into three segments: prewar, war, and postwar. These segments were further identified with stages of life: they had been adolescents before the war; they were young adults between 1914 and 1918; and they had come into the full force of mature life after the war ended. It was the sequence of these segments, the distinctive quality of each, and the way they reinforced one another that gave people of this age group the conviction that they represented a generation and were historically unique.

Like psychoanalysis, generational theory gives priority to the early experiences of life. Each age group awakes intellectually to find itself surrounded by a "world in force," a "vital horizon," within which it takes its first independent steps.[12] In the case of intellectuals born around 1890, the world in which they found themselves was life as it was being lived in large European cities between 1900 and 1914. The outstanding characteristic of this world was that it was in the process of disappearing. Technology and advanced capitalism were transforming and reshaping it beyond recognition. Nineteenth-century organs of perception had difficulty making the transition, for the pace of life had quickened, distances were shrinking, the country was being sucked into the vortex of the expanding city, motor vehicles clanged through crowded streets, airplanes had opened up a third dimension of existence, and moving pictures were impressing their rhythm upon the eye. At the same time that the physical world was changing, political and social structures seemed on the verge of being overthrown. Everything was in flux. Old systems of reference were under attack, old hierarchies were being challenged, and old elites were being pressed to make concessions. Revolution seemed inevitable, and those who had something to lose did not conceal their fear. Finally, this world lived under a threat of war. The generation of 1914 could recall their years of adolescence by counting off the international crises through which they had lived. The men among them knew that one day they would be mobilized and would march; and thus the idea of war had the force of fate and exercised on them a dangerous and powerful attraction.

Hence the generation of 1914 grew up under the triple sign of technology, revolution, and war. If you like, this was their destiny. But these simple facts tell us nothing about the attitudes with which they began adult life. Every generation encounters the world in force in the form of an interpretation made by the generations that preceded it. This interpretation is made up of elements of folk wisdom, common sense, and high culture, and may be full of contradictions. Though educated in the official hegemonic culture and often drawn toward traditional images of what was beautiful, honorable, and good, intellectuals of the generation of 1914 quickly discovered the counterculture of modernism, as it had been developed by the generations of 1875, 1890, and 1905 in their revolt against the conventions and hypocrisy of bourgeois society. It was from the leaders of the avant-garde that these young people took their criticism of contemporary society, their taste for color, shape, and sound, and their visions of the future. Coming along at the moment they did—the moment of Gide's novels, Picasso's paintings, and Stravinsky's music—they grew up *within* modernism in a way that no previous generation could have. Modernism was an essential part of their world in force.

How did modernist culture present itself in the years directly preceding the war? Not in the same way that we would define modernism today. The Anglo-American-Irish writers, now taught in American universities as the exemplars of literary modernism, were little or not at all known. Nietzsche, Dostoevsky, Bergson, Barrès, D'Annunzio, and Shaw were the spiritual guides looked up to by the young of 1914. And the message they taught was one of antimaterialism. Reality, they said, was a perspective and a construction rather than a verifiable fact or thing. Man was not the executor of natural and historical laws, but a creator of his life. There were no limits on the individual except those imposed by lack of imagination or weakness of will. The new culture was skeptical of science, when not outright antiscientific. Scientific analysis was considered a mental instrument of severely limited validity; intuition into the multiplicity of human realities was recommended in its place; and action rather than contemplation was valued as a source of knowledge. The new culture was subjectivist and relativistic; truth was both personal and temporary. Contradictions were not to be avoided but to be embraced. And, finally, the new culture was fiercely antibourgeois and, by implication, antidemocratic, if only because the cultivation of the spirit was such an austere discipline that only small elites could be expected to undergo it. There was a paradox here: young intellectuals often wanted to educate and lead the masses forward to new levels of sensibility, but all too frequently they discovered that the taste of the masses was irreconcilable with the obscurities of modernist culture. The result, in most cases, was despair and the plunge into ever more private forms of expression.

It was with these beliefs that the intellectuals of the generation of 1914 marched off to war. Few had given much thought to what the war might mean. They had been too preoccupied with their education, their love affairs, and their dreams. In that sense, the war came as a surprise and a shock. But some of their older brothers, who had anticipated war in their poems, plays, and paintings, had seen a major European conflict as a possible solution to the unbearable tedium and mediocrity of bourgeois life. And young men born in the late 1880s and 1890s had unconsciously absorbed these apocalyptic attitudes and internalized these images of a beneficent war. Like their older brothers, they hoped that the war would break the impasse of prewar politics, create a sense of national unity where none existed, nurture the virtues of sacrifice, fortitude, and boldness, and destroy bourgeois civilization, thus paving the way for the emergence of a new, more vital culture.

The war was a great disappointment. It could not provide what the young of 1914 had wanted from it. Instead of being exciting, it was tedious; instead of being glorious, it was horribly destructive; instead of raising humanity toward a higher level of existence, it threatened to cast it down among the beasts. Yet whether intellectuals from the generation of 1914 denounced or affirmed the war—and there were many in both camps—they all underwent its impact and carried the experience with them into the postwar world. And one effect of the war was to confirm those modernist doctrines that they had encountered before 1914: that reason was weaker than instinct and feeling; that action was superior to and relatively independent of thought; that spirit was stronger than flesh; that personality was multiple rather than unitary; that time was a subjective state rather than an objective measure; that truth was relative and that therefore absolute truth was nonexistent; that language was opaque and manipulative; that conflict was endemic to humanity and strife the midwife of virtue; and, above all, that history was discontinuous, progress an illusion, and destruction the prerequisite of cultural renovation. The generation of 1914 would never free themselves from these apocalyptic visions. One world had died before their eyes; another labored to be born. Meanwhile the task of the "modernists" within this generation was to contribute to the destruction of the old and work toward the construction of the new.

The war then confirmed and legitimated the modernist thesis of a cultural break. It called into question the continuity and viability of the traditional European cultures. It intensified feelings of generational uniqueness extending across European boundaries and created a sense of international community among the proponents of modernist culture.[13] It raised to a higher and more dangerous power that hostility to bourgeois culture that had been one of the chief characteristics of modernism before the war. Moreover, the events of the immediate postwar period— the creation of a communist regime in Russia, the attempt to spread revolution to Central and Western Europe, the collapse of liberal democratic regimes in countries like Italy and Spain, and the emergence of fascism, which identified itself culturally with futurism—reinforced the feeling that the restoration of prewar values and political and social structures could only be fleeting. The bourgeoisie was on its knees. The old official culture was doomed to be swept away into the dustbin of history. It was in this atmosphere of "fin-du-monde" that the generation of 1914 began their careers and made their first collective initiatives in cultural life.

Given the experiences the generation of 1914 brought with them, therefore, when they embarked upon the creative period of their lives, it is not surprising that they should be extraordinarily receptive to the essays of Freud, the novels of Proust, Mann, Woolf, and Joyce, the poetry of Rilke, Pound, and Apollinaire, and the paintings of Picasso and Chagall, nor that they would apply themselves to winning acceptance for these works in wider cultural circles. Indeed, it would be tempting to argue that the chief function of the generation of 1914 within the modernist movement was not so much the creation of new techniques or the realization of modernist masterpieces, but the defense and diffusion of modernist works by members of previous generations. And I think it is true that the generation of 1914 became certifiers of what was authentically modern and guardians of the modernist canon. Witness the literary criticism of Edmund Wilson (1895) and the art criticism of Herbert Read (1893); or the campaigns of the surrealists, the most important modernist movement to come out of the generation of 1914. André Breton may not be remembered chiefly for his poems, but as an impresario, organizer, and conservator of a certain kind of modernist sensibility.

Yet tempting as it might be to dismiss the generation of 1914 as the epigones of modernism, such an interpretation would be wrong. For if one looks once more at the list of names that I have given as constituting a representative sampling of modernist intellectuals and artists from the generation of 1914, one will notice that in Europe, though this age group continued to produce important painters (Chagall, Miró, de Chirico, Grosz, Dix) and novelists (Céline, Broch, Roth), it was above all in the fields of poetry, architecture, design, theater, and film that it made its most distinctive contributions to the modernist sensibility. The poems of Eliot and Montale, the buildings of Le Corbusier, Mies van der Rohe, Nervi, and Neutra, the designs and photographs of Moholy-Nagy, the theater of Toller, Brecht, and Piscator, the film of Chaplin, Eisenstein, Pudovkin, Cocteau, Gance, and Renoir became binding examples of modernism in these fields of artistic activity.

A more exhaustive listing would also reveal a geographical shift in the relative importance of the Western nations in the modern movement. Paris remained a site of modernist activity throughout the 1920s, and an important refuge for painters and writers from all countries; but in many fields (theater, film, and architecture certainly and, arguably, the novel as well) the French themselves had ceased to lead the way. The real centers of modernist vitality lay elsewhere: in Berlin, Weimar, Dessau, Dresden, Leningrad, Moscow, London, and New York. Vienna had lost definitively the critical importance it had had for the generations of 1890 and 1905 as a matrix of modernist innovation. Style-setting buildings continued to go up; but the clustering of talent and the hothouse atmosphere of the years before the war were no longer to be found in the former imperial capital. Most surprising perhaps is the sudden rise of the United States within the modern movement. American novels were among the greatest produced by the generation of 1914, and many of the greatest buildings, though designed by architects of European formation, were realized in the United States. The designs and images of the modernists were scooped up into the great mill of American capitalism and, after being processed, were diffused to the world as they had never been before. By 1940, thanks to Hitler, faraway Los Angeles had become one of the major modernist centers of the Western world. Who could have predicted this in 1914?

In addition to championing modernist masterpieces and establishing the criteria for the modernist canon, then, the generation of 1914 oversaw the transfer of modernism from the Old World to the New. They also probed the limits of modernism and initiated the reaction against it that would become such an important characteristic of the following generation. Here also I think the experience of the generation of 1914 was decisive. Malraux (1901) once said that history drove over his generation like a tank. This was even truer for the generation that preceded his. And history took the form of war and revolution. The great modernist masterpieces of the generation of 1905 had been produced by people who were indifferent to politics; but indifference to politics was a luxury few members of the generation of 1914 could afford. Even those unpolitical by temperament, like Huxley, and Céline, and many surrealist poets, were driven into political stances. Louis Aragon, one of the most promising modernist poets in the 1920s, became during the 1930s a practitioner of socialist realism and a communist propagandist. By the early 1930s artistic experimentation was giving way to a new concern for representation. The techniques of modernism were not abandoned; but the limits had been drawn and the vision of the new culture considerably reshaped. History had imposed itself on the consciousness of the generation of 1914 and forced a return to more realistic conventions. And thus one could argue that it was the generation of 1914, the first truly modernist generation, that first felt the limitations of modernism and drew back before its most extreme implications.[14]

Notes

1. José Ortega y Gasset, "La deshumanización del arte," in *Obras completas* (Madrid: Revista de Occidente, 1966), 3:359; *The Dehumanization of Art and Other Essays,* major essay trans. Helene Weyl (Princeton, N.J.: Princeton Univ. Press, 1968), 12–13.

2. See, for example, the collaborative volume *Crises of Political Development in Europe and the United States,* ed. Raymond Grew (Princeton, N.J.: Princeton Univ. Press, 1978), esp. pp. 5–7 and 42–43.

3. Theodore Zeldin, *France 1848–1945* (Oxford: Oxford Univ. Press, 1977), 2:1124, 1127–28.

4. See my review of the second volume of Zeldin's history of modern France in the *Journal of Social History,* Fall 1980, 137–42.

5. For the cultural situation in this period and the relationship of modernism to it, see Maurice Crubellier, *Histoire culturelle de la France XIXe–XXe siècles* (Paris: Colin, 1974), and Malcolm Bradbury and James McFarlane, eds., *Modernism* (New York: Penguin, 1976).

6. I have discussed the principal generational theories in *The Generation of 1914* (Cambridge: Harvard Univ. Press, 1979). See also Anthony Esler, *Generational Studies: A Basic Bibliography* (privately printed, 1979), 21–65.

7. Within the limits imposed by the structure of the life cycle, any individual may find her- or himself drawn toward younger or older generational groups.

8. See Samuel Hynes, "What is a Decade? Notes on the Thirties," *Sewanee Review* 88 (Summer 1980): 506–11. For an outstanding example of a decade history, see John Willett, *The New Sobriety 1917–1933* (London: Thames & Hudson, 1978).

9. Figures in parentheses are dates of birth.

10. For the generation of 1890, see H. Stuart Hughes, *Consciousness and Society* (New York: Knopf, 1958); Gerhard Masur, *Prophets of Yesterday* (New York: Macmillan, 1961); and Roger Shattuck, *The Banquet Years* (New York: Harcourt, Brace, 1958).

11. There was also a fifth modernist generation, consisting of intellectuals born after 1900, who inherited modernism, absorbed it, and then called it into question in the changed historical circumstances of the 1930s and 1940s. See James D. Wilkinson, *The Intellectual Resistance in Europe* (Cambridge: Harvard Univ. Press, 1981).

12. For the concepts of "vital horizon" and the "world in force," see José Ortega y Gasset, "En torno a Galileo" (1933), in *Obras completas* (Madrid: Revista de Occidente, 1970), 5:21–54.

13. It was precisely these qualities of discontinuity and internationalism that Hitler disliked in modern art. In his speech inaugurating the "Great Exhibition of German Art 1937" in Munich, he complained that by the modernists "art,

on the one hand, was defined as nothing but an international communal experience, thus killing altogether any understanding of its integral relationship with an ethnic group. On the other hand its relationship to time was stressed, that is: There was no longer any art of peoples or even of races, but only an art of the times. According to this theory, therefore, Greek art was not formed by the Greeks, but by a certain period which formed it as their expression. . . . Consequently, art as such is not only completely isolated from its ethnic origins, but it is the expression of a certain vintage which is characterized today by the word 'modern,' and thus, of course, will be un-modern tomorrow, since it will be outdated. According to such a theory, as a matter of fact, art and art activities are lumped together with the handiwork of our modern tailor shops and fashion industries. And to be sure, following the maxim: Every year something new. One day Impressionism, then Futurism, Cubism, maybe even Dadaism, etc." In Herschel B. Chipp, *Theories of Modern Art* (Berkeley and Los Angeles: Univ. of California Press, 1968), 476.

14. For the preoccupation of French novelists with history and politics in the 1930s, see Maurice Rieuneau, *Guerre et révolution dans le roman français 1919–1939* (Paris: Klincksieck, 1974), 313–14; for the limitations of modernism, Thomas S. Hines, *Richard Neutra and the Search for Modern Architecture* (New York: Oxford Univ. Press, 1982).

Matei Calinescu

Modernism and Ideology

There are three themes I should like to develop here. One concerns the notion of commitment in modern literature. Is there such a thing as political commitment in literature? In what shapes does it appear, and, ultimately, what sense does it make literarily and politically? The second theme is an assessment of the theory, affirmed in recent decades by Anglo-American critics, and occasionally by continental Marxist critics, that there is a close connection between modernism and fascism— is this theory valid? Is it in any way helpful to critical understanding? Does it stand in need of serious revision, or would we be better off if we simply discarded it? My third theme will be rather an argument in favor of considering the relation between literature and ideology in the modern age in terms of dialogic consciousness, a working model of which is offered by Bakhtin's philosophy of language and, more specifically, by his approach to the constitutive polyphony of Dostoevsky's writing.

Commitment

Elsewhere I have argued that within the sphere of modernity there is little substantive disagreement between the proponents of "art for art's sake" (if we take this phrase as meaning more than a mere passing fashion) and the most dedicated theorists of "committed art" in regard to their ultimate goal: the *aestheticization* of the world.[1] With this broad realization in mind, we can better understand some of the paradoxes linked to the idea of commitment, a pivotal element in the problematic of modern literature and politics.

One of these paradoxes is the willingness of certain modernist artists, particularly of some representatives of the aesthetic avant-garde, to commit themselves to causes promoted by tightly-knit organizations that quite openly expect them to surrender their intellectual freedom and to submit themselves to the most rigid kind of ideological control (some of the rebellious surrealists, like Paul Éluard and Louis Aragon, became disciplined members of the staunchly "orthodox" French Communist Party). In some of their politically committed works such writers illustrate the extreme but not infrequent case of sacrificing even art "for art's sake," that is, for the sake of the fully liberated and inherently aesthetic world of the future.

The strong aesthetic component of utopian thought can also have another paradoxical consequence: it can lead, and has led, to the notion that art in and of itself is a *revolutionary* force and even that it is the only authentic revolutionary force (hence, politics, and specifically leftist revolutionary politics, should imitate art and not vice versa, as the French philosopher Jean-François Lyotard once suggested).[2] The idea that poetry can change the world is implicitly contained in many romantic statements concerning the "mission" of the artist, statements that cover the whole range between what we may term "progressive attitudes"—such as Shelley's—and "regressive attitudes"—such as those espoused by many of the German romantics, who, to use a phrase coined by Novalis, were intent on "romanticizing the world." In our century and from a different perspective, the surrealists were no less intent on rendering the world "surreal," by setting free the boundless oneiric imagination and erasing the difference between dream and reality, or by eliminating the very possibility of the "reality principle."

If art is by itself able to "change life"—as Rimbaud urged—then obviously there is no need for the artist to make any commitment politically and to obey the orders of leaders or organizations, orders that are bound to be narrow-minded and detrimental to the fulfillment of true art's spontaneously revolutionary vocation. From this standpoint, the artist, involved in the great work of imaginative destruction and reconstruction of the world, is specifically called upon to resist all appeals to commitment. André Breton's view that "true art is unable not to be revolutionary" (beyond and even *against* any specific ideological "commitment")[3] was shared, in the post–World War II period, by many representatives of the New Left, from Herbert Marcuse to Gilles Deleuze to Jean-François Lyotard. For the latter, the artist, engaged in an ever-renewed work of "deconstruction," is, in right and in deed, a politician of *desire,* that is, in fact, an antipolitician, the only kind acceptable from the point of view of the revolutionary force of universal desire or libido.

If the idea of political commitment is not flatly rejected by the artist, there seem to be two main positions in regard to how such commitment is to be envisaged. (Needless to say, in reality these positions are not completely separate and all sorts of overlaps can and do occur.) The first and more interesting approach is characteristic of avant-garde artists who, in their dream of overcoming the older split between the two avant-gardes, the political and the aesthetic (a split that Renato Poggioli places around 1880), try to reconcile their political commitment with their bent toward formalist experimentalism. This is what I will call form-oriented commitment. The second position, content-oriented commitment, is advocated by writers and critics (in many cases identified with the political as opposed to the aesthetic avant-garde) who are uninterested in, or downright suspicious of, questions of form.

Let us first examine the politics of avant-gardist formalism. If art has a revolutionary function, argues the politically minded formalist, this function should be consciously performed primarily on the level of form, by dislocating, disrupting, or dispersing the old forms and by inventing forms which, by virtue of their newness, are solely capable of embodying a truly new content. The fact is that even when it is not overtly concerned with politics, the formalist attitude has a political dimension that should not be ignored. The formalist dialectic of literary change, as elaborated by the Russian formalists of the 1920s (Viktor Shklovsky, Roman Jakobson, Boris Tomashevsky, Boris Eichenbaum) or by the Prague School structuralists of the 1930s is based on such notions as "defamiliarization," "violation of the norm," or "foregrounding of the device," all of which can be interpreted politically (in spite of the fact that the formalist critics themselves went only occasionally in that direction). Actually, the Russian formalist approach, which is largely a critical assessment of the iconoclastic manifestations of the artistic avant-garde (we know that formalists were very close to the cubo-futurists, Khlebnikov, Mayakovsky, etc.) can be said to consist of the application of a *formal political model* to the question of literary development.

A good literary example of political commitment consistent with the polemical formalism of the avant-garde is Bertolt Brecht. An expressionist in his youth, Brecht became a self-consciously committed Marxist writer without giving up his allegiance to the idea of formal novelty.

Significantly, Brecht arrived (how independently?) at some of the cardinal notions of the Russian formalists, offering directly politicized versions of "defamiliarization" (his famous *Verfremdungseffekt*), or "violation of the norm" (taken in the more general sense of a rejection of *mimesis,* or the Aristotelian rules of imitation and empathy), or of the "foregrounding of the device" (art should openly recognize its "conventional" character, it should not conceal its true nature behind a veil of "realistic" illusions). Even Brecht's well-known didacticism profits from its inclusion in a polemical-formal context, where it can be seen as an element in the larger pattern of foregrounding. In this case, content, without sacrificing any of its distinctive qualities, becomes artistically more effective by being overtly and unexpectedly treated as a formal device among other formal devices in the general formal strategy of the work. As T. W. Adorno put it, "The primacy of lesson over pure form, which Brecht intended to achieve, became in reality a formal device itself."[4]

Both the pursuit of art as an inherently revolutionary activity, from whose perspective commitment can only be a dangerous illusion, and the kind of form-oriented committed art practiced by a Brecht have been strongly criticized by proponents of political literature both on the Right, and, more significantly, on the Left. Limiting ourselves to the "orthodox" Marxist view, formalist aesthetics (even when it claims to promote clear-cut Marxist ideas) cannot but lead to the creation of works that are, in the world of "real" politics, irrelevant at best, dangerously confusing at worst; works that, "objectively" if not subjectively, end up playing into the hands of the Enemy.

But is the alternative, namely, content-oriented political commitment, any less irrelevant, confusing, or even "objectively" detrimental to the cause of the revolution? There are two major versions—existentialist and Marxist—of the content-oriented theory of committed art. I will briefly examine here only the existentialist (Sartrean) version, which, while largely subsuming the one advanced by "mainstream" Marxism, manages to avoid some of the latter's ritual banalities and clichés and brings into clearer focus its constitutive contradictions and aporias.

Sartre's famous concept of "littérature engagée," although repeatedly criticized for its "idealism" and "petit-bourgeois individualism" by numerous orthodox Marxists, and even by more sophisticated representatives of this line like Georg Lukács, comes close to mainstream Marxist political-aesthetic doctrine in at least two fundamental respects: one is the strong emphasis on subject matter or ideological content; the second is, given the sweeping ethical claims of both Sartre and the Marxists, an unavoidably high degree of self-righteousness. The latter aspect is significant in that it reveals the concealed but undeniable theological-dogmatic foundation of both theories. Ironically, this dogmatism (precisely because it is revised to fit the secularism of modernity) renders the very content to which the artist is supposed to commit himself essentially problematic and eventually unimportant.

In his perceptive critique of Sartre, Adorno points out that the apparent advantage of Sartrean commitment over mere ideological "Tendenz" cannot but render "the content to which the artist commits himself inherently ambiguous. In Sartre, the notion of choice—originally a Kierkegaardian category—is heir to the Christian doctrine 'He who is not with me is against me,' but now voided of any theological content."[5] Content-oriented commitment, then, ends up as dogmatism—a dogmatism in search of an ever-elusive "authentic" content in the case of Sartre, a merely simulated dogmatism in the case of the disciplined Marxist who is "committed" not in fact to anything specific, but only to following the shifting party line. Adorno claims that "even if politically motivated, commitment in itself remains politically polyvalent so long as it is not reduced to propaganda, whose pliancy mocks any commitments by the subject."[6] Content-oriented commitment turns out to be, in both cases, fundamentally empty: its intended content is eroded and finally lost in the simple-minded and noisy formalism of propaganda.

Modernism and Fascism

A point frequently made by Anglo-American critics of modernism, irrespective of their own persuasion or methodology, is that the modernists were attracted, by and large, to a staunchly conservative and often fascist political philosophy—so much so that this attraction tends to appear as one of the major distinguishing features of modernism. On the continent, such a view would be highly qualified, unless it were advanced by communist critics following the Moscow line and therefore prone to label anything they dislike as "fascist." The fact is that in Europe, with the exception of Mussolini's Italy (where people such as Marinetti's futurists or more independent modernists such as Papini or Pirandello supported fascism), few writers whom we could call modernist favored the various extreme right-wing movements that swept the continent in the 1920s and 1930s. It is true that in Germany some of the expressionists, the most prominent of whom was Brecht's friend, Arnolt Bronnen, became Nazis, but Bronnen reconverted to communism after the war and died in East Germany. More ambiguous and more intriguing were the cases of Ernst Jünger, who, after a period as a Nazi sympathizer, turned against the regime long before its collapse, or of the great philosopher Martin Heidegger, who was partially and briefly co-opted by the government in his capacity as a university administrator but whose thought remained untouched by Nazi ideology. (Interestingly, in the postwar years, Heidegger became one of the seminal influences on clearly left-oriented philosophers in France, from Sartre and Merleau-Ponty to some of the structuralists and to such diverse representatives of post-structuralism as Jacques Derrida, Gilles Deleuze, and Jean-François Lyotard.) In France some—but by no means all—members of the *Action Française* group collaborated with the German occupants during the last war. On the other hand, staunchly conservative Catholic writers such as Georges Bernanos (a one-time activist of *Action Française*) were deeply horrified by the murderous politics of fascism as soon as they saw them put into practice (as Bernanos's account of the Spanish Civil War in *Les grands cimetières sous la lune* testifies). By far the most puzzling case of a fascist writer in France is Céline. Although after the publication of *Voyage au bout de la nuit* (1932) he allowed himself, perhaps reluctantly, to be embraced by the leftists (he even traveled to Moscow to collect his royalties for the Russian translation of *Voyage*), his increasingly rabid anti-Semitism led him to espouse the Nazi program and to welcome the German invaders of his country. But this was the welcome of a man clearly out of his mind and, through its cranky excesses and violent *sauts d'humeur,* it embarrassed even the German occupation authorities. To what extent did Céline's intensely personal paranoia (which mysteriously did not prevent him from continuing to be a major writer) coincide with Nazi paranoia, greater and infinitely more cunning by virtue of its demonic mediocrity? Can we speak, in regard to Céline, of "commitment"? I would go along with George Steiner in *Language and Silence* and say that while posing an extraordinary challenge to the humanistic mind (how can unspeakable moral evil result in, or coexist with, the creation of great literature?), Céline remains an enigma.

Given all these exceptions and certainly others (less spectacular and therefore easier to ignore), continental modernism, including the avant-garde, was *not* attracted to fascism. A much stronger case can be made that it was repelled by fascism, and this reaction explains in large part why so many modernists (even when they were not particularly politically minded or politically knowledgeable, the best example here being André Gide) were drawn to leftist ideologies: anarchism, Marxism, para-Marxism (in the case of the Frankfurt School), or even communism. There is no point in making a list of prominent writers and critics who opposed the various European fascist ideologies of the 1920s or 1930s. Is it really necessary to recall that, in France, from representatives of the older generations such as Gide, Roger Martin du Gard, or Alain to the surrealists (Breton, Éluard, Desnos, Péret, Char), to the personalists (Mounier, de Rougemont), to the existentialists (Catholic like Gabriel Marcel or atheist like Sartre, Camus, or de Beauvoir), to such hard-to-classify authors as Simone Weil, Malraux, or Georges Bataille, the majority of the intelligentsia were antifascist and in many cases joined the Resistance during the war? Is it necessary to recall the vast intellectual exodus from Nazi Germany and the rich chapter of German culture constituted by *Exilliteratur?*

The argument that European modernism was fascist holds only if we accept Georg Lukács's distinction between "critical realism" (good) and "modernism" (bad because decadent), and his orthodox Marxist assumption that the political opinions of writers do not really count, being mere forms of ideological self-deception. Thus, for Lukács, anti-realist modernism was bound to be—"objectively"—an expression of fascist ideology or, more recently, of the ideology of the cold war, irrespective of the declared allegiances of its representatives.

Since Lukács's *The Meaning of Contemporary Realism* (published in German in 1957 and translated into English in 1963), and particularly the often-anthologized opening essay, "The Ideology of Modernism," has had some influence in English-speaking countries, a few comments on his views are in order. Although his book was written in the period of de-Stalinization, Lukács still approaches literature in terms of the black-and-white dualism of Zhdanovist aesthetic ideology: the evolution of literary consciousness from the latter part of the nineteenth century on appears to him the result of a "struggle" between two radically opposed tendencies, realism and antirealism, i.e., modernism. On the one hand we have realism, with its sense of social perspective and hierarchic structure, its understanding of history and its adherence to an objective principle of selection, its critical detachment and its ability to convey "concrete typicality." Modernism is in every respect the symmetrical opposite of realism: what it manages to convey is "abstract particularity," and this is so because it is uncritical and naive, because, lacking a principle of selection, it can only achieve a distorted, anxious, arbitrary, and eventually absurdist view of reality. Hence the modernist's subjectivist denial of history, his loss of any concept of the future, his dissolution of dynamically structured time into an amorphous, inexplicable flux or *durée,* his sense of meaninglessness, *Geworfenheit,* and *angst.* Derived from the twin experiences of deep depression and manic fits, Lukács argues, the modernist vision of life is essentially psychopathological, as illustrated in such movements as naturalism, symbolism, futurism, constructivism, Neue Sachlichkeit, and surrealism. The modernist, wittingly or not, is "objectively" on the side of fascism. Lukács writes: "I do not suggest that there is a direct connection between modernist literature and political attitudes of this kind [fascist or Cold War ideology]. The works of Joyce and Kafka were written long before; and Robert Musil is known to have been a strong opponent of Nazism. We are not concerned here with direct political attitudes, but rather with the ideology underlying these artists' presentation of reality. The practical political conclusions drawn by the individual writer are of secondary interest. What matters is whether his view of the world . . . connives at that modern nihilism from which both Fascism and Cold War ideology draw their strength."[7] And from Lukács's perspective it certainly does.

In the same essay, "Franz Kafka or Thomas Mann?" the critic goes even further when he states that, again "objectively," any artist whose work is based on *angst* cannot "avoid . . . guilt by association with Hitlerism and the preparations for atomic war. It is, indeed, of the nature of literature's social significance that it reflects the movements of its age even when it is—subjectively—aiming to express something different."[8] On the strength of such an argument, Kafka, whose work Lukács discusses specifically in terms of *angst,* would appear somehow as a precursor of fascism! But no, Lukács generously exonerates Kafka himself of such culpability, since Kafka "wrote at a time when capitalist society, the subject of his *angst,* was still far from the high mark of its historical development."[9]

Superficially, a somewhat more coherent case can be made for the protofascist or fascist leanings of Anglo-American modernism. Although— or perhaps because—fascism was less of an immediate political reality in England or in the United States, some of the outstanding English-speaking modernists, unlike their continental counterparts (if we leave aside the exceptions I have discussed), rather freely and often foolishly gave verbal support to fascist ideas. The evidence for the connection between high modernism and fascism, without being overwhelming, is there. Thus one may speak of the fascism of English modernists without resorting to contorted arguments of the Lukács type. Incidentally, such arguments could have little appeal to the English or American critic who, even when he or she enjoys theorizing, usually prefers not to do so in an empirical vacuum.

Going from the general to the particular, let us see what some critics of Anglo-American modernism have had to say with regard to its fascist orientation. Frank Kermode, for instance, distinguished what he calls "paleomodernism" from the post–World War II "neomodernism" in the following terms: "Early modernism tended toward fascism, later modernism toward anarchism. . . . The anti-humanism . . . of early modernism (anti-intellectualist, authoritarian, eugenicist) gives way to the anti-humanism (hipsterish, free-sexed, anti-intellectualist) of later modernism."[10] Kermode believes "that there has been only one Modernist Revolution" and that the distinction between its two stages, however striking, is not radical. Modernism, in his view, is constitutively authoritarian, antihumanist, and anti-intellectualist; the anarchism of neomodernism appears as the result of a change in "tactics" rather than in "strategy."

For Ihab Hassan, modernism ended some time ago and has been replaced by postmodernism; the two movements may have many affinities but they remain essentially separated—modernism having "created its own forms of Authority" while postmodernism "has tended toward Anarchy in deeper complicity with things falling apart."[11] Leaving aside the question of postmodernism, Hassan's characterization of modernism itself, and particularly the politics of modernism, is very close to Kermode's: the modernists were "crypto-fascist," elitist, committed to a hierarchial vision of culture and society.

On a lower level of generality, there is no dearth of studies focusing on the appeal of fascism to individual modernist writers. The repeated profascist statements of W. B. Yeats—which alternate, however, with his no less strong expressions of contempt for all ideologies and practical politics—have been discussed in detail by Conor Cruise O'Brien.[12] John R. Harrison has grouped five outstanding modernists (W. B. Yeats, Wyndham Lewis, Ezra Pound, T. S. Eliot, and D. H. Lawrence) in a book entitled *The Reactionaries* (1966) in which the label "fascist" is used quite profusely. More limited in scope than Harrison's essay on "the Anti-Democratic Intelligentsia," but also more sophisticated and more sensitive to the intricacies of aesthetic consciousness, is William Chace's *The Political Identities of Ezra Pound and T. S. Eliot* (1973).

Quite recently the equation between modernism and fascism has been reaffirmed, with larger if more confusing theoretical ambitions, by

Fredric Jameson in his neo-Marxist and poststructuralist essay *Fables of Aggression: Wyndham Lewis, the Modernist as Fascist* (1979). Jameson's interpretive strategy is interesting in that, beyond the theme of modernism's fascist connection, it provides us with the curious example of a leftist critic who, through *esprit de contradiction* and a sort of fashionable unconventionality, praises someone whom he takes to be a quintessentially fascist writer not for the independent literary qualities of his work but precisely for the direct expression (and supposed "unmasking") of the fascist spirit through those very qualities. For Jameson, Wyndham Lewis typifies the "affinities between protofascism and Western modernism" but, at the same time, "the articulation of this crisis of the subject in the objective form of a protofascist denunciation of parliamentary corruption . . . provides Lewis with an active and aggressive system of figuration which is quite distinct from its more symptomatic and subjectivizing expression (solipsism, the monad, schizophrenic dissolution) in conventional modernism."[13] So Lewis is, in spite of what the title of the essay tells us, not so much a modernist (at least in the conventional sense) as a postmodernist *avant la lettre,* an early herald of "the emergence of some new, properly postmodernist or schizophrenic conception of the cultural artifact."[14]

The question one might ask is: are we to see postmodernism as a direct outcome of protofascist (unconventional) modernism? Is postmodernism some kind of neofascism, and in what precise relationship does it stand to old fascism? And, more disturbingly, was fascism itself— or fascism as espoused by Lewis—all that bad when it allowed the author of *The Apes of God* to do a better critical job than literally all the Marxists of his time in exposing "subjectivism, . . . establishment modernism, . . . the illusions of the stable subject or ego, . . . [and] the ideological dishonesty of hegemonic liberalism"?[15] About the effectiveness of Lewis's critique ("more powerful and damaging than anything formulated by the Marxism of that period") there is so little doubt in Jameson's mind that we might ask ourselves the old question: with such (literary) friends, did fascism really need any enemies? The general thrust of Jameson's argument might be summarized as follows: Lewis is a great artist *because* he is a fascist; as a fascist, he is able to see not only the hypocrisies of liberalism but also (albeit unwittingly) to unmask fascism itself better than any antifascist or nonfascist. Leaving aside the trendiness of Jameson's terminology (for which his main model, Gilles Deleuze, can be blamed as much as he[16]), leaving aside the minor and not-so-minor confusions of which his essay is full, I cannot help feeling that his way of reasoning is highly bizarre if not perverse and even pernicious.

What, then, was the rationale of the sympathy of some important English-speaking modernists toward right-wing politics and specifically fascism during roughly 1900–1930? In his article "Writers and Politics" Stephen Spender is right, I believe, when he says in direct reference to Harrison's *Reactionaries:* "The most important thing common to the reactionaries was that they had a kind of shared vision of the greatness of the European past which implied hatred and contempt for the present. . . . Often their politics only shows that they care less for politics than for literature."[17] Even Pound, who came closest to political activism, cared more for his art than for his inexcusable fascism. Typically, as Stephen Spender remarks on another occasion, the admiration expressed by W. B. Yeats for Hitler and Mussolini did not prevent him from regarding them as "liveried major domos" and did not "impose on him the slightest obligation to refrain, at a moment's notice, from kicking them downstairs."[18]

Incidentally, such a view of political leaders as mere domestics of the Artist (a striking example of aestheticist wishful thinking!) may explain why Yeats's expressions of support for various politicians, and his equally strong views of politics as a contemptible thing, are not so incompatible or discontinuous as one would be tempted to think. "The reactionary traditionalist," Spender goes on to say, "stood outside fascism while supporting it." While he does not exonerate a Yeats or a Pound from personal "responsibility for the things Hitler and Mussolini did," Spender praises them for having "observed standards in their work which were independent of their politics."[19]

The plain fact is that the Anglo-American modernists who advocated fascist ideas misunderstood fascism and never grasped its darker, more sinister nature. The critical generalization based on selective pronouncements of such modernists, namely, that literary modernism on the whole showed a propensity toward fascism, stands in great need of qualification if not complete revision. And, at any rate, there are other writers, even plain antifascists—*pace* Jameson—like Thomas Mann, from whom we can learn a lot more about fascism than from Yeats, Eliot, Lawrence, Lewis, or even Pound.

Dialogy

There are certainly great political writers, but no writer is great *because* of the politics he or she embraces. Clearly good politics (even from a partisan perspective) does not necessarily result in good art, nor bad politics in bad art. These are truisms. To say, like Engels about Balzac or Lukács about Conrad, that the great writer somehow manages to see the (political) *truth* beyond, or even against, his or her own expressed political creed does not advance us either. The latter theory could become more interesting if it were freed of two of its basic assumptions, one being the notion of "genius" (the poet is a "seer," whose mind's eye pierces through the deceptive veil of ideological appearances), and the second being the purely political definition of "truth" (the truth of history, the truth of the "totality" of the social process, etc.). Once we eliminate these two assumptions, the theory might be reformulated as: a great writer is one who feels a constant urge "to think against himself," to borrow E. M. Cioran's suggestive phrase. It hardly needs to be said that a host of other qualities are required, but most of these are already contained, at least as potentialities, in the rich and strange ability—call it inner dialogy—of thinking against oneself. Good literature in general—including of course good political literature, which is always also good apolitical literature—can therefore be judged according to the extent to which it embodies effectively a dialogic principle.

Seen from this vantage point, and subordinated to the higher idea of dialogue, commitment paradoxically regains the importance that it can only lose when it is reduced to mere ideological "alignment" of whatever sort. This regained importance does not derive from commitment per se but rather from the severe tests to which its strength is submitted by being confronted with a wide variety of other, divergent or flatly contradictory, views.

It is perhaps not fortuitous that the first comprehensive formulation of the literary aspects of dialogue originated in Mikhail Bakhtin's commentary on the works of possibly the greatest political novelist of all, Dostoevsky. Dostoevsky makes his writing a space of dialogue, Bakhtin argues in his *Problems of Dostoevsky's Poetics* (1929), a space in which the most diverse opinions are fully and forcefully articulated by the various characters while the novelist himself, with his own opinions, is merely one of the voices heard in the complex polyphony of his novels. This polyphony could not exist if the voices that make it up were treated unequally or if any one of them were denied its fundamental dialogic freedom.[20] The deep force of Dostoevsky's novels derives neither from the "realistic" gift of the author nor from his own strong theological-political opinions, but from the dialogic compulsion of his imagination to invent convincing opponents of his views and to endow them with unforgettable fictional identity. From a different angle, Ortega y Gasset makes a similar observation in his essay "Notes on the Novel" (1925), when he writes that Dostoevsky's "religious and political ideas are not operative agencies within the body of his work; they appear there with the same fictious character as the faces and the frenetic passions" of the other figures.[21]

So if there is any real commitment in Dostoevsky it is to the spirit of dialogue and to its rules. In more general terms, it is the intellectual drama of an ongoing and unending dialogue among possibilities that makes good literature—including good political literature—transcend, and by transcending *expose*, the inherent limitations of any particular ideology. As Bakhtin perceptively notes, an internally persuasive discourse (as opposed to the "authoritarian" discourse of "monologic consciousness") always enters "into a strong interaction, a *struggle* with other internally persuasive discourses. Our ideological development is just such an intense struggle within us for hegemony among various available verbal and ideological points of view. . . . The semantic structure of an internally persuasive discourse is not finite, it is open; in each of the new contexts that dialogize it, this discourse is able to reveal ever new ways to mean."[22]

Extrapolating from Bakhtin, I will conclude by saying that the "internally persuasive" discourses of Yeats, or Eliot, or Pound, or the other "reactionaries" of Anglo-American high modernism are *not* "dialogized" when placed within the context of European fascism. Their own pronouncements on fascism, careless or superficial in many cases, more stubborn and cranky on occasion, certainly deserve to be studied, but not as a key to understanding the internal persuasiveness of their major works. The conventionally defined politics of the great Anglo-American modernists can show us the limitations and failures of their "dialogic imagination," but can tell us nothing about the truly dialogic tensions, agonies, and joys of their best writing.

Notes

1. The twin topics of the politics of aestheticism and the aestheticism of radical politics are discussed at some length in my essay, "Literature and Politics," in *Interrelations of Literature*, ed. Jean-Pierre Barricelli and Joseph Gibaldi (New York: MLA, 1982). For the use throughout the present paper of such terms as "modernity," "modernism," and the "avant-garde," as well as a discussion of broader issues of aesthetics and politics, see my *Faces of Modernity: Avant-Garde, Decadence, Kitsch* (Bloomington: Indiana Univ. Press, 1977).

2. Jean-François Lyotard, *Dérive à partir de Marx et Freud* (Paris: Union Générale d'Éditions, 1973), most specifically in "Notes sur la fonction critique

de l'oeuvre," where the (politically) exemplary character of art is a direct consequence of the fact that "the function of art is *immediately* revolutionary" (p. 235).

3. Breton writes in the "Manifesto for an Independent Revolutionary Art" (1938): "True art is unable not to be revolutionary. . . . In the realm of the artistic creation, the imagination must escape from all constraint and must under no pretext allow itself to be placed under bounds. If, for the better development of the forces of material production, the revolution must build a socialist regime with centralized control, to develop intellectual creation an anarchist regime of individual liberty should from the first be established. No authority, no dictation, not the least trace of orders from above." In *What is Surrealism?* ed. and introd. Franklin Rosemont (New York: Monad Press, 1978), 184–85. Breton does not seem to be aware that centralized "revolutionary" control in economic and political life is under no obligation to tolerate the intellectual anarchism he is advocating. This kind of aestheticist wishful thinking on the Left is paralleled on the Right by Yeats's view of Hitler and Mussolini as mere domestics who, through their fascist politics, were actually serving the cause of a new artistic Renaissance (see p. 89).

4. T. W. Adorno, "Commitment," in *The Essential Frankfurt School Reader,* ed. A. Arato and E. Gebhardt (New York: Urizen, 1978), 308.

5. Ibid., 303–4.

6. Ibid., 301–2.

7. Georg Lukács, "Franz Kafka or Thomas Mann?" in *The Meaning of Contemporary Realism,* trans. John Mander and Necke Mander (London: Merlin, 1963), 71.

8. Ibid., 81.

9. Ibid., 77.

10. Frank Kermode, *Modern Essays* (London: Collins/Fontana, 1971), 61.

11. Ihab Hassan, *Paracriticisms* (Urbana: Univ. of Illinois Press, 1975), 59.

12. Conor Cruise O'Brien, "Passion and Cunning: The Politics of W. B. Yeats," reprinted in *Literature and Revolution,* ed. G. A. White and Charles Newman (New York: Holt, Rinehart & Winston, 1972), 142–203.

13. Fredric Jameson, *Fables of Aggression: Wyndham Lewis, the Modernist as Fascist* (Berkeley and Los Angeles: Univ. of California Press, 1979), 18.

14. Ibid., 20.

15. Ibid., 19.

16. In fairness to Deleuze one must admit that, however idiosyncratic, his use of terms is never quite so arbitrary or unexplained as is Jameson's. Let us take the word "schizophrenic," employed honorifically by Jameson. In Deleuze and Guattari's *Anti-Oedipus,* the reader is duly reminded of the word's etymology ("schizophrenia"—"divided or split mind"), an etymology which is the key to understanding the new philosophical-anthropological acceptation in which the term is used by the authors. Furthermore, the reader is cautioned not to confuse "schizophrenia" as employed in the *Anti-Oedipus* with the current clinical meaning of the word. One might argue that Jameson's book—by, among other things, the casual way in which it introduces the epithet "schizophrenic"—presupposes

familiarity with Deleuze/Guattari. But even someone who happens to be familiar with Deleuze/Guattari cannot make much sense of such a phrase as a "properly postmodernist or schizophrenic conception of the cultural artifact." This is simply pretentious and very loose language.

17. Stephen Spender, "Writers and Politics," *Partisan Review* 24, no. 3 (1967): 373.

18. Stephen Spender, foreword to Alastair Hamilton, *The Appeal of Fascism: A Study of Intellectuals and Fascism, 1919–45* (London: Blond, 1971), xii.

19. Ibid., xiii.

20. For a broad definition of dialogic consciousness, see M. M. Bakhtin, *Problems of Dostoevsky's Poetics,* trans. R. W. Rotsel (Ann Arbor, Mich.: Ardis, 1973), ch. 4 and esp. pp. 87–113. For broader literary applications of the dialogic model see M. M. Bakhtin, *The Dialogic Imagination,* ed. M. Holquist, trans. M. Holquist and C. Emerson (Austin: Univ. of Texas Press, 1981), esp. "Discourse in the Novel," pp. 259–422. In some of my recent essays I have proposed a dialogic (and dialogically pluralist) definition of postmodernism. See in particular my "Ways of Looking at Fiction," in the 1980 *Bucknell Review* special issue on *Romanticism, Modernism, Postmodernism,* vol. 25, no. 2, pp. 155–70, and my essay, "From the One to the Many: Pluralism in Today's Culture," in *Innovation/Renovation,* ed. Ihab and Sally Hassan (Madison: Univ. of Wisconsin Press, 1983), 263–88.

21. José Ortega y Gasset, *The Dehumanization of Art and Other Essays,* trans. Helene Weyl (Princeton, N.J.: Princeton Univ. Press, 1968), 45.

22. Bakhtin, *The Dialogic Imagination,* 346.

Russell A. Berman

Modernism, Fascism, and the Institution of Literature

During the two decades following World War I, important representatives of literary modernism drew close to the burgeoning fascist movements. T. S. Eliot proclaimed his preference for fascism over communism, and the introduction to his lectures at the University of Virginia in 1933 reads like a program for an American *Blut und Boden* culture.[1] One thinks in addition of Pound's enthusiasm for Mussolini's Italy, Céline's hostility to the French Third Republic, Hamsun's calls for collaboration with the German occupation in Norway, and Gottfried Benn's initial support for the National Socialist regime. The issues I shall address involve the relationship between the literary works of the modernist authors close to fascism and the characteristics of the modernist project in general. It is not difficult to describe the varied (and often mutually contradictory) fascist or protofascist sympathies of these authors. One can also attempt to explain the genesis of these political predilections in terms of individual biography and ideology, as Fredric Jameson has done in his study of Wyndham Lewis.[2] Nevertheless, central aesthetic-historical questions remain: is the ideological polarity implicit in these works fundamentally external to their modernist aesthetics, or are the characteristics of their modernisms somehow tied to—or engendered by—a fascist project? Can one describe specifically aesthetic features of a fascist work of art, and is that work of art specifically modernist?

It is crucial to differentiate these questions from alternative, perhaps more obvious approaches to the enigmatic hybrid "fascist modernism." The partial confluence of modernist literary programs with aspects of fascist thought could of course suggest an investigation of the specific ideologies of the individual authors in order to examine the nature of their attraction to political movements. Instead of this biographical focus, one might follow Georg Lukács in his attempts to delineate categories of certain literary works which, so it was argued, objectively corresponded to fascist tendencies regardless of the subjectively expressed political allegiances of the author. This essay, however, will place neither the person of the author nor the singularity of the work in the center of its analysis. Rather, modernism, as will be shown in a moment, will be taken as a radical shift in the institutional framework of literature, in which the fundamental status and function of the literary work in society were called into question, new definitions were evoked and, among these, a program for a fascist modernism emerged. In particular this institutional approach to the question of a fascist modernism will focus on the reorganization of the relationship between the text itself and the reader. The concrete politics of literature are not at all exhausted by the ideological intentions of the author; on the contrary these intentions precede the real political act, the unfolding of a realm of social interaction around the recipient.

As Peter Bürger has argued, modernism developed in the context of the obsolescence of the bourgeois institutions of art which had arisen during the eighteenth century and which collapsed under the attack of the early twentieth-century avant-garde movements.[3] The traditional autonomous work of art had flaunted its independence from the practical concerns of the recipient; above it was inscribed Mörike's dictum: "Was aber schön ist, selig scheint es in ihm selbst." Modernism articulated alternative models in which precisely this autonomy of the work was rejected: life and art were to be merged. Bourgeois art had reached its apogee with the symbolist "l'art pour l'art" movement and its insistence on its distance from everyday life. The avant-garde's efforts to escape this golden cage of irrelevance led to a surfeit of new conceptions of the social status of art that in turn evoked a wealth of formal innovations during the early twentieth century. Of course, even the antisocial self-definition of autonomous art had a social function; for modernism in any case the social character of the various aesthetic endeavors was constantly underscored, and among these socially motivated literary projects a fascist version arose to compete with the other varieties of modernism.

The political character of all modernist projects centered on the reader. Bourgeois aesthetics had traditionally presumed a passive audience only because it could unquestioningly assume the presence of literate recipients sharing homogeneous backgrounds, values, and attitudes. The disappearance of the stable, communicative relationship between the literary intelligentsia and its public appeared to the readership to be the result of the bohemian irresponsibility of the artists,[4] while for the latter it was tantamount to the collapse of the public. The realist author had been able to speak to an audience whose presence seemed as unproblematic as that of a natural resource; the modernist author encountered a literary community which was no longer fully functioning, having lost much of its public character in the course of the socioeconomic transformations of the nineteenth century.[5] Capitalist secularization trapped the formerly autonomous literary public in the Weberian iron cage, from which modernism sought, in one way or another, to emancipate its audience. Modernism addressed an audience not for the sake of a message but in order to produce a reader, and the various forms of modernism engaged in this production in radically differing ways. Fascist modernism ascribed to the work the role of imitating a reactionary revolution. If the fascist political movements intended to overcome the alleged chaos of liberal capitalism by returning to the ideological vision of a primitive stability and homogeneity, the fascist work of art appropriated this regenerative goal for itself. No longer an autonomous object of beauty to be contemplated by the passive recipient, it was designed to transform the status of the recipient in order to reunite him or her with the primal order of race and the permanence of unquestionable values.

This regenerative aesthetics can be traced to one variety of mid-nineteenth-century anti-capitalism. Richard Wagner bequeathed not only a political legacy which led, via the institution of Bayreuth, directly into the *völkisch* circles close to Hitler; his program for the work of art too was a central precursor of the fascist cultural vision. His traumatic experiences in Paris, then the capital of modernity, and his sense of exclusion from the rudimentary culture industry explain his formulating a negative model of the contemporary work as solely formal, superficial, and sensational—a model he associated, by the way, exclusively with his Jewish competitors in the music market. In contrast, his *Gesamtkunstwerk,* which was to gather together the isolated arts, would also gather the atomistic individuals of the laissez-faire world and forge them into the organic unity of the folk. Hence Wagner's characteristic language, artificially antiquated and allegedly original; hence also his attraction to the national mythology. The Wagnerian work was the magic swan that would carry the German folk out of the land of bondage and liberal alienation and return it to itself. The regenerative work claimed to set the stage for the people to come into being. For Martin Heidegger, eight decades later, only through the work of art "does the nation first return to itself for the fulfillment of its vocation."[6] The art work was not the object of aesthetic contemplation but the locus of the generation of a national project. The recipient ceased to represent an individual sensibility capable of interpretive activity and disappeared into the mysterious unity of the folk. The fascist work did not produce the reader in order to provide a consumer of aesthetic pleasure but in order to organize him or her within the national rebirth.

This political goal, far beyond the realm of aesthetic autonomy, indicates the distance between fascist literature and traditional bourgeois art, and therefore points to the fundamental shift in the institutional character of literature associated with modernism. The identifying modernist feature of fascist literature was not its political character but its refusal to restrict itself to an aesthetic realm and its efforts to penetrate social life. This anti-aesthetic prejudice, shared of course by other varieties of modernism, where, however, the specific regenerative program was absent, necessarily colored the literary criticism generated within fascist circles. Thus in his review of Hans Grimm's *Volk ohne Raum*, Paul Fechter insisted explicitly that the novel no longer corresponded to the model of purposeless bourgeois fictionality but instead could actively "contribute to the creation of the folk, our still present task."[7]

The model of the regenerative work is a modernist or protomodernist model in Bürger's sense because it rejects the functionlessness of bourgeois aesthetic autonomy; it is modernist, however, in an apparently non-innovative manner, since it claims to reinstitute a traditional identity. It manipulates the recipient in order to rejuvenate the nation; indeed it claims to be the link between individual recipient and folk collectivity, or, rather, that the individual must disappear within that collectivity. Thus Nietzsche, one of the earliest critics of this regenerative aesthetics, counterposed Bizet to Wagner in order to suggest competing reception models: while Wagner disciplined his audience with a formless music and authoritarian gestures, Bizet's classical sensuousness heightened the rational intellectuality of the listener. For Nietzsche, Wagner's "*espressivo* at any cost," the tedious repetition of central ideas in the recurring leitmotifs, eroded any legitimate musical structures, while attempting to overpower the recipient with the nonmusical contents. Wagner's efforts to convert his audience anticipated twentieth-century efforts to organize a *völkisch* public via the propagandistic character of fascist literature, where directly expressed ideological stances were defended in lengthy diatribes that constantly interrupted the ostensible narratives: the disappearance of substantial form implied the manipulation of a reader no longer called upon to exercise discrimination. On the other hand, Nietzsche's critique of this tendentiousness and his preference for an independent, self-possessed recipient foreshadowed the aesthetics of the late Benjamin and Brecht: instead of regeneration, the production of an active readership or audience as the telos of a work. The modernist Brecht envisioned a public—yet to be created—capable of active thought and, therefore, of rational action; but for the fascist modernists, regeneration, and not activation, became the central thematic concern: the overcoming of sterility in *The Waste Land* or *Lady Chatterley's Lover,* the return to the land in *Growth of the Soil,* the images of utopian nature in the *Cantos.* More important, the fascist modernist works declared themselves to be the mechanism of the return, not only its description. As in Wagner's critique of his musical competitors, Lawrence for example rejected the conventional versions of the novel as superficial gossip, arguing instead that "the novel properly handled" must return the reader "to the most secret places of life [where] the tide of sensitive awareness needs to ebb and flow, cleansing and refreshing."[8] It rejuvenates and regenerates, awakening an occluded organicity as surely as does Mellors's penis. In a parallel manner, Céline presented himself as "le grand libérateur du style," emancipating lived language from the oppressiveness of form. His novels became the eruptions of a primal experience against any of the mediating mechanisms of society: "faudra raconter tout sans changer un mot de ce qu'on a vu de plus vicieux chez les hommes," and only such a primal narration, in which petit-bourgeois ressentiment cloaks itself in vitalist pretense, was deemed capable of providing a final resolution: "on ne sera tranquille que tout aura été dit."[9]

It is the world of change and exchange that the fascist work denounces; neither the diversity of difference nor the transformation of history is tolerated. Instead, an eternal stratum of racial existence is represented and remembered. Thus one may speak of the monumental character of fascist works, for they present themselves precisely as monuments to an experience denied, it was claimed, by a superficial liberalism and expelled from bourgeois art but nevertheless always present. This explains the antimodernist gesture of fascist modernism. On the level of ideology, the present is rejected as liberal, rational, and capitalist, while an image of a wholesome and thoroughly stable past is unfolded: Eliot's seventeenth century, Pound's China, or Hamsun's primitive agrarian world. This nostalgia profoundly obscured the objective character of the sociohistorical transformation in the twenties and thirties: the literature that claimed to oppose a liberal present in the name of a preliberal past immanently reflected the transformation to postliberal social forms under the bureaucratic administrative state and therefore rejected the categories of the anachronistic bourgeois culture of the nineteenth century, development and mediation.

Autonomous bourgeois literature of the previous era had been regularly concerned with development, most saliently in its key genre, the *Bildungsroman,* as well as with the harmonious integration of diverse elements; the hero of the novel of development can pass through qualitatively different settings and undergo fundamental transformations. The fascist modernist corollary, by way of contrast, is organized around the absence of change. Events and situations are repetitive, and the hero never truly grows. In *Growth of the Soil*, Hamsun's peasant Isak remains fundamentally the same throughout the course of his career; he learns nothing new, while his initial knowledge is constantly reconfirmed. Despite the author's insistence on the primacy of nature and in particular on growth as a natural process, the implicit model of nature is not one of romantic organicism, which always sketched a transformation from an origin to a qualitatively new morphology. Rather, Hamsun's nature is the cipher for immutability and permanence, and it is this fear of change, a key theme, which also organizes the novel's formal structure.

Fascist literature rejects the developmental character of the bourgeois narrative and replaces it with the seriality of changelessness. Unlike other modernisms, its insistence on the priority of homogeneity bars it from the principled juxtaposition of heterogeneous materials in the montage form.[10] Similarly it must thematize a hostility for the fictional figures who represent the potential of difference: Jews and women. Anti-Semitism and misogyny emerge therefore as logical consequences of the aesthetic project and cannot be reduced to peripheral issues that an antipolitical literary scholarship might prefer to ignore as merely extrinsic. The basic thrust of the literary endeavor leads Eliot to his Bleistein and Lawrence to his Connie.

This is an auspicious point at which to underscore the relationships among competing types of modernism. Bourgeois autonomous literature regularly displayed a developmental character; modernist nonautonomous works replaced development with repetitive seriality, a term which can be applied not only to Hamsun's prose but to the works of Kafka or Brecht, or, most obviously, to dodecaphonic music as well. In the context of the monumental fascist work, however, seriality functions in a unique and precise manner. It embodies the insistence on an unchanging existence; the message is proclaimed repetitively, both in content and form, and the recipient is reduced to the passive receptacle of the author's tendentiousness. Elsewhere, in other modernisms, seriality leads in a diametrically opposite direction in order to evoke the recipient as an active subject; the radical repetitiveness of the serial composition becomes, in a dialectic inversion, the prerequisite for an authentic transformation and the emergence of the fundamentally new realm of freedom. This metamorphosis, not the often belabored metaphysics of parody, is the central statement of *Doctor Faustus;* in one of his more lucid moments, Serenus Zeitblom could aptly characterize the *magnum opus* of his friend, the paradigmatically modernist composer, in the following terms: "a formal treatment strict to the last degree, which no longer knows anything unthematic, in which the order of the basic material becomes total . . . there is no longer any free note. But it serves now a higher purpose; for—oh marvel, oh deep diabolic jest!—just by virtue of the absoluteness of the form the music is, as language, freed."[11]

For the modernist Thomas Mann, seriality bore the hope of transcendence; for the fascist modernist seriality meant the fundamental absence of change. This fear of difference furthermore could radically influence the narrational structure of prose and the character of fictionality. The novel of the earlier period was marked by an omniscient narrative perspective which was able to organize disparate voices harmoniously. In the modernism of montage forms, where the juxtaposition of heterogeneous elements became the central principle, the harmony was exploded but the diversity of material was maintained; with its polyphonic structure Mann's *Doctor Faustus* can again serve as an obvious example. In fascist modernism, however, diversity—and therefore harmony— disappears, and one finds instead a tendentious reduction of prose fiction to a monotonal voice. Thus Connie Chatterley rapidly adopts Mellors's language, whose message is nearly indistinguishable from that of the narrator. Thus also in Hamsun's later novels the hero ceases to function as an independent character and becomes solely the carrier of the narrator's speech. Finally an extreme example of narrative reductionism: in the central work of German *völkisch* literature, Hans Grimm's *Volk ohne Raum,* not only has the difference between narrative voice and central figure shrunk to a minimum; in addition, the fundamental character of fictionality—the necessary distance between the narrated cosmos and the life-world of the recipient—is disclaimed; the author as narrator appears immediately as a figure in the text and thereby transforms it into a purported memoir. The autonomy of bourgeois fiction gives way to a pseudo-document that presents itself to the reader not as an imaginative mirage, protected and sequestered by the quotation marks of aesthetic form, but rather as authentic experience, unmediated and unquestionable.

The fascist attacks on the literary tradition, however, were never as radical as the iconoclasm of competing versions of modernism. Adrian Leverkühn radically negates Beethoven's Ninth Symphony; Thomas Mann cites the tradition in order to overcome it. In contrast Eliot and Pound quote earlier works in order to resuscitate a preliberal orthodoxy of values. The alternative modernisms ascribed alternative intents to montage: parody or preservation. Fascist literature, as rebellious as it may have presented itself to be, therefore tied modernism ultimately to a cultural conservatism. In the midst of Ernst Jünger's futurist paean to mechanized war, the hero still reads Renaissance poetry at the front, and this thematized conservatism corresponds to a more general loyalty to the inherited literary institution, despite the modernist break with the past. Of course, fascist literary programs denounced the traditional work, the beauty of which the bourgeois recipient contemplated in entranced passivity; replacing the autonomous work with the allegedly unmediated experience of the pseudo-document, fascist literature did not, however, transform this passive recipient, who was then called upon to contemplate not the work of art but the world as art work: Benjamin's "aestheticization of politics," Riefenstahl's Nürnberg, Jünger's battlefields as fiction-become-real. Fascist modernism rejected autonomy but preserved the recipient of the autonomous work as the passive spectator of an immutable reality: the regressive realization of the modernist project as the transformation of life into art. In the totally secularized world, all modernisms were concerned with positioning the reader not only vis-à-vis the text, but also within fluid social structures no longer legitimated by traditional values. Once the public could no longer simply be assumed as the natural context of literature, modernist literature was forced to undertake the production of its own recipients. The text located the reader within a social relationship and thereby ascribed to him or her an identity, the character of which was inextricably tied to the sociopolitical environment. Modernism might produce the reader as an ironic intellectual by presenting paradoxes or as a rational activist by presenting contradictions. Fascist

Berman

modernism presented an unbroken myth and produced the reader as victim, as an immobile voyeur, prepared to embrace both the work of art and his or her own destruction as moments of pleasure.

Notes

1. T. S. Eliot, *After Strange Gods: A Primer of Modern History* (New York: Harcourt, Brace, 1934).

2. Fredric Jameson, *Fables of Aggression: Wyndham Lewis, the Modernist as Fascist* (Berkeley and Los Angeles: Univ. of California Press, 1979).

3. Peter Bürger, *Theory of the Avant-Garde,* trans. Michael Shaw (Minneapolis: Univ. of Minnesota Press, 1984).

4. See Levin Ludwig Schücking, *The Sociology of Literary Taste,* trans. Brian Battershaw (Chicago: Univ. of Chicago Press, 1966).

5. See Jürgen Habermas, *Strukturwandel der Öffentlichkeit* (Neuwied: Luchterhand, 1968), and Richard Sennett, *The Fall of Public Man* (New York: Knopf, 1977).

6. Martin Heidegger, *Poetry, Language, Thought* (New York: Harper & Row, 1971), 42.

7. Paul Fechter, "Ein deutsches Volksbuch" in *Die Neue Literatur* 32 (1931): 467.

8. D. H. Lawrence, *Lady Chatterley's Lover* (New York: Grove, 1959), 117.

9. Louis-Ferdinand Céline, *Voyage au bout de la nuit* suivi de *Mort à Crédit* (Paris: Gallimard, 1962), 27 and 323.

10. See my "Montage as a Literary Technique: Thomas Mann's 'Tristan' and T. S. Eliot's *The Waste Land,*" in *Selecta* 2 (1981): 20–23.

11. Thomas Mann, *Doctor Faustus* (New York: Vintage, 1971), 488.

SECTION 2
The Practice of Modernism

presented by
Monique Chefdor

La vision nouvelle est un déménagement, un changement de domicile, on entre dans un autre logis.

(The new vision is a displacement, a change of address, you move into a new home).

—Gabrielle Buffet

Un de mes amis, esprit mobile et exalté me disait trouver des différences entre les oeuvres littéraires, picturales ou musicales, je n'étais pas de son avis et nous eûmes une longue conversation sur ce sujet; notre délire dura près d'une heure, jusqu'au moment où nos cervelles transformées plus ou moins en bouillie, nous permirent de constater le néant de toutes théories physiques ou métaphysiques!

(A friend of mine, a swift and exalted mind, told me he perceived differences between literary, pictorial or musical works, I did not agree with him and we had a long conversation on the subject; our ravings went on for about an hour until our brains more or less reduced to mush enabled us to ascertain the void of all theories, physical or metaphysical!)

—Francis Picabia, *Jésus-Christ Rastaquouère*

Apart from matters of periodization, identification, ideology, beyond history, "theory and system," first and foremost Modernism is a practice, a practice of styles in the broadest sense of the term. In all its simultaneous and successive variations Modernism unites music and the verbal and visual arts in the common pursuit of alternative modes of expression.

Leaving aside the distinctions of both chronology and medium, this section offers a variety of approaches to some aspects of Modernist experimentation in an effort to underline continuity in discontinuity, wholeness in fragmentation, unity in only apparent disunity. Instead of using an inventorial and revisionist method, the following contributions reflect the overall tone of this volume by turning attention to a few selected moments of Modernist practice in poetry and the novel, theater arts, painting, music, and photography. In that same spirit a reconsideration of the major achievements of the High Modernists has been avoided in favor of an exploration of less frequently assessed trends.

Anna Balakian sets the tone for a proper comparative approach with her demonstration of how a French, a South American, and a German poet, nurtured by the same revolution in poetics, contributed to a redefinition of the "apperception of reality," an intensification of "aesthetic co-experience" and the return of language to its "logos-function." Although connections between Huidobro and Reverdy have often been noted, as Balakian herself points out, they have not been established at the level at which we see them here. Hugo Ball, more frequently known for his bruitist poem *Karawane* than for the splendid pieces introduced here, is also presented in a new light. By probing into the core of their mature writings, Anna Balakian's analysis frees all three poets from the labels of dadaism, cubism, and creationism usually attached to them and places them in the mainstream of what she deems to be the more constructive direction of Modernism, as opposed to the more destructive one. Some might take exception to an implicit endorsement of the charge of negativity frequently made against many avant-gardes. On the other hand, Balakian's judicious denunciation of the misreading of tone poems as mere expression of the absurd invites us to take a closer look at the assumptions on which those charges are commonly made. The thesis she develops in these pages brings the reader to a better understanding of the process by which the Modernist poet, whether he experiments in so-called nonsense poems or uses standard structures (as her three models eventually did), used "language as a power generator to provoke the imagination" and create a "cameo of the struggle for synthesis." Such ambitions or dreams, as we know, pervade Modernism from symbolism to surrealism, two familiar worlds for Balakian.

Along the path from artist/mirror to artist/god (predicted for modern times by Huidobro), the Faustian temptation of a pact with the devil cannot be escaped. The next essay thus appropriately starts with a recollection of Adrian Leverkühn's dialogue with the "compound ghost" in Thomas Mann's *Doctor Faustus*. Harvey Gross's concern, however, is not with thematic aspects of Modernism but with its stylistic dilemma, best exemplified in its use of parody and self-critique in the form of allusion, quotation, reminiscence. Reminding us of familiar examples such as Picasso, Eliot, and Joyce, Gross focuses on Mann's critique of myth in two of his early stories, *Tristan* and *The Blood of the Walsungs*, and illustrates the mode of parody with Mahler's complex network of musical intertextuality. One cannot emphasize enough the central importance of these techniques in the entire spectrum of Modernist artistic and literary productions, which, if by nothing else, are unified by ironic reflexivity. Beyond the exposition of these pervasive stylistic modes, Gross's essay evokes the specter of the true nemesis of modernity: its compulsive need to establish itself against tradition.

Nowhere was this tyranny of the new more acutely felt than in Apollinaire's Paris, which, as Margaret Davies recalls in her essay, was a true "melting pot of . . . changes." Apollinaire, the spokesman for *L'Esprit Nouveau,* and Cendrars, who printed his first works at his own "Editions des Hommes Nouveaux," were both past masters in the art of literary reminiscences and collage. Against the background of a wide framework of reference, Davies focuses on these two champions of *modernité* together with a third poet, Max Jacob, to analyze some of the techniques by which these Paris poets met the "challenge of being modern" in the first two decades of this century. Parallel with the international triptych which opens this section, we can detect a hidden dualism in this Parisian triptych. Whereas both Apollinaire and Cendrars share a sense of simultaneity, elasticity, randomness, Cendrars does not join Apollinaire and Max Jacob in their experimentation with the "material aspect of language." A virtuoso in the use of *image-associations* to convey the tension between centrifugal and centripetal forces at the core of modern experience, Cendrars stretched the modernist sense of irony to the point of making poems out of newspaper items and serials, but he rarely resorted to calligrammatic devices and then only with parodic intent. Apollinaire's contribution to *modernité,* on the contrary, also points toward the autonomy of the artist, the move away from representation. In both directions, however, we find precedence given to a "central faith in the poet's creativity."

Almost as a homage to simultaneity (which "seemed to be synonymous with *modernité,*" as Margaret Davies puts it) the drive toward the autonomy of the artist is immediately echoed by Jo-Anna Isaak's study of autotelic aesthetic praxis in Russian futurism and English vorticism. Here Modernist trends toward abstraction are exemplified in full BLAST, so to speak! In addition to an analysis of the various means by which art, verbal and visual, was relieved of its semantic function by the futurists and the vorticists, Isaak's essay brings out another point of tension, another paradox inherent in the Modernist vocation: the basic difference between playful abstractionism (the *jeu* noted in the preceding essay), illustrated here by Lewis, and the Russian futurists' commitment to the idea that "form conditions content" and, therefore, that aesthetic revolution will and *must* bring social change. We are reminded of Matei Calinescu's allusions to the theories of Lukács and Jakobson in the opening section. As is well known, this major source of division among the Modernists tore asunder the surrealist movement and continues to split apart contemporary aesthetics.

Turning our attention, in the same period, to this side of the Atlantic with Jay Bochner's essay on the New York Secession, we discover a sort of inverted mirror of the aesthetic playfulness/social commitment dilemma. Experimentation with machinery art took on radically different significance for a European artist such as Picabia, for instance, who used machines with irony, and for American painters and photographers like the Secessionists, for whom the machine had to "serve in the founding of an indigenous art." The instructive comparison Bochner makes between Williams's poems and Marin's paintings reveals techniques of fragmentation formally similar to their European counterparts, but semantically altogether different. What marked a move toward abstraction in Europe here had representational qualities. In New York, the "first city of modernity," as early as 1902 abstraction was reality.

After these worldwide wanderings through early styles of Modernism in various areas of literature and the arts it seems appropriate to focus on a single key figure who combined theory and practice, poetry and painting: Paul Klee. Renée Riese Hubert's essay sheds light on Klee's unique position within Modernism, central by the scope of his conceptions and marginal in the reception he encountered. It also further illuminates several of the paradoxes recurrently underscored in this volume. Indeed, Klee's isolation from his fellow Modernists because of his attachment to romantic concepts of artistic creation is part of the basic dichotomy noted earlier (by Balakian and Davies). In all three facets of his work (theoretical essays on art, paintings, and poetry) the recognition of the autonomy of art, a common theme throughout this section, is coupled with a need to establish order, to "overcome chaos," a trend found only in the more orphic tradition of Modernism. Of special interest to analysts of Modernism, as explored by Hubert, are the links between verbal and visual arts illustrated by Klee's works.

A fundamental feature of Modernism, both in literature and in the arts, is its questioning of representation. By emphasizing the mannerist character inherent in the practices of iconicization, elliptical effects, fragmentation, and final "reading of the partial as holistic" Mary Ann Caws brings into focus an important unifying feature of the Modernist kaleidoscope. Achieving a fusion of past and present, visual and verbal, concrete and abstract, she also combines theory and practice by offering readers a model of a Modernist criticism. If ever a style of Modernist criticism were to be identified, her re-creative use of the critical eye as a union of both the reader's and the viewer's eyes would constitute an appropriate parallel to Modernist experimentation. This swift, penetrating scanning of the creative horizon points to essential techniques of Modernist visual and verbal arts; it also brings to life the body of texts too often left to the annals of esoteric writing although they epitomize Modernist sensibility (Artaud, Bataille, Leiris, and Desnos, for instance, among others). Her evocation of Proust at the end of an exploration of more extreme forms of Modernist expression appears highly emblematic of the search for unity in diversity pervading the entire volume. Indeed, whether we turn to the iconoclastic attacks against language and form or to the more "Olympian" style of High Modernism, we find that all Modernists share an avowed or concealed desire to free art from ephemeral temporality.

Let us hope, in conclusion, that the parts of the Modernist "body unveiled" by the following essays will help to "re-member and re-collect" the body entire.

Anna Balakian

A Triptych of Modernism: Reverdy, Huidobro, and Ball

Three poets of the early decades of this century shed
light on the major paradoxes of modernism. I am not trying to establish
this triptych to exercise random intertextuality nor as a basis for a study
of influences. Geography separated these poets; the age connected them.
From Paris to Zurich, to Santiago and Buenos Aires, the clocks were
synchronized. Their affiliation resulted from a common cultural source
that nurtured them and that they recognized: the revolution that had
occurred in poetics in the previous century and that was to bifurcate
modernism in our time.

In the context of modernism these poets have made the following
permanent contributions, evidenced both in their poesis and their poetry:
they have relied on the power of the image to generate rather than
reflect sense or sensation, they have attempted to redefine the apperception
of reality, and they have focused their efforts on returning language to
what Hugo Ball called its logos-function: "You may laugh, language
will one day reward us for our zeal, even if it does not achieve any
directly visible results. We have loaded the word with strengths and
energies that helped us to rediscover the evangelical concept of the 'word'
(logos) as a magical complex image."[1]

The other road of modernism leads of course to rebellion, deconstruction, relativism, non-anthropocentrism, collage, dehumanization,
and the cult of the abstract. This bifurcation, which becomes more and
more clear as the century nears its end, justifies references to the avant-

gardes in the plural rather than in the singular, for indeed modernism has pulled in two different directions in the twentieth century.

The deterioration of culture and its reflection in the arts is comprehensively described by Hugo Ball in his article on Kandinsky in 1917:

> A thousand-year-old culture disintegrates. There are no columns and supports, no foundations any more . . . churches have become castles . . . convictions have become prejudices. . . . There are no more perspectives in the moral world. . . . Above is below, below is above. The meaning of the world disappeared. . . . The world showed itself to be a blind juxtaposition and opposing of uncontrolled forces. Man lost his divine countenance, became matter, chance, an aggregate. . . . He became a particle of nature . . . no more interesting than a stone; he vanished into nature. . . . A world of abstract demons swallowed the individual utterance, . . . robbed single things of their names . . . psychology became chatter.[2]

If one believes that in the total scheme of the cosmos all are condemned to remain ignorant of the whole and are driven by unconscious forces, why should not art display these same forces of automatism and insufficiency of structure? The processes involved in these forms of the modern arts, then, are in a sense imitations of nature. When Boileau and Pope advised the artist to hold the mirror up to nature, the Cartesian or Newtonian assumption was that nature was orderly in its operations— and even in its aberrations—meaningful even in its destructive forces, intentioned by a superior will. Now holding the mirror up to nature reveals a nature that is random, purposeless, uncontrolled by any unifying consciousness. Thus the modern artist who sees this change in our perception of the universe is aiming at the same target as his predecessors; what has changed is his understanding of the character of nature.

But in the case of Hugo Ball's verbal painting of the disintegration of a world, the intention was not to hold the mirror up to this desolation. In fact, Ball's notion of the modern was neither to reflect the chaos nor to identify with it, but rather to react to it and offer an alternative— an optional universe. In the second part of the same article on Kandinsky he tells us that the artists are dissociating themselves from "this empirical world. . . . They become creators of new natural entities that have no counterpart in the known world. They create images that are no longer imitations of nature but augmentations of nature by new, hitherto unknown appearances and mysteries. That is the victorious joy of these artists— to create existences, which one calls images but which have a consistency of their own that is equivalent to that of a rose, a person, a sunset or a crystal."[3]

In an equally prophetic stance, Vicente Huidobro was saying: "The epoch just beginning will be eminently creative." His attitude toward nature was summarized in his famous cry: "We will not serve." A bit more jaded than his two contemporaries, Pierre Reverdy hoped that the abject human plight might push the imitative faculties of the artist to the limit at which even if he was not capable of pure creation he might become convinced that he had acquired such a faculty.[4] Resistance to chaos in the search for creative powers was the alternate direction of modernism, strongly visible in the works of this triptych. The inherent motivation of their writings was anchored in the belief that modern society's major forces of aggression would be directed against the physical universe rather than remain engaged in fratricide; there was a vision of man fighting blind forces rather than man fighting man. This spirit is indicated in the very titles of their major works. Written in wartime, none of them refers directly to the war. Huidobro's *Altazor*, the supereagle, born at the age of thirty-three, the day of the death of Christ; Reverdy's *Les Epaves du ciel*, a viewing of earth as a sky fall-out; Ball's *Das Flug auf der Zeit*, flight out of time? Perhaps, but also flight out of the age. In all three the fate of humanity drives the poet to a defiance of the process of representation itself, whether of humanity, of society, or of the universe, rather than to an expression of disgust, to a visionary reality contiguous or adjacent to the natural universe but independent in its purposes.

Mallarmé's theory of creative communication had pointed in two directions: one from the interior, nonverbalized state of consciousness to verbalized exterior configuration, the other from the discovery of an arresting exterior object to interior distillation. The implementation of this dual optic is the basis of the dialectics of modernism, expressed on the one hand as the figurative and on the other as the abstract in the arts. The triptych here discussed opted for figuration. These poets expressed in almost identical language their faith in the image as the central edifice of the work of art, whether in poetry or in painting. Analogical communication produces a confluence of objects whose associations with each other are totally dependent on the author's will and his capacity to reshuffle word associations. These are *achieved* associations, not random ones. As Reverdy said in *Le Livre de mon bord*: "Art begins where chance ends."[5] Chance simply flirts with the artist but as an opportunist the artist exploits chance for his own designs. Huidobro calls this facility "superconsciousness."[6] In other words, as André Breton was to find out, automatism is nothing without *vigilance*.

The tolerance of object associations translated into image associations is well known as a gauge of modernism. From Lautréamont's spectacular metaphors to the much-quoted definition of image by Reverdy, repeated by Breton and Max Ernst, the technique had actually been expressed some ten years earlier by Huidobro, who had traced it back to Voltaire's *Philosophical Dictionary* in its definition of the imagination. Regardless of who said it first or best, the fact remains that in the early part of the twentieth century the theory of the image received recognition as the cradle of a hermetic process of creation. The association of disparate realities in the image was practiced for different reasons by different people. It was random game activity for many collage artists. It was divination for oracular ones; it was a process of gestation for still others. This last-proposed function is most significant in the case of Ball because he is generally known for his dada interlude, and for the dadaists collage was a derisive activity. Ball, participating in dada performance and talking about Rimbaud's powers of language at the same time, strikingly demonstrates as a simultaneously deconstructive and constructive artist the dichotomy of modernism. But his deeper adherence to the constructive is evident in his theoretical statements about language and its function in the creative process: "The new art is sympathetic because in an age of disruption it has conserved the will-to-image." He goes further to proclaim: "In principle the abstract age is over."[7] Although much was to happen thereafter to disprove Ball's contention, as late as the 1930s Reverdy was of the same conviction as Ball: "Thought can only recognize itself and judge its limits in the concrete."[8]

But before going further, we have to overcome a taboo of modern criticism: the so-called intentional fallacy, i.e., the relevance of the artist's intentions to the actual work accomplished. Those who object to the serious consideration of intentions argue that whatever intentions there may be should be inherent in the work itself and that outside of the work they have no validity. In the case of poetry, however, particularly modern poetry, the expression of intentions is in fact part of the poesis. Some, of course, include their awareness of process in the poem itself, turning such poems into poem-manifestos; Apollinaire and Wallace Stevens are two important practitioners of this genre. Others manifest their awareness of the process of the poetic act in their prose, considering poetic intention almost as significant as, and more consistent with their innermost being than, the individual sparks of the generative process that we call "poems." Reverdy said: "No creation is perfect except in its hypothesis."[9] The implication is that too often the artist's self-assigned commissions in this world are beyond his power, however brave—or arrogant—to deliver. The poetic process is itself the experience; the single poem gives signals that go beyond what is recorded.

Intentions and their less comprehensive implementations are virtually inseparable in considerations of the features of the modernism of the triptych here in question: problems of reality, image, and language, both in their poesis and their poetry.

The demolition of the concept of reality was not something new in the twentieth century. In the midst of a loudly declared school of realism in the arts, Baudelaire, Maxime du Camp, Champfleury, and Courbet connived to distort the definition of the obvious and static connotation of the word. Realists are dreamers, said Champfleury, and he called Gérard de Nerval a "realist" in his revised definition of the word. Had Baudelaire developed his fragment, "Puisque réalisme il y a," he might have been the theoretician of surrealism. The desire to redefine reality was for Baudelaire an epistemological need and search. "Every good poet is a *realist*,"[10] he said, thus dislodging that well-determined signifier from the commonly signified. Many years later Reverdy was to say: "The true poet . . . is he who has as his primary force, the sense of reality."[11] In his vision the poet is equipped with a dragnet to harvest his realities out of the miscellany of nature.

While Baudelaire was dislodging that particular signifier, "reality," from common usage, he was in fact opening the way for the poetic manipulation of all signifiers, making of language, rather than of nature, the matrix of poetic reality. And this reality, according to Reverdy, holds its own independent space "among the things that exist in nature."[12] As already observed of the title *Les Epaves du ciel* each part of the composite is easy to envisage but together the unambiguous signifiers create an ambiguity, the cause of which is neither a complicated syntax nor a far-fetched lexicon, nor even some secret mythopoetic reference—practices which were prevalent in the leading poets of the post-symbolist persuasion, contemporaries of Reverdy in his early period.

The "oval" of *La Lucarne ovale*, which has no connection with the content of the poems, illustrates the geometrical preoccupations of both the new artists and the new poets. Reverdy, like Huidobro, who entitled one of his collections *Horizon carré*, paid tribute to Saint-Pol-Roux; this unclassifiable poet had defined the "poet" as a geometrician of the absolute. Elsewhere Reverdy characterizes his eye as lozengical—another reference to geometrical form.

The next title, *Les Ardoises du toit*, seems innocuous on the surface. There appears no tension between *slate*—an earthy substance—and *roof,* equally tangible—and what is more ordinary than a slate roof? Even separating *ardoise* from *toit,* one can conceivably have a blackboard on which to write an ephemeral poem. But, wait, *ardoise* also means a credit account—on which the poet is free to draw for sustenance (elsewhere he has called the dream an exploitable mine), and with this extended connotation not only is the function of *slate* modified but it in turn alters the simple connotation of roof and assumes dimensions beyond that of housetops. Another seemingly innocuous title is *Cravates de chanvre. Cravate* (necktie), however, assumes an ominous change of function when coupled with *chanvre,* a weed used to make rope. The two words considered as individual and separate images are semantically innocent, but their rapprochement creates a lethal composite, for a *cravate de chanvre* is in effect a *noose.* But there is still another meaning lurking behind *chanvre,* for it is also a plant from which hashish and marijuana are extracted; so again we have the combination of the real and the illusion, of man gravitating toward hallucination and yet encompassed in a concrete reality of danger. The logos-character of words creates images that use natural data to mean something more. Curiously, the obvious reality of the moment, World War I, is obliterated from the poetry of this vintage, as it was to be from that of World War II. The same absence of the obvious conditions of life can be noted in the poetry of Huidobro and Ball from the same period.

In a poem called "La Réalité immobile," Reverdy compares the poem to a photo without a frame, thus extending the absence of referentiality from the temporal to the spatial. In a poem called "Minuit," this total lack of referentiality is striking in the presence of specific, concrete signifiers of elementary meaning and comprehensibility. "Minuit / La pendule sans fin sonne à coup de marteau / Sur mon coeur / En entrant dans la maison sinistre et désolée dont j'ai perdu le numéro" (Midnight / The clock endlessly hammers the hours / On my heart / Entering the bleak and desolate house whose number I have lost).[13] Passage from the limited to the limitless is often expressed through negatives and the adjective "last," or through an impossible comparison manipulating the signifiers of limit to cancel out their respective meanings. Such is the case in a poem called "Abîme," where we find a line such as "La chambre s'étendait bien plus loin que les murs" (The room extended far beyond the walls)[14] syntactically obvious, yet semantically unacceptable except as a poetic reality.

Reverdy is also capable of expressing flexibility of time without resorting to linguistic occultism. In "Ronde nocturne" the distant realities brought together are a cloud and a bell. The cloud's passage makes the bell ring. The poem ends with a vision of someone (persons are never named or otherwise identified in his poems) climbing to heaven or sky. The ladder cracks. It is artificial, adds Reverdy: "C'est une parabole ou une passerelle" (A gangplank or a parabola).[15] The phonetic wordplay cannot, unfortunately, be communicated in English. The final line: "L'heure qui s'échappait ne bat plus que d'une aile" (Now the escaping hour beats only one wing) is neither linguistically nor referentially subject to interpretation—and no psycho-criticism will help! *S'échapper* is a verb simple both in its literal and figurative meanings. Time and bird escape in different images, the hour and the bird beat time also in separate configurations. In association with "wing" both verbs carry simultaneously both levels of meaning. This communication is both existential and aesthetic, and if one were to examine reader reception, one would have to do so qualitatively rather than quantitatively.

If there are such associations, there are also total annulments of established relationships between objects and their meanings. A startling revision of perception is achieved by the dislocation of meaning in simple words and uncomplicated syntax. "Regarde / Les étoiles ont cessé de briller / La terre ne tourne plus / Une tête s'est inclinée / . . . / le dernier clocher resté debout / Sonne minuit." (Look / The stars have stopped shining / The earth stops turning / A head is leaning / . . . / the last bell tower upright / Strikes midnight), as we find in "Son de cloche" for instance,[16] or in "Minute": "La pendule les bras en croix / s'est arrêtée."[17] Do these seemingly apocalyptic pauses in human activities, according with the cessation of nature's movements, proclaim a world of absurdity, associable with Jean-Paul Sartre's gratuitous world? Some critics have suggested as much, but I would reject such a conclusion. Reverdy's poetry creates existential states of consciousness, but Reverdy is not an existentialist in the French sense of the word. If he sees emptiness around him, he is not seized with nausea by the indifference of nature and the universe. He populates it with a network of activities controlled by his own awareness of the dynamics of existence. Such is the case in a small poem called "Feu": "L'espace s'agrandit / Et là devant? quelqu'un qui n'a rien dit / Deux yeux / Une double lumière / Qui vient de franchir la barrière / En s'abattant." (Space grows big / And there up front? someone who said nothing / Two eyes / A double light / Which has breached the barrier / And is collapsing.)[18] If some twentieth-century writers have sought to compensate for the random character of the universe by appropriating social purpose in their writing, this is not the case for Reverdy any more than it was for Mallarmé; self-fulfillment occurs strictly on aesthetic terms.

The bridges or "passerelles" that Reverdy creates through verbal strategies between his inner state and the objects his eye absorbs are in keeping with one of the two modes proposed by Mallarmé, i.e., from the indescribable, spiritual state sensed in the abstract to objectification without psychological elaboration or intellectual analysis of the condition that gave impetus to the creative act. A line from Mallarmé's *Crise de vers* is often quoted to demonstrate that the voice of the poet must disappear into his work; but that need not be taken to imply that subjectivity is lost and detached from the poem. No poet worth his salt would make such a concession. On the contrary, subjectivity penetrates the language so thoroughly that it no longer needs the identity of the poet to do its work. It is a fermented entity that cannot return to its inert and flat form. The objects the poem designates have assumed the imprint of the writer.

If in studies of poetics Reverdy has remained somewhat marginal, Vicente Huidobro is hardly better known among readers of Latin American literature, let alone among those of general literature. The first major collection of his poems to appear in English came out only in 1981. To date the best references to him and his development are to be found in the comprehensive introduction to his *Complete Works* by a compatriot and sometime avant-garde writer, Braulio Arenas; the other solid source is a book devoted to the study of his poetic language by George Yudice.[19] These are in Spanish; in addition there are a few comparative studies in dissertations in French and English. The basic biographical data that interest us here are that Huidobro's voice was heard for the first time outside of his native Chile in Buenos Aires, then during World War I in Madrid, and then in Paris, where he arrived in 1916 and where he stayed for the next ten years, contributing to the same avant-garde journals as did Pierre Reverdy. The poetry of Rimbaud and Mallarmé was his literary matrix. There was also a strong philosophical factor in his development, namely the impact of Hegel and Heidegger. This double affiliation is evident in all of Huidobro's poetry. Like a Hispanic Victor Hugo, he provides such a prolific body of poetry as well as prose that the choice of references here becomes strictly eclectic, as one selects significant pieces in what is, not surprisingly, an uneven work.

I am particularly drawn to his *El Espejo de agua*, which marks a distinct break with his earlier symbolist-oriented poetry. Like the titles of Reverdy, those of Huidobro have intricate connotations in their apparent simplicity. The objective realities do not seem too distant here: mirror, of course, has had from time immemorial metaphoric affiliations with water. So here we see two reflecting agents juxtaposed. But is reflection a *state* or a visionary agent? Are we involved with a new kind of mirror? The very first poem, entitled "Arte poetica," initiates the animistic intimacy of the indeterminate "also," like the "quelqu'un" of Reverdy. The referential discontinuity is accompanied even more than in the case of Reverdy by clear delineation of objects, be they man-made or natural: "Que el verso sea como une llave / Que abra mil puertas" (Let poetry be like a key / Opening a thousand doors).[20] But *llave* also means *faucet*, which brings us back to water, although on the rational level suggesting that poetry may be a key to open many doors is more acceptable. But in the wider circumference of double connotation the poem touches the broad notion of unlocking restrained energies, thus manifesting the process of poetic creativity. "Inventa mundos nuevos y cuida to palabra" (Invent new worlds and watch your word). Obviously this is not to be a subconscious or intuitive pouring out of words if the poet is to mind his words, but a process strictly under control. We are reminded of Reverdy's "Art begins where chance ends." This advice is reinforced later in the poem by the simple statement that true vigor resides in the *head*. And when he concludes that everything under the sun lives for us, this is not to be taken for a spiritual anthropocentrism. To live for us really means to him: to be at our disposal. He had heard an indigenous poet say: "Don't sing of the rain, poet, make it rain." Rain is a result; *making it rain* is a creative process. In line with this image, Huidobro says in his "Arte poetica": "Por que cantais la rosa, oh Poetas! / Hacedla florecer en el poema!" Why sing of the rose, make it flower! Everything is there, in other words, not to be admired but to be manipulated because the poet, that agent of manipulation, is, as the final line of the poem tells us, "a small god."

In the second poem, having the same title as the collective work, "El Espejo de agua," the tranformational capacity we guessed in the title, "the mirror," makes of it a river, then a watery globe, a fishbowl where all the swans drown, and as we go from one image to the next we notice that the orb, which also means globe, becomes more than a reflecting object; it causes an active assault on the swan-poetics of symbolism.

Mi espejo, corriente por las noches,	(My mirror, flowing through the night,
Se hace arroyo y se aleja de mi cuarto.	Has become a brook streaming out of my room.

Mi espejo, más profundo que el orbe	My mirror, deeper than the globe
Donde todos los cisnes se ahogaron.	Where all the swans drown.)[21]

In *Poemas articos*, where the contamination of cubism becomes evident, we can find two kinds of poems; on the one hand the passive juxtaposition of objects (what painters call nature-morte) and others more relevant to the pattern here described: images in movement, displaying the process of creation rather than the crystallization of the art process. This effect is produced, for instance, in a poem called "Marino," where the sailor demonstrates godlike activities in concordance with the image of a bird about to soar in initial flight. The creations are a series of displacements not of vision but of human and cosmic phenomena; it is indeed a broader extension of the "making roses" proposed in his "Arte poetica." An ancient mariner (Huidobro was familiar with English romanticism) intrudes upon the cosmography and disturbs the temporal structure of the earth as well:

Hice correr ríos que nunca han existido	(I made rivers run Where none had been before
De un grito elevé una montaña	With a shout I made a mountain rise
Y en torno bailamos una nueva danza	And now we do a new dance around it ...
Y enseñé a cantar un pájaro de nieve	And I taught a snowbird how to sing
Marchemos sobre los meses desatados	Let us depart upon the floating months
Soy el viejo marino que cose los horizontes cortados	I am the old sailor Who mends torn horizons.)[22]

Like Victor Hugo's *La Légende des siècles*, Huidobro's *Adán* and *Altazor* encompass the first and last man. Although in *Altazor* there are many references to God and to Satan, these are not personal identifications of divinity; rather, they embody the powers of generation and destruction. The sense of apocalypse that has been associated in this poem with modern tendencies toward deconstruction can only result from a partial reading of the poem. The devastation is described only to give the god-poet an opportunity to rethink the universe. The seismograph has taken note of his birth. The sun is born in his right eye and sets in his left eye,[23] meditates Altazor, and he suggests that if God exists at all it is thanks to the poet. This echoes what he had earlier questioned in *Adán*: whether the poem exists because of the water perceived, or the water exists because the poet has perceived it. He wonders: "Si tu agua forma el canto / O si tu canto forma el agua."[24]

Independent in his breathing and in his nourishment, the new god-poet knows it is late: "there is no time to lose," "no hay tiempo que perder" becomes a refrain in canto 4 of *Altazor*.[25] His last image is that of a mill, but a mill reaching out eventually to constellations; distant realities again combined, the earth-power creating energy and by extension nourishment, and the cosmic power providing another form of energy, i.e., luminosity.

The epic poems of Huidobro rise to an ecstatic pitch at which the aesthetic experience of creativity becomes a substitute for religious communion. The line between the messiah and the antichrist of magic, as he describes himself in *Altazor*, grows very faint.

But if the struggle between spiritual communication and aesthetic expression is evident in Huidobro, the artist's confusion between aesthetic ascesis and religious ecstasy was in the case of Hugo Ball to lead actually into religious conversion. In the interval, however, between Ball's dada activities and the religious identity he eventually assumed, there is a body of writing consisting of two plays, two novels, articles, and what has been termed "a handful of poems." It just happens that the handful of poems consists of a hundred and twenty-three poems. One might say that Baudelaire and Mallarmé are also guilty of having written a handful of poems! Ball's commentators associate him with dada and expressionism, just as Reverdy and Huidobro get swallowed up in cubism and creationism. Ball's poetry is passed over simply as "obscure" and his spiritual experience passed off as a "bad trip."

I have examined these poems closely and see no overt rebellion of the social type that would associate him with the expressionists. These are not ideological poems that might illustrate Ball's previously quoted fresco of social devastation. Basically, they can be divided into two parts, those addressed to love in general and to Emmy, his wife, in particular, and those in which he struggles with a universe in shackles and tries to apprehend those shackles for his own purposes. When the task becomes too difficult he calls upon a sort of divinity, using the names of God, Maria, Seraphin, and so on, much as Rimbaud used the word "genie" or "force" and Rilke "the angel." It is an appropriation of name and concept rather than an evocation of creed, baffling to the general reader just as the word "God" in *Le Gant de crin* has made many attribute a deep Catholicism to Reverdy. It is also a suggestion of the godly quality toward which Huidobro aimed in *Adán* and *Altazor*.

One of Ball's poems actually appropriates the structure of the Twenty-third Psalm: he tries to define the presence that operates transformation upon this world and concludes with "Willst du die neue Welt erbauen." It could be considered a religious poem except that we are not at all sure that the *du,* written with a small "d," is not self-reflexive. Ball had not yet reached the moment of his religious crisis.

Clearly, the poems of Ball, like those of the other two here observed, implement the second process posited by Mallarmé: he goes from awareness of unease outward to its objectification. There is no verbal ambiguity or abstraction in Ball's poetry. These concise poems, studded with meaning, are chiseled in concrete. No mystification is created by syntax or lexicon. But in Ball's case the encounter of distant realities is achieved with the word itself. Through the miracle the German language permits him to perform, he produces what I would like to call a "bildungsgedicht." The permitted, legitimate practice of coining new words by tying together substantives into single words is here stretched to comply with the dictum of the whole new era that new words are necessary to create a new state of existence, and new objects to occupy legitimate spaces in the cosmos. The words Ball coins by combining those in the standard lexicon come as close to a new built-in figurative discourse as I have ever seen. Ball ties substantives together that annul each other's power to signify or that create a tension among multiple significations. The fact that he wrote sound-poems in his short dada period has been overstressed as his only distinction in the annals of the avant-garde. Incidentally, these tone-poems are often attributed to primal cries of fury or expressions of the absurd. This in itself is a gross fallacy. Even a brief examination will convince the reader that structurally they are phonetic and phonemic patterns probing the nature of language, and not intended for simple shock effects. When the special role of the so-called nonsense poems is recognized in the totality of Ball's poetry, then perhaps his poems in standard structure will be approached with more respect and serious consideration. Baudelaire and Mallarmé also used standard poetic structures. But adherence to standard forms does not thereby exclude these poems from the category of the avant-garde, any more than the open structures or nonstructured utterances of so many poems in the twentieth century constitute new forms of poetic discourse. Many an open-ended poem of our day is very standard and banal in its signification.

The neat compliance of Ball with form and rules of prosody belies the explosively far-reaching steps he quietly took toward polysemy and the composition of his personal epistème. After all, he was nurtured by both Rimbaud and Hegel. Like Rimbaud, Ball knew the power of transformational semantics, and like Hegel he knew the spiritual tension that two contradictory forces can create when pitted against each other. When these two conditions meet—the manipulation of language to support the existential tension—great poetry is in the making even if in small, unassuming bundles as in Ball's case.

There is a poem of Ball's called "Mallarmé's flowers," which reveals Ball's subtle understanding of Mallarmé. This is quite a different response to Mallarmé than one finds in Huysmans' *À Rebours*. It is not a simulation of character, but a response to style. In the first line the first substantive, which is a composite, combines a number of the most important qualities of the poetry of Mallarmé: the word means literally "golden avalanche," metal or riches and permanence, associated with the coldness and movement simultaneously implied by the second part of the word. Then, the genitive "des," combining *from* and *of* interchangeably, introduces "alten Azur," containing the obsession with *Azur*, and the cult of the ancient that evokes Hérodiade—the name not to be mentioned until some lines later. In the next line *star, snow,* and *eternity* are cohabiting with a search for beginning, and as each flower dear to Mallarmé is conjured in the next lines, the sense of *toil* emerges; Mallarmé's power to create a rose is likened to the creation of the flesh of a woman, thus directly referring to a divine maker. The verbs he uses are more applicable to the actions of a sculptor than to those of a writer, and the evocation of Christian symbols is a device whereby he transfers the aesthetic to the kind of religious terminology more likely to be understood by his readers. The short poem terminates in the celebration of the death of the poet in an atmosphere in which the immanence of flower-essence is as permeating as it is invisible.

Mallarmés Blumen

Auf Goldlawinen des alten Azur,
Aus der Sterne ewigem Schnee nahmst du im Anbeginne
Für eine, vom Weh noch unberührte, jungfräuliche Flur
Die großen Kelche deiner Schöpferminne.

Der Zynnien helle Hälse, die falben Gladiolen
Und jenen göttlichen Lorbeer der seelisch Verbannten,
Hochrot erglühend wie eines Seraphs Sohlen,
Die von der Scham zertretener Morgenröten entbrannten.

Die Hyazinthe beriefst du, die Myrthe geistern und bleich,
Gleich dem Fleisch einer Frau schufst du als Rose

Grausam jene Herodias, die noch im Gartenbereich
Vom strahlenden Blut des Propheten träumt überm Moose.

Und bildetest aller Lilien schluchzende Blässe,
Daß sie im Weihrauch verblauender Horizonte
Aufstiegen über die Seufzermeere der Messe,
Um zu verschmachten im Anblick weinender Monde.

Hosannah, Maria, in deinem Garten und Schoß,
Daß das Echo verebbe in himmlischen Abendlüften,
Wo der Heiligen Gloriolen schimmern extatisch und groß.

Selig, o Mutter, sind deiner blühenden Brüste
Erhabene Kelche voll Wein und voll Brot.
Selig der Dichter, daß es ihn siechend gelüste
Nach künftigem Leben in einem balsamischen Tod.

Orpheus

Oh, königlicher Geist, dem aus den Grüften
Die Leoparden folgten und Delphine
Im Tiefgeschlecht sahst du die Menschenmiene,
Gegrüßt von allen Brüdern in den Lüften.

Die Leier eingestemmt in junge Hüften,
So standest du umbrandet auf der Bühne.
Vom Tode trunken summte deine kühne,
Berauschte Stimme mit den Blumendüften.

Du kamst aus einer Welt, in der das Grauen
Die Marter überbot. Da war dein Herz
Zerronnen erst und dann erstarrt zu Erz.

Durch jede Sehnsucht drang dein liebend Schauen.
Es führten dich die Vögel und die Fische
Im Jubelchor zum höchsten Göttertische.

In view of the innumerable powers of Orpheus that had been generated during the symbolist era, it would seem impossible to expect of Ball any originality in the handling of this myth. Yet Ball's "Orpheus," written just before Rilke's *Sonnets to Orpheus*, is a small masterpiece. If God is the doubling suggested in the image of Mallarmé, the image of the king of heights and depths is associable with Orpheus, the dialectics of position resolved in a unity of concrete brotherhood. From the depth to the heights, the recognition of the human countenance is envisioned not as an abstraction but as a composite of leopard, dolphin, and bird. In the lines that follow, the interplay between fauna, flora, and the mineral world is identified with the torture of Orpheus. The struggle ends in his resurrection in what could have been an abstraction but instead is a physical intoxication at a table (concrete object) belonging to God. If the theme of the Orpheus legend is death and transfiguration, the poem achieves it in the encounter of the most concrete objects connected by the power of Orpheus, who thus creates a unity in a divided world, one might add; but the generalization is in the reader's mind and not in the poem, for the poem has cleared a space where naming directly refers to Orpheus alone.

This concrete quality is apparent in Ball's characterizations of dreams. In view of his German romantic heritage, one would expect the dream to be a strong poetic factor in Ball's work and the techniques of veiling and fantasy to be devices of his dream transcriptions. He does indeed get from Novalis the notion of *Dursichtigkeit*, but he is not peering through veils. Rather he sees through bright and concrete entities. His dreams are, as he says, "evergreen": "immergrünen Traüme."

The process whereby dream becomes poetry, and the ordinary globe-dweller takes flight, is strikingly represented in a poem called "Like a Caterpillar." The worm collects mulberry leaves and sucks deep their juice—an image reminiscent of Mallarmé's faun sucking the grape pulp and peering through the skin. Here we see silk-foam oozing out of the worm's mouth. With the nourishment of dreams, equated here with the silk-foam, the worm weaves a net in its underground abode, and it whiles away its time in puppet shows and masquerades until it pierces the darkness of its covering and soars with wings stretched out into a new sun where death and joy converge. My paraphrase goes no further than to suggest the very concrete character of the transformation of the earthbound into a soaring being and the risks involved in the process. The linguistic movements creating the transformation are much more important, poetically speaking. The contradictions of lowly and lofty, sublime reality and delusive fantasy, are in Ball's poem verbal strategies, and the break that brings about the transformation is expressed by a verb which is generally connected with the breaking of a solid substance into particles. Equally, the spreading out of the wings is described in a word that denotes the stretching of something of a material nature rather than a spiritual one. And most notable is the fact that the dream is not an ineffable state but as real as grass and silk, and as intoxicating as champagne. The poem demonstrates once more the power of the poet to manipulate natural objects: to make them do and be according to the orders of the poet, who does not serve but is served.

Preoccupations with polysemy and polyvalences, as well as reader reception, may seem associable with the work of these three poets because of the use of similar terminologies and a common interest in the functioning of language. Astute critics, acting as heroic mediators between author and reader, decipher meaning by decoding the writer's use of language and recoding it for the new reader. But at the threshold of the century, the cult of linguistic structures as a source of creativity had as its objective a different sort of hermeneutic operation. The poet did not seem concerned with the production of a text laden with multiple meanings, intended for a reader smarter than himself, who would extrapolate them in order to create his own rational subtext. Instead, as evidenced continuously in the writings of these poets, language was a power-generator; the poet used it to provoke the imagination, primarily his own, and to release creative energy intrinsic to poetic achievement, associated in his mind with some form of divine process. The *process* of language generation— which Reverdy called "a high voltage transformer"[26]—fascinated these writers much more than did the actual production of multiple meanings for themselves or for anybody else. From artist/mirror to artist/god was the path predicted for modern times by Huidobro. The analytical exercise that fascinates literary critics, namely the transfer of a rational communication to a rational reception thereof in some modified form, is an ideological exchange, not a great concern to poets. On the other hand the stimulation of the reader's power to create images by getting involved in the creative process of the poet is an *aesthetic* experience. Empirical criticism has encouraged the confusion between informative communication and aesthetic co-experience. In the climate of the modernism discussed here language was interesting only as a source or pool for the creative process, and hermeneutics was writer-oriented rather than aimed at reader reception. Language was important only as it illuminated the poetry; when the tables are turned around, poetry becomes interesting only as it illuminates language! For this particular set of poets, of which the current triptych delineates a model, aesthetics was much more than a preoccupation with art. Their metaphysics was encrusted with and encapsulated in their aesthetics because at that point poetry had become much more than discourse about beautiful things or unusual emotions. It was a counterproposal to ordinary living. In trying to emerge from the linguistic labyrinth, these poets thought they were leaving the poem, not as a testimony to their struggle with language, but as an opening created in the darkness, a passage to freedom. So the poem itself was not an exercise in analytical thinking but a cameo of the struggle for synthesis, not an object reflecting the writer but a system to revise the cosmos through the potentials of naming. These poets converging from three different national cultures identified a major step beyond the attribution of sign-meaning to objects or states of consciousness; they made meaning a variable in the establishment of equations between signs and between writer and reader.

Notes

1. Hugo Ball, *Flight Out of Time* (New York: Viking, 1974), 68.
2. Ibid., 224–25.
3. Ibid., 226.
4. Pierre Reverdy, *Le livre de mon bord* (1930–36; reprint, Paris: Mercure de France, 1948), 95.
5. Ibid., 94.
6. Vicente Huidobro, "Manifiesto de Manifiestos," in *Obras completas* (Santiago: Zig-Zag, 1963), 1:664.
7. Ball, 60.
8. Reverdy, 227.
9. Ibid., 83.
10. See Balakian, "Fragments on Reality by Baudelaire and Breton," in *Fragments: Incompletion and Discontinuity*, ed. Lawrence D. Kritzman (New York: New York Literary Forum, 1981), 101–9.
11. Pierre Reverdy, *Le Gant de crin* (1926; reprint, Paris: Flammarion, 1968), 64.
12. Ibid., 47.
13. Pierre Reverdy, *Les Ardoises du toit*, collected in *La Plupart du Temps, Poèmes 1915–22* (Paris: Gallimard, 1945), 136.
14. Ibid., 164; trans. Mary Ann Caws and Patricia Terry, *Roof Slates and Other Poems of Pierre Reverdy* (Boston: Northwestern Univ. Press, 1981), 45.
15. Ibid., 168–9; trans. ibid., 53.
16. Ibid., 170; trans. ibid.
17. Ibid., 178; trans. ibid., 55.
18. Ibid., 153; trans. ibid., 65.
19. George Yudice, *Vicente Huidobro y la motivación del lenguaje* (Buenos Aires: Editorial Galerna, 1978). In English see *The Selected Poetry of Vicente Huidobro*, ed. David M. Guss (New York: New Directions, 1981).
20. Vicente Huidobro, "El Espejo de agua" in *Obras completas*, 1:255; trans. D. M. Guss, *The Selected Poetry of Vicente Huidobro* (New York: New Directions, 1981), 3.
21. Ibid., 255; trans. ibid., 3.
22. Ibid., 319; trans. ibid., 51–52.
23. Ibid., *Altazor*, canto 4, p. 394.
24. Ibid., "Adán ante el mar," *Adán*, 240.
25. Ibid., *Altazor*, canto 4.
26. Reverdy, *Le livre de mon bord*, 153.

Harvey Gross

Parody, Reminiscence, Critique: Aspects of Modernist Style

"My dear fellow, the situation is too critical to be dealt with without critique."

—The Devil

In chapter 25 of Thomas Mann's *Doctor Faustus*, Adrian Leverkühn holds "an unexpected but long expected"[1] dialogue with the Devil. Mann's Devil is a composite figure, "a compound ghost"[2] who appears to Adrian in three questionable shapes: first, as the allegorical traveler who haunted *Death in Venice*; then as "a member of the intelligentsia . . . a writer on art and music . . . a theoretician and critic" (231); and finally as Privat-docent Eberhard Schleppfuss, the demonic theologian whose teachings had intrigued Adrian and Serenus at Halle.

The Devil has come on his traditional mission: to exact from Adrian acquiescence in the Faustian bargain. He also comes, as he comes to Ivan Karamazov, with insolent familiarity, confronting Adrian with his own most secret thoughts. To Adrian's great annoyance the Devil uses the intimate form of address, and Adrian demands to know, *"Wer sagt Du zu mir?"* (Who said thou to me?) (217). But the *Du* is justified; in Mann's shifty, many-layered allegory, Adrian *is* the Devil as he *is* Germany and as he *is* his creator Thomas Mann.

In his guise as critic and theoretician (his second appearance), the Devil discusses with Adrian the crucial problems of style and technique facing a composer in the first decade of the twentieth century. The discussion takes place in 1911, in the Italian town of Palestrina. The theoretical wisdom he expounds is largely the work of Theodor Adorno, "who himself composes, so far as thinking allows him" (231). Adorno was Mann's neighbor in Los Angeles during the writing of *Doctor Faustus* and served as his adviser on musical matters. Mann incorporated large sections of Adorno's *Philosophy of Modern Music* directly into the text of *Doctor Faustus*; the difficult problems of technique and style that the Devil and Adrian rehearse are presented as Adorno formulated them and often in Adorno's own words.

I take the situation of music, as Adrian and the Devil discuss it, to be representative of the general problems of style that were also facing literature and painting. As Ortega expressed it, the period presented "a compact unity";[3] practitioners in all the arts were facing similar difficulties. Basic was the shared awareness that the present age stood in sharp separation from the previous one; with the turn of the century, there developed a self-conscious epochal sense and "a radical consciousness of modernity which freed itself from all specific historical ties."[4] This radical consciousness inaugurated a vigorous search for new styles and techniques that might confirm and legitimate modernity.

The Devil offers an analysis of the stylistic dilemma in music based on what he names "the technical niveau" (232). The composer no longer has available the entire spectrum of possible tonal arrangements; certain combinations, like the chord of the diminished seventh, have gone stale. "Every composer of the better sort carries within himself a canon of the forbidden, the self-forbidding, which by degrees includes all the possibilities of tonality, in other words all traditional music" (232). This exhaustion of technical means, though related to changes in culture and society, does not exclusively depend upon them but has also been determined by the history of music itself. Adorno argues that music follows neither the laws of nature nor of psychology; it changes and develops in accordance with an irreversible and immanent historical process.[5] "The prohibitive difficulties of the work lie deep in the work itself" (*DF*, 233). Consequently the very idea of a self-sufficient "musical work" is no longer tenable; indeed, the Devil declares himself "against 'works,' by and large" (233).

Style is the incarnation, through the means of technique, of a content, an articulate substance, or an ideology. Throughout the nineteenth century, though styles varied and changed, there were fundamental stabilities. Painting was representational and depicted the perceived realities of the human and natural world. The novel was also representational; its structure, based on so-called laws of cause and effect, organized itself on the principle of diachrony, that things followed each other according to the logic of time. Music still operated within the limits of the tonal system despite the assault made on it by Wagner's most radical work, *Tristan und Isolde*.

But as the Devil points out, those musical genres—sonata and symphony—which depended on tonality and its manipulations could no longer sustain themselves on "the once bindingly valid conventions" (235). Late nineteenth-century composers such as Brahms approached the problem of style through conscious archaism—as in the baroque passacaglia that concludes his Fourth Symphony—or through an elaborate network of allusions, quotations, and references. Thus Charles Rosen observes: "With Brahms we reach a composer whose music we cannot fully appreciate—at a certain level, at any rate—without becoming aware of the influences which went into its making . . . [Brahm's persistent use of allusions to Beethoven] acknowledges the existence of a previous classical style, an aspiration to recreate it, and an affirmation that such a recreation is no longer possible on naive or independent terms. The control of style is now not merely willed but self-conscious."[6]

The Devil allows that Adrian, through "the self-conscious control of style" (*DF*, 234) might function as a composer despite the alleged exhaustion of all technical means and strategies. Such functioning would be in the nature of a holding operation: Adrian might write compositions that were "the solving of technical puzzles. Art becomes critique. That is something quite honourable, who denies it?" (233). Or Adrian, at his own suggestion, might "recognize freedom above and beyond all critique. He could heighten the play by playing with forms out of which . . . life has disappeared" (235). And the Devil retorts that such free play would be a parody which "might be fun, if it were not so melancholy in its aristocratic nihilism" (235).

Art becomes critique and parody. The dialectical twist of modernity is that art becomes the critique of itself: we have had in the twentieth century music about music, poetry about poetry, and, in the last generation, criticism about criticism. In the decade of modernism before the First World War, composers, painters, and poets all experimented with outright parody and the subtler forms of critique: allusion, quotation, and reminiscence. I can think of nothing more "melancholy in its aristocratic nihilism," nothing more emblematic of the period in which it was painted than Picasso's parody-painting, *Les Demoiselles d'Avignon*. Painted in

1907, it shows five naked women arranged without regard for perspective, and with lumpy bodies depicted without regard for anatomy. The colors are harsh and unmodulated; the women's faces are distorted into primitive masks, their bodies into geometrical shapes. On the left three of the women (they were actually prostitutes) awkwardly assume the classic posture traditionally associated with the three graces. The iconographic intent is clear and the ironic contrast between past and present is as sharp as Eliot's in *The Waste Land*:

> But at my back from time to time I hear
> The sound of horns and motors, which shall bring
> Sweeney to Mrs. Porter in the spring.

Eliot's technique of allusion, as a specific device of compositional rhetoric, was at first critically excoriated—he was called by the uncomprehending a plagiarist. (Mahler, whose technique of allusion is similar, was also denounced as a thief of others' tunes.) Later it was understood that the use of allusion showed the contrast between a decadent and godless culture—our own twentieth century—and a vigorous, more ordered past. On the ideological level, such a recognition is incomplete or superficial. Eliot's use of allusion will often establish generic mode and offer an interpretive key. When Prufrock asks,

> Would it have been worth while,
> To have bitten off the matter with a smile,
> To have squeezed the universe into a ball
> To roll it toward some overwhelming question,

we recognize the altered quotation from that other love song, Marvell's *To His Coy Mistress*. The poet in Marvell's poem makes a lively verbal attack on his lady's virginity, and puts the overwhelming question to her directly. Prufrock dare not sing out loud his love song for fear that *his* lady might say

> "That is not what I meant at all,
> That is not it, at all."

The allusion recalls the genre, the persuasion-to-love poem, and its conventional motif, *carpe diem*. In a sense Eliot is reconstructing a literary past that has been interrupted by a cultural break. Here we would also emphasize Adorno's point about the immanent historical tendencies in the materials of art themselves. The altered and parodied allusions function formally: they help to establish genre, organize narrative, and arrange patterns of motifs and symbols.

The large-scale parodies of myth, Joyce's *Ulysses* and Eliot's *The Waste Land*, expand the techniques of quotation and allusion. Joyce's Homeric infrastructure provides a point-for-point analogue and critique of the "real" happenings in *Ulysses*; Joyce's tightly systematic double ordering of his materials resembles an allegory or expanded metaphor. Eliot's use of the Grail legend and fertility rituals is less systematic and somewhat after the fact; he had been reading *Ulysses* during the composition of *The Waste Land* and realized that "the mythical method" would be an important stylistic means for ordering "the chaos that was modern history."

Thomas Mann and the Critique of Myth

Nearly two decades before *Ulysses* and *The Waste Land* were published, Thomas Mann was experimenting with the parodic treatment of myth. Some critical thinking would exclude Mann from the movement of modernism: Lukács sees him as a bourgeois realist standing as a bulwark against such modernist evil as Franz Kafka.[7] I see Mann differently. He stands in the mainstream of modernism because his work, in its style and *Weltanschauung*, commits itself to the problematic and the perverse. Two early stories, *Tristan* (1902) and *Wälsungenblut* (*The Blood of the Walsungs*, 1905) are richly detailed, exuberant parodies of Wagnerian materials.

Both stories deal with the torments of desire. *Tristan* tells of two patients in a sanatorium who carry on an affair that is on the level of actuality entirely platonic. The man involved is Detlev Spinell; he is a failed writer, a dilettante, one of those Mann characters whom life has defeated. He is affected and self-conscious, with the temperament of an artist but neither the will nor the talent to create anything of significance. The woman is Gabriele Klöterjahn, who has come from the Baltic coast with her businessman husband. Gabriele has recently given birth to an obscenely healthy baby but the effort has cost her her own health. Her husband, Herr Klöterjahn, is a bourgeois vulgarian, "a connoisseur both of food and wines" who demonstrates his sexual vitality by making passes at the chambermaid.

Detlev is our *fin de siècle* Tristan, Gabriele a fatally ill Isolde, and Klöterjahn a stupidly insensitive King Mark. Complementing the mythic parallels are typical details of style and tone. Mann uses, with some lack of subtlety, the technique of the Wagnerian leitmotif. Dr. Leander's eyeglasses always glitter; Klöterjahn always stuffs his hands into the pockets of his easy-fitting English trousers; an odd little pale blue vein always pulsates in Gabriele's forehead, etc. The tone of the story, with one significant exception, is heavily ironic. Herr Klöterjahn insists, almost to the moment of her death, that Gabriele is suffering only from some minor impairment of the trachea. But the omniscient narrator makes it clear from the very outset of the story that Gabriele is doomed.

Detlev and Gabriele consummate their love in an act that can be interpreted as "symbolic" but whose issue has shattering emotional consequences. On a gloomy February afternoon they find themselves together in the salon of the sanatorium; the other patients have gone on a sledding expedition. Detlev has learned that Gabriele is a pianist and persuades her to try the piano in the salon. She at first hesitates: "Glauben Sie nicht, dass ich spiele, Herr Spinell! Ich darf nicht. Wenn es mir nun schadet?!" ("Pray do not ask me to play, Herr Spinell. I must not. Suppose it were to be bad for me—").[8] But she finally yields to Detlev's passionate wooing. She first plays Chopin's Nocturne in E-flat major, op. 9, no. 2. She is not only a brilliant technician but is able to bring out the deep sensuality of the music: "Unter ihren Händen sang die Melodie ihre letzte Süssigkeit aus, und mit einer zögernden Grazie schmiegten sich die Verzierungen um ihre Glieder" (183). ("Under her hands the very last drop of sweetness was wrung from the melody; the embellishments seemed to cling with slow grace about her limbs" [p. 343]).

Detlev discovers a piano score of *Tristan und Isolde*. He shows it to Gabriele; her reticence gone, she begins the Prelude. Mann drops his usual mode of irony as he describes Gabriele's playing and the highly-charged music, Wagner's hymn to human sexuality.

> Sie spielte den Anfang mit einer ausschweifenden und quälenden Langsameit, mit beunruhigend gedehnten Pausen zwischen den einzelnen Figuren. Das Sehnsuchtsmotiv, eine einsame und irrende Stimme in der Nacht, liess leise seine bange Frage vernehmen. Eine Stille und ein Warten. Und siehe, es antwortet: derselbe zage und einsame Klang, nur heller, nur zarter (184).

> (She played the beginning with exaggerated and tormented slowness, with painfully long pauses between the single figures. The *Sehnsuchtsmotiv*, roaming lost and forlorn like a voice in the night, lifted its trembling question. Then silence, a waiting. And lo, an answer: the same timorous, lonely note, only clearer, only tenderer . . . [343–44]).

Gabriele plays through the second act, when "das heilige Geheimnis vollendete sich. Die Leuchte erlosch, mit einer seltsamen, plötzlich ge-deckten Klangfarbe senkte das Todesmotiv sich herab, und in jagender

Ungeduld liess die Sehnsucht ihren weissen Schleier dem Geliebten ent-
gegenflattern, der ihr mit ausgebreiteten Armen durchs Dunkel nahte"
(185) ("the holy mystery was consummated. The light was quenched;
with a strange clouding of the timbre the death-motif sank down; white-
veiled desire, by passion driven, fluttered towards love as through the
dark it groped to meet her" [345]). At one point in her performance
Gabriele pleads lack of understanding; she can play the music but does
not know what it means. Detlev explains, and in full innocence she
remarks "Ja, so ist es.—Wie kommt es nur, dass Sie, der Sie es so gut
verstehen, es nicht auch spielen können?" (185) ("Yes, yes. It means
that. How is it you can understand it all so well yet cannot play it?"
[345]). Detlev shrinks under this question: he is the artist manqué, the
dilettante who knows, who can criticize but cannot himself create.

Despite her innocence, Gabriele has the carnal knowledge that enables
her to penetrate to the meaning of Wagner's music. She plays through
Isolde's love-death and those final pages of Wagner's score when we
hear, for the last time, the Sehnsuchtsmotiv; and the restless harmony
resolves into a clear tonal center—to paraphrase Browning—the B
major of love and death. The tension released, Detlev falls to his knees
and bursts into a spasm of silent weeping. Gabriele is transfixed: "Ein
ungewisses und bedrängtes Lächeln lag auf ihrem Gesicht, und ihre
Augen spähten sinnend und so mühsam ins Halbdunkel, dass sie eine
kleine Neigung zum Verschissen zeigten" (187) ("Her face wore a dis-
tressed, uncertain smile, while her eyes searched the dimness at the back
of the room, searched painfully, so dreamily, she seemed hardly able
to focus her gaze" [347]). All passion spent, both are in a state of what
we can only describe as postcoital shock. Without ever touching each
other, the protagonists, through the mediation of Wagner's allusive,
psychologically shrewd, potent music, come to know each other.

What I am suggesting here is that Mann assigns the role of Galeotto[9]
to Wagner's mythmaking and music; that the content of Wagner's art,
its powerful conjunction of hyperexpressive musical textures and always
ambiguous use of myth, lends itself to such assignment. In *The Blood
of the Walsungs*, written a few years after *Tristan*, Mann makes an even
more explicit assignment of the Wagnerian content. The pathos of Gabriele's love-death and the swooning ecstasy of Mann's descriptive prose
tend to blunt the parodistic elements of *Tristan*. But *The Blood of the
Walsungs*, in the sharpness of its social comment, its brilliance of descriptive
detail, and its total lack of sentiment, does not so much parody but
caricature the Wagnerian materials.

In this tale—perhaps Mann's most overtly "decadent" performance—
the author casts a very cold eye on the milieu and mores of a wealthy
Jewish family, the Aarenholds. Mann plays variations on some of his
earlier themes: spiritual alienation, the artist manqué, the artist's need
to suffer in order to create. But the focus is on the lavish style of life
the Aarenholds enjoy, and its effects on their twin children, Siegmund
and Sieglinde. Mann narrates in meticulous detail the elaborate furnishings
of the house, the menus of their meals, the elegance and luxury of their
clothes. Intersecting this world of minutely presented reality is a mythic
and symbolic line issuing from Wagner's *Die Walküre*, the second opera
of the *Ring* cycle. If, as Harry Levin many years ago pointed out,
modernist style represents a fusion of realism and symbolism, then *The
Blood of the Walsungs* ranks as an early and nearly perfect example of
modernist style.

The plot of the story is quite simple. We are introduced to the
Aarenholds at lunch; we meet Herr Aarenhold, who has made an immense
fortune in Silesian coal, his ugly wife, and their four children, Märit,
Kunz, and the twins. The seventh at table is von Beckerath, a government
official who is engaged to Sieglinde. The unlikely Hunding of the piece,
he is not allowed to use the familiar with Sieglinde: "sie liebte das nicht"
("she did not like it" [294]).

Lunch is served. "There was bouillon with beef marrow, sole *au
vin blanc,* pheasant, and pineapple. Nothing else." With a dead pan
Mann comments "It was a simple family luncheon" (295). Conversation
is lively, passionate, sharp; the children are adepts in the school of *nil
admirari,* and attack everything that poor von Beckerath says. Siegmund
and Sieglinde ask von Beckerath's permission to attend the opera that
evening; he misunderstands and, eagerly granting permission, assumes
that he is also invited. In tones of heavy irony, Siegmund explains:
"Sieglinde und ich, wir bitten, vor der Hochzeit noch einmal *allein
miteinander* die 'Walküre' hören zu dürfen" (296) ("Sieglinde and I
were asking you to permit us to hear the *Walküre* once more *alone
together* before the wedding" [300]). The family has long understood
that a special relationship exists between the twins: they are never apart;
they move about always holding hands; and they communicate in an
unspoken language. Yet because of their own isolation and self-absorption
the Aarenhold family does not recognize anything abnormal in the twins'
behavior.

Rings um den taktfest hurtigen Hufschlag ihrer Pferde, um die lautlose
Geschwindigkeit ihres Wagens, der sie federnd über Unebenheiten des Bodens

trug, brauste, gellte und dröhnte das Triebwerk des grossen Lebens. Und abgeschlossen davon, weichlich bewahrt davor, sassen sie still in den gesteppten, braunseidenen Polstern,—*Hand in Hand* (302).

(The twins are transported to the opera in the family carriage: Their horses' hoofs rhythmically beat the ground, the carriage swayed noiselessly over the pavement, and round them soared and shrieked the machinery of urban life. Quite safe and shut away they sat among the wadded brown silk cushions, hand in hand [307]).

From this comfort and security, Mann catapults us into the savage world of *Die Walküre*. The twins are "exactly in the right mood" (307), and Mann is hinting at what he later treats in *Doctor Faustus*, the nexus between aestheticism and barbarism. But Mann does more than contrast the primitive vigor of the Walsungs with the effete decadence of the Aarenholds: he gives us a multilevel paraphrase which is both a comic description of the performance and a typological forecast of the story's startling ending. The tenor and soprano are typical full-fleshed Wagnerian singers; he wears a blond wig, "Sie hatte einen alabasternen Busen, der wunderbar in dem Ausschnitt ihres mit Fell behangenen Musselinkleides wogte" (303) ("She had an alabaster bosom which rose and fell marvelously beneath her muslin robe" [308]). Uncertain of their entrances, they keep their eyes riveted on the conductor.

Despite the comic aspects of the performance, Mann allows us to feel the psychological allusiveness and perverse power of Wagnerian art. In this art myth is justified and redeemed by the music; nothing is in itself absurd or implausible. We accept Hunding's uncomprehending, primordial stupidity as we accept the brother-and-sister love of Siegmund and Sieglinde; the moral imagination is suspended as long as the music is playing. When the Aarenhold twins leave the opera they are in the grip of the enchantment: "Nichts konnte an sie, was sie der wilden, brünstigen und überschwenglichen Welt hätte abwendig machen können, die mit Zaubermitteln auf sie gewirkt, sie zu sich und in sich gezogen. . . . Sie begriffen nicht gleich, warum der Wagen stand; sie glaubten, ein Hindernis sei im Wege. Aber sie hielten schon vor dem elterlichen Hause" (308) ("Nothing was there which could alienate them from that extravagant and stormily passionate world which worked upon them with its magic power to draw them to itself. The carriage stopped; they did not at once realize where they were, or that they had arrived before the door of their parents' house" [314]).

The house is deserted and the twins prepare for bed. Intoxicated by their memories of the music, they lose themselves in kisses and caresses. In Siegmund Aarenhold's fashionably decorated bedroom there is a bearskin rug—as there was in Hunding's primitive hovel—and on it the twins become the Siegmund and Sieglinde of Wagner's myth.

The Blood of the Walsungs was—and still is—a shocker. Mann had second thoughts about the story and it was not officially published until 1921. Those interested in literary gossip have interpreted the story as an exposé of Mann's family and the mores of those wealthy Jews living in the *Tiergarten* district of Berlin.[10] But that was scarcely what Mann was up to. The story is a critique of myth: a story about a story, and about art itself. And what more appropriate symbol could Mann have found for art become critique, for art turned in upon itself, than incest?

Gustav Mahler and the Art of Evocation

One of the surest of tests is the way in which a poet borrows. Immature poets imitate; mature poets steal; bad poets deface what they take, and good poets make it into something better.

—T. S. Eliot

A contemporary cartoon—with the caption *Mahlers Metamorphosen*—shows Mahler wearing the features and costumes of his celebrated predecessors. We see Mahler depicted as the Abbé Liszt, in clerical garb and looking smugly ascetic; as Meyerbeer, looking sleek and prosperous; as Schubert, looking lyrical and serene; as Beethoven, with a characteristically exaggerated glower; and, finally, as Wagner wearing his celebrated *Meistermütze*.

The cartoon makes satiric reference to a specific feature of Mahler's style: his use of quotations and allusions to previous music, and his many modes of irony, parody, and reminiscence. These are integral features of his compositional procedures; they offer clues to understanding the structure of his music as well as the interpretation of its expressed content. I shall cite examples of his borrowings and their sources in previous music not to demonstrate Mahler's skill as a plagiarist, but to show how quotation, parody, and reminiscence fulfill a variety of connotative functions.

Example 1 (see Appendix) is the powerful opening statement of the Third Symphony. Eight horns together, *fortissimo*, announce a slightly disguised version of the string tune from the finale of Brahms's First Symphony (example 2). Mahler rearranges the intervals of Brahms's tune, but the first five measures exactly duplicate its rhythmic shape. Our attention is immediately caught by the great volume of sound and the familiarity of the tune. The score is marked *kräftig, entschieden:* with power and decision.

This is an instance of deliberate pilfering, and we can only believe Mahler intended that we recognize the source. Brahms's tune itself alludes to Beethoven's *Ode to Joy*; when this was called to Brahms's attention, it elicited the well-known rude retort that any ass would know *that.* Mahler's citing of the tune establishes a context of reference and strengthens our recognition of prior musical discourse. Mahler felt he had been severed from tradition; he once remarked (doubtless with ironic intent) that while Beethoven had been able to start as a modified Haydn and Mozart, and Wagner as Weber and Meyerbeer, he had had the misfortune to be Gustav Mahler from the start. The opening of the Third Symphony says, in effect, "I, Gustav Mahler, am beginning where Brahms and Beethoven left off."

Example 3 is also an opening statement: the slow introduction to the first movement of the First Symphony. Here Mahler is not so much quoting but alluding to a familiar tonal ambience: the intent of the passage is the arousal of expectation as we pass from the world of silence to the world of sound. So gradual is this passage that we are not exactly certain when the music begins. We hear, in the long pedal on the dominant, a reminiscence of the opening of the first movement of Beethoven's Ninth Symphony; however, the motif in descending fourths that Mahler first assigns to the oboes and bassoons (example 4) is derived from the slow introduction to Beethoven's Fourth Symphony (example 5).

The opening of the Second Symphony (see example 6) is a shattering assault on silence. We hear a powerful string tremolo on G and running figures in the bass. Mahler may have been thinking of Schubert's *Erlkönig;* or, more likely, of a work he had often conducted, Wagner's *Die Walküre* (example 7). (Wagner was himself an inspired pilferer.) Mahler makes something different and striking out of his source. The rhythmic figures in the bass become thematic: what were neutral accompanying materials in Wagner become basic elements of structure. Mahler's allusion to the opening scene of *Die Walküre* and its raging storm also adds a specific representational dimension. Not that we necessarily recall the image of the storm-battered Siegmund struggling into Hunding's house, but we certainly retain a strong sense of nature in vehement eruption.

New and informed with the critical bias of modernity were Mahler's many modes of parody. Some of his most characteristic movements are deliberate distortions of the Austrian Ländler, the military march, and the funeral procession. The third movement of the First Symphony is a burlesque funeral march conceived in a spirit of corrosive irony. Its main theme is the children's round, "Frère Jacques," grotesquely played in the minor on a solo double-bass (example 8). A contrasting section, played by the winds, bass drum, and cymbals, is pointedly marked *mit parodie* (example 9). Mahler handles with extreme brilliance the violent contrasts between lugubrious solemnity and raucous vulgarity; this is one of his most original and effective movements.

Infinitely more subtle is the use of what I would call "transcendental reminiscence" in Mahler's Ninth Symphony. The theme of this work and of the two works associated with it—*Das Lied von der Erde* and the unfinished Tenth Symphony—is valediction. The Ninth is an elegiac song, a continuation of *Der Abschied*, which concludes *Das Lied von der Erde*. The opening movement, marked *andante comodo*, recalls the intense mood of regret and resignation that concludes *Das Lied*; Mahler's music is often self-referential in ways that enforce the literary and autobiographical aspects of his work.

The persistent and structurally prominent reminiscence in the first movement of the Ninth is derived from Beethoven's program sonata *Das Lebewohl* (no. 26, in E^b major, op. 81a). Beethoven begins the sonata with a three-note motif framing the syllables LE-BE-WOHL (example 10). Mahler does not quote the motif literally, but disguises it, works it into inner voices, and writes descants above it. The effects are quite magical; the reminiscences of the motif evoke a specific pathos and the many moods of valediction (example 11).

I would also single out for special mention the ghostly and insistent references to the first movement of Schubert's Unfinished Symphony in the finale of Mahler's Sixth Symphony (example 12). First heard on the bass tuba, this fragment of Schubert's theme gradually assumes a most poignant significance: an anguished memory of a lost world. The effect is like the one Eliot evokes in *The Waste Land* with his thematic use of Shakespeare's "Those are pearls that were his eyes."

Theodor Adorno has this to say about Mahler's acts of creative appropriation: "Everything with which [Mahler] occupies himself is already there . . . his themes are expropriated ones . . . nothing sounds as it should; all things are diverted as if by a magnet. What is worn out yields pliantly to the improvising hand; the used parts win a second life as variants . . . the expression of a . . . melody, straining under the pressure of [oboes and English horn] arrives where the approved musical language could never safely reach. Such music crystallizes the whole . . . into something new."[11]

Adorno tends to bestow praise through negation. He also points out that those critics who attack Mahler for lack of originality—or, even worse, plagiarism—are exercising bad faith. Their complaints against Mahler are not based on musical or aesthetic considerations, but are informed by "the bourgeois idea of property . . . unmusical judges condemn musical thieves."[12] But the matter can be differently proposed and argued. Harry Levin, speaking of the compositional methods of Joyce, Eliot, and Mann, puts it positively: "The best writing of our contemporaries is not an act of creation, but an act of evocation, peculiarly saturated with reminiscences."[13]

Nonconcluding Postscript

Parody, reminiscence, and critique can all be subsumed under a generalized concept of irony. I am not referring exclusively to irony as a particularized gesture of language, a rhetorical device, but irony as Nietzsche understood it: as the period style of the modern world and of its spiritually deprived inhabitants, the epigones. In that indispensable essay *On the Use and Disadvantage of History*, Nietzsche argued that an excess of historical knowledge placed an intolerable burden on human consciousness:

> Durch dieses Übermass wird der jederzeit schädliche Glaube an das Alter der Menschheit, der Glaube, Spätling und Epigone zu sein, gepflanzt; durch dieses Übermass gerät eine Zeit in die gefährliche Stimmung der Ironie über sich selbst.

> (Through this excess is planted the always damaging belief in the old age of mankind, the belief that we are latecomers and epigones; through this excess an age reaches a dangerous mood of irony toward itself.)[14]

A few pages later scholars are referred to as men who behave as:

> praktische Pessimisten . . . welche die Ahnung eines Unterganges leitet . . . so empfinden sie und leben eine *ironische* Existenz (257–58).

> (practical pessimists, as men guided by a sense of imminent catastrophe . . . [they] feel and live an ironical existence.)

Aware of themselves as latecomers, and bearing the unhappy knowledge that the materials and forms of art were approaching exhaustion,

Mann and Mahler developed a new style of embarrassed self-regard, the varied techniques of irony. (It may not be irrelevant to point out that no writer used irony with more brilliance than did Nietzsche; modernity's most passionate critic, he never overcame "the fatality of being modern.") Through fragmented or distorted references to the past, they generated new energies, set up richer contexts, created new resonances. Modernity, especially in its late nineteenth-century manifestations, negated the possibility of the autonomous masterpiece. The modernists of the first decade of the twentieth century redeemed the time with parody and reminiscence. It was an art indeed, as the Devil sneered, "melancholy in its aristocratic nihilism." But it prepared the way for the achievements of High Modernism and the masterpieces of the post–World War I decade.[15]

APPENDIX: MUSICAL EXAMPLES

Ex. 1

Ex. 2

Ex. 3

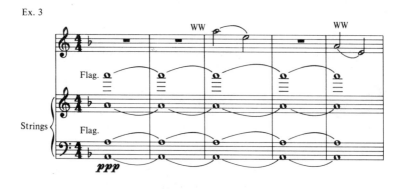

Ex. 4

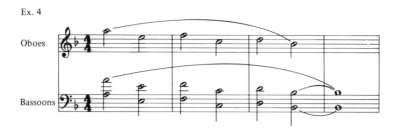

Ex. 5

Strings

Ex. 6

Violins, violas

Celli, bassi

etc.

Ex. 7

Violins, violas

Celli, bassi

Stürmisch. Schnell und sehr heftig

Ex. 8

Solo Bass *8vb*

Kettle Drum

Feierlich und gemessen

etc.

144

Gross

Ex. 9

Ex. 10

Ex. 11

Ex. 12

Notes

1. Thomas Mann, *Doctor Faustus*, 4th ed., trans. H. T. Lowe Porter (New York: Penguin, 1974), 215. Page numbers will be indicated in the text for all subsequent citations from this book, cited as *DF*.

2. T. S. Eliot, *Little Gidding*, 1. 95. There are interesting parallels between Eliot's "compound ghost" and Mann's triple devil. Both come in a version of hell to discuss the theory of art and eschatological matter: damnation and salvation.

3. José Ortega y Gasset, *The Dehumanization of Art* (New York: Anchor, 1956), 4.

4. Jürgen Habermas, "Modernity versus Postmodernity," *New German Critique* 22(1981): 4.

5. T. W. Adorno, *The Philosophy of Modern Music*, trans. Anne G. Mitchell and Wesley V. Blomster (New York: Seabury Press, 1973), 32ff.

6. Charles Rosen, "Influence: Plagiarism and Inspiration," in *On Criticizing Music*, ed. Kingsley Price (Baltimore, Md.: Johns Hopkins Univ. Press, 1981), 27–28.

7. Georg Lukács, *Realism in Our Time* (New York: Harper & Row, 1971), 47–92.

8. Thomas Mann, *Die Erzählungen*, band 1 (Frankfurt: Fischer Taschenbuch Verlag, 1976), 182; *Death in Venice and Other Stories*, trans. H. T. Lowe Porter (New York: Vintage, 1963), 342. Page numbers given in the text for all following citations from this text and *The Blood of the Walsungs*.

9. Or Pandar; see Dante, *Inferno* 5, 1. 137.

10. In writing this story Mann, as he always did, worked close to his own experience. His wife Katia Pringsheim had a twin brother, Klaus; they were the children of wealthy, cultivated, and highly assimilated Jewish parents. Fearing a scandal, Mann withdrew the story from publication. However, the story was leaked to the Munich literary community and Mann was accused of anti-Semitism. For details, see Richard Winston's *Thomas Mann: The Making of the Artist, 1875–1911* (New York: Random House, 1981), 207–11.

11. T. W. Adorno, "On the Fetish-Character in Music," in *The Essential Frankfurt School Reader* (New York: Urizen, 1978), 298.

12. T. W. Adorno, *The Philosophy of Modern Music*, 182. See also Rosen, 17: "Plagiarism has an interest for ethics and law, but little for criticism."

13. Harry Levin, *James Joyce: A Critical Introduction* (New York: New Directions, 1944).

14. Friedrich Nietzsche, "Vom Nutzen und Nachteil der Historie für das Leben," in *Friedrich Nietzsche: Werke in Drei Bänden*, ed. Karl Schlechta (Munich: Carl Hanser Verlag, 1954), 1:237. My translation.

15. This paper was written during my tenure as a fellow of the National Humanities Center in Research Triangle Park, North Carolina. I thank the Ladies of the Scriptorium for their care in typing and retyping the manuscript. I also thank Kathy Logan, music librarian of the University of North Carolina, Chapel Hill, for allowing me to borrow scores and recordings.

Margaret Davies

Modernité *and Its Techniques*

The focus of discussion here will be that most concentrated awareness and expression of modernity which crystallized in Paris
at the turn of the century, developed with increasing intensity, reached
its apogee in 1913–14, and continued to be felt at the end of the war
before it merged into the new movements of dada and surrealism. The
figure of Guillaume Apollinaire will serve as a sort of "instrument d'op-
tique" to scrutinize some of the techniques invented to express the sense
of a whole change in Western humanity's way of looking at and being
in the world. From time to time, however, a brief look will be given at
other writers who were experimenting on similar lines in order to try
to discover what were the constants, what the variables in the expression
of *modernité*.

Much has been written about the convergence of ideas and attitudes
stemming from sources as diverse as Planck and Einstein, Nietzsche and
Freud, as well as from the development of modern technology and the
power of the machine. Paris at the turn of the century, as we know,
was a veritable melting pot of these changes, and it was here that
Apollinaire made his début in 1902. Everything about him made him
particularly susceptible and even exemplary: his age, twenty at the beginning of the century, his mixed blood, his lack of roots, his cosmopolitan,
unsettled background, his own restless, mercurial nature, his great gifts,
his ambition, his impressionable temperament, perhaps even a certain
opportunism. And it is noticeable that even in early poems, despite the
heavy symbolist influence, there are certain characteristics which, with
hindsight, can be seen to be modern. In *La Chanson du Mal Aimé*

(1903–4), in particular, there is a marked discontinuity in time, space, and emotion. Also, long before the technique of collage developed in painting, there is a structural use of auto-collage in order to represent another point in time and another strand of emotion, for instance the insertion of earlier pieces such as "Aubade," and the crude outburst of the Zaporogue Cossacks against their Sultan. Written most probably in 1902, the Rhineland poem "Les Femmes," built uniquely out of fragments of conversation, provides another example of something akin to the technique of collage. As yet, however, these give the appearance of not being entirely random, but in fact simulated, the "vraisemblable" rather than "le réel."

Perhaps the most modern of the works Apollinaire wrote at that time, 1903–4, though it did not actually see the light of day until 1917, was *Les Mammelles de Tirésias*. But here certain modern tendencies were mediated through Jarry, who, along with Rimbaud and Lautréamont, was one of the real founding fathers of *modernité*. *Les Mammelles*, like *Ubu*, is totally unrepresentational and, as is now well known, it is in the preface to this play that Apollinaire coined the word "sur-réalisme." Regarded for long as perhaps a trifle, certainly a romp, it now has to be considered seriously in any study of the development of modernity in the theater.

It is, however, toward 1905–6 that the seeds of modernity really begin to germinate, and this occurs particularly in the realm of painting and is dominated by the researches and experiments of Picasso and Braque. This is of course a vast and by now familiar subject. I should like, however, to underline just one detail that helps to illustrate the way in which the visual arts and poetry were constantly interacting in their evolution toward modernity. Picasso always declared that as a painter he had been concerned with finding plastic solutions to plastic and visual problems, in particular those created by the rejection of perspective and chiaroscuro. Nevertheless, in his early days in Paris in 1900, he had been very affected by Rimbaud and Mallarmé. What struck him was the way both poets had emphasized the autonomy of the artist's imagination, the importance of the inner eye: and it was Picasso's own drive toward autonomous creation in the early cubist experiments which, in turn, fired Apollinaire's enthusiasm, even though the actual forms it took sometimes disconcerted him. When he first saw *Les Demoiselles d'Avignon* in 1907, for instance, Apollinaire was as shocked as most others; and in his own work between 1904 and 1907 he seemed to be torn by the same dichotomy. On the one hand there was a passionate desire to embrace the concept of modernity, on the other a reluctance, even an inability, to cut adrift from the known symbolist modes and create totally new forms. "Pourquoi faut-il être si moderne?" (Why must one be so modern?) runs a revealing line, later to be deleted, in the draft of *Le Brasier*.

In fact in Montmartre Apollinaire was often mocked for still being "trop symboliste," and it was Max Jacob who seemed to be more modern in his prose poems, which were later to be published in *Le Cornet à dés* in 1916, but which were already being read aloud to friends who were not always above exploiting their new ideas. His modernity seems to reside mainly in a total break away from representation and in the construction of fragments of fantasy that are nevertheless solidly welded together by the form of the prose poem. Jacob also notably exploited the actual material aspect of language itself, allowing the sounds of words and their associative power, in particular the ambiguity present in homophony, to generate theme and meaning. A prime example of this is "Fausses Nouvelles Fosses Nouvelles," in which the Balkan war is transposed into and parodied in a theatrical war, "la guerre des balcons," between critics and journalists with their different aggressions, the whole effect being of an ironical attack on the idea of war itself. "Il y a eu des sièges de loges, le siège de la scène, le siège d'un strapontin et cette bataille a duré dix-huit jours. . . . Cet épisode de la guerre des Balcons a beaucoup fait pour les engagements volontaires en province." ("There were sieges of boxes, the siege of the stage, the siege of a folding seat and the battle raged for eighteen days. . . . This episode of the Balcony war did a good deal for voluntary enlistments in the provinces.")[1]

Although Apollinaire was always eager to exploit ambiguity, puns, wordplay, anagrams, and acrostics at this stage, this was not such a conscious technique for expressing a modern vision as it already was for Jarry and Jacob, or as it was later to become in his own work. In 1907 and 1908 (and, interestingly, again under the combined influence of Rimbaud and Mallarmé) he became overtly obsessed with the much more general idea of the autonomy of the artist, what he, interpreting this as the divine, demiurgic, creative force, termed in *Les Trois Vertus Plastiques* the artist's "inhumanity." In the two big poems of 1908, *Le Brasier* and *Les Fiançailles*, Apollinaire treated this notion thematically by opposing a modern idealism to the inevitable regressive pull of mortality and the human emotions. More important from my standpoint of technique is the fact that, to express this opposition, he uses elemental imagery— fire to express the modern and the divine, water and earth to express the past and the mortal—and allows them to work together in blocks, like the big blocks and shapes in Picasso's early cubist paintings, without any support from narrative or ratiocination. The whole poem is in fact created out of the relationships among these images, without any linking threads of explanation. In *Les Fiançailles* there is a more complex, fragmented structure, a more subtle interaction, in which elements from one block shift and mingle with those of the others, and which again could be paralleled with Picasso's later pictures of 1908. Also, more consciously now, there is an important use of auto-collage to represent Apollinaire's own past, from which he is now evolving. For instance, he begins the poem with a piece written in 1902 in order to represent the old symbolist aesthetic he has left behind, quoting from it again just before the final apotheosis. These poems represent an important development, not only as an "art poétique" but as instances of a growing concentration on the image and its central generating role. From time immemorial the imaging power of humanity, and particularly of its poets, has been its most effective means of transcending the corporeal limits imposed upon it by time and space. It would seem to be no accident that when the Einsteinian space-time, this new dimension, had become such a talking point, and the need to transcend time and space was seen to be already partially fulfilled in the modern world, the self-conscious poet, eager not to be pipped at the post by the scientist, the technician, even the gardener, should more than ever prepare to exploit its free-ranging, associative powers. Science for Apollinaire had always been the great rival; the poet would now prove that he could be as positively creative.

By concentrating like this on Apollinaire my intent is not to give the impression that he alone was responsible for the development of *modernité*. I only wish to stress that he is to my mind one of the best mediums for reflecting the different ideas and techniques then abroad, as well as a brilliant inventor himself. One of the concepts which Apollinaire took up with great enthusiasm in 1909–10 was that of unanimism, the brainchild of the Groupe de l'Abbaye de Créteil, which counted Jules Romains, Georges Duhamel, and Henri Hertz among its members. What emerges predominantly from their work is the sense of the oneness of human life containing the multiple. For them an individual should be able to embrace simultaneous, multiform human experience at different points in space, just as through one's ancestry one was the sum of all past times. It is a powerful and inspiring idea that was later to spread in many other ways and link up with other influences to become the all-important and ubiquitous "simultanéité."

It certainly inspired Apollinaire conceptually. To express the sense

of life being lived all over the globe at one and the same time seemed
to be the great challenge for the modern poet, the ideal way in which
he could convey the swiftness of communication, the intensity of modern
life. Again it is through the medium of the image that this impression
can best and most obviously be created. Thus techniques are now developed
not only to juxtapose images from different times and different places
("ailleurs, ailleurs"), but to pare them down, to split them off into
fragments (as the cubist painters were doing with their analysis of forms)
to achieve a many-faceted kaleidoscopic effect, a swift movement through
notations, sometimes reduced to one single word standing out like the
tip of an iceberg of associations.

In Apollinaire's *Le Voyageur* (1910–11) one can see clearly the
development of the simultaneist technique. Fragments of memories slip
by unexplained:

> Vagues poissons arqués fleurs surmarines
> Une nuit c'était la mer
>
> (Vague arched fish, super marine flowers
> One night was the sea)
>
> Quelqu'un avait un furet
> Un autre un hérisson . . .
>
> (One had a ferret,
> Another one a hedgehog)
>
> Deux matelots qui ne s'étaient jamais
> quittés
>
> (Two sailors who had never parted)[2]

These would seem to serve as the objective correlatives of a many-
layered private experience, of the journey of the restless traveler through
life.

There may well be another influence at work here from another
important area of experimentation. Although Apollinaire in these years
affected to dislike the futurists, and their noisy publicity and chauvinism,
maintaining that under their desire for movement, dynamism, and speed
they were still painting "états d'âme," he was undoubtedly aware (indeed
that may well have helped to occasion his animosity) that they had
much to offer, for instance in the realm of actual, innovative poetic
techniques. Marinetti's *Technical Futurist Manifesto of 1912* in particular
stressed just the role of the image I have mentioned in *Le Voyageur*.
For him it was the "Imaginazione senza Fili" which was all-important,
and which expressed itself through isolated images, some of them reduced

to one word only. They were, in fact, to be used like a shorthand by the teeming, creative mind, and their associations would flower and then generate a host of others, once language was freed from the constraints of logic. Not only is imagination liberated to chase a random simultaneity, but to this end language itself is let off the leash. It is now clear that attention is being fixed ever more on the nature of the signifier itself and its creative potential—as opposed to the abstract signified—a trend already exemplified in Jacob, and one which will become progressively more important throughout the century.

At the same time, however, there is also felt the urgent need of some controlling factor, some new order in disorder, some imposing synthesis. At the existential level the correlative of being aware of "le tout dans le tout" is of the "rien" at the heart of things. Already in *Les Poésies d'O. Barnabooth* (written between 1902 and 1908), the urgent traveler Valéry Larbaud had, despite the excitement and urgency, also expressed his sense of solitude, the void in the individual heart. And in his long poem of 1912, *Les Pâques à New York*, Blaise Cendrars is confronted and overwhelmed not only by his own solitude and despair at loss of faith, but also by the task of expressing the simultaneous despair of the mass of poor immigrants who are centered in that modern city par excellence, New York. There he meets the challenge of creating a synthesis out of these disparate impressions by the predominantly traditional means of powerful rhyme and meter and a skillful interweaving of contrasting images. In Apollinaire's poem *Zone*, which was undoubtedly sparked by *Les Pâques*, the centrifugal fragmenting force proves overwhelming thematically. It is nevertheless aesthetically controlled at the center of the poem by the poet's vision of simultaneity, the birds of mythology and of his own invention seeking *their* center and guide in the figure of Christ, made superbly modern by virtue of the modern poetic image of Christ as airplane, as well as by the ironic, subversive "jeux de mots" between voltigeur/voleur, pupille de l'oeil/pupille des siècles. In even more violent fashion Cendrars turns his irony into blasphemy:

> Votre sang recueilli, elles ne l'ont jamais bu
> Elles ont du rouge aux lèvres et de la dentelle aux cul.
>
> (Your blood in a cup, they never drank from that glass
> They have rouge on their lips and lace on their ass.)[3]

For a while the two poets seemed to be sharing not only the same inspiration of simultaneity, but the same deployment of techniques. Their

Davies

mutual friend, the painter Delaunay, also identified *le simultané* not only as his inspiration but also as a means, "le métier," that he used to convey it. And it would seem clear that his use of simultaneous contrasts of complementary and noncomplementary colors with their different dynamic effects helped both poets to experiment with using language in an analogous fashion. Apollinaire's *Les Fenêtres* simply juxtaposes images, alternating the slow-moving associations of memory and emotion with the brief, swift sense perceptions of the outside world and holding them together with the Ariadne's thread of a perception of light, color, and dynamism opening out on to the modern, juicy, golden world. What is new in his evolution here, marking the transition between *Alcools* and his poems of 1913 onward, is this turning outward, and the application of the simultaneist technique of the fragmented image not only to memory but also to sense perceptions of the present, modern world.

The technique of free association already known in Freud's treatment of the mentally ill is carried further by Cendrars in *La Prose du Trans-sibérien*, that magnificent monument to modernity. The train journey, with the sound patterns of its wheels, is the ordering theme around which cluster simultaneous impressions of time and space, and from which fan out what Cendrars calls "image-associations" snatched from both inner and outer worlds, and reduced to their most extreme short-hand—the word. Characterizing the modern poetry of this period, Cendrars himself said later in *Aujourd'hui*: "On a beaucoup joué avec les *lapsus psychae* aussi bien que les *lapsus linguae*,"[4] and the conscious manipulation of the apparent Freudian slip has a definite generating role to play: "J'ai aussi joué aux courses à Auteuil et à Longchamp-Paris-New York. . . . Et j'ai perdu tous mes paris / Il n'y a plus que la Patagonie, la Patagonie qui convienne à mon immense tristesse" (I also played the races in Auteuil and Longchamp-Paris-New York. . . . And I lost all my bets / Only Patagonia now, only Patagonia remains to suit my immense sadness).[5] Sound and sense jostle together to spin out the web of the image-associations, and indeed the sense of failure, of being a "mauvais poète," of not being able to hold the much of modern life in the little of the individual which haunts the poem with its refrain is identified as the inability to push the image-associations far enough:

> Autant d'images-association que je ne peux pas développer
> Car je suis encore fort mauvais poète
> Et l'univers me déborde.

> (So many image-associations which I cannot develop

Because I am still a pretty bad poet
And the universe overwhelms me.)[6]

The specifically modern tension of wanting to stretch out ever further in time and space, in outer speed and inner intensity, and at the same time of needing to hold this multiplicity in control, is enacted through a veritable sorcerer's apprentice vision of the war's amputated limbs let loose and madly dancing together, before the whole poem is finally integrated and dominated by that totally modern symbol of vigilance, communication, and male energy, the Eiffel Tower.

It would seem that increasingly the problematic of modern technique was situated in the search to open up the space of the poem in order to encompass the multiple, random, simultaneous disorder of lived experience, and at the same time to find ever more supple and subtle ways of containing it. The old order had broken up, long live the new "raisons formelles!" For Cendrars it was the tension itself between the centrifugal and the centripetal forces, "elasticity," which became the structuring principle, the control of the creative mind always underlined in the *19 Poèmes élastiques 1913–1914* by a return to the artist or the work of art in the final line.

Throughout 1913–14 Apollinaire, like so many others, seemed to be inspired by a veritable experimental fervor. Each poem of that time explores a different avenue, as if he were approaching the problem from varying angles in the manner of the scientist with his experiments. In *Lundi Rue Christine* he takes up again the form of the "poème-conversation" and exploits the simultaneous sounds of real life, stringing together snippets of conversation in order to see whether they will make a poem. The fact that they do is thanks first to the poet's selection, then to his way of dispersing them on the page as lines of verse, but also for good measure to his own inserted, self-reflexive comment, "ça l'air de rimer," and the presence of the mellifluous line, "La fontaine coule noire comme ses ongles," which while advertising itself as poetry with its regular cadence nevertheless subverts the whole concept of poetry by its non-sense and its irony—a black one to boot. Cendrars went further, and, as M. Duchamp alias Richard Mutt did with the urinal, chose as one of his "poèmes élastiques" an already existing real object, a newspaper item in *Paris Midi* from which he carved out the telegram poem "Dernière heure" without any further comment.

The mood of experimentation was general and generally harnessed to the concept of simultaneity; for in many ways simultaneity seemed then to be synonymous with modernity. One major line of approach to creating an effect of simultaneity was through sound, and Henri Barzun, against whom Apollinaire waged a bitter polemic, exploited the use of polyphony, with different voices reciting simultaneously. Again, this could be seen as inspired by and dependent on a relatively modern invention, the gramophone, and, again, the experiment is focusing on the material aspect of words themselves, the signifier rather than the signified.

Apollinaire was now to exploit the other main aspect of the materiality of words, namely the visual effect they create on the page and the possibilities of meaning that can be engendered by their spatial relationships. One could trace all sorts of influences at work here, the most obvious being Mallarmé with *Un Coup de Dés*, as well as previous word-picture poems throughout literature. There had also been a recent general interest in the Chinese ideogram, which may well have originated in the 1914 contact with the imagists from Fenellosa, although it is clear from Flint's article in *Les Soirées de Paris* in July 1914 that the imagists felt that they were working along lines which had already been exploited for some years in France. Furthermore there was an important contact in the early summer of 1914, through Larionov and Goncharova, with the Russian cubo-futurists, who were also making experiments with picture-poems. Then there were the futurists themselves, who for some time had been experimenting with typographical effects and geometrical patterns, and Apollinaire's first "idéogramme lyrique" does in fact exploit the geometrical pattern formed by the Eiffel Tower and the radio waves emanating from it. Last but not least, perhaps, there was for Apollinaire the desire to do something different from what Henri Barzun was doing: "Zut pour M. Zun" runs one snippet from "Lettre-Océan," significantly placed at the topmost point of the circle surrounding "La Tour Eiffel."

It is, however, an entirely logical and characteristic development in Apollinaire's own desire to transcend time and space that he should claim for words, which necessarily evolve in time, their less obvious spatial powers. In the same way the cubist painters had attempted to annex the dimension of time for the visual, spatial art of painting by fusing together in one picture aspects which can be seen only at different moments. It was also closely connected with another crucial point: the ambition of inducing a whole other way of reading, a "lecture synthético-idéographique" rather than "linéaire-discursive" which would take in the whole page at once and read its overall spatial meanings as well as the unfolding in time of its semantic associations. Apollinaire himself stressed that these spatial meanings were just as important as the others.

This to my mind highlights one of the very important aspects of Apollinaire's contribution to modern techniques. It has in fact taken us a long time to realize the full importance of the calligrams which were until the last decade or so regarded simply as amusing games, pretty doodles that sometimes interfered with the appreciation of the poem itself. They were certainly not developed immediately after Apollinaire. Although Reverdy, for example, used typography and spacing to create meaning he repudiated any attempt actually to fuse the arts, saying that the souls of the artist and the poet were far apart and should be left like that.

Perhaps too this particular path was occulted by surrealism, with its different emphasis on the inner world. But it is not only because of its exploitation of space that I am stressing the calligram as a vital modern technique, nor because I wish to imply that concrete poetry is the apogee of modernity—but because it revolutionizes not only the relationship between author and text but also that between reader and text. The reader is now brought into the actual production of the text, a text that becomes "scriptible" (writable) rather than "lisible" (readable) in Barthesian terms: and there is no need to stress how central this notion is to modernist and even postmodernist preoccupations. The reader now has to work to produce meaning out of many possible meanings, to hold all of them together simultaneously, to decide which to stress and when, in short to experiment with the text rather as the writer had done. The love of ambiguity which had been obvious from the beginning in Apollinaire's exploitation of the double meanings of words, of puns and wordplay generally, and which he had encouraged with his sudden suppression of punctuation on the proofs of *Alcools* at the end of 1912, becomes now the creation of a whole network of association working at the many levels of different perceptions, invoking now a truly simultaneous reception of simultaneity.

La Montre[7] is an excellent example of the way the reader is invited to create for him- or herself the different layers of meaning, which are held together by the circular shape (figuring synthesis) of the clock marking man's trajectory from cradle to grave. Within this notation of the numbers there is a play between associations: one in "mon coeur," two in "les yeux," l'enfant as the third product, Agla, one of the four graces, the five figures of the hand, and the obvious pun in Tircis. These associations also begin by referring to Apollinaire himself but increasingly work toward references not only to the elements of his own poetry, "la semaine," "les Muses aux portes de ton corps," "le bel inconnu," but to poetry generally: "le beau vers dantesque" with its eleven feet. Then this whole *jeu créateur* of association, of intra- and intertextuality, is seen to depend on the watch-chain—"Comme l'on s'amuse bien" written in larger type—and the words of transcendence are inscribed, as it were, outside the time and space of the watch: "La beauté de la vie passe la douleur de mourir." Life, death, creative play, the wheel (or the clock) comes full circle.

Even here, within the calligrammatic form, each poem explores different possibilities. One particularly instructive example is *La Mandoline, l'Oeillet et le Bambou*.[8] Here one can see clearly the generation of meaning from the shapes alone—the circular female shape of the *mandoline* and the male shape of the opium pipe giving rise to the flower, which announces the new "loi des odeurs." Also significant is the way each shape is placed on the page: there generally seems to be an evolution from left to right representing the progression from the old art of sound to the new "loi des odeurs." Then there are the different ways of reading the circular shape of the *mandoline,* depending on where one starts, each one giving a slightly different emphasis. Verbal rhymes are created as well, in addition to messages which can be put together from the morphemes which stand out in large letters: "bal," "tra, la la."

I shall, however, merely point to the revolutionary effect of the opium pipe. The norms of grammar are completely violated if one attempts a linear reading, nor does one fare better with a "lecture en zig-zag." Instead the random, discrete associations billow out like the opium smoke, but are held in synthesis by the visual shape, the O that figures the mouth of the pipe, the mouth of the poet, and the great O of the universe. It is in itself a particularly striking and concentrated "mise en abîme" of the continued search for ever more tenuous "raisons formelles" that will condense and hold together the ever-varying, multiple, and new perceptions of the poet.

The drive toward the autonomy of the artist that was seminal to the early development of *modernité* is now clearly seen in a further stage of development. The semireligious tone of the 1908 poems, conveying a faith in the artist as demiurge which still owed something to the nineteenth century, even the drive toward simultaneity which had seemed to be the mainspring of *modernité,* flower now with a celebration of the creative process itself as "jeu." The search for new "raisons formelles" is seen to be a valuable contribution to man's knowledge of himself and of his relationship with the world around him. "Comme l'on s'amuse bien"—"on," that is, both writer and reader engaged together in an endless game of exploration. For if from the point of view of the sun there is nothing new, as Apollinaire said in *L'Esprit Nouveau* in 1917, for us there are "mille et mille combinaisons qui n'ont jamais été inventées" (thousands and thousands of combinations which have never been invented).

External events, however, were now to have a profound effect. The heady excitement engendered at the turn of the century by the feeling that everything was possible had been accompanied by the tension I have called the sorcerer's apprentice complex. In the event the First World War seemed to be proving that humanity had indeed lost control, that machines had turned against their masters, that the forces of destruction, rather than those of a new creativity, had been unleashed. Two immediate reactions seemed possible: one was the way of dada, to face destruction with destruction, to negate, to annihilate even art itself—or if not actually to destroy it, at least to turn away from it as Cendrars did, to the documentary, the lived. The other, that of Apollinaire, Jacob, Reverdy, and Pierre-Albert Birot, was to continue to search for the new, thus expressing a faith in man's essential creativity, but to undercut this idealism with a particularly sharp edge of irony. In his late prose works, in particular, Apollinaire seems intent, like Baudelaire in his *Petits Poèmes en Prose*, to subvert all of his own poetic themes. The series of false artists who appear in the late "contes" in fact parody all the cherished modern aims of Apollinaire's earlier poetry: simultaneity and the transcending of space and time are travestied in the figure of Justin Couchot, made divine because of the truncation of his limbs; the search for new "raisons formelles" in the new arts of "amphionie" and "gatroastronomie"; the power of science and machines to create a Brave New World in *Traitement Thyroïdien* and *La Chirugie Esthétique*. After the all of aspiration comes the nothing of realization. "Une profonde statue en rien" is the monument to Croniamental, the hero of *Le Poète Assassiné*. The same bitterness pervades the enclosed and somberly beautiful work of Reverdy, with its solitary, faceless, failed central figure, lines even the exuberant fantasy of a Birot, and had always been the mainspring of Jacob's self-depreciation and mordant wit.

That strange and very modern late work of Apollinaire I have just mentioned, however, *Le Poète Assassiné*, perhaps contains an indication of a way forward after the collapse of idealism, indeed a whole development wherein one can see a real similarity with Anglo-Saxon modernism. For it essentially celebrates that "jeu créateur" on which the clock of life has been seen to depend, the free-ranging play with the artist's actual material, the stuff of words, the signifier actually taking over from the

158

Davies

signified. This autobiography, in the lineage of Rabelais, positively coruscates with puns and wordplay, and could be seen actually to be engendered by them. A mother called Macarée is obviously intended to become a "macchabée"; if Croniamental is "né d'un pet" his story is bound to be one of "contrepèteries," or vice versa. Here the analogy with surrealist writers, in particular Desnos and Roussel, is obvious, as are the resemblances to Joyce.

To sum up, these then are the specific techniques exemplified by Apollinaire, initially arising from his search for simultaneity: The development of the structuring power of the image through its associative range; the reduction of the image to fragments, even of a single word, in order to create effects of speed and dynamism; the kaleidoscopic faceting effect that enables the poet to switch from outer to inner world and back; collage and auto-collage to weld those outer and inner worlds, and to transcend them; a whole new exploitation of space through the exploration of the visual effects of the image on the page, and thence a new kind of relationship between text and reader; and finally the endless "mise en abîme" of the *jeu créateur*.

What finally emerges as perhaps the most impressive contribution not only of Apollinaire but of the whole early period of *modernité* of which he is an exemplar is the central faith in man's creativity to the point where when all other ideals have crumbled human language itself is let out on the rampage to turn even the blackest of irony into a source of invention, liberation, and laughter.

Notes

1. Max Jacob, *Le Cornet à dés* (1917; reprint, Paris: Gallimard, 1967), 30–31. Trans. Judith Morganroth Schneider in Sydney Lévy, *The Play of the Text* (Madison: Univ. of Wisconsin Press, 1981), 133.

2. Guillaume Apollinaire, *Alcools, Oeuvres poétiques* (Paris: Gallimard, 1965), 78.

3. Blaise Cendrars, "Les Pâques à New York" in *Du monde entier* (Paris: Gallimard, 1967), 17. Trans. Scott Bates in *The Selected Writings of Blaise Cendrars*, ed. Walter Albert (New York: New Directions, 1966), 51.

4. Blaise Cendrars, *Aujourd'hui, Oeuvres complètes* (Paris: Club Français du livre, 1980), 6:82.

5. Cendrars, "Prose du Transsibérien" in *Du Monde Entier*, 33.

6. Ibid., 40.

7. Guillaume Apollinaire, "La cravate et la montre," in *Calligrammes, Oeuvres poétiques* (Paris: Gallimard, 1965), 192.

8. Apollinaire, *Calligrammes*, 209.

Jo-Anna Isaak

The Revolution of a Poetics

Soleil, prends garde de toi.
　　　　—A. P. Wiertz

I fear we shall never be rid of God, so long as we still
believe in grammar.
　　　　　　　　　　　　—Nietzsche

"What strikes me as beautiful, what I should like to
do," Flaubert wrote, "is a book without external attachments, which
would hold itself together by itself through the internal force of its
style." Flaubert's dream of an order of art independent of the referential,
the representational, was actualized within certain developments of abstractionism in the early 1900s—when art took to analyzing its own
ontology. The movements that follow Flaubert's imperative, creating
not art contingent upon empirical experience but art as process and
mode of perceptual and formal experience, have one characteristic in
common—their strategies of abstraction evolved out of a complex nexus
of linguistic and plastic media. It is as though what Roman Jakobson
refers to as the "bared medium" could only be realized by investigating
the devices of *other* media. In particular, strikingly similar traits can be
observed among the group of English vorticists associated with Ezra
Pound, Wyndham Lewis, and the manifesto *Blast* (1914)[1] and the group
of Russian futurists, an alliance of writers and painters who displayed
a comparable urge to write manifestos which would function as "A Slap
in the Face to Public Taste" (1912).[2] In the *Blast* manifesto, Pound

attempted to delineate what he called the "ancestry" of vorticism by quoting Pater's famous phrase on the etiology of abstraction in art: "all arts approach the condition of music." In the same chapter of *The Renaissance* Pater goes on to make two other much more explicit statements. The first is that "art is always striving to become a matter of pure perception, to get rid of its responsibilities to its *subject.*" In the second, abstraction in one medium is seen to be capable of suggesting a means of aesthetic autonomy in another. Pater notes that "in its special mode of handling its given material, each art may be observed to pass into the condition of some other art, by what German critics term an *Anders-streben*—a partial alienation from its own limitations, through which the arts are able, not indeed to supply the place of each other, but reciprocally to lend each other new forces."[3]

The notion of the autonomy of the artistic material was developed by the Russian futurists into a fully articulated aesthetic. Kasimir Malevich's assertion that the object of painting was the expression of its own "body as such" ("The idea is to combine the variety and multiplicity of lines, space, surface, color and texture into one body as such")[4] had its direct linguistic counterpart in Velemir Khlebnikov's and Aleksei Kruchenykh's insistence on the idea of the "word as such,"[5] the self-sufficient word, free of its referent. Just as all the other arts consist in the shaping of self-validating material, so too does poetry: its "material" is words, and thus poetry is characterized as obeying immanent laws and its semantic function reduced to a minimum. "Before us there was no art of the word," Kruchenykh wrote in *The Three* (*Troe*, 1913), and he asserted the autonomous value of the "autotelic word." The raw material of literature was to be allowed to stand by itself, no longer chained in slavery to meaning, philosophy, psychology, or reason: "The word is broader than its meaning. Each letter, each sound has its relevance. . . . Why not repudiate meaning and write with word-ideas that are freely created? We do not need intermediaries—symbols, thought, *we give our own new truth and we do not serve as the reflections of some sun.*"[6] And Benedikt Livshits wrote that now poetry was "free from the sad necessity of expressing the logical connection of ideas."[7] In 1911 Pound had launched a comparable attack against the burden of reference imposed upon poetry, complaining that for over two hundred years poetry in English "had been merely the vehicle . . . the ox-cart and post-chaise for transmitting thoughts poetic or otherwise."[8]

The assertion of the right to an autonomous or autotelic aesthetic praxis should not be understood as synonymous with the solipsistic principle of "art for art's sake," but rather should be accompanied by the following qualification of Jakobson's:

> Of late criticism thinks it fashionable to stress the uncertainty of what is called the formalist science of literature. It seems that this school does not understand the relations between art and social life, it seems that it promotes *l'art pour l'art* and proceeds in the wake of Kantian aesthetics. The critics who make these objections are, in their radicalism, so consistent and so precipitate that they forget the existence of the third dimension, they see everything in the same plane. Neither Tynyanov, nor Mukarovsky, nor Shklovsky, nor I have preached that art is sufficient unto itself; on the contrary, we show that art is part of the social edifice, a component correlating with the others, a variable component, since the sphere of art and its relationship with other sectors of the social structure ceaselessly changes dialectically. *What we stress is not a separation of art, but the autonomy of the aesthetic function.*
>
> I have already said that the content of the notion of *poetry* was unstable and varied over time, but the poetic function, *poeticalness,* as the formalists stressed, is an element *sui generis,* an element that cannot be mechanically reduced to other elements. This element must be laid bare and its independence stressed, as the technical devices of cubist paintings, for example, are laid bare and independent. . . .
>
> But how is poeticalness manifested? In that the word is felt as a word and not as a mere substitute for the named object or as an explosion of emotion. In that words and their syntax, their signification, their external and internal form are not indifferent indices of reality, but have their own weight and their own value.[9]

As the manifesto titles suggest, (*Blast, A Slap in the Face to Public Taste*) it is as a reaction against the pluralism of bourgeois taste that these artists posit their stylistic dissent. The enthusiasm and exaltation with which they announce this stylistic dissent indicates that the formal revolution—the radical shifts in modes of aesthetic production, theoretical positions, and treatment of perceptual and linguistic conventions—is the pretext for hurling a Promethean challenge, repudiating their determinate role in producing representations of the ideological world. According to Malraux, modern artists ventured into the field of abstractionism with the intention of escaping the hegemony and homogeneity of that "museum without walls" in which they had found themselves since photographic reproduction provided the technology of pluralism—the immediate assimilation and dissemination of the work of art. Although I do not agree with Malraux's teleology of abstract art, what is important to our discussion here is his observation of the intention of abstractionism as reaction against the dominance of now easily reproduced "high art"—traditional academic culture providing a fictitious, but authoritative, universality and continuity with the past—and against mass culture, which is wholly divorced from any culture created by the people, but which is "art" produced and packaged for the masses. Edmund Wilson has given these two types the contrasting names "classics" and "commercials."

The most famous apostle of the creed of the "classics" is T. S. Eliot, who, in appropriating mythified cultural fragments to shore against his ruin, attempted to appropriate the work of Ezra Pound and James Joyce and to marshal them under the retrospective utopian banner of new literary classicism. "It is simply a way of controlling, of ordering, of giving a shape and a significance to the immense panorama of futility and anarchy which is contemporary history," Eliot writes in *"Ulysses, Order, and Myth."* This is perhaps the most candid revelation of the true compensatory impulse behind the eclectic historicist's static notion of history, which enables him to create a false synthesis of cultural fragments and endow them with notions of grandeur, nobility, universality, authority—all the old verities no longer to be found in the modern world, but which, we are asked to believe, obtained in the past. The mythic method, Eliot claims, is a step toward "making the modern world possible for art."[10] In the *Slap in the Face* manifesto this mode of artistic production, along with Pushkin, Dostoevsky, Tolstoy, et al., is the first to be thrown overboard from the "Ship of Modernity," a reaction analogous to Pound's assertion that you needn't read Shakespeare, you could find out all you needed to know about him from "boring circumjacent conversation." "Better mendacities than the classics in paraphrase."[11]

The greatest ad-man of the "commercials" is F. T. Marinetti, who, in his zeal for "the new," heroically and hysterically attempted to acculturate the entire avant-garde to the modes of production and theoretical positions of commodity capitalism in order to develop devices that would facilitate the swift communication of propaganda for that thoroughly modern merry-go-round—reification. This is borne out in Marinetti's adulation of all forms of capitalist technology and in his attempts to convert the whole Italian futurist movement into propagandists for Mussolini's fascism.

The ostensibly dissimilar artistic or pseudo-artistic production practices of mass culture and high art converge on the level of the common cult of the cliché.[12] For Pound, whose *Make It New* poetics[13] is shared by the Russian futurists, who used the same slogan, Marinetti's futurism was "only an accelerated sort of impressionism,"[14] implying that it is only a new form of mimeticism. But as Jakobson maintains, "Poetry is renewed from within, by specifically linguistic means," and he treats poetic language throughout his essay on "Modern Russian Poetry" (1919) as a kind of metalanguage.[15] Like Pound, who asserted that "a work of art has in it no idea which is separable from the form,"[16] Jakobson, too, denies the distinct existence of subject matter or "content." Analyses of innovations based upon external or social causation are therefore erroneous. Both Pound and Jakobson fault Marinetti for the way he directs poetry to the task of recording new facts in the material world: rapid transit, speeding motor cars, locomotives, airplanes, and so on. "But this is a reform in the field of reportage, not in poetic language," Jakobson observes, and contrasts Marinetti's new mimeticism with Kruchenykh's assertion that "it is not new subject matter that defines genuine innovation. Once there is new form, it follows that there is new content; form thus conditions content. Our creative shaping of speech throws everything into a new light."[17]

Thus Marinetti's futurism and Eliot's neoclassicism—the symbolic modes of concrete anticipation and the allegorical modes of internalized cultural retrospection—are understood to be comparable devices of stultification that reinforce and reinvent the cultural power structure. They are the aesthetic manifestations of the psychic mechanisms of anticipation and melancholy. At the origin of the allegorical is an enforced and incapacitating melancholy, the result of prohibition and repression; at the origin of the valorization of reactionary power and of reification is the continual generation and denial of expectations. When Pound, in an interview in Mayakovsky's magazine, *The Archer* (*Strelets*, 1915), dissociates himself from Italian futurism he does so in a way that specifically addresses these ideologically induced psychic states and the manner in which they thwart the development of any genuinely innovative artistic activity capable of critical negativity.

> We are "vorticists." . . . Everything that has been created by nature and culture is for us a general chaos which we pierce with our vortex. We do not deny the past—we don't remember it. It is distant and thus sentimental. For the artist and the poet it is a means to divert the instinct of melancholy which hinders pure art. But the future is just as distant as the past, and thus also sentimental. It is a diversion of optimism which is just as pernicious in art as melancholy. The past and the future are two brothels created by nature. Art is periods of flight from these brothels, periods of sanctity. We are not futurists: the past and the future merge for us in their sentimental remoteness, in their projections onto an obscured and impotent perception. Art lives only by means of the present—but only that present which is

not subject to nature, which does not suck up to life, limiting itself to perceptions of the existent, but rather creates from itself a new, living abstraction . . . our task is to "dehumanize" the contemporary world; the established forms of the human body and all that is "mere life" have now lost their former significance. One must create new abstractions, bring together new masses, bring out of oneself a new reality.[18]

Concomitant with this insistence on the new and the present, so central to both Russian futurism and English vorticism, is their interest in primitive and folk art. Russian neoprimitivism was to have considerable influence on the inception of abstract art in England. Although ostensibly it arose in Russia out of nationalist sentiments and the need for a viable indigenous art form in opposition to the invasions of Western culture, it was precisely this aspect of Russian art that found the most favorable reception in the West—in fact, it was what the West demanded. Diaghilev's first ballet performed in the West was criticized in the French press for its lack of national atmosphere: "The French desired a folk-lore element, expected a special, almost exotic flavour in the performances. In short, they wanted what they, as Frenchmen, understood to be 'du vrai Russe.' "[19] It was in response to this demand that Diaghilev launched *L'Oiseau de Feu* (1910)—a colorful although unconvincing pastiche of various Russian fairy and folk tales. Nevertheless, it was what the West called for, and by 1911 the influence of the Ballets Russes had spread far beyond the confines of the London and Paris elite. How great this influence was may be judged by the following extract from "Painters and the *Ballets-Russes*" by André Varnod: "In any case, it was a perfect enthusiasm which, sweeping away the artistic, literary and social worlds, reached the man in the street, the wide public, the gown-shops and stores. The fashion in everything was *Ballets-Russes*. There was not a middle-class home without its green and orange cushions on a black carpet."[20] In 1913 Diaghilev very shrewdly enlisted the talents of Goncharova, and in spite of Larionov's declaration of 1913 that "we are against the West, vulgarizing our Oriental forms and rendering everything valueless,"[21] by 1914 Goncharova had burst upon Paris and London as the creator of the decor of the *Coq d'Or*—and Larionov too had begun to work for Diaghilev.

The appropriation by the West of ancient Russian art cannot, of course, be attributed wholly to Diaghilev's cultural transportations. T. E. Hulme's complaint about the way in which "elements taken from the extremely intense and serious Byzantine art are used in an entirely meaningless and pointless way"[22] was a response to the Byzantine-style screens, rugs, inlaid tables, and paintings that proliferated in the wake of the Bloomsbury group's visit to Constantinople in 1911. Fry's enthusiasm for the art he saw while on this trip may have resulted in his decision to include the work of Russian artists in his Second Post-Impressionist Exhibition (1912). Here the works of Nikolai Roerich, Mikalojus Ciurlianis, Nataliya Goncharova, Mikhail Larionov, and other Russian artists of what the catalog referred to as the "New Byzantine Group" were exhibited together with the works of Vanessa Bell, Frederick Etchells, Duncan Grant, Cuthbert Hamilton, Wyndham Lewis, and Edward Wadsworth.

In spite of Hulme's justifiable complaint, the English artists' "adaptations" of Byzantine art forms enabled them to familiarize themselves with the use of nonrepresentational design. Roger Fry spoke of the "incredible phenomenon" of Goncharova and Larionov's stage decor, pointing out that now artists could go to the theater "to see experiments in the art of visual design—still more, experiments which indicate new possibilities in the art of picture-making."[23] The early abstract compositions of Bomberg in particular were inspired by Diaghilev's ballets (fig. 1). And certainly a great number of the works produced at the Omega Workshop, plans for which began immediately after the Second Post-Impressionist Exhibition, show the influence of Russian folk art and crafts. These connections explain in part the precociousness of the development of abstract art in England. For example, Wyndham Lewis's *Portrait of an Englishwoman* (fig. 2), which was reproduced in *The Archer* (1915), is markedly similar to Malevich's later suprematist paintings, for example *Dynamischer Suprematismus* (Suprematist Composition, 1916 [fig. 3]); and David Bomberg's *The Dancer* (1914) can be compared to Rodchencko's compass drawings of 1915. Examples such as these illustrate how similar influences can lead to morphologically comparable effects.

The adaptation of Russian neoprimitivist art in England has very different ideological implications from the same activity in Russia. This phenomenon was diagnosed in the twenties by Russian productivist artist and theoretician Boris Arvatov, who writes in *Art and Production*:

> While the total technology of capitalist society is constructed on the highest and latest achievement and represents a technique of mass production (industry, radio, transport, newspapers, scientific laboratories, etc.), bourgeois art in principle has remained on the level of crafts and therefore has been pushed out of the collective social practice of mankind into isolation, into the realm of pure aesthetics. . . . The individual, lonely master, that is the

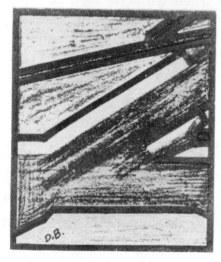

David Bomberg, *The Russian Ballet Lithographs* (1914–19). Reprinted by permission of Anthony d'Offay Limited. (Fig. 1)

Wyndham Lewis, *Portrait of an English-woman* (1914). Estate of Mrs. G. A. Wyndham Lewis. By permission. (Fig. 2)

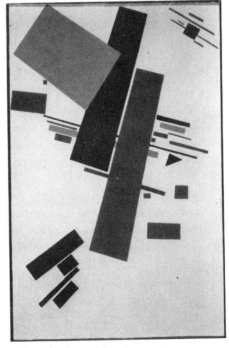

Kasimir Malevich, *Dynamischer Suprematismus* (1916). Reprinted by permission of the Wallraf-Richartz-Museum, Köln. (Fig. 3)

only type of artist in capitalist society, the type of specialist in "pure art" who works outside of the immediately utilitarian practice because this practice is based on machine technology. From here originates the illusion of art's purposelessness and autonomy, from here its whole bourgeois fetishistic nature.[24]

Arvatov's analysis could apply to industrial England, but in post-czarist Russia the development from neoprimitivism to abstract art to constructivist and productivist practices follows a very different trajectory.

In part, this can be explained by analyzing the reasons for the Russian avant-garde's renewed interest in primitive and religious art— particularly orthodox icon painting. Malevich's enigmatic announcement that *The Black Square* (1914–15) was "the icon of our times"[25] was followed by his statements in *The Non-Objective World* that "art no longer cares to serve the state and religion. . . . It wants to have nothing further to do with the object as such and believes that it can exist in and for itself."[26] The paradox of Malevich's position is resolved through a consideration of the semiotic function of the ancient icon itself. The controversy between the iconoclasts and iconodules, of fundamental significance for Orthodox Christianity, may, to a great extent, be seen as a controversy concerning precisely the semiotic character of the icon— the central point of which was the attitude toward the sign.[27] In spite of the icon's extremely formalized but nevertheless figurative form it was originally understood to be nonrepresentational, in that its "referent" was regarded as ineffable—the face of Christ could never be known. Malevich's *Black Square* lays bare the absent referent as the source of the nonreferentiality of the icon and calls into question the whole problematic of any sign's relationship to the phenomenal world. In so doing Malevich exposes the idealism of the theological debate, its assumption of what Derrida calls the "transcendental signified," "which supposedly does not in itself, in its essence, refer back to any signifier but goes beyond the chain of signs, and itself no longer functions as a signifier." Rosalind Coward and John Ellis's discussion of Derrida's critique of the sign is useful here:

> In this way, the distinction or equilibrium of the notions "signified" and "signifier" in the sign allows the metaphysical belief of a reserve or an origin of meaning which will always be anterior and exterior to the continuous productivity of signification. . . .
> [Thus Derrida asserts] that a philosophy of language based on such a notion of the sign is "profoundly theological." "Sign and deity have the same place and same time of birth." The pyramid (referent—signified— signifier) ends by resolving itself into the hypostasis of a signified which always culminates in god: "the epoch of the sign is essentially theological."[28]

Malevich conflates the signifier and signified, not as is customarily the case to let the concept present itself in a supposedly unmediated manner, but rather to reverse the process and foreground the signifier, thereby circumventing the idealist problematic that supposes the preexistence of meaning. When Malevich speaks of the primitive tendency in modern art, he does so in terms appropriate to his own use of the icon and makes it clear that the modern adaptation of primitive art is not an atavistic activity, but rather what he calls a "decomposition": "It is the attempt to escape from the objective identity of the image to direct creation and to break away from idealism and pretense."[29] Primitivism, as it was to be employed by the Russian avant-garde, was one of the major strategies for facilitating the creation of the autonomous, autotelic work of art, a work of art relieved of its semantic or representational function, precisely because meaning with an *a priori* existence had been repudiated; signification was now understood to be dependent upon the passage of signifiers themselves.

The repudiation of the transcendental signified appears as the Promethean declaration of *Victory Over the Sun* (1913)—the theatrical collaboration of Kruchenykh (text), Malevich (costumes and set designs), Matyushin (music), and Khlebnikov (prologue). It is extremely significant that Malevich claimed that suprematism originated while he was working on the sets for *Victory Over the Sun*. It has been suggested that Malevich's sketch for the backdrop for the first act (fig. 4) may be part of the sun against the dark universe, especially since the diagonal line is actually curved and may be the horizon line of the sun.[30] Also, parts of the sun appear on the cover for the libretto (fig. 5). If this reading is valid then the *Black Square* may be read as the total obliteration of the sun, the climactic event of *Victory Over the Sun*.

Victory Over the Sun is remarkably similar in title, theme, structure, charactery, stage design, and linguistic innovation to Wyndham Lewis's play *Enemy of the Stars*, written less than a year after *Victory Over the Sun* and Mayakovsky's play *Vladimir Mayakovsky, a Tragedy* had caused a riot at the Luna Park Theatre in St. Petersburg. Lewis may have learned of the plays from Marinetti, who visited Russia a couple of weeks after they were performed. In his memoirs Livshits details the debate Kulbin had with Marinetti concerning the importance of *zaum* or trans-rational language, which Kruchenykh had just developed in *Victory Over the Sun*.[31] What account Marinetti gave of all this when he returned to England a few months later, and whether he brought with him the illustrated text of *Victory Over the Sun* published while

Isaak

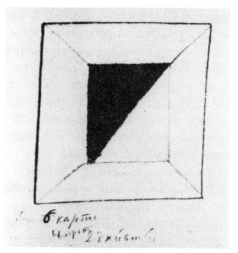

Kasimir Malevich, backdrop sketch for the
opening of *Victory Over the Sun* (1913).
(Fig. 4)

Kasimir Malevich, cover for the libretto of
Victory Over the Sun. (Fig. 5)

he was in St. Petersburg is not known. But it is clear that the innovations of the Russian futurists would be a subject of considerable interest to the English vorticists.

Lewis wrote *Enemy of the Stars* because, as he said, his "literary contemporaries [were] not keeping pace with the visual revolution,"[32] yet he did not adopt Marinetti's theories and practices nor his typographic experiments, but instead utilized a great many devices comparable to those employed by the Russian futurists. Mayakovsky's canvas cubes and "slightly slanted"[33] sets may have been the inspiration for Lewis's stage arrangements, in which "overturned cases and other impediments have been covered, throughout arena, with old sail canvas." In the second scene the "audience looks down into scene, as though it were a hut rolled half on its back, door upwards, characters giddily mounting in its opening."[34] A picture of the setting for *Victory Over the Sun* shows an unmatched drop and wings hung upside down; in the sixth scene there is the unusual stage direction that the fat man "peeps inside the watch: the tower the sky the street are upside down—as in a mirror."[35] The colors of the setting in both *Victory Over the Sun* and *Enemy of the Stars* are stark, unmodulated contrasts—predominantly black and white. In the second scene of *Victory Over the Sun* there is the addition of "green walls and floor" for the set of scene 2, on which Malevich had written "green until the funeral"; and in Lewis's play there are "the Red Walls of the Universe . . . till the execution is over" (E, 61).

The artificial light from the spotlights used in *Victory Over the Sun* played an important part in creating its dramatic effects. Malevich had at his disposal a modern console-controlled lighting system that had just been installed in the Luna Park Theatre. Livshits describes how the "tentacles of the spotlights" cut up the bodies of the actors into geometric sections: the figures "broken up by the blades of light . . . alternately lose arms, legs, heads," presumably because the colored spotlights absorbed similar colors in the costumes. These blades of light, which light up what Livshits called "a night of creation for the world"[36] sound remarkably close to the bizarre, tremendously forceful and threatening lighting which pierces the night in *Enemy of the Stars*. "A white, crude volume of brutal light blazes over" the characters, crushing them. The stars, "machines of prey," shine "madly in the archaic blank wilderness of the universe" (E, 64).

The characters are grotesque abstractions of people, their bodies no more resistant to the powerful restructuration than is the rest of the environment. In Mayakovsky's play there is a man without an ear and one without a head; in *Victory Over the Sun* the fat man complains that his head lags two steps behind his body; in *Enemy of the Stars* a disembodied boot appears regularly to kick the protagonist, Arghol. Characters who are not parts of people wear masks and move like animations of monumental statues or distorted half-machine, half-human figures. Arghol "walks like wary shifting of bodies in distant equipoise." In one variation he is described as a "creature of two-dimensions, clumsily cut out in cardboard by coarse scissor-work,"[37] a description appropriate to Malevich's costumes, which were made of cardboard and resembled armor. The one illustration Lewis gives of the Enemy of the Stars (fig. 6) could be a somewhat modified side-view of Malevich's Futurecountry Strong Man (fig. 7). These are the protagonists of the plays.

The Futurecountry Strong Man, like Lewis's Enemy, is engaged in a Promethean struggle. Man against the sun is the paradigm of the poet's desire to overthrow the agency of meaning—the prohibitionary seat of representation, "the sun of cheap appearances" as Matyushin calls it,[38] or an "immense bleak electric advertisement of God" as Lewis calls it (*E*, 66). "We pulled the sun out by its fresh roots / they were fatty permeated with arithmetic," the victors sing (*V*, 117). *Victory Over the Sun* is a restructuration of an entire cosmology—language users, not space, time, or causality, determine the order of the universe. "Lookers painted by an artist, will create a change in the look of nature," the prologue promises. Once the victory over the sun has been accomplished the Elocutionist announces: "How extraordinary life is without a past . . . what a joy: liberated from the weight of the earth's gravitation we whimsically arrange our belongings as if a rich kingdom were moving" (*V*, 121).

The language and structure of both plays is closely akin to that of the carnival. As Julia Kristeva points out:

> Carnivalesque structure is like the residue of a cosmogony that ignored substance, causality, or identity. . . . Figures germane to carnivalesque language, including repetition, "inconsequent" statements (which are nonetheless "connected" within an infinite context), and nonexclusive opposition, which function as empty sets or disjunctive additions, produce a more flagrant dialogism than any other discourse. Disputing the laws of language . . . the carnival challenges God, authority, and social law; insofar as it is dialogical, it is rebellious. . . .
>
> The scene of the carnival . . . is . . . both stage and life, game and dream, discourse and spectacle. By the same token, it is proffered as the only space in which language escapes linearity (law) to live as drama in three dimensions. At a deeper level . . . *drama becomes located in language.*

Wyndham Lewis, *Enemy of the Stars* (1913). Estate of Mrs. G. A. Wyndham Lewis. By permission. (Fig. 6)

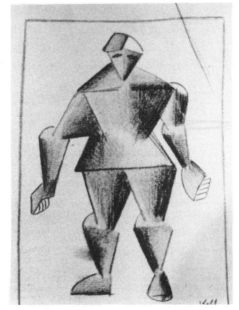

Kasimir Malevich, Futurecountry Strong Man costume sketch for *Victory Over the Sun* (1913). (Fig. 7)

On the omnified stage of carnival, language parodies and relativizes itself, repudiating its role in representation.[39]

It is exactly at this level—the drama located in language—that the two plays bifurcate. In *Victory Over the Sun* phonetic and semantic deformations and new meaning generated by them achieve what Jakobson describes as the "significant potential" of neologism, that is, its potential for abstraction.[40] *Victory Over the Sun* is the creation of the non-objective world. The old order of time, space, causality no longer obtains. Characters travel freely from the tenth to the thirty-fifth centuries of the future or "leave sideways into the 16th century in quotation marks" (V, 111). The final song of the play is pure transrational poetry—*zaum:*

```
luh      luh      luh
Kruuh         Kruuh
       Hee
       Hoomtuh
Krruh         duh       tuh       rruh
       Krruh                      vwubra
       doo             doo
ra luh
       Kuh      buh      ee
              zhub
zeeda
       deeda
```

This is the complete song, as meaningless in English (or rather transliterated, as here) as in Russian.

In Lewis's play, language remains incapable of detaching itself from representation. Even though at times the materiality of language is fore-grounded and we are conscious only of what Lewis was later to call "the finely sculptured surface of sheer words," these "sheer words" are not long at liberty—their referents soon overtake them. Lewis's protagonist is posited in opposition to exactly the same forces as Kruchenykh's Futurecountry Strong Man. His play can be read as an allegorical enactment of Worringer's theory of the two oppositional wills to art—abstraction (Arghol) and empathy (Hanp). Arghol is the abstract artist engaged in "the dehumanization of art,"[41] but as Lewis makes clear in the beginning he is a "foredoomed Prometheus." He is beaten regularly by the "will of the universe manifested with directness and persistence" (E, 66), and is beset by Hanp, to whom Arghol says, "You are the world, brother, with its family objections to me" (E, 73). Hanp is organic nature with its demands for empathy. In both plays "nature is not an origin, but a run-down trope."[42] In *Victory Over the Sun*, "the violets groan / Under the firm heel" of the Strong Man (*V*, 115):

> The flower world doesn't exist anymore
> Sky cover yourself with rot . . .
> Every birth of autumn days
> And blemished fruit of summer
> Not about those, the newest bard
> Will sing.
>
> (V, 114)

In *Victory Over the Sun* the victory over cosmic order and the destruction of nature is the abolition of conventions of representation. In *Enemy of the Stars*, however, there is no victory. Arghol is "imprisoned in a messed socket of existence" (*E*, 68), and his only mode of extricating himself is through language: "Arghol's voice had no modulations of argument. Weak now, it handled words numbly, like tired compositor. His body was quite strong again and vivacious. Words acted on it as rain on a plant. It got a stormy neat brilliance in this soft shower. One flame balanced giddily erect, while another larger one swerved and sang with speech coldly before it" (*E*, 66). Arghol's decisive struggle takes place in the dream scene. It is within the dream, whose characteristic is, as Kristeva points out, carnivalesque discourse, that language could attain its " 'potential infinity' (to use David Hilbert's term), where prohibitions (representation, 'monologism') and their transgression (dream, body, 'dialogism') coexist."[43] In the dream Arghol fails to transgress the prohibitions, to enact the revolution that would transform him and his environment. He remains Arghol (fixed identity) and others recognize him as such in spite of his attempts to "obliterate or turn into deliberate refuse, accumulations of self" (*E*, 78). "He was simply Arghol. . . . He repeated his name—like sinister word invented to launch a new Soap, in gigantic advertisement—toilet—necessity, he, to scrub the soul" (*E*, 80). Nor is he able to rid himself of reality for long. He wakes up to find Hanp has followed him—"Always à deux!" In the end it is Hanp (the world) who kills Arghol, to the "relief of grateful universe." "The night was suddenly absurdly peaceful" (*E*, 84). The execution is over, the universe satisfied.

Enemy of the Stars is Lewis's most daringly experimental approach to language, "a piece of writing worthy of the hand of the abstractist innovator."[44] "If anything extended could be done with it," Hugh Kenner observed, "this early style would be one of the most impressive inventions in the history of English literature."[45] At the same time, the dramatic action located in the language marks Lewis's retreat from the linguistic revolution. "Words and syntax," he decided, "were not susceptible of transformation into abstract terms, to which process the visual arts lent themselves quite readily."[46] This was the first step in Lewis's withdrawal from the abstractionist experiment. His second would come when he decided that "abstract terms" no longer seemed worth exploring in the visual arts either. The war which he had first complained of as having "stopped Art dead"[47] he later praised for having saved him from what he called the "abstractist cul-de-sac."[48]

Many years later, when Lewis looked back on the period just after the *Blast* publication, he expressed a sense of missed opportunity, a recognition that there was some further potential, some next step to the aesthetic revolution which he had failed to actualize—which, in fact, he had failed to see: "I might have been at the head of a social revolution, instead of merely being the prophet of a new fashion in art. Really all this organized disturbance was Art behaving as if it were Politics. But I swear I did not know it. It may in fact have been politics. I see that now. Indeed, it must have been. But I was unaware of the fact."[49] His fellow vorticists were even more reactionary: "The immediate need of the art of today," Christopher Nevinson announced in 1919, is for "a reactionary, to lead art back to the academic traditions of the Old Masters and save contemporary art from abstraction."[50]

The vision of the future, so unformed in the vorticists, was extremely clear to the Russian futurists. They saw themselves as harbingers of a political revolution. The subsequent evolution from Malevich's suprematism to the constructivist practices of artists such as Rodchenko and Lissitsky, and their explicit politicization during the productivist period, confirms their vision of themselves: their work was intricately bound into and supportive of the social revolution in the Soviet Union. As Malevich asserted, the overthrow of bourgeois taste, "smashing the old tables of aesthetic values[,] was the first step in smashing the bourgeois order."[51]

Notes

1. The manifesto was signed by R. Aldington, Arbuthnot, L. Atkinson, Gaudier-Brzeska, J. Dismorr, C. Hamilton, E. Pound, W. Roberts, H. Sanders, E. Wadsworth, and Wyndham Lewis.

2. The manifesto was signed by David Burliuk, Aleksei Kruchenykh, Vladimir Mayakovsky, and Velemir Khlebnikov. Translated in Victor Markov, *Russian*

The Revolution of a Poetics

Futurism—A History (London: MacGibbon & Kee, 1969), 45–46. The term "futurist" causes some confusion in the context of the Russian avant-garde. It is not synonymous with Italian futurism, from whom the Russians dissociated themselves, nor was the term borrowed from the Italians. It is an abbreviation of "Men of the Future," a name they had given themselves before the inception of Italian futurism.

3. Walter Pater, "The School of Giorgione," *The Renaissance* (1873; reprint, New York: Modern Library, 1961), 129, 128 and 132. Actually, Pound misquotes Pater. The sentence should read, "All art constantly aspires towards the condition of music."

4. Kasimir Malevich, "On New Systems in Art," *Essays on Art 1915–1935*, trans. Zenia Glowacki-Prus and Arnold McMilan, ed. Troels Anderson, 2 vols. (London: Rapp & Whiting, 1969), 1:92.

5. This phrase became the title of their 1913 manifesto.

6. Aleksei Kruchenykh in *Troe* (*The Three*) (Moscow: Zhuravl, 1913), trans. Susan Compton, *The World Backwards: Russian Futurist Books 1912–16* (London: British Library, 1978), 56 (my italics).

7. Benedikt Livshits, "Liberation of the Word," in *The Croaked Moon* (Moscow: Osyen, 1914). Quoted by Susan P. Compton, "Malevich's Suprematism—the Higher Intuition," *Burlington Magazine* 118 (Aug. 1976): 577–85.

8. *Literary Essays of Ezra Pound*, ed. T. S. Eliot (London: Faber & Faber, 1954), 11.

9. Roman Jakobson, "What is Poetry?" in *Questions de poétique* (Paris: Editions du Seuil, 1973), 122.

10. T. S. Eliot, "*Ulysses*, Order, and Myth," *The Dial* 75 (1923): 480–83.

11. Ezra Pound, *Hugh Selwyn Mauberley* (London: Ovid Press, 1920).

12. For a detailed analysis of the connections between "mass" and "high" culture see Renato Poggioli, *The Spirit of the Letter* (Cambridge: Harvard Univ. Press, 1965).

13. Ezra Pound, *Make It New: Essays* (London: Faber & Faber, 1934); but the essay as a whole must be dated 1910–31.

14. Ezra Pound, "Vortex," *Blast* 1 (1914): 154.

15. Roman Jakobson, "Modern Russian Poetry: Velimir Khlebnikov," trans. Edward J. Brown, in *Major Soviet Writers*, ed. Edward J. Brown (London: Oxford Univ. Press, 1973), 58–82.

16. "Brancusi" (1921), *Literary Essays of Ezra Pound*, 441. Pound is quoting T. J. Everest and claims that this statement is "the best summary of our contemporary aesthetics."

17. Quoted in Jakobson, "Modern Russian Poetry," 61.

18. Ezra Pound, interview with Zinaida Vengerova, "Angliiskie futuristy," *Strelets* 1 (1915): 93–94. Unpublished translation by John Barnstead.

19. Prince Peter Lieven, *The Birth of Ballets-Russes* (1936; reprint, London: Allen & Unwin, 1956), 106.

20. Quoted in Lieven, 159. Wyndham Lewis was provoked to write a critique of Diaghilev's ballets in which he criticizes Diaghilev for associating

the "finest artists of his time" with the "art of this High Bohemia of the revolutionary rich of his time." He reserves his praise for Diaghilev's early "primitive" ballets. "The Russian Ballet: The Most Perfect Expression of High Bohemia," in *The Enemy: A Review of Art and Literature* (1927–29; reprint, New York: Kraus Reprint, 1967), 54–57.

21. Mikhail Larionov, "Rayonist Manifesto" (Moscow, 1913), quoted in Camilla Gray, *The Great Experiment: Russian Art, 1863–1922* (London: Thames & Hudson, 1962), 138.

22. Quoted in "A Neglected Phase of British Art," editorial, *Apollo*, Mar. 1917, 182.

23. Roger Fry, "M. Larionov and the Russian Ballet," *Burlington Magazine* 34 (1919): 112–18.

24. Boris Arvatov, *Iskusstvo i proizvodstvo* (Moscow: Proletcult, 1926), 95. Unpublished translation by Nathan Smith.

25. Kasimir Malevich to Alexander Benois, May 1916, in *Essays on Art*, 1:45.

26. Kasimir Malevich, *The Non-Objective World* (1926; trans. Howard Dearstyne, Chicago: P. Theobald, 1959), 74.

27. See Boris Uspensky, *The Semiotics of the Russian Icon*, ed. Stephen Rudy, trans. P. A. Reed (1922; reprint, Lisse: P. de Ridder Press, 1976).

28. Jacques Derrida, *Positions* (Paris: Editions de Minuit, 1972), 23–25, quoted in Rosalind Coward and John Ellis, *Language and Materialism: Developments in Semiology and the Theory of the Subject* (London: Routledge & Kegan Paul, 1977), 123.

29. Malevich, *Essays on Art*, 1:90.

30. See Rainer Crone, "Malevich and Khlebnikov: Suprematism Reinterpreted," *Artforum* (Dec. 1978): 38–50.

31. See Markov, 154.

32. Wyndham Lewis, *Rude Assignment: A Narrative of My Career Up-to-Date* (London: Hutchinson, 1950), 129.

33. Markov, 146.

34. Wyndham Lewis, *Enemy of the Stars*, *Blast* 1 (1914): 60; hereafter cited as *E*.

35. *Victory Over the Sun*, trans. Ewa Bartos and Victoria Nes Kirby, *TDR/The Drama Review* 15, no. 4 (Fall 1971): 121; hereafter cited as *V*.

36. Benedikt Livshits, *Polutoraglazyi strelets* (Leningrad, 1933), 187–88; cited in Susan Compton, *The World Backwards*, 55.

37. This is from the 1932 version of the play (London), 40.

38. M. Matyushin, "Futurism v peterburge," *Futuristy: Pervyi jhuranal russkikh futuristov* 1–2 (Moscow, 1914), 156; cited in Charlotte Douglas, "Birth of a 'Royal Infant': Malevich and *Victory Over the Sun*," *Art in America*, Mar./Apr. 1974, 47.

39. Julia Kristeva, *Desire in Language: A Semiotic Approach to Literature and Art* (New York: Columbia Univ. Press, 1980), 78–79 (emphasis mine).

40. Jakobson, "Modern Russian Poetry," 75.

41. This phrase, made popular by Ortega y Gasset, was first used by Wyndham Lewis in *Blast* 1:141 to describe his aesthetic intent.

42. Joseph Riddell, "Decentering the Image: The 'Project' of 'American' Poetics?" in *Textual Strategies: Perspectives in Post-Structuralist Criticism*, ed. Josué Harari (Ithaca, N.Y.: Cornell Univ. Press, 1979), 325–45.

43. Kristeva, 79.

44. Lewis, *Letters of Wyndham Lewis*, ed. W. K. Rose (London: Methuen, 1963), 552. This is what Lewis had hoped *Tarr* (written in the same year as *Enemy of the Stars*) would be.

45. Hugh Kenner, *Wyndham Lewis: The Makers of Modern Literature* (London: Methuen, 1954), 16.

46. Lewis, *Rude Assignment*, 129.

47. Lewis, *Letters*, 69.

48. Lewis, *Rude Assignment*, 129.

49. Wyndham Lewis, *Blasting and Bombardiering* (London: Eyre & Spottiswoode, 1937), 35.

50. Christopher Nevinson, *The Studio*, Dec. 1919.

51. Malevich, "The Problems of Art and the Role of Its Suppressors," *Essays on Art*, 1:49.

Jay Bochner

New York Secession

In an essay attempting to define Modernism Richard
Poirier has written: "Modernism happened when reading got to be
grim."[1] Poirier is referring to certain Modernists, Eliot and Joyce notably,
and while we might lengthen his list, to include Mallarmé for example,
it is clear that he is evolving his definition from the difficult and essentially
self-reflexive work of a very specific group, the great Modernists of
English Literature. But for many of us, Modernism antedates the grim
writers of Axel's castle, even in the English-speaking world. In particular,
there were artists and writers working in New York who embodied
many of the aspects of Modernism but who resisted the artistic isolation
that leads to grim art. They sensed, early on, a trap well described by
Raymond Williams in his *Culture and Society*: "The positive consequence
of the idea of art as a superior reality was that it offered an immediate
basis for an important criticism of industrialism. The negative consequence
was that it tended, as both the situation and the opposition hardened,
to isolate art, to specialize the imaginative faculty to this one kind of
activity, and thus to weaken the dynamic function which Shelley proposed
for it."[2] This group, loosely associated under the aegis of the photographer
Alfred Stieglitz, drew its energy from a fledgling modern society for
which they entertained hopes so high that few citizens of the democracy
could fulfill them. As the century advanced these resolutely American
Modernists attempted to maintain a strong, to them necessary, link
between modern art and modern society; their secession was aimed at
the bourgeois's betrayal of the modernity from which he made his living.

When Alfred Stieglitz declared his "Photo-Secession" in 1902, he went, in various ways, further than had his predecessors in Vienna, Munich, and Berlin, for he was rebelling against much more than official schools. Such organizations in America as the Camera Club and the New York National Academy of Design had much less authority than their counterparts in Europe because culture itself in America had no power. The lineage of tradition and culture embodied in the official associations in Europe did not exist in America, and thus institutions here represented something much more superficial, the *pretense* of culture, a conventional veneer intended to give the American elite a sense of not being entirely devoid of European sophistication and intelligence. Stieglitz did not have to compete with an authentic, official, and well-rooted culture for an audience, but actually had to convince a mercantile society that art had any value at all beyond being a proof of gentility. It is one of the major paradoxes of American society that the Puritans should bequeath it a spirituality that could be assuaged by sitting-room sentimentality and appear unsullied by profits at any human cost.

In a cropped image of a gelding in harness entitled *Spiritual America* Stieglitz indicated Victorian society's obsession with a disembodied spirituality designed to obliterate its sexuality and economic aggression. Mark Twain had greeted the new century thus: "I bring you the state nation named Christendom, returning, bedraggled, besmirched and dishonored, from pirate raids in the Kiao-Chou, Manchuria, South Africa and the Philippines, with her soul full of meanness, her pocket full of boodle, and her mouth full of hypocrisies. Give her soap and a towel, but hide the looking-glass."[3] The academic painter provided soap for the profit-taker's parlor; but Stieglitz proposed, at least as part of his program, the looking-glass. The metaphor is particularly apt in that, until Stieglitz, photographs with pretensions to art had been variously doctored, through the use of soft focus and the application of ink or paint to negative or print, in order to approximate the appearance of painting. Stieglitz led the fight for straight photography, insisting on clarity and definition, the image as most immediately and best rendered by his machine.

It is remarkable that the American Secession should begin with a machine, the camera. In *The City of Ambition, 1910* (fig. 1) we have a mechanically produced work of art portraying the American engineer's dream. The tall, sleek buildings of capitalism tower over a somewhat more human-scaled ferry and port, but smoke as they do, as if the whole city were a factory. The scene is backlit; it appears to be early morning, so the buildings are in semidarkness, somewhat spectral, yet massive,

Alfred Stieglitz, *The City of Ambition, 1910*. National Gallery of Art, Washington: Alfred Stieglitz Collection. (Fig. 1)

while the sun illumines the chimney smoke and the glittering water. There is a sense of great bustle and energy, yet with no human figures. The tip of a railing in the foreground and a wharf on the right which has the effect of a bridge link the city to the viewer and enhance a classical perspective of progressive depth and height. The camera-eye rests at ground level, but is forced to scan upward over a scene no European artist ever saw in land- or cityscape. The slowly rising majesty of tall mountains, with their peaks miles off in the distance, have nothing in common with the abruptly vertical, geometric masses of these buildings built by and filled with unknown people. The viewer pauses over the shimmering water; the exalted city beckons.

In Stieglitz's hands the machine was turned on itself, to show itself. In *The Hand of Man* of 1902 (fig. 2) the locomotive bears down, spewing its filth over a grimy and barren landscape. Can we imagine the merchant's wife hanging this print, or the previous one, in her home, next to the ubiquitous *Death and the Maiden* or a portrait of her virginal daughter? Certainly not, for it is not pretty. Yet it has beautiful movement and determination. The hunched locomotive bears down on a straight line off to the right while the viewer stands to one side, on another track, which is unoccupied and gracefully intertwined with others. This is the perspective of the Secession, standing aside and dissociating itself from commercialism, but still tied to the energy and hope of democracy. In America, commerce replaces authority, and is insidious rather than per-emptory. It makes a slippery adversary. But by accepting the machine as a new and vital development of society, and thus inevitably a part of culture, the Secession was also being subtly aggressive; if the magnate made himself out of machinery and skyscrapers, could he convincingly jettison all that baggage when it came time to look cultured? The portrayal of machinery in art at this juncture in American history strikes me as a *dare* to the buyer, a challenge to hang the looking-glass.

Of course Stieglitz's 291 was a small enough gallery that few buyers were confronted with such a dare. Most modern art was bought by only a few, possessors of advanced and well-primed minds. When the Armory Show opened in 1913 the almost machine-like *Nude Descending a Staircase*, termed by one artist "Staircase Descending a Nude,"[4] was the work that caused the greatest furor; but there was no machinery at the Armory show, nor was there any photography. The prospective buyer was not challenged by American modernity since all the Modernist work was foreign, and radical in another context. Picabia only discovered his machinist style after arriving in New York, where he was struck by

Alfred Stieglitz, *The Hand of Man* (1902). National Gallery of Art, Washington: Alfred Stieglitz Collection. (Fig. 2)

the city's naked, mechanical life, quite lacking in the tempering effects of hundreds of years of unyielding tradition. In an interview in 1915 he declared: "This visit to America ... has brought about a complete revolution in my methods of work. ... Almost immediately ... it flashed on me that the genius of the modern world is in machinery and that through machinery art ought to find a most vivid expression."[5] Thus the joyous yet cynical drawing of machines for the magazine *291*, Stieglitz's one venture into dada—or pre-dada, since we are in 1915 and the term has yet to be coined. Picabia's *Portrait d'une jeune fille américaine dans l'état de nudité* (fig. 3) portrays an *allumeuse* or tease, or flirt (to be precise, a sparkplug is called a "bougie allumeuse"). Picabia's modifications are usually sexual: in this case the brand name has been changed to "Forever," indicating that American girls require too much commitment. The thread is perfectly horizontal, thus this *allumeuse* does not screw; the pun is mine, but I think the visual message is the same. I doubt that the area the spark jumps is correct, but I have no interpretation for that modification. In any case, this is not quite meant as art, but rather caricature in which people are represented as machines relieved of their intended functions. A few touches render the object useless while, at the same time, its relation to sexuality is humorously heightened. In his portrait of Stieglitz (fig. 4) used for a cover of *291*, Picabia portrayed the man who makes art with a machine by this same machine as it fails to attain its "ideal." The bellows are broken off from the lens and hang limp, which has been interpreted sexually, but is usually interpreted, with the help of biographical evidence, to mean that Picabia was *chiding* the photographer for thinking about closing *291* before the job of bringing art to Americans was finished. Presumably this was no time to stop, as symbolized in the lifted hand brake and gearshift in neutral, or "au point mort."[6] The irony of the image seems counterbalanced by the inscription, *Ici, c'est ici Stieglitz, foi et amour,* where the reiterated *ici* underlines Stieglitz's presence in the battle.

The next stage came when Picabia gave up slightly modified or composite machines for almost entirely imaginary ones. In *Voilà Elle,* (fig. 5) an early example of avant-garde poetry and drawing together, there is a definite relation between his completely obscure mechanisms and Marius de Zayas's visual text. Joined at the bottom by "Elle," and "voilà Elle," the two pages share a general stiffened motion from bottom left toward upper right. Both are made of pieces tenuously linked, so that the eye wanders arbitrarily, trying to puzzle out such and such a detail or the relevance of one phrase to another. De Zayas's "Femme"

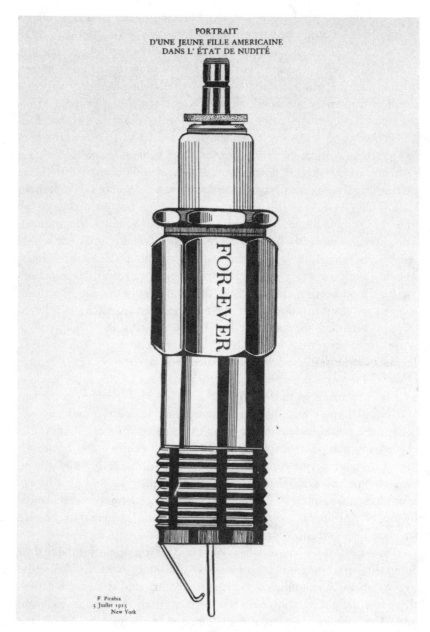

Francis Picabia, *Portrait d'une jeune fille américaine dans l'état de nudité*, from *291*, nos. 5–6 (1915). Philadelphia Museum of Art: The Louise and Walter Arensberg Collection. (Fig. 3)

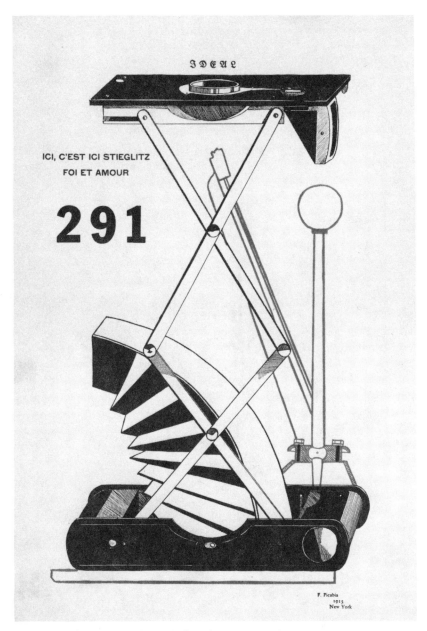

Francis Picabia, *Ici, c'est ici Stieglitz, foi et amour*, from *291*, nos. 5–6 (1915). Philadelphia Museum of Art: The Louise and Walter Arensberg Collection. (Fig. 4)

Marius de Zayas, *Elle*, and Francis Picabia, *Voilà Elle*, double page from *291*, no. 9 (1915). Philadelphia Museum of Art: The Louise and Walter Arensberg Collection. (Fig. 5)

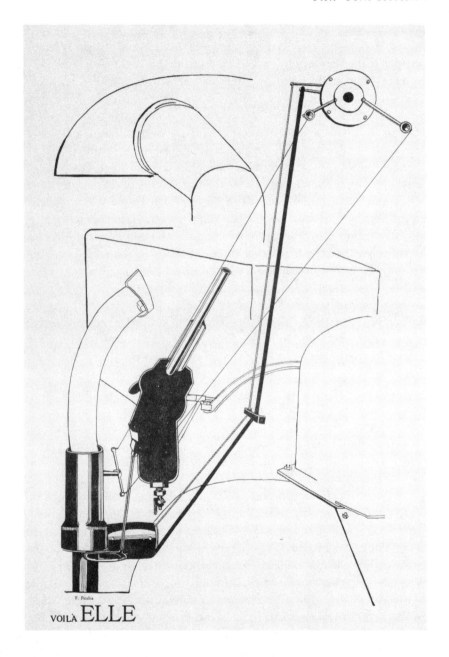

F. Picabia

VOILÀ ELLE

is quite the opposite of our spark plug, as she lives only for pleasure in any and all places, so well separated from social demands that I wonder if the text would have passed censorship in English. The male is represented pretty much entirely by the word "Huluberlu" which holds the center; thus the woman of the portrait is quite dependent upon this crank, or clown. This is a poem composed, or recomposed, after its words were set in type, to go a step beyond mechanical transcription, while one old relic of handwriting survives in a corner. William Camfield suggests what he terms a "sexual" interpretation for the Picabia drawing, with a female target near the top and the object left of center a gun aimed at her.[7] Almost all of Picabia's machinery was purposely erotic, appropriately uncovering the Victorian's displaced sexual energy; however, I find this drawing more obscure. The gun, if that is what it is, will miss the target; it has a three-dimensional, rounded barrel but a flat cross-section of a handle, which doesn't look at all like a handle anyway. The target/disk is both held and manipulated by wires running to the piping at lower left. It seems more likely that we are being led on; since the machine appears to be able to do something, we search for its function. Picabia pursues the logic of the machine's failure, but onto a highly intellectualized plane where the Secessionists, not really that amused by their relation to industry, could usually not follow.

An aristocractic artist well steeped in the European tradition, Picabia uses machinery with irony on his way to dadaism. For him the machine was a means in his fight against art. For the American Secessionists, on the other hand, the machine was the very foundation of society as they had to know it, and it had to serve, very seriously, in the founding of an indigenous art. An artist whose work seems to resemble Picabia's was Morton Schamberg, who was also a photographer. But there is no dadaist mockery in Schamberg, and less humor than fancy and delight. Here we are dealing with machines rendered into art. Shorn of connection to anything (all his machines are well isolated in the middle of the picture), they are immobilized. Whether they are real or invented remains to be shown; most recent criticism tends to see them as real, but the viewer can only consider their intrinsic beauty. They have weight, while Picabia's of this period are more sketchy or schematic; they do not bewilder the viewer, but are rather calm, even friendly. The crash of machinery is stilled. The coloring of *Painting IX (Machine)* (fig. 6), for example, enhances the idea that this machine might be on vacation and not so inhuman after all. Marcel Duchamp, on the other hand, could be both dadaist and relevant, if only by virtue of his knack for scandal.

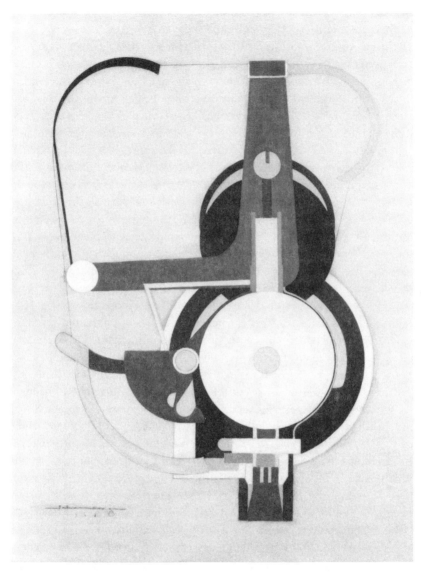

Morton Schamberg, *Painting IX (Machine)* (1916). Oil on canvas, 30⅛ × 22¾″.
Yale University Art Gallery: Collection Société Anonyme. (Fig. 6)

The famous *Fountain* photographed by Stieglitz appeared to its first audience in the *Blind Man*, since the Independent Artists' Exhibition of 1917 had refused to show it; it was deemed both vulgar, or immoral, and a plagiarism. The jury read very well this perfect secession; it dispossesses industry of its product by changing its context, from bathroom to art show, and puts the bodily functions back in view. In this last sense it can be seen as the counterpart of Stieglitz's gelded *Spiritual America*. Shortly after Duchamp created, so to speak, his fountain, Schamberg joined plumbing and carpentry in his *God* of 1918. The title is perhaps excessive, but may refer to the two elements of his assemblage as gods in America. The text defending R. Mutt, presumed creator of *Fountain*, in the *Blind Man* ends: "The only works of art America has given are her plumbing and her bridges."[8] The terms for these objects in Schamberg's sculpture, mitre-box and plumbing trap, or mitre and trap, may lead us further. Both Duchamp's and Schamberg's appropriated objects have been modified: the urinal is on its back, and a sink trap should more likely be underneath, to catch.

However, these were dead ends for the Secession, whose true revolution lay in artistic resistance, whereas dada was beyond art altogether; it could be enlisted in the struggle against puritanism but could not remain a permanent objective in a context where, for the likes of Stieglitz, no serious art yet existed. Stieglitz was not attempting to demolish culture, as his European friends felt obliged to, but rather, through proselytizing and experimentation, to bring America around to authentic, independent, and craftsmanlike artwork. This required moving outside of the buy-and-sell cycle, yet somehow not abandoning the prime goal. In the *Blind Man* Stieglitz penned the suggestion that paintings at the Independents' should not be signed, the purchasers to find out only after they had acquired the work who the painter was. In this way, wrote Stieglitz, "the Society would not be playing into the hands of dealers." "The public would be purchasing its own reality and not a commercialized and inflated name."[9] This attempt at removing oneself from the center of the American action can be seen in most of the artists of the period. For the ash-can school it took the form of looking directly at the seamy side of life, under the el as it were. They changed the subject, and were much denounced. However, the Modernist can be more interesting in that his intention can be reflected in the manner of seeing, so that the very structure of the work secedes from the previously acceptable. In his painting *The Wake of the Ferry, II* of 1907 (fig. 7), John Sloan breaks up the stormy scene with the dark beams of the ferry. He cuts

John Sloan, *The Wake of the Ferry, II* (1907). Oil on canvas, 26 × 32″. The Phillips Collection, Washington, D.C. (Fig. 7)

the presumed scene up, breaks the illusion that the boats in the distance should hold our interest, and brings us closer to the figure of the woman at the right and the ferry we are on, even though we see so little of it. We only know we are rocking as we leave something or someplace behind. It is a painting remarkable for its lack of content, except for the framing forms. An accordion fence further separates us from what we are leaving. A similar division of the image is effected in Stieglitz's *Going to the Post, Morris Park, 1904* (fig. 8), which is even more radical in terms of composition since the sustaining beam goes right up the middle of the frame. Other girders at the top and shadowed spectators at the bottom continue the framing. Rather than a separation of foreground and background, here we have separation of left from right, since all the horses run on the left. The viewer's eye keeps landing in that empty half-ellipse of track, as if the picture lacked something there. Both of these pictures show a removal from the great, fine subject, a development which is discussed at some length in Peter Galassi's *Before Photography*. The artist becomes the victim—but the willing victim—of his position vis-à-vis his subject; he can no longer compose his picture, only take it, as Galassi has it.[10] The array of objects arranged in progressively distant planes, with the prime, glorious object of one's interest occupying a well-calibrated position within the perspective, disappears in favor of what appears to be available. The monument barely peeks out in the distance from behind a myriad of impoverished buildings because we could not find a better place to stand. Though this would seem an attribute of photography, which would thus become *per force* a tool of democratization, Galassi shows that many painters, usually minor ones, chose similar arrangements for their material. Everett Shinn was a popular painter of theatricals and dancing girls, all suffused with the bright, delicate light of his master Degas. In *The Orchestra Pit, Old Proctor's Fifth Avenue Theatre* (ca. 1906) (fig. 9) however, his alluring girls on the stage are behind and cropped, while the center of the picture is occupied by the back of a head. We don't see what instrument this man is playing, and we are further separated from the stage and from him by a curtain. This is a dramatic break with the portrayal of a period's light pleasures, rendered via the presumed bad luck of sitting in the wrong seat. The glitter recedes, and we contemplate our unprivileged position. The contingent point of view of these last three pictures ruins the fine topic and focuses on the broad, abstract structures that limit our view.

While Galassi insists that painters did this before photographers,

Alfred Stieglitz, *Going to the Post, Morris Park, 1904*. National Gallery of Art, Washington: Alfred Stieglitz Collection. (Fig. 8)

Everett Shinn, *The Orchestra Pit, Old Proctor's Fifth Avenue Theatre* (c. 1906–7). Oil on canvas, $17\frac{7}{16} \times 19\frac{1}{12}''$. Collection of Mr. and Mrs. Arthur G. Altschul. (Fig. 9)

the photographer was certainly more apt to feel the pressure of his medium. Even a photographer like Lewis Hine, who seems to have paid little or no attention to composition in his documentary portraits of slum dwellers and new immigrants, could find himself with a negative in which space became structured in dramatic ways; thus *Boys at Work, Manchester, N. H.* (1909), in which most of the picture is in darkness, and a boy's head rests embedded inside the machinery at the right, almost hidden because of the other, more highly contrasted figures and machines. In another instance one of Hine's familiar figures, the young paper boy, *Danny Mercurio* (1912) (fig. 10) is surrounded by the cleanliness and order of Washington, D.C. The heavy matron caught stalking awkwardly off to the left is separated from the spunky Italian boy by a great deal of pavement and class, a distance increased by their respective gaits, the boy's easy stroll toward the camera and the matron's rigid arm and stiff kick, as it were, at the frame of the picture. The street boy is perfect center of this image; considering his small size and classical composition's abhorrence of the static center, he is drastically central, a sort of island of spunk in the wide, rational city, while the dark, veiled bourgeoise has been pushed back to the margin. She may well be miffed at the camera's rejection of her importance; in any case the left edge constantly upsets the picture's balance, as it is difficult for the eye to encompass the boy and the woman at the same time.

Despite such successes as these Hine generally paid little attention to structure, preferring to pose his subjects in clear lighting, matter-of-factly facing the camera in what would have to be called today a *cinéma-vérité* style. Stieglitz, on the other hand, always structured his images and aimed at the full artistic exploitation of his medium. His first interest was not to record, but to make photography an art, and in order to do so he wanted to explore its possibilities. He was first to photograph scenes in rain, in snowstorms, and at night. In such experiments he met face-on the problem of available light, and solved it while never sacrificing composition. The first expectation of photography, the reason some supposed painting was finished, was that it would render every detail perfectly. This meant, as a corollary, that it could leave nothing out. Stieglitz would accept the degree of chance, but also wait hours for other elements to compose themselves as he wanted them. He thus struck a balance between controlled form and uncontrollable contingency. In the Vermeer-like scene of *Sun Rays—Paula, 1889* (fig. 11), as the title indicates, the window blinds have cast a whole different light over an otherwise ordinary, if not sentimental, image. Though the impressionist

Lewis Hine, *Danny Mercurio* (1912). International Museum of Photography at George Eastman House. (Fig. 10)

Alfred Stieglitz, *Sun Rays—Paula, 1889*. National Gallery of Art, Washington: Alfred Stieglitz Collection. (Fig. 11)

might have given as much importance to the lighting here, Stieglitz, without the advantage of color, has done something quite different and new. The scene has been overcome, flattened into abstract bands repeated in various tones on the window, table, and walls, as well as on the wicker chair and the birdcage, where the pattern is further complicated. The figure, tablecloth, and room as a whole have volume but in large areas of the picture the light works against volume. It gives prominence to the candle, which is already ribbed and set against an unlit, rather extravagant wallpaper. The paraphernalia on the wall is massed together against the dark paper but also broken by the strips of light. The sentimentality and nostalgia of the photographs and ribboned hearts here fade before the structural massing. Further, the whole photograph is a band of light across the middle of the frame, with top and bottom lost in darkness. Stieglitz has waited and worked for the precise quality of this light, the moment it could dominate the picture and restructure its banalities, yet not obliterate its objects, which include photographic portraits very different from his own.

It is a commonplace that the literal art of photography freed the painter for nonrepresentation. Certainly this is true for the Stieglitz circle, and Marin, among others, was termed "anti-photographic" in the pages of *Camera Work*, that term being taken to mean "conscious of the existence of photography." Stieglitz encouraged this distancing by constant comparison, if not confrontation, as his numerous shows of paintings at 291 witness. The most adventurous works at the Armory Show, an almost abstract sketch by Picasso and the sole abstraction of the show, by Kandinsky, were both acquired by Stieglitz. However, photography also had a more direct role to play in abstraction, via, for example, the same sort of play of light discussed above. In *Abstraction, Porch Shadows, Twin Lakes, Connecticut, 1916* (fig. 12) Paul Strand shot from so close, and at such an angle, that he had to name the object in his double title. Of course the geometries of buildings and machines lent themselves, if not exactly to abstraction, then at least to a shift toward radical form. Such semi-abstraction made a virtue of the photographer's restricted angle of vision; and the restriction could be sought after, to render the object strange and structure mass and light with the barest nod to representation. There is another version of *Porch Shadows*, taken perhaps twenty minutes later, in which the triangle of light at bottom right cuts a swathe clear across the white surface, and the picture has been cropped at the top to remove the pieces of wood that provided some sense of perspective. With the viewer's loss of bearings, imitation becomes abstraction. Strand's famous *Wall Street, New York, 1915* (fig. 13) shows

Paul Strand, *Abstraction, Porch Shadows, Twin Lakes, Connecticut, 1916.*
Copyright © 1982 The Paul Strand Foundation, Millerton, N.Y. (Fig. 12)

Paul Strand, *Wall Street, New York, 1915*. Copyright © 1971, 1976, as published in *Paul Strand: Sixty Years of Photographs*, Aperture, Millerton, N.Y., 1976. (Fig. 13)

the balance, or perhaps tension, the Secession could achieve between an abstract play of light and volume and social comment. Figures have entered the scene as strictly minor elements, while most of the space is given over to the heavy shadows of stone monitoring their progress. The people are few in number and dispersed, while the building is monolithic and even rational. The perfectly aligned, negative masses in the building so dominate the picture that it seems the figures, also black but small and irregular, are being chastised for some sort of waywardness.

No matter how abstract the photograph became it had to maintain some relation to objects. In fact, the more abstract the image the more solid and palpable its components collected from reality. Abstraction in photography brings out texture, for example the stone in Strand's *Wall Street*. What photography could do less easily was permit the imagination to distort and recombine the objects of reality, to make them thus less solid and secure. Instead of Strand's massive oppression, *Wall Street Stock Exchange* (1924) by John Marin (fig. 14), realistic enough in its facade, appears no more than that—a facade. The frame of the scene is irregular and contracted, and the buildings seem to crash together and explode out the top, their tenuousness enhanced by watercolors. They have power but no cohesiveness. These two renderings of Wall Street make a remarkable contrast, one which we can translate into contrary critiques of the economy; we are oppressed by Strand's image, cannot restrain Marin's. His work seems enthusiastic but it is hard to tell the direction of its energy. His *Brooklyn Bridge* (1910) (fig. 15) is splitting up but also pulling everything into its center. The figures seem to advance confidently enough, and the general rumpled look is rather friendly, particularly with the two outboard streetlamps. The way across this bridge, which was soon to become Crane's symbol of modernity in America, appears difficult, certainly, yet not uninviting. Marin portrays a chaotic energy to which the camera has no access by reducing buildings to elements and lines the camera cannot draw (since the photograph has no lines at all, to be anti-photographic would be, precisely, to draw lines that are not illusions of reality). After Rimbaud's drunken boat and a few years before Cendrars's drunken train of *The Prose of the Transsiberian* we have Marin's drunken bridge, man enmeshed in his creation, attempting to stave off reification. Marin's buildings are always going in two or more different directions at once, collapsing down through the pavements and flinging themselves upward. Nothing goes to the edge, so the buildings are mainly bits and pieces that fly up and back, tottering, or squeezing into the picture. His various Woolworth

John Marin, *Wall Street Stock Exchange* (1924). Watercolor. Collection of Mr. David M. Solinger. (Fig. 14)

John Marin, *Brooklyn Bridge* (1910). Watercolor, 18½ × 15½″. Metropolitan Museum of Art: The Alfred Stieglitz Collection, 1949. (Fig. 15)

buildings particularly are monuments to a five-and-dime society. I reproduce his cover for *291*, no. 4 (1915) (fig. 16), possibly another
rendition of the Woolworth. More contraction into the middle, no frame,
buildings barely outlined in short, unfinished strokes, no top at all to
the highest structure. What holds the buildings together is the way they
seem to huddle away from the edges of the paper.

The requirement Ezra Pound set for modern, imagist poetry, that
it live "close to the thing," might seem at first a far remove from what
Marin was doing. Indeed, a call for images that were "clean," "sharp-
edged," and "dry," to replace the late romantics' "fuzzy," "gummy,"
and "wet"[11] approaches to representation reminds us of Stieglitz's insistence
upon straight photography. No doubt Pound's dichotomy translates
poorly to other media; Marin's shattered objects are not clear, but they
are dealt with clearly. A Secessionist poet like William Carlos Williams
similarly combined the photographer's close-up attention to the thing
at a precise moment of illumination with the modern painter's dismemberment of his means, or syntax. When Williams read "Overture to a
Dance of Locomotives"—probably at the very same Independents' Exhibition of 1917 that rejected Duchamp's urinal[12]—his listeners could
not see what he had done to his line. Words before and after make
sense of "of those coming to be carried quicken a,"[13] but for the book-
reader Williams has insisted upon a break-up. We must read precariously.
What was once a line, or a breath, slips away into the next, which in
turn may send us back to the first for a reconstruction. "Spouts" begins:

> In this world of
> as fine a pair of breasts
> as I ever saw
> the fountain in
> Madison Square
> spouts up of water
> a white tree . . .[14]

This is perhaps less a break with syntax than a purposely disconcerting
breach of the syntactical contract. Each short, unfinished line finds its
surprise in the next, as Williams meshes commonplaces with sensuous
but seemingly unrelated objects. In its larger outlines the poem is a
closely-photographed film in which the eye's angle of vision is drastically
narrowed down, as in Strand's *Porch Shadows*, and forced to follow
the delicate movements of the water before being allowed to draw back
and see the fountain as a whole. And, as each line moves us about this
magnified, sensualized event with openings such as "spouts up," "turns

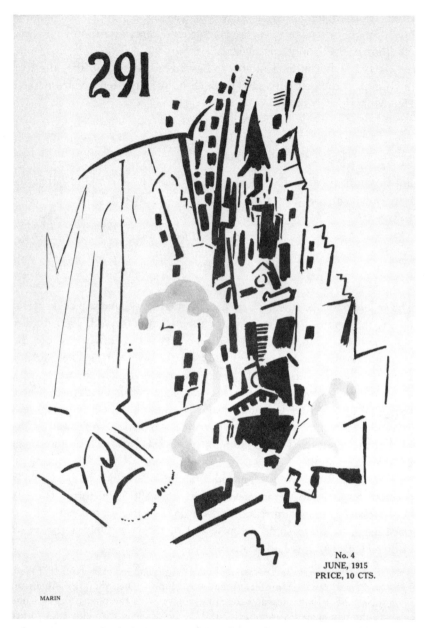

John Marin, Cover for *291*, no. 4 (1915). Probably the Woolworth Building. Philadelphia Museum of Art: The Louise and Walter Arensberg Collection. (Fig. 16)

from," "back upon," "and rising," and "reflectively drops," the illogical but stunning breasts linger in the background, a juxtaposition with some fabulous and enticing contingency.

In "Drink" (1916) a man searches for roots, gropes for some sort of solidity combined with savor, which he sees in groves of fruit trees. His drinking is akin to

> The wild cherry
> continually pressing back
> peach orchards.

But this appears to be the wrong place to look; he will find his strength, roots, body in the tall sexual buildings of the shining city:

> My stuff
> is the feel of good legs
> and a broad pelvis
> under golden hair ornaments
> of skyscrapers.[15]

The sequentiality of such a poem is manipulated for an effect of dispersal during the reading and surprising juxtaposition in the end. The building is humanized, rendered sexual and even loved; the body soars into the sky. Williams's short lines, huddled on the white page like Marin's paintings, leave us expectant, but make us see the objects unfettered, or propose uncommon ways of perceiving linguistically unadorned, simple things; thus the opening line of the celebrated "The Great Figure," "Among the rain," or later the two lines "in gold / on a red." The object, the thing itself, is re-illuminated via this sustained displacement of our expectations.

Marin's *Brooklyn Bridge* and Williams's "Drink" both exhibit a form of fragmentation that nevertheless has centripetal force. The city is aggressive, but not intractable. Ever so tentatively both painter and poet begin to carve some promise out of the city. Only a few years earlier Henry Adams had written:

> Nearly forty years had passed since the ex–private secretary landed at New York with the ex-Ministers Adam and Motley, when they saw American society as a long caravan stretching out towards the plains. As he came up the bay again, November 5, 1904, an older man than either his father or Motley in 1868, he found the approach more striking than ever— wonderful—unlike anything man had ever seen—and like nothing he had ever much cared to see. The outline of the city became frantic in its effort to explain something that defied meaning. Power seemed to have outgrown its servitude and to have asserted its freedom. The cylinder had exploded,

and thrown great masses of stone and steam against the sky. The city had the air and movement of hysteria, and the citizens were crying, in every accent of anger and alarm, that the new forces must at any cost be brought under control. Prosperity never before imagined, power never yet wielded by man, speed never reached by anything but a meteor, had made the world irritable, nervous, querulous, unreasonable and afraid.[16]

This was the first city of modernity, which the Secession chose to wrestle with on the terms of modernity. They faced the machine head-on, by showing its intrinsic beauty or by subverting it. They reframed it, or used it to split the frame and corner the human element as it seemed to them cornered by technology and commerce. They focused down so closely as to sever the object from its function; they atomized it, and reconstituted it in some pristine, unexploited relationship to the body. While they initiated most of the means of High Modernism they put them at the service of the dynamic exchange with industrialism that Raymond Williams sees as their necessary challenge.

Stieglitz's famous *Steerage, 1907* (fig. 17) is composed of broad, powerful lines. The gangway radically separates the two groups of immigrants with an empty but central shining passage. The funnel, boom, and staircase compress the frame, though the gangway cuts through the middle of their triangle. The boom hems down the figures above, which are mainly dark, while there are lighter figures, mainly women, dispersed below. A flimsy triangle of poles supports the gangway. Stieglitz set particular value on the round white hat above on a man peering down on the group below, and on the crossed suspenders isolated against the large dark area. He wrote: "I stood spellbound for a while. I saw shapes related to one another—a picture of shapes, and underlying it, a new vision that held me: simple people; the feeling of ship, ocean, sky; a sense of release that I was away from the mob called 'rich.' "[17]

In this image Stieglitz builds new, already cubist forms, yet clearly embraces a social function. The Secession had to work with modernity but not sell out to it. So Stieglitz wrote of himself: "He is a workman who has been all his life on a strike."[18]

Alfred Stieglitz, *The Steerage, 1907.* National Gallery of Art, Washington: Alfred Stieglitz Collection. (Fig. 17)

Notes

1. Richard Poirier, "The Difficulties of Modernism and the Modernism of Difficulty," in *Images and Ideas in American Culture: The Function of Criticism*, ed. Arthur Edelstein (Hanover, N. H.: Brandeis Univ. Press, 1979), 125.

2. Raymond Williams, *Culture and Society, 1780–1950* (London: Chatto & Windus, 1960), 43.

3. Twain, in the *New York Herald*, 30 Dec. 1900, quoted in Howard Mumford Jones, *The Age of Energy: Varieties of Experience, 1865–1915* (New York: Viking, 1971), 212–13.

4. Gutzon Borglum, quoted in Milton Brown, *The Story of the Armory Show* (Greenwich, Conn.: Joseph H. Hirshhorn Foundation, 1963), 110. Borglum was a very well-known sculptor and an organizer of the Armory Show (though he resigned a few weeks before its opening).

5. Interview entitled "French Artists Spur on American Art," *New York Tribune*, 24 Oct. 1915, sec. 4, p. 2, quoted in K. G. Pontus Hultén, *The Machine as Seen at the End of the Mechanical Age* (New York: Museum of Modern Art, 1968), 83.

6. See Abraham A. Davidson, *Early American Modernist Painting, 1910–1935* (New York: Harper & Row, 1981), 80, for his discussion of analyses by Dickran Tashjian, William Camfield, and William I. Homer.

7. William A. Camfield, "The Machinist Style of Francis Picabia," *Art Bulletin* 48 (Sept.-Dec. 1966): 315.

8. *The Blind Man* 2 (May 1917): 5.

9. Ibid., 15.

10. Peter Galassi, *Before Photography: Painting and the Invention of Photography* (New York: Museum of Modern Art, 1981), 17.

11. As cited by James E. Breslin, *William Carlos Williams: An American Artist* (New York: Oxford Univ. Press, 1970), 33–34. The adjectives are attributed jointly to Pound and T. E. Hulme.

12. Paul Mariani, *Williams Carlos Williams: A New World Naked* (New York: McGraw-Hill, 1981), 106.

13. Williams, *The Collected Earlier Poems* (New York: New Directions, 1951), 194. First published in *Sour Grapes* (1921).

14. Williams, 222. First published in *Sour Grapes* (1921).

15. Williams, 140. "Drink" first appeared in *Others* for July 1916, an issue edited by Williams.

16. *The Education of Henry Adams* (New York: Random House, 1946), 499.

17. Quoted in Dorothy Norman, *Alfred Stieglitz: An American Seer* (New York: Random House, 1973), 76.

18. Quoted in Evelyn Howard, "The Significance of Stieglitz for the Philosophy of Science," in *America and Alfred Stieglitz: A Collective Portrait*, ed. Waldo Frank, Lewis Mumford, Dorothy Norman, Paul Rosenfeld, and Harold Rugg (New York: Literary Guild, 1934), 199.

Renée Riese Hubert

Paul Klee: Modernism in Art and Literature

Although Klee wrote an important essay on modern art, critics prefer other painters, notably Picasso, Kandinsky, and Ernst, to establish the characteristics of and provide a basis for modernism. We may wonder to what extent such choices are arbitrary and whether Klee has the credentials to become a model of modernism. Apollinaire, soon to be followed by Breton, Reverdy, Jacob, and Eluard, saw in Picasso the very incarnation of "l'Esprit nouveau,"[1] which requires above all a complete break with the past, the *sine qua non* for the formulation of a new theory of art or a radically new way of dealing with the problem of representation. Abundantly endowed with the courage to reject the past and with the ability to discover or invent something shockingly new, Picasso assumed heroic stature in their eyes and therefore could serve as a model and a leader for all artists, even those whose creative endeavors had goals widely divergent from his own. "We also know," argues Suzi Gablik, "since the shift into Modernism, that progress in art is not made, as once was thought, by the accumulation of knowledge within existing categories: it is made by leaps into new categories or systems."[2]

Modernism, beginning with Baudelaire, not only questions the past but stresses the importance of the new, the present moment as distinct from any others. "Le plaisir que nous retirons de la représentation du présent tient, non seulement à la beauté dont il est peut-être revêtu, mais aussi à sa qualité essentielle de présent" (The pleasure which we derive from the representation of the present is not only due to the beauty with which it can be invested, but also to its essential quality of being present).[3] Baudelaire, in *Le Peintre de la vie moderne*, refers to the tensions between the invariable, the eternal, and the changing, contemporary present in every work of art. Picasso belongs indeed among those artists who put the greater stress on the present moment, as throughout his career he has constantly surpassed his own artistic discoveries.

In comparison to Picasso, Klee did not find many advocates among writers, though two surrealists, Crevel and Vitrac, wrote penetrating essays on his work, the former focusing on his transformation of the world, problems pertinent to this study.[4] Neither Crevel nor Vitrac described Klee as an adventurer. The Bauhaus teacher did not seek a break with the past, proclaim discontinuity, or openly oppose the institutions of his day. Klee's modernism, less prone than Picasso's to political and social attitudes, owes very little to the exigencies of a given historical moment.

Klee's deep attachment to German romanticism, as opposed to Max Ernst's ironical manipulations of romantic practices, or the cubists' lack of reference to that period, sets him apart from other modernists. Holderlin's concept of poetry, Goethe's idea of nature, and Novalis's conception of cosmic unity made a lasting impact on the twentieth-century painter. They constitute the matrix, though not always easily detectable, for his aspirations.[5] In times of crisis the artist, unable to communicate with his contemporaries, experienced alienation. Herbert Read, in his introduction to Klee's *On Modern Art*, suggests an analogy between Klee and Holderlin: "The final source of power in the artist is given by society, and that is precisely what is lacking in the modern artist."[6] Klee felt the need for an inward drive; he sought communion on a higher level. In spite of his belief in a centered universe, in a unity that could be restored and which was available beyond the fractured surfaces, Klee's views on art and nature diverged from those of the romantics. His allegiance to romanticism, as we shall see, never took the form of nostalgia.

In the "Creative Credo" and *On Modern Art* Klee deals with problems such as the role of artistic creation, the genesis of the work of art, the relation of nature to art, and the basic elements of painting.[7] In *On Modern Art,* product of a Jena conference, he explains his theories to an audience of laymen viewing an exhibition of his works. In the "Creative Credo" he formulates them in terms of a personal act of faith. Both essays provide insights into his own creative process. By stating his artistic theories, which go beyond pure intellectual speculation without following a systematic line of reasoning, he takes stock of himself. He attains lucidity by stages, by means of efforts comparable to those of Paul Valéry in "Les Pas" and "L'Aurore," as well as in some of his critical essays, or those of Wallace Stevens. The artist, according to the "Creative Credo," transforms his experiences, real or imaginary, into pictorial images. The picture does not render these experiences in an immediately recognizable form, but does not completely obliterate them either. The artist, by reducing, channeling, and metamorphosing outer experiences, proceeds on a journey toward the invisible parts of the world.

How do these aspirations manifest themselves in the creative act? The painter states that he has at his disposal dot, line, plane, and space, and that, with the exception of the dot, they represent basic forms of movement, as well as his own gestures. A painting composed of lines and planes becomes an articulation of forms. "Le sens en peinture se définit comme signifiant par le système complexe des éléments plastiques et non par référence aux objets de la perception," says Louis Marin.[8] (In painting meaning is defined as a signifier through the complex system of plastic elements, not as a reference to the objects of perception.) Yet in spite of the absolute rigor of many of his lines and the apparent subordination of representation, formalism never becomes for Klee an end in itself. He argues that forms must be linked to structure and meaning. Thus Klee's practice appears to confirm Gablik's definition of modern art: the "history of art can be seen as a process which has entailed the slow and laborious liberation of forms from their content."[9] Form and content are interrelated in Klee's art though not according to traditional patterns. Form ultimately participates in the demands of a deeper reality. Klee, in his pictorial universe, does not aim at the reaffirmation of an established relation between form and content. "Out of abstract elements a formal cosmos is ultimately created independent of their groupings as concrete objects or abstract things such as numbers or letters."[10] Klee is concerned with both lines and colors, as well as with the passage from forms to subjects. His Jena audience was little accustomed to the notion that the subject or image emerges from the interrelation of formal elements, rather than from models provided by nature or at least by the artist's ideas and imagination.

Klee insists less on the nature of pictorial unity than on the process of creation itself. He gives an account of his experience in the land of deeper insight, narrating not so much a particular adventure as a fundamental quest in deciphering linear constructs that the viewer may behold. Such a journey, captured or recaptured by graphic signs, need not rely on preconceived or *a priori* systems. Linking the accidental to the essential, Klee appeals to chance, advocated by several early twentieth-century avant-garde movements, especially the surrealists, as a means to curtail reason and make everything possible. Chance may lead to the invisible. The first sentence of the "Creative Credo" reads, "Art does not reproduce the visible, it makes visible."

We may well construe Klee's account of his journey to be simultaneous with the commentary or explanation of a painting, the movement generated by its lines, their continuity or lack of continuity, and their interrelation. The narrator's intercourse with the world, his perceptions, his "Stimmung" are transformed into varied graphic expressions: "lines of the most varied kinds, spots, dabs, smooth planes, dotted planes, lined planes, wavy lines, obstructed and articulated movements." The "Creative Credo" links a Weltanschauung uncovered in the course of an inner journey to the discovery of the painter's medium, a conjunction of the creative act with philosophical or critical awareness frequent among modernists from Valéry to Borges and Beckett. In the case of Klee, as with many of his contemporaries, including Picasso and Ernst, the completion of the work of art matters far less than the aspiration toward creation; the act of creation becomes truly fundamental. "Art plays an unknowing game with ultimate things," says Klee, "and yet achieves them." Like Proust, like Picasso, Klee defined art as a metaphor for creation and insisted on process. He showed as little concern as did the surrealists for the notion of a masterpiece, or even of a finished product. Lyotard, speaking of Klee's art in conjunction with his writings, alludes, with a somewhat different terminology, to this process:

> On n'y voit pas, on y travaille. Le trait n'y note pas les signifiants d'un discours, ni les continus d'une silhouette, il est la trace d'une énergie qui déplace, figure, élabore, sans égard au reconnaissable.[11]

> (There is no seeing, there is work in action. The line does not express the signifiers of a discourse, nor the shape of a figure, it is the trace of an energy which displaces, figures, elaborates without taking the recognizable into consideration.)

The work of the artist must be viewed as continuous, as a constant overcoming of stasis, of death, of the "point" or dot as isolated, motionless end. Klee emphasizes energy, vitality. Creation, a moving force that avoids the repetition or reproduction of a model, tends to disassemble and deconstruct it, and although Klee never proposes deconstructive gestures in the manner of Baudelaire's "Mauvais Vitrier," his transformation of a model, namely nature, into art implies not merely metamorphosis, but also transgression. It does not suffice for this artist, as it did for Baudelaire and Delacroix, to read nature as in a dictionary. Nature has lost for the twentieth-century painter that reassuring continuity which the romantics attributed to it and which they sought to emulate. Klee, like other modern artists, expresses his strong awareness of deviations and breaks in artistic creation, but without ever dismissing nature or conceiving of an art completely divorced from it. In his theories and to a certain extent in his paintings he remains attentive to the organic model and its basic functions, viewing them in an open context, for his vision extends beyond the ordinary. The domain that Klee seeks to locate does not violently clash with nature as it does frequently in the works of the surrealists, especially Ernst and Magritte. Klee does not express the same mistrust as those more radical modernists in regard to feeling and perceptions.

Discussion concerning movement naturally leads not only to theories on space but also on time. Klee repeatedly disagrees with Lessing's statement in *Laokoon*, for he questions the validity of a complete separation of art and literature which would relate the visual exclusively to space and the verbal to time. Already in the "Creative Credo" he had advocated as inevitable the orchestration of time and space in the visual arts, to a certain degree equating spatial expansion and growth. In the Jena essay he openly suggests the inferiority of the verbal arts, which do not require such an orchestration. "This is due to the consecutive nature, the only methods available to us for conveying a clear three-dimensional concept of an image in space and results from deficiencies of a temporal nature in the spoken word." The insistence on both spatial expansion and temporal growth leads inevitably to Klee's theory that the viewer cannot grasp a painting at a single glance, that it requires a continuous exposure or reading, a theory that Louis Marin stresses in his essay on the painter:

> A vrai dire, jamais l'expression "lecture d'un tableau" n'a été plus exacte: le tableau se présente comme une page d'un vieux livre, d'un antique grimoire écrit dans une langue et une écriture inconnues.[12]

> (In fact, never was the phrase "reading a painting" used with greater accuracy: the painting stands like a page out of an old book, an ancient scroll written in an unknown language with an unknown writing.)

Marin's method of reading a painting, suggesting a practical approach, is evident throughout Klee's writings. The painter insists on the mobility of the eye as it explores the painting. For Klee the eye is in the painting, in the same way that for Mallarmé it is in the text, and he says in the *Pedagogical Sketchbook* that the eye follows the path that has been prepared for it. Such a path does not reveal itself in any obvious way. Klee, who tends to avoid three-dimensional space, constructs traps or misleads his viewer by false perspective created by intersecting lines, as in *Zimmer Perspective mit Einwohner* (Perspective of a Room with Occupants, 1921 [fig. 1]). Klee in this and other works of art brings the viewer close to the creator, an idea implied in the following quotation from the "Creative Credo": "Occasionally the beholder stops looking and goes away—the artist often does the same thing. If he thinks it worthwhile, he comes back—again like the artist." The analogy between writer and reader, painter and viewer, which in a sense had originated in Baudelaire's "Au Lecteur," recurs in modernist art and literature and attains an even stronger expression in the works of Joyce and Beckett.

In the "Creative Credo" Klee uses the quest, the itinerary, the journey, as a central metaphor to explain the quality of movement governing lines. In *On Modern Art* he further explains the relation of the phenomenal world to art and analyzes the stages of the creative process, suggesting the relationship of art to nature by the metaphor of the tree. He compares the order of nature to the roots, artistic achievement to the leaves. "As in full view of the world, the crown of the tree unfolds and spreads in time and space, so with his word" (13). Both the choice of the tree and itinerary can be detected as recurrent signs in Klee's art. I do not wish to suggest that the painter depicted trees to use them as overt symbols of artistic creation or that any of his paintings narrate his experiences or discoveries. The painter's creative process emerging from the unconscious is fully summarized by Lyotard: "L'art traverse les choses, il porte au delà du réel aussi bien que l'imaginaire"[13] (Art pierces through things, it transports beyond reality as much as the imaginary). In his Jena lecture the painter comments on the creative process as a journey into the recesses of his mind, where the image of the tree alludes to both the visible and the invisible, the conscious and the unconscious, and the slow maturation of the work of art. For his listeners, surrounded by Klee's art, the painter exemplified the transformation by opposing leaves to roots, which, of course, predicates change, movement primarily on the level of creation. The image suggests rejection of mimesis as well as of *ex nihilo* artistic production. The tree's position is humble, and the beauty at its crown is not its own. It is

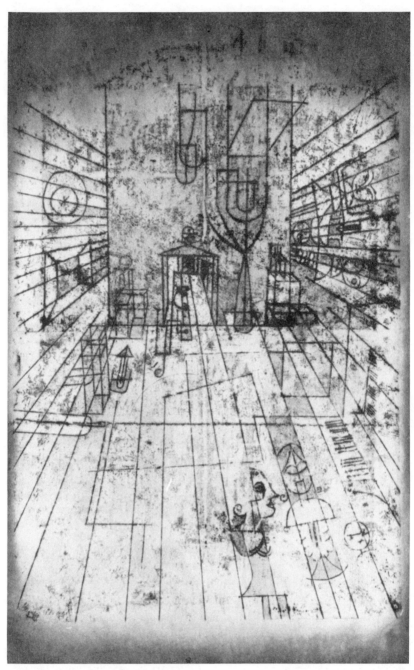

Paul Klee, *Zimmer Perspective mit Einwohner* (Perspective of a Room with Occupants, 1921). © Cosmopress, Geneva, and A.D.A.G.P., Paris, 1985. (Fig. 1)

merely a channel. Lyotard, who also alludes to Klee's image of the tree, comments on this relation but tends to go perhaps too far in separating the two realms:

> Cet objet (le tableau) la nature ne l'a pas produit. Bien loin d'être conforme à son plan, il est dénaturé ou transnaturel. Il atteste que la création excède la nature créée, et que l'artiste est un endroit où elle continue à produire ses fruits. Nature et art sont deux règnes de la création. Mais le second ne dit rien à la première.[14]

> (Nature did not produce that object [the painting]. Far from conforming to its design, it is denatured or transnatural. It attests that creation surpasses created nature and that the artist is a place where it continues to bear fruit. Nature and art are two orders of creation. But the second does not communicate with the first.)

Klee, as I said earlier, never bypasses or dismisses nature, yet he certainly recognized to a large degree the autonomy of both art and nature.

If the metaphor of the tree does not imply complete autonomy of the work of art, it suggests a certain determinism. We detect in Klee's writings, more strongly than in the works of Apollinaire, Picasso, or even Wallace Stevens, the need to attain a certain order. Tensions, dissonances, represent stages to be overcome. This need to establish order, even harmony and equilibrium, might explain why Klee, unlike Picasso or Ernst, rarely created collages, a genre highly representative of modern aesthetics. The aspiration toward order, the need to overcome chaos, entailed a new start, a new discovery in each case, or, to use Gablik's language, a leap into a new category. Rather than reaffirming existing rules, it generated its own by means of its process. In his Jena conference the artist's freedom is affirmed not as a gift, but as acquired by gradual penetration into the inner world. Compared to Picasso's, Klee's modernism seems modest indeed, all the more so because his declarations never become self-assertive. In this context Marjorie Perloff's claim that modernism is a tension between rival strains can help us once more "separate" Picasso from Klee. The following comment would refer to the former rather than to the latter: "Visual artists have consistently resisted the Symbolist model in favor of the creation of a world in which forms can exist 'littéralement et dans tous les sens,' an oscillation between representational reference and compositional game."[15] Klee substitutes an originating gesture for mimesis; this creative gesture on the part of the painter, however, might pertain to a Kantian spatio-temporal *a priori*—an *a priori* that precedes phenomenal impression.

If indeed Klee's two essays, as critics point out, directly reflect his work as a painter, conversely the ideas I have stressed, especially the exploration of the painting by the viewer, should prove to be helpful in reading and decoding specific works of art. I shall at first comment on two pictures which seem almost exclusively formal and which, deprived of their titles, could at first sight be mistaken for abstract paintings.

The oil painting *Architecture* (1923), with the exception of two triangles on the upper part of the picture, consists wholly of rectangles (fig. 2). As the subtitle "Yellow to violet stepped cubes" indicates, the color range is also reduced to a simple scheme: two primary colors (blue and yellow) and two complementary colors (green and purple), relations that Klee discussed in *On Modern Art*. The four shades follow each other in succession on the color scale. The "tones" of the individual rectangles represent variations, shifts, modulations of the basic colors. One rectangle compared to the next is more or less luminous, transparent, opaque or dark. Where do these changes in color come from? No outer light sources determine the patterns: the fluctuations or harmonies come from within. And what causes the different sizes of the rectangles, which vary in elongation and condensation? How are we to read this painting endowed with so many of the qualities of nonfigurative art, when its title does not exclude concreteness? We confront a composition of blocks that do not reveal a recognizable structure, but suggest musical rhythms. Colors barely represent those most frequently encountered in nature. Although this painting by no means corresponds to Picasso's famous saying, "A picture used to be a sum of additions. In my case a picture is a sum of destructions,"[16] we can certainly claim that mimeticism, at least in the narrow sense, has been completely avoided.

The viewer is struck by the economy of means, simply blue and yellow rectangles, avoiding exact repetition, creating rhythms by what appear to be controlled irregularities, and will search for the secret laws lying behind Klee's creation of order. The eyes move along, assembling, separating, reassembling elements. Whether the viewer proceeds from color contrasts to proximity of shades or attempts to establish a vertical or horizontal continuity, he sooner or later runs into obstacles. He cannot pursue the same direction, for his itinerary will require shifts or discontinuity. As the eye moves from rectangle to rectangle, their dissimilarity necessitates constant adjustments.

We doubt more and more that scales, steps, blocks constitute abstractions, for we realize that several energies are at play. As the rectangles are roughly painted on a dark blue surface, gaps, irregular and often minimal, emerge. Their edges appear as uneven fluctuations. These gaps,

Paul Klee, *Architecture* (1923). © Cosmopress, Geneva, and A.D.A.G.P., Paris, 1985. (Fig. 2)

combined with the unevenness of the colored surface, suggest the possibility of movement and change. We confront a moment in time, not out of time. As the rectangles' projected and potential motion suggests breathing or growth, the exclusively formal qualities of the painting are transcended, and organic dimensions emerge. Brushstrokes, increasingly visible and vibrant, retain the creative gesture of the painter. In addition to the fluctuating colors and the vibrating lines, the two-dimensional surface transforms itself into a three-dimensional space in certain areas: a few of the rectangles become cubes; color patches coalesce into a colored wall. The third dimension emerges from the juxtaposition of squares at certain angles, as protrusions and recessions appear at various levels and in different areas. All the while, mobility and change, seemingly propelled by an invisible but magnetic force, aid and abet the interplay of colors. The triangles in the upper region of the painting assert an upward thrust; they appear to be variations of the arrows prevalent in so many of Klee's paintings.

Klee gave titles to paintings only after completion, when the image had fully manifested itself. In modernist terms, the work itself produces the title. By naming a painting, the painter expresses his awareness of the image which has emerged from the formal elements. Klee conveys the notion of architecture not by representation of a building, but as an ongoing process, blueprinted, if not built, by the viewer as well as by the artist, whose eyes have seemingly been magnetized by the wall.

The patches can also be interpreted as the assemblage, serialization, and reduction of a canvas along with its frame. They reveal the arbitrariness of the frame with its perfect rectangular shape, limiting and imprisoning the work of art. In *Architecture* painting seems to be caught in the act of taking over the frame. The "mise-en-abîme" of the work of art, producing tension and questioning its limitations and uniqueness, practically forces us to recognize the painting as modernist. The problems it raises are analogous to those raised by many works of fiction, beginning with André Gide's *Counterfeiters*.

Perhaps the pastel *Blühendes* (Blossoming, 1934), also composed of loosely assembled squares in tones ranging from blues to reds (fig. 3), a work that strikes us by its formal similarity with *Architecture*, relies on similar creative principles. The patterns are arranged to create alternations between similarities and contrasts. The strokes of the crayon suggest once again the vibrating gestures of the artist. Squares placed on the outside are segmented; the "flowerbeds" expand beyond the viewer's field of vision. The flower clusters, made up of bold, non-

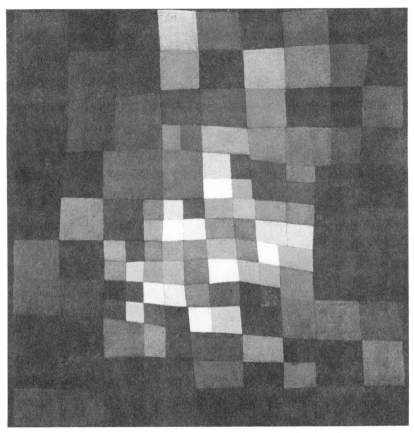

Paul Klee, *Blühendes* (Blossoming, 1934). Kunstmuseum Winterthur. (Fig. 3)

Hubert

blending colored patches, suggesting various stages of growth, have burst forth from a mysterious dream world. Motion is signaled by an allusion to depth rather than by the shifting of squares in relation to each other as in *Architecture*. Klee proposes a different principle of motion in each painting, as Constance Naubert-Riser suggests in *La Création chez Paul Klee*:

> La constitution du champ formel est toujours à refaire, chaque oeuvre d'art doit avoir *sa* genèse, et ne pas transposer simplement des motifs déjà inventés.[17]

> (The constitution of formal space requires constant remaking, each work of art needs its genesis and must not simply transpose already invented patterns.)

In the pen drawing *Zerstörter Olymp*, (Olympus Destroyed, 1926), as in *Architecture* and *Blühendes*, motion can only be assessed by a careful, progressive reading of the work (fig. 4). Klee evokes a state originating in an action that has taken place. He does not depict, in spite of his apparently descriptive title, a recognizable scene. No single mountain rises toward the sky, as fragmentation and chaos spread over the surface. What matters are the formal devices underlying the image of destruction. Whereas color relation determined the two previous paintings, *Olympus Destroyed* is primarily constructed by linear patterns, that is, by parallels. Parallelism would normally be consistent with indefinite linear extension. However, the multiple directions, the fragmenting horizontality, and the interlocking of various diagonals create spatial disruptions and blockages. This threatening lack of a place of refuge or escape is aggravated by the squeezed-in quality of space in the painting and the functionless door. In view of diverse slanting, sinking, or elevating sections, the painting conveys the impression that movement and its threatening effects have by no means come to rest. Contentions about Klee's use of lines seem relevant here:

> Die Linie, in scheinbar spontaner Verwendung, die direkt aus der Bewegung des Pinsels ihre Form erhält, baut die Figur aus ihrer Bewegung auf. So soll sie durch ihr blosses Dasein Bewegtheit veranschaulichen.[18]

> (The line, apparently void with total spontaneity, and directly shaped by the brushstroke, builds up the figure with its own movement. So it must create the feeling of movement through its mere existence.)

In *Olympus Destroyed* any stable and erect position seems impossible in this centerless and eccentric universe. Parallel lines delineate unstable, transparent strata lacking a material presence capable of reassuring

Paul Klee, *Zerstörter Olymp* (Olympus Destroyed, 1926). Galerie-Rosengart, Lucerne. (Fig. 4)

viewers bold enough to enter the maze. They are mere variations of the cosmic image dispersing and concentrating, and no doubt are responsible for the contrapuntal red and blue traces still inscribed in the sky. Nothing prevents the viewer from expanding the thread in time and space where earth and sky, equally involved, have become accomplices in confusion.

Colors and lines are not the prime sources of motion, of spatial and temporal expansion, in so blatant a way in all of Klee's paintings. Signs and various verbal elements often intrude, forcing the viewers in their spatial exploration to decode and decipher. Jean Laude in "Paul Klee: Lettres, Ecriture, Signes" elaborates the painter's statement that writing and drawing are fundamentally identical: "Il n'y a en effet identité de l'écriture et du dessin en leur fond que parce que l'une et l'autre fixent durablement *une idée*."[19] (The only reason that there is a fundamental identity between writing and drawing is that both set *an idea* in a lasting form). The drawing *Ihr habt hier eine Lumpenwirtschaft!* (What a mess you made! 1927) gives, so to speak, triple exposure to such an idea by the use of writings, arrows, and drawing. As we follow the arrows, we take in the handwriting without losing sight of the drawing. The words "What a mess you made" are followed by "You ought to be ashamed." Does the drawing exemplify the verbal exclamation of a parent reasserting order in response to a disorder caused by a child? Such anecdotal contrasts are only superficial. What matters in the drawing is an irreversible force pushing toward the right; even if the power manipulating the lines remains unknown, we may wonder whether the verbal and the visual elements must submit to the arrow or whether figures swerving toward the right freely propagate their own distortions. Each of them outlines a series of impossible contradictory gestures and motions seemingly exempting them from gravity and stability. As the beholder's eye moves toward the right, it encounters greater disintegration, fragmentation, and discontinuity. The figures drawn by hatchings resembling scribbles add once more the originating gesture of the draughtsman to the manifold movements. Writing and hatching drawn into the same orbit seem to become, at least tangentially, identical.

As such an analysis indicates, Klee's art stresses exploratory signs over meaning, and in doing so establishes links with the verbal arts. The simultaneous presence of visual and verbal signs within a given work corresponds to an affinity consciously exploited. Or perhaps he has pushed his virtuosity so far that he can use defunctionalized verbal and other recognizable signs as pure plasticity. In several works, such as *Kommen herein* (Enter, 1937) and *Zeichen für Wachstum* (Signs of

Growth, 1937), both tempera and linear signs resembling letters possess the characteristics of organic figures. A single system of lines creates the structural network of the latter tempera. The black lines can be viewed as partial or complete letters of the alphabet, some nascent, some full-grown, some familiar, others enigmatic. As a few of the lines stretch beyond the borders of an inner frame, they suggest an unlimited possibility of growth. The simultaneous patterns of organic growth and verbal signs are at once punctuated and expanded by round red dots or fruit. White areas surrounding the black lines or wiring, and blue surfaces avoiding sharp edges, protrude into or repulse one another. The blue and the white become interchangeable forces, simulating further forms of growth and other sign systems. As *Blühendes* and *Architecture* seemed to show the painter's gesture opposing the frame, so *Zeichen für Wachstum* signals the transgression of the page. As a result, the work of art appears at once as a reduction and as an unfathomable excess.

In the black and white watercolor *Complexe Zahl* (Complex Number, 1937) Klee has carried the conjunction of sign and representation one step further. The same black lines that compose the number made up of recognizable and enigmatic digits also outline the upper level of a landscape. The superposition of several horizontal levels provides the scheme of the whole page as well as the paradoxical penetration in depth into a space reduced to two dimensions. As the numbers are decomposed, threatened, analyzed, various moments in time are recorded by the changes in design. Klee creates a single language for the verbal and the visual.

In the famous oil painting *Villa R* (1919) the first sign of displacement the viewer experiences results from the use of colors: the green sickle moon, the blue villa, the brown sky (fig. 5). Villa and letter assume the same weight of importance; they share a wall. Although the villa is composed of identifiable parts, whereby walls, roofs, windows, towers, doors, and staircases seem to encourage our penetration, our progress results in a persistent deconstruction of what seems a nonexistent villa. As Rosalind Krauss suggests: "What is systematized in collage is not so much the forms of a set of studio paraphernalia, but the very system of form. ... Picasso's collage was an extraordinary example of this proto-history, along with Klee's pedagogical art of the 1920's in which representation is deliberately characterized as absence."[20] Planes, surfaces, lines assemble in such a way as to abolish any distinction between the inside and the outside, the villa and its surroundings. The eye, engaged in a labyrinth of geometrical lines that never yield or mingle, is prodded

Paul Klee, *Villa R* (1919). © Cosmopress, Geneva, 1985, and Oeffentliche Kunstsammlung, Kunstmuseum Basel. (Fig. 5)

by signs. The letter R would presumably name the villa, reduced to mere signs. But it also corresponds to the green sickle moon by its color and shape. The red cross and the red dot on the roof provide other signs interacting with the letter and other elements of the painting. Louis Marin explains:

> "La lettre" n'interdit pas ce spectacle et sa fonction n'est pas de censurer. Elle n'interrompt pas: la villa est toujours là sous la lune au bord du chemin. "R" s'y surajoute pour décaler le spectacle d'avec sa visibilité, pour le miner par son creusement in-signifiant.[21]

> ("The letter" does not block off the scene and its function is not to censure. It does not break a sequence: the villa is still there under the moon by the roadside. "R" is superimposed to distanciate the scene from its visibility, to undermine it by its insignificant probity.)

As the eye seeks to structure the components of the villa, it discovers or encounters more than one constellation in which the letter is outlined in incomplete or incipient form. The letter assumes a truly organic function in the painting, which reminds us that the landscape belongs to the visible made invisible.

The letter stripped of its relevance to the alphabet generates multiple relations between visual and verbal in the tempera *Pastorale* (1927) or *Ein Blatt aus den Städtebuch* (A Leaf from the Town Records, 1928, oil on chalk, paper on wood). In *Pastorale*, landscape, musical score, and written document overlap (fig. 6); the small blue strip on top belongs primarily to the former, the horizontal lines to the latter. Indecipherable signs, alluding to natural forms, induce the viewer to participate in the creation of a language wherein art reorders nature. Klee multiplies the exchange of characteristics between verbal and visual, treating them as representational systems rather than objects. *Leaf from the Town Records* will lead to a similar process of reading, as written document, musical score, and landscape coincide once again. In the upper part, the viewer will recognize the sky and an official seal. In the remaining eleven lines Klee uses schematization and reduction of means in alluding to the cityscape by its houses, flags, and churches, forms which display the characteristics of verbal signs. The spatial surfaces on which the major events of the city are narrated in repetitious and further repeatable patterns looks like a page carefully handwritten by an ancient scribe. The superimposed eleven lines convey temporal and spatial expansion by the accumulation of strata. Even more than in *Villa R* Klee here engages his viewers in an inquiry into the representational process itself, as they decipher the cosmic as well as the terrestrial, the visual as well

Paul Klee, *Pastorale* (1927). Museum of Modern Art, New York: Abby Aldrich Rockefeller Fund. (Fig. 6)

as the verbal; the conjunction of all these possibilities allows for the creation of a full-fledged story.

Klee's *Schriftbilder* (Scripture Poems) include on the painted surface texts written in ordinary letters. In *Er küsse mich mit seines Mundes Kuss* (Let Him Kiss Me with the Kiss of His Mouth, 1921, water color and china ink, version 1) the Biblical text emerges directly from the sky as an unmediated revelation (fig. 7). The two-dimensional sky divided by parallel lines, on which the letters appear, becomes a page. On the painted surface, where the brushstrokes have left their traces, irregular handwritten letters are inscribed, presenting the viewer with neither a copy nor a conventional form of representation, but, so to speak, with the original itself. Klee, who in his critical writings has pointed out his intent to rediscover an essence equivalent to an origin, who like Faust wonders whether the word or the deed was in the beginning, gives in a sense his answer in this scripture poem, the primacy of the word already stated in the "Creative Credo": "Since infinity has no definite beginning, but like a circle may start anywhere, the idea may be regarded as primary. 'In the beginning was the word.' "

Klee in *Let Him Kiss Me* undercuts meaning. Spatial divisions accentuate shapes and compose a formal unity that absorbs the diversity of the alphabet and its straight lines. The letter O, the only visible circle, coincides with the most luminous spot on the painting, the reddish sun. As we decipher the text, we pass from dark to lighter zones; we repeatedly read not only Biblical words, but we progress with time, moving from the darkness which precedes creation to luminosity and fire, simultaneous with Genesis. The intense lines of the "Song of Songs," including the word "liebe," which is inscribed four times on the azure zones, suggest spirituality and even extend into the invisible as letters are doubled by reflections or transparent spaces.

Commenting on the calligraphic picture *Einst dem Grau der Nacht enttaucht* (*Once Emerged from the Gray of Night*, 1918, watercolor), Laude implies that such works may be read in the context of *On Modern Art*, where line is equated with measure, tone with weight, color with quality.[22] The watercolor depends on duality and division between the black handwritten text inscribed on the upper edge of a white surface and the printed text, repeating the same words on the colored surface with each letter boxed into a square which it both divides and fills (fig. 8). The watercolor also depends on horizontal division by a silver strip, into two uneven parts of ten and nine parallel lines. Contrasts and duality emerge from the text, which at first refers to "once," equivalent

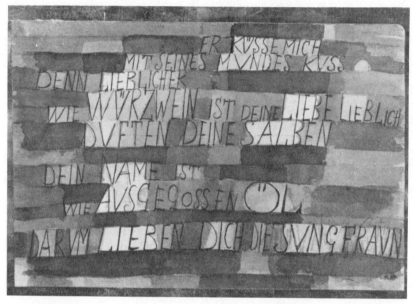

Paul Klee, *Er küsse mich mit seines Mundes Kuss* (Let Him Kiss Me with the Kiss of His Mouth, 1921). Galerie-Rosengart, Lucerne. (Fig. 7)

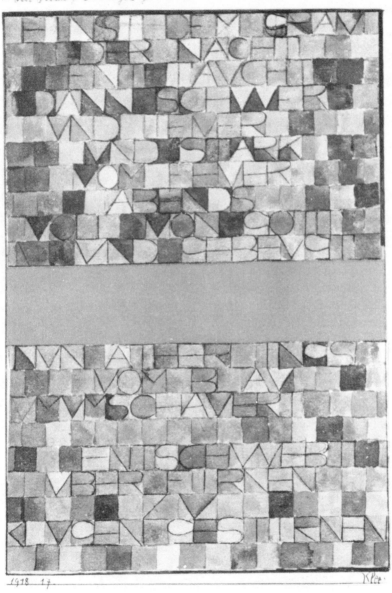

Paul Klee, *Einst dem Grau der Nacht enttaucht* (Once Emerged from the Gray of Night, 1918). © Cosmopress, Geneva, and A.D.A.G.P., Paris, 1985. (Fig. 8)

to the past, the night, and later to "now," the present, linked to ether, flowers, stars; these time sequences are barely reflected in the color panels. The letters integrated into colored fields are made indecipherable; as they appear to shape the squares, they are subordinated to the plastic elements of the painting, yet verbal and plastic duality never fully overlap.

Are we to conclude that, in spite of poetic and verbal allusions to time, stasis, not movement, dominates this work? The gray band, sum of all colors dividing the page, obviously alludes to the beginning of the text as it recapitulates the constellation transported back into invisibility or absence. As we explore or search, beginning, middle, and end, height and depth, require constant displacements, constant substitutions; as in *Architecture*, as in *Zerstörter Olymp*, we constantly have to shift from anticipation to indeterminacy. We participate in the transformations of the banal alphabet into a new code as we read a page where letters, lines, and colors are repeated, anticipating by this device the discrepancies between the first and second acts of Beckett's *Waiting for Godot*.

The entry of verbal codes into Klee's pictorial universe raises the question of to what extent the visual is pertinent to his poetry. The poems, some found in notebooks, others as entries in the painter's diary, were published posthumously. Written in the first person, they refer at least indirectly to artistic creation. Arranged differently on the page, they would form a completely integral part of the diary. Statements composed of short lines, they could almost be uttered in a single breath or "created" by a single gesture. Klee usually explores his relation to the world and watches for the manifestation of the creative act. No lyric flow governs his brief juxtapositions, his concise structures, which are comparable to his painting.

Reduktion!	Reduction!
Man will mehr sagen	One would like to say more
als die Natur	than nature
und macht	and makes
den unmöglichen Fehler,	the impossible mistake
es mit mehr Mitteln	of wanting to say it
sagen zu wollen als sie,	with more means
anstatt mit weniger Mitteln.	rather than fewer.
Das Licht	Light
und die rationellen Formen	and the rational forms
liegen im Kampf,	exist in continuous struggle.
das Licht bringt sie in Bewegung,	Light sets them in motion,
biegt gerade,	bends straight lines
ovalisiert parallele,	makes ovals of parallels

dreht Kreise in die Zwischenräume,	turns circles in intervals
macht den Zwischenraum aktiv.	activates the intervening space.
Daher die unerschöpfliche	Thus the inexhaustible
Mannigfaltigkeit.	multiplicity.[23]

In "Reduktion!" Klee presents a paradox. A selective process takes place as the work of art originates from nature. The resulting selection provides the viewer with a vast range of possibilities. Alluding to pictorial means, light, lines, their interaction, their mobility, the poet conveys the continuity of creation. Lines, light, space are active forces, perhaps not even directed by the artist, rather than conceptual entities underlying the paintings, which are instead created by the activation of space, the opening and closing of passages. Klee implicitly advocates the breaking away from geometric patterns as he rejects mimeticism in regard to nature, and his growing self-awareness constitutes a progressive experience.

The following text is based on precise spatial imagery:

Wasser	(Water
darauf Wellen,	Waves upon it,
darauf ein Boot,	a boat upon them,
darauf ein Weib,	a woman upon it,
darauf ein Mann.	a man upon her.)[24]

Words translate visual creation. The poem graphically constructs a movement from horizontality to verticality, from stasis to mobility, encompassing sexual and cosmic union. Since the poem does not include a conjugated verb, temporality is located within spatial stratification, indefinitely expandable.

Weil ich kam, erschlossen sich Blüten,	(Because I came, blossoms opened.
Die Fulle ist ringsum, weil ich bin,	Abundance all around, because I am
Zum Herzen zaubert meinem Ohr	Spellbound my heart, my ear
Nichtigallsang.	to nightingales
Vater bin ich allem,	Father I am to all
Allen auf sternen,	of all on stars
und in letzten Fernen.	and in the furthermost distance.
Und	And
weil ich ging, ward es Abend	because I went, the evening fell
Und Wolkendleider	and cloud-robes
hullten ums Licht,	shrouded light,
Weil ich ging,	because I went
Schattete das Nicht	the void cast shadows
über allem.	over all
O	Oh
Du Stachel	you thorn
in silbern schwellender Frucht!	in the silver swelling fruit.)[25]

Hubert

"Weil ich kam, erschlossen sich Blüten" is endowed with lyrical qualities: a personal tone, the continuous presence of the poet's voice, if not persona. Its relevance to painting appears more dubious. The poet seemingly proclaims a rational order, relating himself to a world that has meaning, that can be affirmed. As in the paintings, we become aware of the simultaneity of the intimate and the cosmic. The poet, through the repetition of the causal "weil," establishes directions, visible or invisible. The causal vocabulary does not convey a logical meaning or follow the strategy of critical discourse, but confirms movement, change, reversibility. The poet, almost equivalent to the sun, though a shifting center, accepts responsibility for both light and darkness, emptiness and plenitude, fruition and decay. But life does not ban the presence of death; the singular and the universal cannot be indefinitely united. The last, somewhat enigmatic line of the text may be clarified in conjunction with the closure of "I am God," which evokes in a more discursive, less imagistic language the same awareness of a world where life and death become synonymous, and which refers to the act of creation, to its willed continuity:

> Nun aber muss ich leiden   (But now I must suffer
> vor dem Vollbringen.   in the act of fulfillment.)[26]

In spite of analogies with the paintings based on theme and structure, Klee's poems, which significantly include a system of punctuation, tend to record emotional states. This tendency, perhaps a faint testimony of Klee's attachment to romanticism, distinguishes his poetry from the paintings, situating it at a greater distance from the contexts of modernism.

Notes

1. Guillaume Apollinaire, *Les Peintres cubistes* (Paris: Eugène Figuière, 1913); Paul Éluard, *À Pablo Picasso* (London: Martin Secker & Warburg, 1947); André Breton, *Le Surréalisme et la peinture* (New York: Brentano's, 1945); Max Jacob, "Souvenirs sur Picasso," *Cahiers d'art*, 1927; Pierre Reverdy, *Pablo Picasso*, Les Peintres Nouveaux (Paris: NRF Gallimard, 1924).

2. Suzi Gablik, *Progress in Art* (New York: Rizzoli, 1976), 159.

3. Charles Baudelaire, *Oeuvres complètes*, Bibliothèque de la Pléiade, vol. 2 (Paris: Gallimard, 1976), 684. Trans. Jonathan Mayne, *Baudelaire: The Painter of Modern Life and Other Essays* (London: Phaidon, 1965), 1.

4. René Crevel, *Paul Klee* (Paris: NRF Gallimard, 1930); Roger Vitrac, "Le regard de Paul Klee," *Cahiers d'art* 20–21 (1945–46), 53–55. See also my "Writers as Art Critics: Three Views of the Paintings of Paul Klee," *Contemporary Literature* 18, no. 1 (Winter 1977): 75–93.

5. For a discussion of Klee's relation to romanticism see Robert Rosenblum, *Modern Painting and the Northern Romantic Tradition* (New York: Harper & Row, 1975).

6. Herbert Read, introduction to Paul Klee, *On Modern Art* (London: Faber & Faber, 1948). Subsequent quotations refer to this edition.

7. Paul Klee, "Creative Credo," reprinted in *Paul Klee, Watercolors, Drawings, Writings* (New York: Abrams, 1969).

8. Louis Marin, *Études sémiologiques* (Paris: Klincksieck, 1971), 97.

9. Marin, 45.

10. Klee, "Creative Credo."

11. J. F. Lyotard, *Discours, figure* (Paris: Klincksieck, 1971), 238.

12. Marin, 97.

13. Lyotard, 238.

14. Ibid., 237.

15. Marjorie Perloff, *The Poetics of Indeterminacy* (Princeton, N.J.: Princeton Univ. Press, 1981), 32.

16. Quoted in Alfred Barr, *Picasso, Fifty Years of His Art* (New York: Museum of Modern Art, 1946), 272.

17. Constance Naubert-Riser, *La Création chez Paul Klee* (Paris: Klincksieck, 1978), 179.

18. Heinz Mösser, *Das Problem der Bewegung bei Paul Klee* (Heidelberg: Winter, 1976), 59.

19. Jean Laude, "Paul Klee: Lettres, Ecritures, Signes," in *Ecritures*, ed. Anne-Marie Christin (Paris: Le Sycomore, 1982), 363.

20. Rosalind Krauss, "In the Name of Picasso," *October* 16 (Spring 1981): 19.

21. Marin, 81.

22. Laude, 355.

23. Paul Klee, *Gedichte* (Zurich: Arche, 1960), 77. English version in *Three Painter-poets*, (New York: Penguin, 1974), 157.

24. Klee, *Gedichte*, 70. Trans. Walter Sorell, *The Duality of Vision* (New York: Bobbs-Merrill, 1970), 164.

25. Ibid., 94. Trans. ibid., 129.

26. Ibid., 30. Trans. ibid., 137.

Mary Ann Caws

Gestures Toward the Self: Representing the Body in Modernism: Cloaking, Re-Membering, and the Elliptical Effect

Il est décevant, s'il me faut ici me dénuder, de jouer des mots, d'emprunter la lenteur des phrases. Si personne ne réduit la nudité de ce que je dis, retirant les vêtements et la forme, j'écris en vain.

(It is disappointing, if I must lay myself naked here, to play with words, to take on the slowness of sentences. If no one reduces the nudity of what I say, stripping off the clothing and the form, I write in vain.)

—Georges Bataille, *Madame Edwarda*

I want to argue here that modernism develops, as one of its leading presentational characteristics, gestures which designate the self as fragmented but moving toward the holistic. If they seem inordinately self-conscious, that very buildup of consciousness energizes both the presentation and the practice of modernism.

The practice refers back to mannerism, where individual parts of the body served as emblems for the whole, where the conscious self-designation of parts as of whole occasions a particularly pointed pointing gesture. This paper itself functions as a representation of the self as representing, so that its author is irremediably drawn gesturing into the space of seeing and of saying. In some sense the paper is about itself, about the energetic gesture of the self-determining turn.

Presenting and Re-Presenting

What we present or state at first, we then re-present or re-state constantly; the body represented is then already not seen for the first time. There is no way for me to speak of any representation of the body without, at least implicitly, including the representatives of a corpus who then, already again, become metonymic parts for the body entire, the elements already of a signifying system they might wish to refuse. Language is included and implied and roped into language about the body, and representing by language is already linked, by the inescapable chains of language itself, into the body of prior and present and future language events. The picture is made up of bodies and parts, of visual representations and linguistic presentation, of visual presentations and linguistic representations, in the circular vice that is the worst of the bodily vices and not the least of the linguistic ones.

But when we speak or write, inscribing the names we give and the lessons we take within a fleshly and corporeal corpus, the corpus of this text is then subject, as we know, to both deconstruction and decomposition as corpse, and this future possibility is what we are writing on as well as in, and against. All the reservations and caveats about what representation is and how it lasts and how it is undone have to be built into our presenting of it.

Eyeing: The Body of the Text

Now a text separated from its context is said to be disembodied; so in our practice of what we see as modernism, as in our theoretical talk about it and its predecessors, we should perhaps be mindful of our own vocabulary, as it in itself is representative, and not just presentative. Whether or not we notice it, representations matter, however secondary to first-time experience they are, and they teach us how we think. What comes to mind eventually is matter, and what comes down to matter now comes to mind.

The dismemberment suffered by all disjunctive picturing, verbal or visual, is at once iconization and insult. The fetish seems to play the role of a section man or woman, a section person only occasionally remembering a totalizing master text.

In just such a fashion, I shall try here to remember the master or overall picture in picturing part by part the textual body I cite, and shall try at the same time to maintain the pictural order in which the entire scene remains included in the space of the eye, a visual spectacle representing the verbal one or taking it in. Yet necessarily the scene I envisage is here and not here, and to speak of rendering an image as if it were simultaneously and identically represented to the self as to the other is already to overlook, paradoxically, the afterness of reading what is before one. The speaking I is caught in a net suspended between two extremes, one, ideal, of cosmic prevision within individual sight, and the other of cosmic absence within individual blindness.

In the first or adequate vision, as represented in a classical scene upon a viewing terrace, such as Herédia's sonnet "Antoine et Cléopâtre," the whole history about the written may be framed for the hero in the space of the heroine's seeing. (He sees in her wide eyes "toute une mer immense où fuyaient des galères"—a whole great sea where galleys were fleeing.)[1] The eyes include the entire view, not just in seeming; their function is adequate to the description, as all the all-inclusiveness is sufficiently motivated. In just such a manner does the fetish element include the complete desire, projected into present history, of the one seeing, feeling, and taking the part for the whole, with some reason. Such vision presents and represents presence.

At the opposite pole, the eyeing of the text is limited by a shutting off of vision into absence: it is not even a case of blindness and insight, but of the black humor of nonsight for the sighted. I shall only quote Georges Bataille's picture of the narrator's father in *Histoire de l'oeil*:

> Ne voyant nullement, sa prunelle, dans la nuit, se perdait en haut sous la paupière. . . . Généralement, s'il urinait, ces yeux devenaient presque blancs; ils avaient alors une expression d'égarement; ils n'avaient pour objet qu'un monde que lui seul pouvait voir et dont la vision lui donnait un rire absent.[2]

> (Seeing nothing, his pupil, in the night, was lost under his eyelids. . . . Generally, when he was urinating, these eyes became almost white; they had at those moments a lost expression; they had for their object only a world he alone could see, seeing which gave him an absent laugh.)

The shutting off of his vision, for another one, is all the more terrible in its double exclusion, of him from us, and of us from him, and in its detailed concentration upon the eye as part only of a non-membered whole.

In between these two visions, between what we ideally see as entire, in the eyes of another or in our own, and what cannot be seen except on the inside, is located the contemporary view of both icon and object, of the language body as re-seen and re-viewed in modernism.

Saying Too Much or Too Little: What Is Afoot?

The twists and turns of mannerism often already taught a concentration on details, a division of the whole for the part. These teachings demonstrate at once how to read partially in order to read fully, and how to read designs, as well as how to read nakedness (we have only to worry about the odd picture Panofsky shows us of the Naked Woman as the representation of Truth and Simplicity by the side of the Ornamented Woman as Worldliness, and the shifts back and forth from bare and true to bare and false characteristic of the Renaissance, to see a good twist to it all).[3] We read wholeness through the blazons of individual parts. If we read Breton's celebration of his wife-in-parts in "L'Union libre" (my wife with a neck of . . . my wife with breasts of . . .),[4] we see yet another free union, that of the parts into the whole, and that of the mannerist technique with the surrealist.

The portrait in "L'Union libre," having moved from head to foot, then makes a vertical return, so that the concluding picture is held in the woman's eyes as they encompass all the elements, earth, air, fire, and water, for the completion of perception and the poem with it. On the other hand, as it were, and moving once more from head to toe, we might ask what the present literal sense is of the exact modernist vision taken, as the expression goes, "au pied de la lettre"? Now to toe the vertical line as it is usually written is exactly what I feel no urge to do and I will therefore begin by reminding you of that majestic picture of the big toe which Bataille held up before us, for examination. This is surely a modern rendering of an iconic item, the contemporary equivalent of the cataloged parts of the body, each made larger than life and including the all, in much the same way that Winckelmann spoke with reverence, of the feet of statues, or, then, of their navels.[5] More modestly, let me suggest what is now at hand, or better, what has recently been afoot.

We might think of Duchamp's picture of the dada foot, with flies, for a nutty but convincing reverse lyricism is indwelling in those far-from-vertical descriptions of the single parts dwelled on by poets like Robert Desnos, whose unforgettable representation of the feet of women on the sidewalks of Paris in *La Liberté ou l'Amour!* or, elsewhere, of their ankles, is likely to last as long as any full-length portrait. Those sidewalks are celebratable exactly because of his viewpoint: in no way lowly, however erotic, no more than are the stairs, sung in so many of his passages, for the passage of feet.

Nor is Desnos a master only of the picturing of female appendages; we owe also to him the trace of the paws or claws of some age-old sphinx on some staircase at break of day, leaving no trace but in a poem, which builds toward the arrival of their awaited arrival, astonishing in its announcement of its own unsurprising status:

> Aussi ne faut-il pas s'étonner de voir la silhouette souple du sphinx dans les ténèbres de l'escalier. Le fauve égratignait de ses griffes les marches encaustiquées. Les sonnettes devant chaque porte marquaient de lueurs la cage de l'ascenseur et le bruit persistant sentant venir celui qu'il attendait depuis des millions de ténèbres s'attacha à la crinière et brusquement l'ombre pâlit.[6]

> (So there is nothing astonishing about seeing the supple silhouette of the sphinx in the shadows of the stair. The beast was scratching with its claws the freshly-waxed stairs. The bells in front of each door lit the elevator cage by their glimmers, and the continuing noise, feeling the approach of the one it had been awaiting for millions of shadows, attached itself to the mane, and suddenly the shadow grew pale.)

Only the traces in the fresh wax will be left, in the mounting and on the rise, when this daydream, powerful beyond simple reverie, has re-entered the realm of the nocturnal dreams that will reabsorb it.

Nailing It Down the Line

From this to Jacques Dupin's entire poem set in a nail scratch, an "onglée,"[7] there is all the stride of contemporary poetry, on its way, netting in its advance the strokes of Mallarmé, the tracks of the Fauves, the most daily of Apollinairean sounds and traces, and one eyelash or one hair creating the universe of Artaud's obsessional Uccello, the portrait painter of Artaud himself, if there ever was one:

> Que vois-tu autre chose que l'ombre immense d'un poil. D'un poil comme deux forêts, comme trois ongles, comme un herbage de cils, comme d'un râteau dans les herbes du ciel. . . . Mais deux poils l'un à côté de l'autre, Uccello. La ligne idéale des poils intraduisiblement fine et deux fois répétée. . . . Et dans les cercles de cette idée tu tournes éternellement et je te pourchasse à tâtons avec comme fil la lumière de cette langue qui m'appelle du fond d'une bouche miraculée. . . . Avec la distance d'un poil, tu te balances sur un abîme redoutable et dont tu es cependant à jamais séparé.[8]

(Do you see anything else besides the immense shadow of a hair. Of a hair like two forests, three nails, a herb-garden of eyelashes, like a rake in the grasses of the sky . . . But two hairs beside each other, Uccello. The ideal line of hair untranslatably fine and twice repeated . . . And in the circles of this idea you spin about eternally and I chase you groping with the light of this tongue for a thread, this tongue which calls me from the depths of a miracled mouth . . . At the distance of one hair you are swaying over a frightening abyss, from which you are forever separated.)

This major power of reading the all in the minimal space, this ability to focus on still less than "la trace et la naissance d'un cil," permits still now the bodily capture of a whole picture of our epoch within one black or red slash diagonal across a painting by Malevich and recaught in Dupin's poem on him:

> Fatal
> comme en un glissement pur violent
> premier visage diagone[9]
>
> (as in a pure violent sliding
> first diagonal visage)

All may be captured in the slightest space, a whole landscape upon one fingernail, or the thinnest scratch: "Une encoche / dans le buis / seule / signe" (A nick / in the boxwood / alone).[10] What is razor-sharp as long as it is lean and linear seems to lose its incisive power if it should expand beyond that precision of the minimal: "Trahison de la ligne qui s'épaissit" (Treason of the thickening line).[11]

A Shoe-in

Now I would like to suggest that it is not only as a metonymy or reminder of the thing as entire but also as a substitute or coverup for something else that the writer or artist often presents or represents the object focused on. Why not, for instance, describe the whole body? The iconization of one single part is a refusal of the corpus seen entire as much as the classic picture of the surrealists in the forest, refusing to open their eyes upon the naked woman's body, refuses to see what it is in principle about. So does the cloak hide, the nail leave no feminine trace, and the substitute act as coverup. This is, I submit, an advanced and cloaked puritanism, but also cloaked in all the dignity of the metonymic, the paradigm, the representative part. "I show you this: you know I understand, have seen, am thinking of the rest."

Is that not, for example, the way it works with feet? with ankles? with the skirts seen passing over those same Parisian sidewalks? To skirt the issue is already to cloak it, and the issue is this: what happens to representing bodies when all you get is the sound of some sphinxy feet? What happens under the apron, to Simone's "real" naked body in Bataille's *Histoire de l'oeil*? to Marie's under her coat in his "Le Mort"? to Madame Edwarda's under her domino? Or, more lyric by far, under her leopard-skin coat, to the naked body of Desnos's Louise Lame in *La Liberté ou l'Amour!* where the exclamation point at the end of the title points to just that bare flesh of the plot. The leopard lays down his coat with love at her door, but is she in?

Let me give an explicit example of absence and what fills it in. In looking at the advertisement of a boy contemplating, as he lies on his stomach, the empty shoe of a woman, we may well ask: What is admired here? The woman? Certainly not. The absent leg, ankle, foot? Try out a few captions: The Prodigal Son Killing the Fatted Calf? or Now That She is Gone? or Lady Lightfoot? What it says in this specific picture is simply "ecco." A pointer, saying just "behold," or a deictic "ecco." What exactly are we to behold? The mark of the shoe. No trace is left, no footprint even, of the dame who filled it.

Now in the case of shoes, at least Van Gogh painted two of them, whether they were for the same foot or not, whether for a peasant woman or just for Heidegger. Meyer Schapiro had at least six shoes, Van Gogh's and Heidegger's and Heidegger's peasant woman's, and Derrida had by that time a good eight shoes, paired or not;[12] we latecoming readers of those shoes now so many times relaced, knowing we should have all those elements together, have—I would submit—exactly two, the shoes Van Gogh gave us in the first place. No woman and no peasant class exhausted and no brilliant readers are necessary to our own picturing of Van Gogh's poetic painted shoes. Here a shoe is, quite unlike a rose, not a shoe.

"Le poète," said René Char in concluding his elusive *Artine*, "a tué son modèle" (The poet has killed his model).[13] Does not all art do that for the body? Who could have stepped into that advertised and modeled shoe anyway? Or, in the case of Van Gogh, those shoes? It is not only a question of class but of motive: the manufacturer makes, after all, with his *manu* or hand, his product, which is to say, us. Inscribed with his initials or his name, the shoes trot upon the Paris sidewalks with or without content: it seems scarcely to matter.

Fingering the Text, or, What's in a Handle?

Georg Simmel, in his famous essay on "the handle"[14] was not concerned with what we are handling here, not even with a light fingering of the text, but rather with the junction of function and beauty, of matter and the idea, of the pot and of its pouring, of what we call availability. How do we get a handle on our modernist handles for our visual and our verbal texts? How do we entitle ourselves to how they are titled, by word or image, inside or out, that is, to their self-pointers?

Before even looking at the hand, we might look at the indexical function of one part of it. In Michel Leiris's "Le Point cardinal," a sudden gigantic plaster finger comes down from a crack in the ceiling to designate the central point in the room, the private parts of a sleeping woman at the middle of what is presented as vanishing point perspective: "qui attirait à lui les tourbillons moléculaires et les faisceaux de perspective" (drawing to itself the molecular whirlwinds and the light rays of perspective).[15] The finger remains pointing there longer than we would habitually stare, fixed in that "immutable direction": this pointer is inescapable, like any index finger of any pointing statue, in plaster, just as another pointer, slightly more offensive because it makes a gesture rather than a point (and a heavy bronze one), the sculptor Cesar's large bronze thumbnail, makes a token statement about creation and how it puts the finishing touch or stroke on what is made and judged and thumbed over. Such tokens serve as fetish objects whose text is easy to read, and all the harder to play with.

At the opposite pole from, for example, de Chirico's glove, usually left empty and open to interpretations which have been poured into it, the finger seems to designate something specific in the text or outside, designating, to the delight of the mannerists as of the modernists among us, the referral itself. It can be seen to relate to the hand as pointing relates to conscious creation, and so to the author's or the artist's own metapoetic view of the work. Proud, these representatives and self-representative texts often are, and lyric sometimes, and, occasionally, both, as in Desnos's long and lyric soliloquy attaching the hands to the body of the text called by an English title, "The Night of Loveless Nights," and forming an odd handle for dealing with it: I quote only a few lines of the many so handled, beginning with the statement of the catalog as it ensues:

Il y a des mains dans cette nuit de marais
Une main blanche et qui est comme un personnage
vivant

. . . .

Mains abjectes qui tiennent un porte-plume
O ma main toi aussi toi aussi
Ma main avec tes lignes et pourtant c'est ainsi

. . . .

Ah même ma main qui écrit
un couteau! une arme! un outil!
Tout sauf écrire
Du sang du sang![16]

(There are hands in this marsh night
A white hand like a living person

. . . .

Abject hands grasping a penholder
Oh my hand you also you also
My hand with your lines and still it is so

. . . .

Ah even my hand writing
A knife! a weapon! a tool!
Anything but writing
Blood blood!)

The rapid alternation between the collective hand play and the singular writing hand, as between the menace and the invitation—("Main chaude d'amour / Main offerte à l'amour / Main de justice main d'amour" (Hand hot with love / Hand offered to love / Hand of justice hand of love)—and the drastic contrast in colors—white hand against the red of blood and the black of ink—call attention to the role here glorified, of the masculine use of the revolutionary handling of the text of love as of justice.

In strong opposition to Desnos's over-handling of the male hand in its presence, the female hand appears to Breton often a menace even in its absence, especially in its suggested trace. Panicked at the supposed acceptance of the teasing suggestion to a visitor that she leave her sky-blue glove in the office of the "Centrale surréaliste," Breton assumes his fear to be related not only to this one glove, fragile in color and in kind, but to the twinning that glove makes with another which the same lady—known only as "cette dame"—threatens to bring in and leave, a glove of bronze. This heavy-handed potential gift, masculine in its threat, poses its bulk in the ponderous sentence describing it:

Je ne sais ce qu'alors il put y avoir pour moi de redoutablement, de merveilleusement décisif dans la pensée de ce gant quittant pour toujours cette main. Encore cela ne prit-il ses plus grandes, ses véritables proportions, je veux dire celles que cela a gardées, qu'à partir du moment où cette dame projeta de revenir poser sur la table, à l'endroit où j'avais tant espéré qu'elle ne laisserait pas le gant bleu, un gant de bronze qu'elle possédait et que depuis j'ai vu chez elle, gant de femme aussi, au poignet plié, aux doigts sans épaisseur, gant que je n'ai jamais pu m'empêcher de soulever, surprise toujours de son poids et ne tenant à rien tant, semble-t-il, qu'à mesurer la force exacte avec laquelle il appuie sur ce quoi l'autre n'eût pas appuyé.[17]

(I don't know what was so frightening and so marvelously decisive for me in the thought of this glove leaving that hand forever. Still this did not take on its entire and real importance that it was to retain for me until the moment when that lady proposed to come back and lay on the table, in the very place I had so much hoped she would not leave the blue glove, a bronze glove she owned and that I have seen at her home since, a lady's glove also, with its wrist bent, its fingers with no thickness, a glove which I could never help lifting, always surprised by its weight as it seemed to indicate the exact pressure it exerted in weighing on what the other one would not have weighed upon.)

Quite unlike the elegant, complicated, lyric prose usually characteristic of Breton, this clumsy passage that I take as all the more significant for that weighs down the text by its obsessive force. Between these two gloves, one present and one absent, one overstated and one suggested, any putative and potential implicit handshake of agreement, understanding, correspondence, has become a glove of itself, the empty outside gesture and what it weighs on. Nothing weighs in it, but much weighs upon it, even Nadja's vision of the hand flaming upon the water, for if what we are accepting is that the outside counts as inside, then is not the representative *cover* of what represents an intention to be taken as truly representing?

We scarcely need another meditation on clothes as language, but perhaps we should examine the covering or clothing gesture. If we accept the embrace of two gloves, *en puissance,* as the signal of an embrace of minds because symbolically of parts of bodies, how are we to read the embrace of, say, two fingers of two gloves? And then, would not any one finger of a glove suffice, whether or not it covered a "real" finger, to make a pointing gesture? Would it suffice detached from the glove? What if we did not recognize it, so detached: is an unrecognizable part of a recognized emblematic representation of a handshake or a pointing gesture any less a part of body language than two hands shaking, one finger pointing or, more pointed still, that finger wagging waggishly? But here the overstatement is the object of my gaze.

Necking, or Man-Handling the Model

In my steady rise up the body, I arrive at the beribboned thing, that cylindrical part of the body from which the voice itself issues and which is, notably in symbolist and surrealist writers and artists, often roped off. The model wears well, but often we see her neckless.

Hamlet playing Mallarmé's *Igitur* wears a ruff about his throat; he may think more unconstrainedly than he may speak. He is no less laced about than the Olympia of Manet, reposing beribboned as if guillotined, her voice cut off by a thin black velvet ribbon. For Paul Valéry, as quoted by Georges Bataille, she inspires a sacred horror, as she is idol rather than thinking woman: "Sa tête est vide: un fil de velours noir lui vole de l'essentiel de son être" (Her head is empty: a thread of black velvet steals her essential being from her).[18] Bataille himself, in speaking of Olympia, speaks of suppression, that of the link which connected her existence—including her reference back to Titian's *Venus of Urbino*—"aux mensonges que l'éloquence avait créés" (to the lies that eloquence had created). She cannot speak, so she cannot lie; the freedom of representing prostitution liberates the tongue or the brush of the artist, while the woman lies mute. Oh happy art.

At the source of Manet's painting, says Bataille, is his agreement with Baudelaire's delightful declaration, so fittingly uttered across from the naked model severed from her existence: "nous sommes grands et poétiques dans nos cravates et nos bottes vernies" (we are great and poetic in our ties and our polished boots).[19] Oh happy fashion!

As for Michel Leiris, gazing with the same fascinated gaze at the lying lady, he celebrates first and foremost the color of red in the picture: "Le goût de la couleur rouge . . . la couleur du drame si celui-ci, pour être vraiment le drame, doit impliquer effusion de sang" (The taste of the color red, the color of drama if it implies the effusion of blood in order to be properly dramatic).[20] I proceed right away to a mental striptease in dealing with immediate realities like these, he says. Setting things properly naked is setting them aright, and the writer has his seigneurial rights to the *mise-à-nue*.

Her ribbon and its bow imply the infinite knot, in a "conventional sign," but also tie him to his own labyrinthine project of writing, guaranteeing, in that maze, the straying step and the loss of self, guaranteeing, at the same time, by pointing to its visibility, the newness of this picture of its time, an accurate representation on which to reflect. The endless rebeginnings of the sentence, like so many reknottings, serve to beribbon the text and slow it down in order to frame the picture, where the knot itself reads like another decoration of the text whose neck it encircles, slowly styled, hesitating and halting, as clumsy as Breton's unusual flat-footed passage already quoted:

> Le ruban qui, sans l'étrangler, encercle le cou d'Olympia et que son noeud ... distingue du serpent qui, se mordant la queue, illustre l'éternel re-commencement, ce ruban qui, à moi qu'un désir double d'exactitude réaliste et de compacité n'empêche pas d'être séduit par les aléas de l'analogie, suggère bien plus que ce qu'exige sa stricte nature, ce ruban de largeur et de longueur modestes a-t-il été le fil qui me gardait de totalement m'égarer dans le dédale où l'écriture m'entraînait. ... Que le nu peint par Manet ... atteigne à tant de vérité grâce à un détail minime, ce ruban qui modernise Olympia et, mieux encore qu'un grain de beauté ou qu'un semis de taches de rousseur, la propose plus précise et plus immédiatement visible, en faisant d'elle une femme pourvue de ses attaches de milieu et d'époque, voilà qui prêtait à réflexion, si ce n'est à divagation![21]

> (The ribbon which encircles Olympia's neck without strangling her, and whose knot ... distinguishes it from the serpent biting its tail and illustrating eternal rebeginning, this ribbon which, for my own taste whose double desire for realistic exactitude and compactness has never prevented me from being seduced by the vagaries of analogy, suggests far more than is required by its nature, this ribbon modest in its width and length has been the thread keeping me from getting totally lost in the labyrinth into which I was being drawn by writing. ... That the nude Manet painted ... attains so much truth thanks to a minimal detail, this ribbon modernizing Olympia, and, even better than a beauty spot or a scattering of freckles, offers her as more precise and more immediately visible by making of her a woman provided with her exact ties to a milieu and an epoch, that is what was offered to reflection, in fact to diversion!)

Pointing to the face and the ear and the neck and its severing from the face, this ribbon is the detail that counts, this deictic marker signaling her time, and at once permitting her to stretch out in what seems the reality of her time. Just so, at the borders of surrealism, and in their time, the brightly pink-bowed Delvaux heroines with their necks so ornamented call attention to their own vestimentary lack or to that of the neighboring nudes, and to their very modernity in so calling attention to it, stretching themselves out as does Olympia ... This is surely the deliberate extreme of de-privation, the snatching away and spoliation of privacy, calling attention to the show.

Guys and Dolls

Far more dolls sprawl over the pages and the scenes of surrealism than over the spaces of other movements. Hans Bellmer removes not just the walking possibilities but the gesturing ones and the thinking ones: what is left in his dolls? The body of these texts is only handlable, in an ultimate passivity. But who recognizes the self here? These trunks and torsos can be read, I think, as scandalous only once; what is cut off and is simply absent may be less offensive than what is gagged off or singled out and off. The habit of the broken body has to be broken all over again, perhaps by re-membering. On the other hand, Beckett's characters in their ultimate deprivation, as they drag along, do no dragging of the text and bear no mute witness to the suppressions of an unwitting author or artist; they are far from mute, and so are no more part of the body of the suppressive glance or pen then a dis-membered character celebrated by Apollinaire.

A ribboned neck with a fair face above and a fair unclothed body below invites some kind of play, even if of the same sugary sadistic kind as Desnos's spanking of the rosy behinds of the child boarders in the Humming-Bird Garden of *La Liberté ou l'Amour!* (brand spanking, it is, if not new, and should be handled as such). But as for hands again, on the other one, the excessive melodrama of Bellmer quenches the wit of the rosy play in tones fiery and sepulchral, black and red. Humor can hang very heavy when so colored, losing at once the glint of black humor with a sparkle and the corporeal gleam of the celebrated Duchampian rosy joke: after all, "Rrose Sélavy."

What crosses from one gender to the other, from Rrose as Marcel Duchamp in drag to Rrose as Desnos in his would-be penning of a distantly-dictated text, can be read as a transgression of the separating slash, pre–S/Z, a forbidden and therefore fatally attractive crossing of the bar. A bar in Michel Leiris's *Aurora* highlights another transgressive crossing, from the whole to the parts, for it is entitled or programmed like a collective intention, a foregathering of the de-matched: "Au rendez-vous des parties du corps" (At the meeting-place of the body parts). There, unsurprisingly, congregate all sorts and conditions of parts illuminated by the veiling of all other parts of the body but the particular variant, "qui pouvait être n'importe quel fragment de cette défroque humaine: la main, le pied, la bouche, l'oreille ou bien simplement la phalange d'un doigt" (which could be no matter what fragment of this human in undress: the hand, the foot, the mouth, the ear or just quite simply part of a finger).[22]

Women, says Leiris, specifying that the one spot they do not veil is chosen as the most beautiful, make no exception here. In his re-assembly, the representation is made up of members partial; and in fact it appears, when a second glass of liquid is consumed, that what had seemed to be a stress upon one part of the body, representing by metonymy the whole, is in fact the entire self, partial as it is. If the mane of hair floats casually about—like the manes of hair in Desnos's poems, waving their farewells and signaling their loneliness—it refers also backward and forward to all those other manes of hair being combed before mirrors by surrealist heroines, seated with their fingers "sur l'aile du peigne" (on the wing of the comb), like Breton's lady dreamed of ("Je rêve je te vois indéfiniment superposée à toi-même" [I dream I see you seated indefinitely superposed upon yourself]), or then Aragon's Mire, in *Anicet*, or then Desnos's combing lady to whom the algae are brought, as she dreams of the sea.[23]

But the analogical mind of this striptease artist, this voyeur of Olympias and this celebrator of the manes of hair and the parts of bodies, inserts within a town of a body, transgressed and rendered incorporeal and inhuman (the windows for the eyes boarded over, rough emery paper replacing the hair and the soft parts, lances sticking out through the breasts), a testament-text of the narratorial adventurer constructing the mockery of the body as an enormous town.

> Depuis longtemps déjà, j'oriente mes recherches dans ce sens du corps humain. J'observe passionément ces antres, dans lesquels plus d'un monstre s'est caché. Au sommet de ce haut monticule de vertèbres, quel veilleur a allumé ces feux? Le troupeau des sensations tactiles paît dans les prés illimités de la peau. Ce soir il s'en ira dormir dans le fumier de son étable, couché avec les chèvres de l'odorat, les porcs du goût, les taureaux de l'ouie, les chevaux de la vue. Plus tard, masqué d'une cagoule d'abrutissement et de fatigue, tout ce bétail ira de lui-même se donner au boucher.[24]

> (For a long time now I have been directing my research along the lines of the human body. I have been passionately observing these caves in which more than one monster has come to hide. At the summit of this high rise of the vertebrae, what watchman has lit those fires? The herd of tactile feelings is grazing in the unlimited meadows of the skin. This evening it will go off to sleep in the dung-heap of its stable, sleeping with the goats of smell, the pigs of taste, the bulls of hearing, the horses of sight. Later, masked with a hood of stupefaction and fatigue, all this cattle will go of its own accord to offer itself to the butcher.)

This, says the text, is the proper picture of Man described.

The Recovery of the Subject:
Supplement and Gathering

The subject, perfect or imperfect, may, however, be recovered, by just what is covered over, and oddly. What covers up points to what is beneath; the Sabine Poppeia is exposed and gorgeous, as she allures; the veil that covers only serves to reveal. On the other hand, certain pictorial coverings of the body, like the stripes Man Ray photographs as decoration, de-sign the naked body with the signature of the artist, in other words, place over it the mark of a man-on-the-prowl, as if hunting the big catch, the leopard of the season. Under the skin marked like a coat, the body remains exposed, sold by whatever name.

By an added twist—again modernism takes its clue from mannerism—the division of wholes into parts, for the iconization of the parts, can, upon surrealist occasion, lead to the addition of the wrong part, like a supplement, as in some of Wilhelm Freddie's photomontages. This kind of special and often obscene supplement serves then as the focus for vision.

The supplement itself brings supplement: the training of the sight upon and by what is extra permits the addition finally of the same part in a self-reflexivity characteristic of modernism, after mannerism. Its very embodiment might be a tabled piece wherein Marcel Duchamp is seated several times around a table, as if added to himself: fiat Man Ray, luxuriously, as the self is recovered and made entire by the self multiplied as in a circular mirror.

The Elliptical Effect

Now among the possible ways of recovery is that of saying too much or too many times, or then covering over and *re-gathering in a pleat* the evidence of what has been excised. I wonder if by an odd circumvention the self, put to flight by codes and icons, disenchanted with disembodiment, might not find it high time to reappropriate, by re-membering, the needs of the language of the body. For these representing bodies represent also something else, available only by its own cloaking off into memory, that is, representation itself, as it is from occasion to occasion embodied and re-constituted or re-incorporated; disembodiment knows, after all, no sex.

The paradox presented here of representing bodies is that something of the naked must be covered for the nakedness to appear attractive, with the shoe or the glove or the ribbon or the veil, or the draped sheet, or the decoration as pointer, but that precisely behind that shoe or glove or ribbon or veil or sheet or stripe, the appendage or part, or even the whole, may disappear. The member of the august body seen here in assembly metaphoric and literal may represent his or her own personal corpus prior to corpsedom, but that representation is really only itself assuming its rightful place in the imagination. The matter here is not one for Velasquez or his genial side-kick Foucault, not a matter of where the artist stands or the king, neither a matter of doorways or mirrors, nor a matter of stance and vanishing point. The elliptical effect I am presenting here in its final embodiment passes through the necessary implied disappearance of the body to be represented for the efficacy of the representational effect. Presented face-on, it fades; suppressed, it reappears, in strength. Seen entire, the body seems to say nothing; seen naked, it seems to spark no story. Seen in part, it speaks whole volumes; seen veiled, it leads into its own text.

When too much is shown, it veils what is not shown; when too much is said, the side that comes short or makes its own ellipsis says, by implication or unfolding, all the more. This double contradiction is what the elliptical effect is all about; now when I speak of the elliptical effect, I am taking ellipsis in its two major senses, both coming from the Greek "to come short": first, the omission of one or more words in a sentence that would have been needed to complete the grammatical construction; second, the oval generated by two foci, one side being shorter than the other. Then the compensating element of the ellipsis on the short-changed side might be the *pleat,* a densification or accumulation, an awkwardness or stylistic clumsiness which has to be "taken up" into the material and is then noticeable, pointing thus the way to the ellipsis by its very opposition. As it works in style of art and of writing, so it works in the body of language itself, which is their substance.

The elliptical effect, presented for both eyes and ears, and with its double generative focus, enables us to come, as it were, full-oval, to a double-focused paradox that characterizes the peculiar rendering and peculiar handling of certain passages and products remarkable in their intensity. First, that what activates the fullest imagination may be itself as fragmentary as a torso, as empty as an empty shoe—provided the foot be remembered with what it stands for; that what sparks the liveliest desire may be as dead as the coat of some sacrificed leopard—provided it lies over the most naked of skins, or even marks it; that the barest sign representing the smallest part may by a classic metonymy, supplemental or not, suffice to flesh out the whole body of memory. Simultaneously, the convex full text on the thicker side of the oval depends upon the concave or empty token, the one that comes short; these paradoxes form together the elliptical form. The very emptiness of the token shoe or coat or glove or hat, with all it fetishistically or emblematically resumes, guarantees that what it represents is more than body, clothed or unclothed, and is never trivial, being text. So the rendering of the empty shoes, preceded necessarily by a knowledge of woman, leg, foot, in descending order, appears to be a representation of absence based on a cover-up and a loss, a negative representation, of a body long gone, and yet, in its recalling, re-present.

There occurs in Proust a scene I read as the opposite correspondent to any scene of adulation of any empty shoe or sign. For in one Carpaccio painting, a cloak upon one of the figures restores finally to Marcel what he had lost, in memory as well as in history. Carpaccio brings back, into the text that began with attraction to a mother, obsession, and the waning of innocence, those elements thought to be lost. For he has included in the canvas Proust calls *The Companions of Calza* just the cloak Albertine had taken to go with Marcel to Versailles fifteen hours before she left him; Carpaccio had, as it were, given the cloak to Fortuny, so that Fortuny could bestow it upon all the Parisian shoulders, among which were Albertine's. And now Carpaccio, as Marcel sees the cloak again, returns to him Albertine lost, in more sure a fashion than any other way of recapturing the erstwhile prisoner: "J'avais tout reconnu, et, le manteau oublié m'ayant rendu pour le regarder les yeux et le coeur de celui qui allait ce soir-là partir à Versailles avec Albertine, je fus envahi pendant quelques instants par un sentiment trouble et bientôt dissipé de désir et de mélancolie" (I had recognized it all, and the forgotten cloak having returned to me the eyes and the heart of the one who was about to leave for Versailles that evening with Albertine, I was overcome for a few moments by a disturbing and soon dissipated feeling of desire and melancholy.)[25]

And so again, still paradoxically, the rendering of the Carpaccian and Proustian cloak, as that which contains now the memory of Albertine present, although lost, is also a positive representation of an experience past but forever inscribed in the present and the body of the text. The combined possibilities of representation, taken together, themselves form a corpus of representing bodies by their signs, which is not less than fully alive in its reading. We do not see in Carpaccio, but through Proust.

Representation as Illumination

Covering over in Proust works as illumination; separation does no less in other texts. The body veiled or the body partial is as resplendent as the world of the mind. In this perspective, the mannerist de La Tour points with a candle as bright as that of the surrealist Magritte, turning back again to the flame as the illumination, in the historic series of Vanitas paintings, of the body dying out. The back can be turned to the sight, as in a Magritte canvas where the man stares out to sea while the candle burns on the table behind him, but the memory of the candle and its significance remains in full view. Magritte's own *Representation,* the heavy framing of the central part of a woman's body, separates out what it shows as a full sign, saying it all by showing only some, forcing the reader to re-member and to re-collect, that is, to re-present.

In the final representation as the closing resource, the recall goes out to the gravest and most joyous assembly of representative and representing bodies—called upon now to speak for their entire selves. Here, the wanderer in whatever temple or baptistery, by whatever mosaic of text, may be given to see, while reading the body, the only fleshly body reincorporated into the whole glorious corpus reappropriated by the imagination as by the spirit it embodies and renders present, re-presented as signs simple, partial, and minimal, now entirely given to representing and remembering, before being given over to the stillness presented in the ellipses, even within this text on representation, now about to fall silent.

> Deux ou trois signes dans l'air, quel est l'homme qui prétend vivre plus que ces trois signes, et auquel, le long des heures qui le couvrent, songerait-on à demander plus que le silence qui les précède ou qui les suit.[26]

> (Two or three signs in the air, who can claim to live more than these three signs, and from whom, in the length of the covering hours, would one think of asking more than the silence preceding them, and following them.)

Notes

1. José-Marie de Herédia, "Antoine et Cléopâtre," *Penguin Book of French Verse* (New York: Penguin, 1974), 422. My translation.

2. Georges Bataille, *Histoire de l'oeil* (Paris: Pauvert, 1967), 176.

3. Erwin Panofsky, "The Neoplatonic Movement in Florence," esp. pp. 151–60, in *Studies in Iconology: Humanistic Themes in the Art of the Renaissance* (1939; reprint, New York: Harper & Row, 1972).

4. André Breton, "L'Union libre," in *Poems of André Breton,* trans. Jean-Pierre Cauvin and Mary Ann Caws (Austin: Univ. of Texas Press, 1982), 48–49. "Ma femme à la chevelure de feu de bois," it begins, and can be translated as "My wife with . . ." or "My woman with," and so on. See also my *Eye in*

the Text: Essays in Perception, Mannerist to Modern (Princeton: Princeton Univ. Press, 1981).

5. See Johann Winckelmann, *History of Ancient Art* (New York: Ungar, 1968), 2:296. For more on fragments, see the *Fragment* issue of *New York Literary Forum* (Winter 1982).

6. Robert Desnos, "Désespoir du soleil," in *Domaine public* (Paris: Gallimard, 1953), 135–37.

7. Jacques Dupin, "L'Onglée," in *Dehors* (Paris: Gallimard, 1956), 49–58.

8. Antonin Artaud, *Oeuvres complètes* (Paris: Gallimard, 1956), 1:138–39.

9. Jacques Dupin, *Dehors* (Paris: Gallimard, 1975), 149.

10. Ibid., 131.

11. Ibid.

12. Jacques Derrida, *La Vérité en peinture* (Paris: Flammarion, 1978), 279ff.

13. René Char, *Artine*, in *Le Marteau sans maître* (Paris: Corti, 1970), 44.

14. Georg Simmel, "Der Henkel," in *Philosophische Kultur: Gesammelte Schriften* (Leipzig: Alfred Kramer, 1919), 116–24.

15. Michel Leiris, "Le Point cardinal," in *Mots sans mémoire* (Paris: Gallimard, 1969), 94–95.

16. Robert Desnos, "The Night of Loveless Nights," in *Domaine public*, 232.

17. André Breton, *Nadja* (Paris: Gallimard, 1964), 64.

18. Quoted in Georges Bataille, "Manet," in *Oeuvres complètes* (Paris: Gallimard, 1979), 9:141.

19. Ibid., 144.

20. Michel Leiris, *Le Ruban au cou d'Olympia* (Paris: Gallimard, 1981), 140.

21. Ibid., 285–86.

22. Michel Leiris, *Aurora* (Paris: Gallimard, 1973), 30–31.

23. André Breton, "Je rêve," in *Clair de terre* (Paris: Gallimard, 1966), 160; Louis Aragon, *Anicet ou le panorama* (1921; reprint, Paris: Gallimard, 1949), esp. pp. 164–65; Robert Desnos, "L'Idée fixe," in *Corps et biens* (Paris: Gallimard, 1968), 110.

24. Leiris, *Aurora*, 120–21.

25. Marcel Proust, *À la Recherche du temps perdu* (Paris: Pléiade, 1954), 3:647.

26. Artaud, 140.

SECTION 3
The Far Side of Modernism

presented by
Albert Wachtel

Though the separations between Modernism and earlier cultural isms are more like twilight than like boundary lines, there are definite differences among such isms, distinctions on which not only critics but the authors who typify the movements are clear. While attention to individuality characterizes both romanticism and Modernism, for example, the former exalts individual subjective experience, whereas the latter regards the individual as our ineluctable means of apprehending the world and subjectivity as a consequent problem. Works that treat of subjectivity do lead into the twilight area between romantics and Modernists, but they enter on the nineteenth-century side as celebrations, and come out on the twentieth as case studies, records of individual experiences that aspire to the condition of scientific truths.

Joyce, for example, when he attempts to produce epiphanies, so records their unique elements as to embody or render incarnate (never forget the religious source of the word) not their subjective but their objective essence, their innate nature or significance. (Similar values lead Stephen Dedalus in Joyce's *Portrait of the Artist as a Young Man* to prefer a list that locates him in the universe to a poem that makes "heaven [his] expectation.") Joyce tries through a careful selection of events and of the words by which they are conveyed to make artfully captured experiences themselves convey their meanings. His benefactor and admirer Pound has a term of his own for such an accomplishment, dubbing it presentation. Their mutual admirer Eliot has a related sort of activity in mind when he declares that literature should convey whatever it intends by means of objective correlatives, and Amy Lowell seeks the same ideal when she extols imagism. Even Lawrence counsels readers to trust the tale rather than the teller.

If Joyce, Pound, Eliot, Lowell, and Lawrence are correct, then, epiphanies, presentations, objective correlatives, images, and tales convey individual experiences in such a way as to place their significance concretely before the reader. Yeats, who begins his distinguished career as a late-Victorian romantic poet, comes to see the value of his younger contemporaries' approach to writing and himself moves through the twilight between the two artistic periods, his poetic revisions often constituting touchstones of differences between them.

Similarly, the fascination with abominations among the Modernists is not linked to romantic conceptions of correspondences between mundane or corrupt realities and otherworldly mental or spiritual realms. Instead, expanding on the aims of the protomodernist Flaubert, who seeks for the exact words to convey the precise shades of meaning he has in mind, Modernists seek an integral presentation of vehicle and meaning—a unity between the concrete experiences or images of art and their significance, the emotions or ideas they contain. Rather than producing seductively corrupt impressions of the present containing "universal analogies" to a spiritual world, the Modernists seek precise images or correlatives by which to embody the inherent meanings of mundane (or abominable) experiences. Some Modernists use a "mythic method," but in its modern context the myth's purpose is not fanciful; rather, it provides a yardstick of values against which to measure contemporary events, and writers like Yeats, to the extent that they use myth or legend otherwise, keep a foot dragging in an earlier movement.

Though commitments to "objective subjectivity" do not provide us with a definitive set of Modernist traits, they do help to characterize both the period and the difficulty, evident in the various papers in our first section, of assigning a beginning to Modernism. Consider, then, the difficulty of defining its end—specifying the last moment of a process in whose midst we continue to live and struggle. For the most part, periods are named after the fact, when succeeding generations recognize a significant unifying set of concerns that may serve to distinguish one group of humans in the continuum of historical time from a preceding group. Even this, of course, presents difficulties, the difficulties of definition itself. Every definition proves also on some level to be an unjustified exclusion, every gain also a loss. Moreover, a zeal for defining, refining, and redefining can eventually produce webs of self-reflexive iterations so complex that they entirely obscure what they are intended to disclose.

Fortunately, we have no such works among our essays, yet the flavor of such speculation cannot but touch them, particularly when the subject is Modernism, or *modernité*. How is one to conclude, to move beyond or overthrow a movement which has for one of its cardinal principles, as Claude Leroy points out in "Modernity and Pseudonymity," the questioning of those principles? Leroy's intelligent essay, the first of this small final grouping, sets forth the problem. The concluding chapters, Charles Baxter's "Assaulting the Audience in Modernism," Marc Bensimon's "Apocalypse Now or in the Magic Hole?"—of which even the title questions itself—and Ihab Hassan's "The Culture of Postmodernism," no less cogently undertake to solve it.

Leroy properly assumes the existence of Modernism (though he prefers its seductive feminine form, *modernité*) on the near side: at some point in the nineteenth century, *modernité* began. But that is not the crucial question for him; instead he undertakes to examine the inexhaustibility of the Modern, its broad inclusiveness and elusiveness, its "ever-renewed power of fascination," and its cap-a-pie quest to become self-definitive—to include itself. He sees the period as real, as inclusive of specific artists, Baudelaire, for example, but so inclusive as to be self-contradictory—as to take for its imperative "a rupture with any imperative." Leroy thus leads us playfully (playfulness is a characteristic of his *modernité*) to the conclusion that the Modern is not only real but inclusive of postmodernism, which he regards as "a symptom rather than a real bet."

If Leroy is right, *modernité* will be the movement that ends movements, lasting as long as new art continues to be generated, and therefore no real period at all. For a movement that lacks even twilight boundaries on its far side is not *one* thing, but rather an undifferentiated something—unordered rather than disordered, perhaps, but in any case characterized by a lack of definition.

Charles Baxter undertakes to set bounds to this omnivorous period by providing a precise account of its purpose or effect, that is, its relationship to an audience. Here too, Flaubert, who decries Emma Bovary's "poisonous" reading habits, anticipates the movement: for Modernism begins, Baxter suggests, when authors discredit and provoke instead of courting an audience—in Flaubert, then, perhaps, or in Kierkegaard's division of authorship into the genuine and the fraudulent. Modernist stirrings can be felt in the deceptions perpetrated by Melville's confidence man and in Nietzsche's attacks on conventional values, even, Baxter cleverly demonstrates, in the oft-criticized ending of *Huckleberry Finn,* in which a convention-bound Tom Sawyer enslaves Jim by forcing him to "play" his former self. In any case, for Baxter Modernism is in high gear when art produces political, moral, or aesthetic outrage—art riots, for example, whether at a play by Synge or an opening of Picasso or a performance of Stravinsky—and has ceased to exist when the audience, inured against attack, is co-opted, taken up into the art itself, frequently to be attacked there in the interest of entertainment. Thus Baxter leads us to Barth, Barthelme, and such nonactivist protest films as *Network.*

Though some of their conclusions are similar, the approaches of Marc Bensimon and Ihab Hassan differ from Baxter's and are almost diametrically opposed to each other. Bensimon negotiates the labyrinths of contemporary theoretical, critical, literary, and artistic production from the early seventies to the eighties, using as his compass the trans-valuations in the *Anti-Oedipus* of Gilles Deleuze and Félix Guattari, who see capitalist society as abetted by Freudian psychology in the production of such false and death-dealing distinctions as those between self and other, human and natural. Such distinctions, they argue, result in false relations between "desiring machines" and the "body without organs" that together constitute the world in production. Bensimon perceives elements of the Deleuze and Guattari vision in Baudrillard, in Serres, in Duras, among others, but he acknowledges it also to be present in Joyce's *Finnegans Wake*, which was a "work in progress" in the clearly Modernist twenties and thirties and published as a volume in the year of the second great war. In addition, the *Anti-Oedipus* division of the world into three stages, the savage, the barbarian, and the civilized, rings curiously of Vico and the Greeks, of gold, silver, and bronze, with a patina of Marx, whom Deleuze and Guattari use as a cudgel against Freud.

Hassan has an explanation for such temporal stretchings of the defined area; "The Culture of Postmodernism" provides Modernism with a terminus by rigorously separating out strands of contradiction on our contemporary far side of Modernism. Hassan sees as crucial to an understanding of postmodernism a certain attitude toward death, namely an awareness of its inevitability; for to him creativity itself, viewed as contact with the unknown, is an "exercise in dying." When Barthes calls for an "escape forward" into the new, Hassan hears a call for escape into death, whether that death be the demise of high culture in favor of the Pop (Leslie Fiedler) or Hassan's own concern with "self-unmaking," *post* rather than *beyond* its predecessor.

Hassan regards postmodernism as more than self-reflexive; he sees it as both self-aware and self-destructive. As part of the critical dimension of these characteristics he isolates ten problems with conceptualizations of the period. Not the least of these is a certain atemporality, for "we are all . . . Victorian, Modern, and postmodern, at once." But Hassan is not led by this awareness to despair of such distinctions. He perceives both "continuity *and* discontinuity" between periods and asserts that one of the special characteristics of postmodernism is an embracing of apparent contradictions, the Dionysian and the Apollonian, for example. (Nietzsche, of course, saw this embrace as characteristic of Classical Greece in the fifth century B.C.) On a theoretical level, Hassan recognizes, different periods frequently share some characteristics; they are distinguished from each other historically by time and theoretically by those characteristics they do not share. His approach, like the postmodernism he champions, is inclusive and tends toward the use of lists—compiling features, authors, ideas, and images—which mark out the boundaries of periods and movements. Hassan thus manages to distinguish the post- from the modern in a convincing way.

In the course of his argument, however, potentially dangerous components of both the Modern and the postmodern surface. Though hard on audiences, Joyce was individualist in a democratic sense: he loved everyman. But Yeats, Pound, Eliot, and Lawrence had hierarchical impulses. In different ways, they all endorsed hierarchies of value, one of the most dismal possibilities of which was realized when Pound embraced fascism. The postmodern in its inclusiveness opposes totalitarianism; but as Hassan formulates its principles, in its tendency to establish inclusiveness through dichotomies it can be thought of as opposing totalitarianism by embracing terror. When Hassan asserts that "we cannot afford to choose between the One and the Many, any more than we can accept *either* totalitarianism *or* terror," he can as easily be thought to mean that we should tolerate and even embrace both as that we should accept neither. Ultimately he advocates, under the apparently benign umbrella of "imagination," a realm in which "discord and concord coexist."

If restricted to art and prevented from being implemented in a political world, such a program remains harmless. But Hassan is doing more than discussing artistic movements; he is developing the taxonomy of a time, talking literally, as he points out, about matters of life and death. Willy-nilly our considerations of art and literature have political implications, and one of the implicit areas of permissibility in discussions of postmodernism is precisely this tolerance for terror. Modernists and writers about Modernism (despite its allegedly apolitical posture) cannot escape the grave social problems of our times.

Claude Leroy

Modernity and Pseudonymity

Artists and critics, normally quick to revive their quarrels
of precedence, have a peculiar passion in common: since Baudelaire,
they have incessantly defined and redefined *la modernité*—even through
its latest avatar, postmodernism.[1] Most likely, the persistence of this
debate is, to a large extent, fueled by a structural difficulty which Michel
Leiris has recently pointed out: "Doubly transitory *modernité* . . . since
it is the grid of a notion, and a shifting one at that, which we apply
to the elusive object to be apprehended."[2] This dual evasion of the
object and of our perception of it (and one no longer knows if our
perception actually apprehends the object or constitutes it) appears as
the source of lures, misapprehensions, and fascinations, which, as the
avant-gardes have experienced it, have an impact one cannot discount.
One hesitates, however, to attribute to this evanescence alone the tenacious
prolongation of an exercise that opposes such a strange resistance to
the systematic identification (that is to say, the denunciation) of its
contradictions. Should not this propensity for precarious definitions,
which appears to be the distinguishing characteristic of *modernité*, be
questioned in its turn? For, in the quest for this new Grail, the eclipse
becomes the rule, as if the act of definition itself were voluptuously
undergoing a process of metamorphosis into its own object of study.

Must it be concluded from this that *modernité* is nothing other, as
a word and as an idea, than an avant-garde version of the famous
Spanish inn where the guest never consumes anything except what he

himself has brought? Obviously not. But one might, perhaps, be forgiven for beginning the inquiry into this system of fortunate disappearances by an inventory in the manner of Prévert.

What then is *modernité*?

It is an aesthetic principle as well as a theme for sociologists.

It is the tenet of the modern world, when it is not its criticism or its condemnation.

It is an instrument of analysis, a concept, unless it is a fetish, a mythology.

It is the same thing as modernism or, rather, its opposite.

It is an imperialist schedule imposed by Western culture on the rest of the planet, and it is an ever-shrinking security on the stock exchange of critical value.

It is, for a Frenchman at least, always to a certain extent Baudelaire's daughter; it was for a long time the mistress of all the avant-gardists; it is, today, their wife, somewhat neglected in favor of the charms of a newcomer: postmodernism.

It is a crisis of the sign and a sign of crisis, and among other things it is an excellent subject for a colloquium. It is as pliant as can be and easily lends itself to metamorphoses. To a certain extent, *modernité* and paradox are one and the same thing. *Modernité* provokes definition, but only in order better to elude it. It pushes toward formulation and while doing so slips away from it, as if, by special vocation, it appeared less as an object to define than as a pure object of definition. Neither external nor preliminary to the discourse that strives to apprehend it, *modernité* presents itself as the never-completed sum of its formulations, each of which contains an act of baptism, a proclamation of new rights (often by way of a manifesto), and a gesture of appropriation to the profit of the informant. The locus of *modernité* is nowhere else than in the discourse held upon it—one would more willingly say, in the discourse that does its utmost to hold *modernité* within itself.

Thus the question: what has made and still makes *modernité* an idea, and, especially, a word, so enduringly, so extraordinarily fascinating for writers, artists, and critics?

My hypothesis will be that none of the proposed definitions of *modernité*, whatever degree of actual legitimacy it might possess, can account for *modernité*'s ever-renewed power of fascination. Nor could adding or cataloging these definitions be of any more use. What is at stake here could be the slippage or undulation of meaning itself, the fugacity of reference, the vagrancy of definitions, in which the trace of another vagrant factor, that of desire, can be discerned. Independent of the ideological and aesthetic conflicts it has very effectively revealed, *modernité* appears, in time as in prestige, as the first of the names taken by the pleasure of the text.

This evasive *modernité*, unpropitious to a discourse of unity, seems to me better suited to the principle of the fragment, undoubtedly because the fragment today is considered the textual mode *par excellence* of *modernité*, but also, and perhaps especially, because the practice of the fragment, although related to that of the maxim, conflicts with definition. What separates it from the maxim is the fact that the fragment does not attempt to establish a definition, but rather to interrupt it, to defer it, to open it, according to Braque's expression, to "infinition."

Let us break apart, then, a few fragments.

As a motto for *modernité*, we could consider this aphorism of Georges Braque:

One must always have two ideas, one to destroy the other.

We could then say:

One must always have two ideas of *modernité*, one to destroy the other, to which a Frenchman could add this corollary:

The option in favor of *modernité*, in aesthetics, is less that of the modern man than that of Baudelaire; or even:

Modernité (along with dandyism) is one of Baudelaire's pseudonyms.

What *modernité* underscores since Baudelaire is the tradition of the new (Harold Rosenberg), the principle of which is yielding to the imperative of rupture.

What the modernist impulse first disrupts, it would appear, is the preeminence of tradition. But what is more seriously broken by this inaugural rupture is the mimetic pact linking art with nature, to such an extent that *modernité* is generally confused with the crisis of representation.

The denial of tradition, like the rejection of mimesis, participates, however, in a more general attitude of denunciation, which calls into question everything that could serve as a model for the text and thus risk reducing it to the status of a copyist's exercise.

The imperative of rupture reverts, by that logic peculiar to *modernité*, into a rupture with any imperative.

Among the models, or types of legislation, which threaten the modern creation with their definitions, are

—the referent: the ally of representation;

—the author: the distributor of expression;

—meaning: the vector of communication;

—truth: the alibi of persuasion;

—tradition: the geometric locus of authority.

The model for these models is, perhaps, provided by the proper name in which we see the power of designation paired with the will to dominate, that is to say, functional necessity with magical operation.

The models appear as possible names for the text, and the motivations they advance (the rules of the trade, the poetic program, etc.) conceal a maneuver to co-opt the reader. As a crisis of the representative sign, *modernité* throws into crisis as well the proper attribute of the name (still unacknowledged), which, under the pretext of establishing the law, qualifies the practice of reserving this pleasure for the sole disposition of the legislator.

Modernité should be read as a succession of attempts, or attacks, aimed at checking the arrogance of definitions, and, through this arrogance, exposing the power that every act of definition usurps.

The crisis of the model (which is *modernité*'s distinguishing characteristic) has been, for thirty-odd years, the object of successive interpretations. These models of crisis, henceforth inseparable from the idea of *modernité,* belong to its corpus.

In their diversity, these rereadings vie with each other in placing *modernité* under the sign of the hecatomb. Thus have we seen proclaimed, one by one, the death of the author, that of literature, of meaning, of genre, of the referent, of the real, of truth—without forgetting, among other assassinations, the death of the reader. The identity of the terrorists as well as that of the necrologists is known to all. How shall we name this marked propensity of *modernité* to eliminate its models: narraticide, scripticide, or texticide?

Like the sorcerer's apprentice, the idea of *modernité* does not escape unscathed from this hecatomb by involution. For the model of the "crisis" is still a model, and what is more legislatorial than subversion? One would be tempted to define the postmodern period (so voluptuously welcomed and described today) as the moment when modernity undertakes its own destruction, by the strict application of its very principles, in a kind of double boomerang (at least, a crisis within the crisis).

At this threshold of irreversibility, what underlies the diverse contemporary readings of the idea of *modernité* pertains, perhaps, to the imagination of exorcism, where the symbolism of the number three (and such ternary maneuvers) plays a determining role.

In this interpretive game, one could thus distinguish three periods and three types of models: a *modernité* of auto-representation, a *modernité* of anti-representation, and a *modernité* of hyper-representation (that which is fulfilled or repudiated in a postmodernism).

With the assistance of some modernologists (Deleuze, Lyotard, Baudrillard, and, naturally, Barthes) one may identify the *modernité* of auto-representation—that of the *noveau roman*—as essentially a practice of criticism, attempting to substitute for the model of mimesis that of the text, without calling into question the model of the model. Bartering one law (that of verisimilitude) for another (that of the text, decreed by linguists), this *modernité* does not modify the regime of legislation. It trades one name for another without challenging the status of *naming* itself. Thus it is with good reason that this version of the modern has long been fascinated by the placing of mirrors.

As a counterpart to this, anti-representation may be considered an ironic practice, determined to destroy the validity of the model in the name of a concealed or unrecognizable higher principle. It is the projection (as per the old *Tel Quel*) onto the text of a principle of negative theology derived from Bataille and from Lacanian psychoanalysis. The text is no longer, then, another name for a literature finally restored to itself, but rather (to paraphrase Blanchot) its other: the other of literature, designated and concealed by the obsessing figure in the carpet of the spider's web.

One will recognize, finally, in hyper-representation, a humorous practice, characterized by the increasing use of the themes of simulation, trickery, optical illusion, and seduction. By way of a specious conformism, it is no longer the model (or the name) that hyper-representation attempts to alter. Nor is it a case of a return to origins: what is rather at stake here is the effect produced, and a particular mode of reading. By hypothesis, we propose to define this hyper-realist, wily, simulative, and humorous *modernité* as an extension to the text of a generalized principle of pseudonymity.

What is a pseudonym? For writers, according to an apt expression, it is a pen-name. This designation can be justified in several ways. Literally a pen-name is a name designating the pen, which is the emblem of the pen, and, by metonymy, that of the writer's trade. But it is also a name which comes from the pen, by a special genealogy which makes the writer the child of his works. Finally, and more obscurely, the pen-name is a name made of writing, a writing which has made itself name, a name-text that disrupts the established order of nominations.

What enables us to identify the pseudonymic principle of current (post-) modernism, what signals the pseudonymic regime which governs its discourse, is, first of all, the abandonment of binary tactics, which function as much in the pairing of model and copy, the true and the false, as in the couple of master and slave (or disciple).

Against the alternate, but also against dialectics, pseudonymic writing develops the exorcistic strategies of the ternary and promotes the countervalues of the indirect, the oblique, the transverse, the drift, the traverse—multiple figures of the slanted projection, composing in this way the rhetorical paradigm of the pseudonym, the slanted projection of the name.

One can note the following pseudonymic practices of writing:

—The fragment, of course, which is a pseudonym for the maxim. Like the maxim, the fragment proposes a brief text, inclined toward the formula. But, in contrast, the fragment turns the weapons of definition against the maxim.

—Simulation, which is a pseudonym for imitation. Like imitation it is an analogic operation, but it revokes the idea of a hierarchy between model and copy.

—Hyper-realism, which is a realism oriented toward the pseudonym.

—Optical illusion, which is the other aspect of verisimilitude.

—Seduction, which is the pseudonym of seduction (seduction is always a pseudonym).

—Humor, almost a double for irony and often confused with it; humor, too, is inclined toward paradox and unmasking, but—and this separates them radically—it includes itself among the targets. Humor: hyper-realism of the law, as the pseudonym is a hyper-realism of the name.

Like hyper-realism in the visual arts, the discourse of humor functions in a ternary system. Whereas between the real and his painting the painter inserts the perverse mediation of photography, which tones the whole of the representation into an optical illusion, the practitioner of humor—and more particularly the humorous fragmentizer—insinuates between his discourse and that which is outside the text the screen of a subtle quotation which is difficult to identify but which ends up, here and there, by vampirizing the order of the reference and establishing the reign of the double.

Humor, a clown among texts? But one should add that this clown is a clone.

As a clone of writing, humor, in the scenography of the modern, holds the position of an operator of pseudonymity. It interferes with the secure allotment of designations, it invites the reader to view the real as a mere effect of discourse, it seriously undermines the relevance of filiations.

Pseudonymous humor turns the oblique into a parricide.

Forms of parricide—socially acceptable because they are symbolic, just like that other crime which is love, if one is to believe Baudelaire—the pseudonym and humor-as-pseudonym nonetheless require the assistance of an accomplice. This accomplice is none other than the reader.

It is, indeed, up to the reader to accredit, to ratify—by the action of reading—the change of name, or rather the change in the regime of the name which the choice of a pen-name initiates. It suffices that the reader agree to say, as Reverdy does before a painting, "Look, this is Braque," for the entire system of naming to topple into pseudonymism.

Modernité and modernism: how can we avoid drawing this parallel, as full of pitfalls as it may justifiably appear? But we will not confront them here as if they offered two slopes of the same hill, two versions, or two visions of the modern. Their confrontation is also (and perhaps primarily) a linguistic confrontation. We are not exactly alluding here to the inevitable opposition between Anglo-Saxon modernism and a French *modernité*—not easily translatable outside their respective cultural histories. This is rather the concern of a poetic of language, if one thus wishes to designate, with Genette, the entirety of linguistic constraints which, often unperceived, determine the structures of the imaginary. Moreover, as far as French is concerned, *la modernité* is the feminine of the modern, incomparably more desirable—as a word—than its dreary confederate *"le modernisme."*

Would not the history of *modernité* be merely a secret amplification, the trajectory of a figure subtly deduced from the constraints of grammar?

Modernité parading toward modernism. Modernism as congealed *modernité.*

Might not modernism come into its own just after the rupture, at that moment of high risk when *modernité*, barely freed from its debt to the preceding model, would be tempted to supplant it? Under the pretext of being avant-garde, modernism might then be simply a diverted form of institutionalization, the replacement of one stereotype by another. Might modernism be the Thermidor of any practice of *modernité*?

This Charybdis in *modernité* is, naturally, coupled with a Scylla, which is the flight forward, the accelerated rotation of figures, emblems, effects—that is to say, fashion: a reef less apparent than the preceding one but against which the enterprise of *modernité* seems to be crashing today.

Leroy

Sartre chastised Baudelaire the man for having abdicated his liberty by submitting himself to a system of tutelage. Could this idea of *modernité*, a revolutionary idea, be, henceforth, the victim of the tyrannical hold of the new that it has spawned itself? An unexpected threat, which sets up a barrier against its humorous enterprises, such a tyranny would lead to the extinction of all models. To define the text as an indulgence in parricide, by means of dismemberment, deconstruction, fragmentation, is, by a paradox only too apparent, to make a pact with tutelage. Without a model to alter, what would become of the pleasure of the text?

Such would be the dilemma: all the models, all the laws, all the avatars of the father's name have (at least, let's suppose it) been altered. Metamorphosed into a vast fabric of pseudonymity, writing has produced optical illusions, illusions of meaning, of genre, of truth, and finally illusions of the name of the father. Is not the last law remaining to be falsified that of the text itself, which is pseudonymity? A vertiginous operation practiced today in the name of postmodernism.

Postmodernism: the expression supposes a preceding *modernité* that has been superseded, recycled hereafter to the state of citation. It is an overextension as well as a renewal, a disavowal and yet a remake, whose slightly kitsch colors do not fully conceal its disarray, a symptom rather than a real bet. Let us imagine, if it is possible, modernity as a player, playing at seducing itself, throwing into crisis the crisis of representation, striving to apply to simulation itself a principle of simulation, bound— in the name of the imperative of the rupture—to break with its own project, without, however, trampling academicism underfoot . . . This proliferation of second-degree figures metamorphosed into forms of the double belongs all at once to apotheosis and endgame, perhaps in the barely acknowledged expectation of a new order which it would then be wise, in utter delight, to begin distorting all over again.

Bringing about the involution of the modern, postmodernism is condemned to undertake its own vampirization. This is the ultimate cannibalism of the reflexive.

From what arises this power of fascination that the idea and especially the word of *modernité* exercise upon critics, artists, and writers (and the fact that even in the word postmodernism, "modern" takes precedence)? This fascination is rebellious, it seems, as rebellious to reasons as to definitions. In the midst of proofs and refutations, of infatuations and second thoughts, eel-like it makes its way, a way that even leads to conferences.

That which excludes, fascinates, it has been said. Fascinating indeed must be that *modernité* that succeeds in excluding definition through sheer excess of it. It recalls another great fascinating woman, Madame Récamier, of whom Benjamin Constant, with good reason, said that she was satisfied with distributing dividends without ever touching her capital.

Or, one might also wish to think of a very famous young American girl.

Modernité is the *grande allumeuse* (the "big tease") of writing.[3]

Notes

1. Although the French *modernité* is frequently better translated by the Anglo-American term *modernism* rather than its cognate *modernity,* for both semantic and ideological reasons the terms are not interchangeable, as several of the contributions to this volume demonstrate. In view, moreover, of the special grammatical as well as philosophical distinctions that Leroy makes between these terms, we shall retain the French *modernité* throughout. We shall, however, keep the phrase postmodernism in place of *post-modernité.* —Ed.

2. Michel Leiris, *Le ruban au cou d'Olympia* (Paris, Gallimard, 1981), 234.

3. An explicit reference to Picabia's portrait of a young American girl as an *allumeuse* (a flirt or tease)—the spark plug (*bougie allumeuse* in French) of *Portrait d'une jeune fille américaine dans l'état de nudité* in *291,* no. 5-6: 5— was already made earlier in this volume by Jay Bochner (see p. 185). Another famous *allumeuse* in Picabia's collection of American girls is the light bulb sketch entitled *Américaine* on the cover of *391,* no. 6 (July 1917), reprinted in *Francis Picabia, 391,* ed. Michel Sanouillet (Paris: Pierre Belfont & Eric Losfeld, 1960), 49.—Ed.

Charles Baxter

Assaulting the Audience in Modernism

If all literary movements create within themselves a class structure of readers, critics, and writers, Modernism does so in a particularly pronounced way. One glance at Pound's *ABC of Reading* will show, for example, how intently the poet divided his audience into segmented hierarchies, based on talent, intentions, and a willingness to follow directions. The literary audience thus becomes a political one, with identifiable friends and enemies. This dimension of Modernism has been seen in part as a reaction and response to the ascendancy of the mass audience in the industrial era, Modernism positioning itself as the dialectically opposed shadow-self of the commercial market.[1] In this sense, Modernist procedures have often placed the concept of art patronage in question and have forced the consumer of art into an ironically adversarial role. It is not just that some audiences are unready for innovations in subject and technique or are too lazy to appreciate the best of what the past offers (one of Pound's constant charges); what is more particularly at stake is the audience's recognition that its status as an audience is morally suspect. When the audience in the theater perceives that it is being accused, the result is that Modernist event, the art riot.

The art riot, with its division of the audience into political and aesthetic factions, formed pyramid-like with the resentful, excluded mass audience at the bottom, has become a historical relic associated with *theatrical* premieres. The argument I am proposing here is that with the rise of the mass audience, the consumer of art becomes the adversary, no matter what his or her class may be. This development is apparent but hard to isolate in the case of fiction and the novel, which is typically identified with the middle class. The forms of public discourse that arose (particularly in journalism and fiction) in the late eighteenth and early nienteenth centuries were persistently attacked by such writers as Tolstoy, Nietzsche, Coleridge, and Whitman (of all people, in *Democratic Vistas*); these attacks repeatedly claimed that the new audience, and not the artist, was destroying the possibility of art.[2] Of these attacks on mass public discourse, the one I wish to single out is Kierkegaard's, in his book *On Authority and Revelation: The Book on Adler* (1847).[3] This study attempts to discredit a Danish person named Adler who has had a false (as Kierkegaard believes) revelation of God and has gone on to expound at length his resulting theological views. Kierkegaard feels that Adler's revelations are fraudulent but that his case is a model for the times.

In attempting to discredit Adler, Kierkegaard proposes a division between what he calls genuine and fraudulent authorship, a division that in one form or another moves historically through most phases of Modernist aesthetics. The fraudulent author, according to Kierkegaard, has a premise but no conclusion: since he does not know his own mind, he does not know what he means and has only a general sense of why he writes. He thus requires publicity and worldly success to validate himself by means of his work. The fraudulent author speaks to his audience by feeding it sensations, but neither the author nor the audience understands the nature of these sensations; moreover, the audience does not see the language of sensations as anything but natural, as if nature were a dictionary of sensations. Generalized mystification results. The fraudulent author is characteristically in a hurry. He can be recognized by his impatience, his rush to get his work out so that he can see what effect it will have. Though he may horrify his audience, he will do so in a way that pleases them, since they will not be moved to act upon their feelings.

The false author, then, gives the age what "the age demands," though this gift is ambiguous, because the age cannot know itself and thus cannot formulate its need with clarity. (The particular logical difficulty of Kierkegaard's position begins to be apparent at this point.) In any case, the "true" author, by contrast, does not need an audience and does not wish to become an author at all; he becomes one by default when his obsessions and his moral relation to their truth drag him unwillingly toward speech. The true author, in these terms, is a proto-modernist. If the world does not accept his work, his attitude is, "So much the worse for the world." The true author thus stands in principle as an adversary to his audience, as its corrective.[4] Kierkegaard's special difficulty at this point has to do with establishing the terms under which an individual, prophetic author finds an audience and keeps it, sharing with that audience a truth he knows it will come to recognize. The whole issue of what constitutes a community is gradually shifted to a Christian context, where audiences are more properly speaking *congregations* who have in common the sharing of a mystical bond. In turn, the authority of an author in this context can be gauged by the relation of his words to Scripture; the author's authority is earned by passing on the irreducible truth of revelation.

Kierkegaard's author, then, is by no means a secular author, but his description of fraudulent authorship—which has no "authority" behind it to give power to its claims—is, point for point, parallel to Alexis de Tocqueville's clinical description of American art in *Democracy in America*. In a secularized market, authority is granted to those who have anticipated the values of the marketplace and earned the power it can bestow. The problem here is that patronage is a matter of guesswork. In modern capitalism there are no eternal "values" held universally, and such values cannot be instilled through education. In a fickle market, the writer discovers that his integrity is threatened by the evanescent nature of commercial authority. When Modernism attempts to oppose what "the age demands," it attempts to restore the artist's authority and to reduce guesswork. But the author's authority is grounded on circular arguments, since nothing outside his work can grant him his power (Pound, in *ABC of Reading*, argues that his authority as a poet originates in his having written successful poems, an argument that will win over those who have already been won over.)[5]

In those instances in which a writer loses his or her public, or never succeeds in winning it, there may be a temptation to mix together a wish to gain an audience with an expression of hostility toward that audience. In the examples I wish to cite, the narrative draws the reader in at the same time that it pushes him back out, offering up "meanings" that are immediately cancelled out, in a sequence of invitations and rejections that ultimately mocks the reader for having been curious about fiction to begin with. I am concentrating on fiction here, since it is a latecomer to the literary aristocracy; the power of the novel has always been located in the marketplace, in hunger, sensation, and recognition.

Its formal values were not "discovered" until Henry James found them in *The Art of the Novel*. It is the reader's role as emotional tourist and spiritual glutton—in short, as an addict and consumer of the sufferings of others—that makes writers contemptuous of those who grant them power, and in its effort to escape the marketplace Modernist fiction, ironically, creates a veritable parade of fraudulent authors and bad readers.

Kierkegaard's impatient bad reader, the archetypal antimodernist, eager for sensation and effects, can be introduced by way of French literature, in Emma Bovary. Spiritually poisoned by her reading of fiction, Emma Bovary literalizes her condition by taking poison, which in a cosmic joke tastes like ink. Emma exemplifies Flaubert's apparent conviction that there is hardly a villainy that can compare with indiscriminate reading. Published the same year as *Madame Bovary,* in a country where aristocratic values have never successfully competed with commercial ones, Melville's *The Confidence-Man* (the last novel he was ever to complete) presents a steamboat full of impatient bad readers, all of them eager to buy fraudulent fictions from the shapeshifting con man. This buying and selling by largely unnamed characters, described in a double-talking legalistic style, puts a ban on intimacy and depth and reduces all relations, including the one between author and reader, to an empty commercial context. In another work by a classic American author, the narrative is, for the most part, in the hands of a writer who does not wish to be one, who does not care to be interpreted, and who wants to end his pact with the audience and with fiction almost as soon as he has entered into it. Despising fame, he is, in Kierkegaard's terms, a true author, having suffered a radical revision of his own moral relation to his life, but his story is finally taken over by a fraudulent author who, poisoned by his addictive reading, wishes to perpetuate suffering and to supply cheap effects.

This true author is Huckleberry Finn, in the book named for him, and the fraudulent author is Tom Sawyer. The novel's final section, the Phelps farm episode, is conventionally considered a failure of some sort, but as a protomodernist episode, critical of fiction's interest in conventionalized suffering as spiritual entertainment, it succeeds in assaulting the audience that has fallen under Huck Finn's influence.[6] The book regularly conflates commerce and literature, doing so in a way that brings out the worst in both. Every time literature of whatever sort appears in the text, it is to signal the onset of cruelty, monstrous pretentiousness, or spiritual sickness: Emmeline Grangerford's poetry precedes the shooting of Buck, the pseudo-Shakespeare of the King and the Duke precedes the sale of Jim for "forty dirty dollars." The imagination of business in the book cannot attend to Huck and Jim's friendship, where, properly speaking, there are no audiences or commerce, only silence. Their friendship gets short space compared to the attention devoted to counterfeits, as if all the literature the book examines were a species of fraud.

A similar rhetoric-for-gain strategy is at work in the Phelps farm episode, engineered by Tom Sawyer, who has been corrupted by fiction but who masks as an innocent, the mischievous preadolescent boy. What occurs in this section, however, is a working-out of ideas about commerce and fiction that the novel has already set down at some length. Tom Sawyer *is* Tocqueville's American artist, and Kierkegaard's fraudulent author: unoriginal, devious, insistent upon the natural origin of convention, slavish toward his audience. He is, in Kierkegaard's phrase, a "premise author," and unimpeachably second-rate. He relives the events of the novel twice over, as if they had occurred in books he has read: elegies are revived, snakes are brought back, and Jim's tears, once private, are now made into stage properties to water imaginary plants.

After two hundred pages, during which time the reader has been invited to feast on cruelty that leads to enlightenment only for Huck, the reader is invited to see all these events over again as fictions, with the cruelty reenacted against Jim. This time, however, the conventions are irritatingly conventional, meant to supply entertainment. Tom Sawyer, the representative reader of fiction, victim and perpetrator of mass culture, is every bit as confounded in his fictions as is Emma Bovary in hers, derealizing free human beings in the act of turning them into stories, of which he will be the hero. In order to fit Tom's plot, Jim must be made a slave again, a slave to fiction. Huck's nonplot frees Jim but doesn't go anywhere or make rhetorical gestures; it is discarded in favor of a crowd-pleaser.

It is as if honesty has no place in fiction, because there is no tension in honesty. Mark Twain has introduced an alienation-effect in the Phelps scenes by intimating that Jim is already free and that Tom's charades are pointless. In the theatricalization of suffering, Jim is forced into the role of actor, but the only part he is permitted to play is his former self as slave. Tom Sawyer's nostalgia for fiction is thus a "literalized" nostalgia for slavery. In any case, the novel's relentless critique of audiences, who are seen at the beginning as interpreters and at the end as mobs ready to riot on cue, has at last moved outward: when a painful story is told twice, the second time as a manipulative charade, the reader is forced to consider the scenes as fake performances concocted by the fiction-maker in collusion with the audience's expectations. Huck withdraws from the last third so that popular fiction can take over. If fiction entraps, the only way for Huck—who is anti-fictional—to get free involves getting out of fiction, out of the book he has just written, away from his dangerous pact with words, which he says is the last such pact he will ever make. As the novel has asserted, as long as we are audiences, no quantity of suffering will satisfy us for long.

One notable feature of the book, impossible to ignore, is the belligerent NOTICE with which it begins. Signed by "G. G.," by order of the author, it threatens violence against anyone who attempts to interpret what follows. This notice, and Huck's urgency about getting free of his own story at the end, are markers, setting boundaries around a condemned, crime-filled area, the locale of the story. The book's "meaning" escapes Huck, since he is not a reader, hungry for sensations.[7] He simply wants to get away from readers and meanings. It is as if Huck is trying to imagine what it might be like to speak without the demands of listeners but cannot arrive at that point; this, I think, is part of Huck's interest in the Territory, to which he claims he is going to light out "ahead of the rest." In one of his late notebooks, Mark Twain imagined Huck coming back from the Territory, silent and insane.[8]

A novel published seventeen years later, and more properly considered a cornerstone of literary Modernism, is Henry James's *The Sacred Fount*, written at a particularly difficult point in his career, after the commercial and public failures of his plays and most recent novel, *The Awkward Age* (1899). Like much of James's work at this period, the novel seems designed not so much to tell its story as to maneuver the reader into an unhappy position in which he cannot "master" the text's materials or his own need to overpower them but must instead confront his own curiosity. The novel's plot, such as it is, originates in the narrator's speculations concerning the exchange of sexual energies between lovers. As a celibate bachelor, the narrator cannot pretend to be a participant in the game he observes, but he does recognize that his theory requires much snooping and prying on his part in order to dig up fresh evidence. Eight times in the course of the novel he asserts that his investigation is none of his business, and, by implication, none of the reader's. At the end of the novel he is rewarded for his overstepping of boundaries by being told by a former confidante that his theory has no basis, that he is crazy to have thought it up. Soon after this episode, the novel ends.

Priding himself on his observational skills, the narrator nevertheless sees nothing. A game is being played with empiricism, in which empiricism and the structures associated with it are bound to lose. The narrator promises a revelation about the side-effects of sexuality; at the same time, he announces that the investigation is in bad taste. The reader is invited in *and* pushed away. He is brought to the keyhole while being warned against keyhole-peeping, and what he has forgotten is that anyone who peeps at the keyhole *is* the story; he has become the thing he observes. He thus experiences the loss of the subject in a literalized way: he comes to the end of the story doubting that anything has been represented except himself, the reader at the keyhole. Thus the novel creates what might be called a "bad" audience, an audience that has come to fiction for the wrong reasons, for "real life" viewed through a transparent glass. This is the realist error, and it is the basis of the faith that defines the bad audience, the one that lacks cunning.

In Modernist fiction, the reader may often feel the eyes of the bad audience looking back at him—the gaze of Madame Bovary, Tom Sawyer, Ford Madox Ford's John Dowell in *The Good Soldier,* and many others—but fiction cannot say, "Don't read on." A system cannot criticize itself in such a way as to leave the system intact, continuing without the reader's consent. As long as the novel continues, the reader reads. That is his role, and thus the system continues to function. Though fiction cannot put an end to fiction, however, it can mirror the reader's participation in it in such a way as to make that participation seem imbued with numerous fallacies. In Nathanael West's *The Day of the Locust,* the story is organized to frustrate conventional expectations and to indict those expectations created from narrative art. In the oddly puritan texture of the novel, all image-making, from house-building on, becomes a form of idolatry, a substitute order that leaves its consumer perpetually manipulated and unsatisfied, trying to do with images what can only be done with physical objects; even Faye Greener, the novel's anti-heroine, is more a collection of images than a human being. It is completely characteristic of this book that its protagonist goes to a house of prostitution in order to see a movie, which breaks halfway through. This provokes a mock riot, a foreshadowing of the apocalyptic riot at the book's end. The climactic riot outside a theater takes over from the presentation inside; it is a riot created by fiction, by images, a hypnotic organism of irresolution, seeking any physical object on which to stake its claim.

As the storyteller, Matthew O'Connor, in Djuna Barnes's *Nightwood* says, "Now that you have all heard what you wanted to hear, can't you let me loose now, let me go?" Until the entire apparatus of fiction stops, the answer is always, "No." When writers have learned to feel contempt for their audiences' addictions and must for their survival satisfy those addictions in any case, the resulting literature has a particular cast, with certain fixed attributes. Reading (and reading in) cannot stop; unsatisfied needs pile up; the tension snaps instead of being resolved. Above all, the act of reading (or, lately, viewing) is felt to be unstoppable, as in Nabokov's *Pale Fire*, where it is simply satirized, or in the following paragraph from another work, where it is described: "The reader! You, dogged, uninsultable, print-oriented bastard, it's you I'm addressing, who else, from inside this monstrous fiction. You've read me this far, then? Even this far? For what discreditable motive? How is it you don't go to a movie, watch TV, stare at a wall, play tennis with a friend, make amorous advances to the person who comes to your mind when I speak of amorous advances? Can nothing surfeit, saturate, turn you off? Where's your shame?"

But of course this story (John Barth's "Life-Story," from *Lost in the Funhouse*)[9] does not end here but falls into bemusement. After a century of outrage, outrage is packaged inside the work. At last the riot becomes the primary subject that only professional writers enact for entertainment value. In the trickle-down aesthetics of postmodernism, in which the anger of Modernism is packaged and merchandised for mass consumption, the riot is the entertainment and is considered safe because the audience's addiction is taken for granted. Virgil Thomson has noted in his autobiography that the modern composer is threatened not by the public's ignorance of music but by its addiction to it. "They are a conditioned lot," he writes, "responding to appreciation propaganda . . . and they all look either vacant or preoccupied."[10]

A final example of the packaging of outrage comes appropriately not from literature but from film. Here one must imagine a work in which the viewer is repeatedly accused of idiocy, infantilism, and general dull-mindedness so extreme that he will accept any social outrage— provided it is packaged properly—as entertainment. His own statements of social anger are merchandised and depoliticized, so that they become anomalous, no matter how large the ranks become. All this appears in a commercial work that decries commercialism, providing at the same time all the standard commercial values. The work is the Paddy Chayefsky-Sidney Lumet film, *Network*. In this film, potent social anger is defined as entertainment. Having taken that initial step, the film's efforts to preach become another form of entertainment. The film participates in what it accuses television of doing and provides the viewer with a self-satisfied detachment, largely fueled by the script's ubiquitous irony. The film's motto for the angry citizen, "I'm mad as hell, and I'm not going to take it anymore," empties both anger and action of all content; anger is thus frozen and stylized, converted into a pose or posture. Robbed of its content, anger becomes vaudeville, and the would-be social activist becomes the nightly comedian. Part of his anger, of course, is directed against the audience for its dull unresponsiveness, but since his accusations have become part of the show, they do not in any sense need to be acted upon. It is as if packaging permits anything by neutralizing specific content.

The vacant, preoccupied look of the audience described by Kierkegaard, Mark Twain, Nathanael West, and others suggests that the mass audience may reach a point where it cannot be insulted—has, in fact, been educated to be Modernist—and that Modernism dialectically has managed to lose its spontaneous furor, its adversarial stance. Modernism's ability to insult the audience has become a historical property, which no longer obtains. "It is difficult to keep the public interested," the narrator of Donald Barthelme's story "The Flight of Pigeons from the Palace" complains. He then goes on to say that "the public demands new wonders piled on new wonders. Often we don't know where our next marvel is coming from. The supply of strange ideas is not endless."[11] Modernism perhaps evolves into something else when everyone, from high to low, agrees to sit passively, alarmed by nothing, and to buy its products.

Notes

1. See, for example, Renato Poggioli, *The Theory of the Avant-Garde*, trans. Gerald Fitzgerald (New York: Harper & Row, 1971), 17–59.

2. On this problem, see Stanley Cavell, "Music Discomposed," in *Must We Mean What We Say?* (Cambridge: Cambridge Univ. Press, 1969), 180–212. Cavell's thinking on the problem of the audience here has suggested certain lines of my own argument. Cavell's essay on Kierkegaard in *Must We Mean What We Say?* establishes the importance of *On Authority and Revelation*, a text usually passed over in discussions of Kierkegaard's work.

3. Sören Kierkegaard, *On Authority and Revelation: The Book on Adler, or a Cycle of Ethico-Religious Essays,* trans. Walter Lowrie (Princeton: Princeton Univ. Press, 1955).

4. See, for example, the stance taken by Pound toward his readers in *ABC of Reading,* in which both standards of taste and the substance of one's education are set by the poet; there are uncanny similarities between Kierkegaard's and Pound's thinking here, though one is ecclesiastical and the other secular.

5. *ABC of Reading* (1934; reprint, New York: New Directions, 1960), 30–31.

6. On the question of the reader's indulgence in fiction, and his punishment for it by the writer, see Irving Massey, "Escape from Fiction: Literature and Didacticism," *The Georgia Review* 32, no. 3 (Fall 1978): 611–30.

7. A point also made by Leslie Fiedler in *Love and Death in the American Novel,* rev. ed. (New York: Delta, 1966), 285.

8. Quoted in the *Mark Twain–Howells Letters: The Correspondence of Samuel L. Clemens and William D. Howells 1872–1910,* ed. Henry Nash Smith and William M. Gibson (Cambridge: The Belknap Press of Harvard Univ. Press, 1960), 748. Huck's insanity is listed in notebook no. 25, TS, p. 24, of the Mark Twain Papers.

9. John Barth, *Lost in the Funhouse* (Garden City, N.Y.: Doubleday, 1968), 127.

10. *Virgil Thomson* (New York: Alfred A. Knopf, 1966), 421.

11. Donald Barthelme, *Sadness* (New York: Farrar, Strauss & Giroux, 1972), 139.

Marc J. Bensimon

Apocalypse Now or
in the Magic Hole?

Apocalypse Now, Francis Ford Coppola's film, is not the subject of this paper, although, given current atrocities, it would not be altogether impertinent; neither is our faithful companion, the daily thought of thermonuclear devastation. There are, however, related problems of anxiety and numbness which have to do with attitudes in recent years regarding desire in the modern world; these shall be discussed briefly here. The terms "holocaust" and "apocalypse" appear more and more frequently in recent titles dealing with the dangers of atomic warfare as well as in the works of the thinkers and artists mentioned here.[1] As we draw closer to the end of the twentieth century, the accumulated "crises," with their usual accompanying anxiety and guilt, are being read as signs that the End is near, just as formerly eclipses or comets were thought to be manifestations of a God ready to judge, reward, or punish. Whether old or new, eschatological representations are somehow linked to some impossible status of desire, hence to paranoid anxiety and death phantasies.

Deleuze and Guattari's *Anti-Oedipus: Capitalism and Schizophrenia*[2] stands at the turn of the 1970s as a revolutionary attack on the institutionalized discourses on Marxism and on psychoanalysis. It is a mad book, another "toll" for all meaning, mirroring the madness of these years of ours, but its madness is different from the one they encourage. When published, the work was acclaimed by some as a symbol of liberation, while others, such as René Girard, read in it the end of the modern world.

Traditional psychoanalysis had been able to claim a special progressive position in that, since it uncovered hidden material, it liberated and encouraged progress: indeed, by correcting infantile regressive desire, it allowed reactionary and phantasmatic choices to be abandoned, permitting adult choices in daily reality.[3] Deleuze and Guattari claim the opposite: desire is not that which distracts from the real, it *is* the real. Essentially revolutionary, it is repressed by our capitalist society through the Oedipus complex, which encodes it with the private familial triangle to hide the threat wild desire constitutes.[4]

For Deleuze and Guattari, the distinction between man and nature, self and non-self, is meaningless; there are only partial objects, desiring-machines, which produce and are produced. Opposed to these binary entities is a "body without organs," an "enormous undifferentiated object" that constitutes the death instinct and immobility. It is the attraction experienced by the machines for the body without organs that serves as a surface of distribution, for the production is, they say, *miraculated* while the body itself is *miraculating*.

Marx's idea of the inert role of capital in the production of surplus value inspires the authors here.[5] This "bachelor machine" is a product of consumption, experienced as sensual pleasure by a subject without any "fixed identity" which, like its Nietzschean model, wanders about the body without organs, all around the edge of the "circle, the center of which has been abandoned by the self."[6]

The Oedipian triangulation is for Deleuze and Guattari the metaphysics of psychoanalysis, invented to bring order to an "explosive desire" that knows neither law, nor lack, nor castration. Hiding the fact that repression is social, the Oedipus complex suggests that one must see the father in the colonel and not the reverse. If masses elect tyrants, it is less out of ignorance than out of desire. These internal contradictions stem from the very mechanism of attraction and repulsion.

Historically, Deleuze and Guattari distinguish three stages of society, the savage, the barbarian, and the civilized. With the savages, the flow of the desiring-machines is completely coded, the body without organs being the "body of the Earth," the socius. The latter, as anti-production, becomes the agent of a secondary repression. With barbarian society, the fear of decoding creates an overcoding, a repression, which channels all surplus values toward the "body without organs," now the despotic "body," which functions as socius. Finally, with modern capitalism, the investment of the desiring-machines is made on the body of capital as money. However, the abstract flows of commerce and money become decoded because coding cannot exist where there is no extra-economic intervention. Capital's relation to production is now such that the code surplus becomes a flow surplus, and the "falling tendency" has no end, its internal limits being constantly displaced. This internal contradiction in capitalism is pointed out by Marx. Capitalist production erects barriers which it trespasses only to erect new and larger ones. "The real barrier of capitalism is the capital itself,"[7] says Marx.

Now Deleuze and Guattari see modern capitalism tending toward a "deterritorialization" of the socius, toward a more decoded limit. The flows become more and more schizophrenic. Schizophrenia is seen by them as a necessary requirement for the functioning of capitalism, though at its very limit it would mean the death of capitalism. The system therefore oscillates and represses with a paranoiac violence. The energies are bound as evidenced by reactionary groups, state institutions, the army, the police, etc. "Privatization" of the unconscious finds its place in this repressive machine.

Psychoanalysis, born with capitalism and from it, decodes and re-presses. The psychoanalyst in us has learned how to deconstruct the old symbolic productions—which were coded—and to pass them into the modern unconscious as decoded material, a phantasmatic theater.[8] In short, the "secondary" repression is of social origin. As for the "primary" repression, it comes from the desiring production. Deleuze and Guattari do admit the existence of an incest prohibition in primitive societies, but, they say, it was a *displacement* of real desire for the "intensive germinal flow," a sort of fascination with returning to the womb or rather to the Body of the Earth, a frightening prospect for the primitive. In short, the Oedipus would have existed as a necessary negentropic mechanism, a "neg-Oedipus," a negation of entropy; a positive incest desire, rid of all guilt, one would assume.

The origin of this machine-desire can be found in Reich's *Function of the Orgasm*. For Reich, a cosmic energy creates on the body a difference of electrical potential; this, combined with a mechanical process, creates the following cycle: "mechanical tension/electrical change/electrical discharge/mechanical release." This notion of a circular unconscious factory, innocent, free from black forces which are dreamed up by "insomniac rationality," is attractive but naive, and so is the acceptance of the multiple concatenations of the Lacanian symbolic order of the unconscious coupled with the denial of the "single signifier" subsuming everything. For Deleuze and Guattari the signs of these chains have no meaning: "Dad's moustache, Mom's raised arm, a ribbon, a cop, etc." They therefore implicitly maintain Lacan's idea that the complicated mechanisms of the Symbolic reach us only through "imaginary incidences,"[9] but reject the notion that the repressed can only produce, as Lacan says, a "flow of meanings which rush into the hole to be closed." For Lacan, "any interpretation is indeed to fill this hole."

The Deleuzian unconscious is impersonal, and since for our authors the Real is the unconscious and its production, the Lacanian Real can no longer exist.[10] On the other hand, Freud included in his 1923 id an unconscious participation of the ego and affirmed that there existed also a "non-repressed unconscious."[11] Further, his theorizing about the opposed life/death instincts raised many contradictions.[12] Deleuze and Guattari criticize the view that no longer opposes a wild desire to a repressing civilization but makes of civilization that which, though guilt-laden like ours, dares in the name of sexuality to defend sexuality against the death instinct. Deleuze and Guattari reject the death instinct and say that the model of death is not without but "within the unconscious."[13]

Their book expresses a sincere exasperation with capitalism and institutional psychoanalysis as tradition and as epistemological bases. The new schizo-analysis proposes no systematic program except an intensification of the schizo attitude, yet its coloration and therapeutic program suggest stronger, if ambiguous, ties with the tradition than they will admit. Freud's and Lacan's authority are contested, but with specious arguments that do not overthrow any fundamental positions, as René Girard points out in an article criticizing their "delirium."[14] The latter, however, makes no mention of their libidinal economy and maintains triangularity, stripped of its object relations, which is fundamental to *his* interpretation of desire. For Girard, it should be recalled, desire is a mimesis of the desire of the other, of a model whose appropriations are desired. The other becomes the rival who can be interiorized as a threatening double. Rivalry means violence, violence exasperates desire. To quench this desire for violence without guilt, an innocent victim is selected and sacrificed. Peace returns. The scapegoat is believed to have power of peace and war and so is worshipped. Hence the establishment of a society around an object of religion (that which links individuals). Girard sees in Deleuze and Guattari's praise of folly a mimesis of folly rather than real madness, a mimesis of the romantic hero, of the hero of difference. He sees in the importance given difference the continuation of a cultural tradition rather than the opposite and, in its end, the dissolution of differences: "What is dying here, is the totality of what we call modernism." A cultural rather than an individual aberration, the work of Deleuze and Guattari, for him, is a summary of former cultural forms. "It is the destiny of modern culture, of the modern end of any culture in the historic sense to live its successive moments—madness included—in some relative lucidity before the death of the cultural which should reveal to us the entire truth of the cultural if our thought does not die with it."[15]

At first glance the two positions seem diametrically opposed, for Deleuze and Guattari want to detriangularize desire, making it innocent; to liberate madness, to encourage it, in order to accelerate the destruction of a repressive and paranoiac system. And yet these opposite views are like the two sides of one coin. Both reject the Oedipus. Despite the profound difference between the two discourses, they have a similar explanation of the process of desire: it is a cyclical tension/release/tension mechanism. As for the nature of desire, the fact that any differentiation must be denied makes of it a perverse desire (in the medical sense) with Deleuze and Guattari, who encourage it by the reification of the object and the alienation of the subject. And is not Girard's reduction of all forms of desire to a desire of appropriation perverse in a sense, outside of the model of Christ, the mimesis of whom will show a non-mimetic way?

Deleuze and Guattari, like Girard, have an apocalyptic vision of the world. Girard sees mimetic desire and violence as essential in human nature but, with the loss of the religious with its regulating function, the modern world is shaken with rivalry and violence,[16] while innocent desire is yearned for, and sacrifice is practiced on Freud, on capitalism, or on religion itself. Man must cease projecting and assume this schizo-phrenic double of his. Girard would like to see the advent of a "true apocalyptic eschatology."[17] For him, cyclic history ends with the coming of Christ, who reveals its inner mechanism. With the "end of the modern world," another cycle is ending: "For Christ is before us, more still than behind us . . . psychoanalysis is completely the Old Testament: castration, the role of the father as rival, the impossibility to grasp the coherent contradiction of desire as identity of the model and of the obstacle in the mimetic process." The "nihilism of old modernity" will disappear to permit a new Christianity, a new rationality based on faith. "In ignorance . . . believe in this *detour* which comes from the *hollow* of the Being / Which one seeks and flees in hatred and in love."

Deleuze and Guattari see at the limit of the deterritorialized body without organs a "desert where decoded flows of desire run free, end of the world, apocalypse." Their work is but a vast metaphoric construction, a theory-fiction, which could have been illustrated by another metaphor, for example that of a gigantic cancer whose mad and absurd metastasis constructs, with its life, its very death. The only solution they propose is the exasperation of schizophrenic oscillation in the hope of accelerating a breakdown which will bring one day "the place of the cure," the "new earth," where will function the "eternal return of the desiring-machine as experience . . . of all the cycles of desire."[18] The term *revolution* should therefore retain here its first meaning also. The utopian *return* to a *post-apocalyptic* state evokes the reign of the same (just as in Girard's work, by the way). As for their madness, it is only a mimesis of madness. Far from being delirious, the *Anti-Oedipus* is a lucid, coherent book. The Deleuzian madness is motivated by a fixed idea, bound to a temporal development incited by the desire to pursue, in order to destroy, this menace incarnated by Freud and by a universalized persecuting system from which is not excluded, as we have seen, an apocalyptic prophetism. But the Girardian thesis also is built on the notion of mimetic desire, of rivalry with the model (which would be for Freud a particular case). Girard, putting the triangle on its head, so to speak, enlarges the case, making it a universal truth with a network of proofs. Is it not the haunting ghost of a truth and a reality no longer here that provokes such discourses?

That is Baudrillard's opinion, in his *Symbolic Exchange and Death* (1976).[19] He thinks Deleuze and Guattari's theories are like "floating moneys," signs, with no reference but the mirror of their own writing. Yet for him also, modern capitalism is the "outcome of a spiral" where the law of exchange value no longer has meaning. He sees everywhere an alienating gratuity. Work, salary, production, and the relations among these lose their meaning, just as do the relation between signified and signifier, and therefore all knowledge and meaning. Hyper-realism, in-determination, and simulation rule everything. Linear discourse, contemporary of the linear and cumulative time of production, disappears, replaced by reproductivity, with its metaphysics borrowed from the genetic model of cloning, while the system recycles implacably this obsession with a past reality and applies it to the modern world as phantasy. For instance, fashion, undetermined but haunted by the ghosts of the past—or of the future—subsumes everything and dissolves all value in a perverse aesthetic enjoyment.

One thinks of "pluralism" in art. For Baudrillard, hyper-realism consists precisely in this attempt to reproduce a reality which ends up vanishing. It might be in the deconstruction, or in the *mise en abîme* (splitting or repeating the object), in the serial form, in the reproduction of a reality defined by its very reproduction, or better by "that which is *always* reproduced." Guilt, anguish, and death-obsession remain. This is also the point of view of the American artist, Robert Morris, of whom I shall speak later. For him, the realist, like the decorative and repetitive tendency in art, expresses the nostalgia of representation, the horror of the void, and the obsession with death.

For Baudrillard, in this universe of signs, of mirrors, the "liberation" of sexuality is but an arbitrary and meaningless abolition of repression, reflecting a fetishistic activity whose purpose is the vain casting off of the threat of castration. At the epistemological level, the whole quest for "truth," which consists in unceasingly removing so many phallic alibis to attain in vain the "bottom of things," is a sham covering up the refusal to face up to the fear of castration.[20]

As for the modern unconscious, whether "bourgeois" or "revolutionary," it is also like floating money. It had given birth to psychoanalysis, but now, psychoanalysis itself, turned into a fashion, programs the unconscious with clichés, libidinal hyper-realism that excludes the symbolic. For Baudrillard, the symbolic is the process of exchange which abolished the break between the real and the imaginary, two terms distinguished because of a conceptual disjunction. So it is with modern life and death. Death is excluded from the symbolic, and as a result life is defined as *survival,* but then death phantasies obsessionally haunt us and invade everything. Modern society takes a perverse pleasure in the daily spectacle of its own destruction.[21] Patrice Covo, a collaborator on the jounal *Tel Quel,* in an article entitled "De quelques impasses," speaks like Baudrillard of death in this world of reproduction. Bourgeois and personal death is no longer satisfying; we must be supplied daily with the luxury of dying on the screen by the millions (corpses of starved millions, war victims, horror movies); and he prophesizes rites that will magnify us more and more: "The last fashionable, *fin de siècle* thing to do will be to rent for a honeymoon a palatial hotel room decorated as a morgue. As for the dogmatic crank, no longer satisfied with dreaming a place at the Pantheon, he will rush to the psychiatrist where he will vomit his struggle with the Angel on the mortuary couch."[22] Like Deleuze and Guattari, Baudrillard emphasizes the coincidence of Freud's discovery of the death instinct with the change from production to reproduction in modern capitalist society. The death instinct is given such priority that it functions as a myth[23] whose meaning is the death of the law of value, which comes back as a ghost to contradict and destroy the psychoanalytic structure completely; it is invaded and overwhelmed by death.

Beyond psychoanalysis, the symbolic processes found in poetic language, as evidenced by the anagrammatic mechanisms (reversibility, dispersions, nonresidual resorption), are opposed to the psychoanalytic processes (displacement, condensation, repression), and this is why a dream and a poem are different and why also neither psychoanalysis nor Marxism really has a thing to say about the work of art. When symbolic, art is exchange, enjoyment, reversibility.

This reversibility, cyclical as is all symbolic form, is what one must strive for in order to put an end to the irreversible processes of hyperrealism and simulation which are heading toward their own death. In fact, "the" linear revolution is already *bending* to produce its own simulation. Revolution, says Baudrillard, is just like Kafka's Messiah, who arrives on the morrow of the Last Judgment, one who waits for it when *it is already here.* "Power is a lure, truth a lure. All is in the *flash-like short cut* where an entire cycle of accumulation is ending, or a cycle of power, or a cycle of truth. The cycle must end. But it can be ended instantly. Death is at stake in this short cut."[24]

Like Baudrillard, Michel Serres's "La Thanatocratie" (1974) denounces a modern world destined for its own self-destruction. Indetermination (simulation and phantasy of determination) is for Serres overdetermination, but he has the same vision of an irreversible drive. A "death instinct" prepares for humanity, with the help of industry, science, and strategy, a genocide from which perverse enjoyment is not excluded, fed by knowledge that has lost its object. Fragmented and enslaved, this knowledge is geared on one track, the "apocalyptic holocaust." Here also, salvation is inscribed in a short cut, a curve. Like a "flash," he says, the "mortiferous past" and the "gaping hole" of the future encounter each other. "History finds in this *place* its involution of which it can be said that if it does not take *place,* our survival will be short."[25]

The "non-thanatocratic" solution Serres proposes is to go upstream by repudiating the universal and by practicing pluralism, polymorphism— a subversive attitude of consumption in the face of power which reminds one of Deleuze. One must, he says, "defragment space," "disconcert energies," a magic solution, which is explained by Serres's Lucretian notion of existence.[26]

For him, all life is deviation, disequilibrium (balance would mean death). Life flows toward death, but it fights against this entropy. Serres evokes the image of the river, whose eddies go back upstream, constituting negentropy. This turbulence is the "knot of all times." The organisms are synchronic, they are a "cloverleaf of times." This pattern, which he sees in everything, is that of Lucretius' *clinamen* (deviation in the fall of atoms responsible for the cohesion which primes the *dine* or eddy). Things are born, drift to their decline, are maintained a moment by turbulence before their inevitable end.[27]

Desire, conforming to the "eddy solution," is a cyclical process, a "spiral unceasingly deviating from itself." For Serres, the "fields of the subjective and of the objective fuse, being together 'order and disorder' as the real produces the conditions and the means of its own knowledge." In fact, everything, man and universe, drifts toward the noise and the black hole of the universe, knowledge being "nothing but this reversal of the drift, this strange exchange of time."

Baudrillard explains the death instinct in Freud by the symbolic exclusion of death in our own civilization, and Serres finds, in a generalized scientific model, a justification of Freud's theory. But both see salvation no longer inscribed in a linear time, which is that of life/death, but in the curving of time.

Like Serres, Marguerite Duras also indirectly attacks the establishment by "disconcerting energies," by destroying all possible satisfaction of desire, which is for her a synonym for possession, for power. This she achieves with characters who, like herself, have "the desire to tear what has gone before to pieces,"[28] and who, destroying all, including their own identity, flee into amnesia and alienation. Constantly excluded from the protean fantasies of triangular desire, the mad Lol V. Stein, an eternally empty center, "rebuilds the end of the world" and dreams of a bliss, "inexpressible for want of a word": "It would have been a word-absence, a word-hole where all the other words could have been buried. . . . With this word lacking, all other words are spoiled, contaminated."[29] Without this signifier, "she is not God, she is no one." In *L'Amante anglaise* (1967), Claire refuses to the end to confess where she hid the head of the body she has butchered. She fears that by allowing them "to take away this *word*, all the others will be buried alive with [her] in the mental institution."[30] She in fact has dismembered all meanings and even characterization since her madness allows her to be both her lover and her dismembered rival. With *Détruire dit-elle* (1969), where sentences are destroyed, and with *L'Amour* (1971), which is a reduction to its symbolic essentials of the *Ravissement de Lol V. Stein,* Duras lucidly goes even further into the fragmentation of characters and narrative. In these "remains," three ghostlike characters, a dream constellation, wander mad on a beach shore, a "dead point of space at a dead point of time."[31] Signs of an oceanic cataclysm and of apocalyptic fires in the adjacent and hostile city echo the characters' inner drama as well as Duras's own obsession with imminent holocaust: "Wherever I go, I see everywhere the signs of society's death, it is hallucinating . . ."[32] After fleeting, shredded images of love, madness, and horror, the text ends with the madwoman watching, as the fires grow pale, the glaring sun. Is a new beginning evoked? With the past now sealed off, this can only point ironically to the inexorable circularity of alienation.

India Song (1973) creates a special "narrative space" in the center of an India ("immobilized in a daily paroxysm") with its "pestilential . . . monsoon" and the infernal circles of its "zones" of leprosy, of famished crowds, and of burning-ghats. Voices of ghosts and characters from other Durasian texts convene to repeat their eternally impossible love story, also "immobilized in the culmination of passion." One of them, the Vice-Consul, unable to "bear the idea" of this India, attempts in vain to shoot leprosy, famine, and even his own image in one of the many mirrors. He also suffers from a desperately "absolute love" for Anne-Marie Stretter, who, "born from this horror," "stands in the midst of it with a grace which engulfs everything . . . a grace which is porous and dangerous."[33] Anne-Marie is a ghost who left her English cemetery to reenact her death. The various fragmented endings (parts 4 and 5) suggest that, as she leaves behind the mad lover and the spectator, she has destroyed the triangle to drown herself in the warm waves of the monsoon. This self-denial and the purifying presence of the beggar woman, with whom she could also be identified, point to Duras's wish to turn the denial of desire into a mystique.

In *Le Camion* (1977), love no longer exists, there is only a potential story, told in the conditional tense, and the would-be characters will never be seen on the screen (i.e., the lady who could have hitchhiked and the truck driver who would have picked her up), but the film shows a truck whose destination is unknown. With its mysterious load, it becomes as symbolically absurd as the hopelessly expanding machinery of the modern world and as absurd as the backdrop of "mortuary buildings" of the Parisian suburbs. Before this spectacle, the end of the world, the return to the sea, is evoked with great relief. Besides, "it is already finished," answers Duras, to the one who asks her how it is all going to end. Does the endless and fascinating turning of the truck wheels—a leitmotiv—function as a symbolic recuperation?

For the American artist Robert Morris, the future is just as hopeless and anguish has turned into a sort of lassitude which is reflected by the contemporary artists whose motions have become dulled. The individual, says Morris, is less preoccupied with his own mortality, while for him there reigns "a growing awareness of the more global threats to the existence of life itself. Whether this takes the form of instant nuclear detonation or a more leisurely extinction from . . . exhaustion of resources . . . (and pollution) . . . that sense of doom has gathered on the horizon of our perceptions and grows larger every day."[34]

In his work, Morris attempts to shake the spectator into awareness. For example, his ironic *Labyrinth* (1974) should suggest the infinite, like the celtic mandalas which inspired it, but it traps and frustrates the spectator.

In some of his recent works, Morris will place the spectator in the midst of distorting mirrors, in order to make him or her lose the sense of distinction between the real and the non-real, the subject and the object, the interior and the exterior; and, in order to rouse in the viewer a reaction, uses raw materials presented in all sorts of unusual methods. One will appreciate his ironic use of the shroud, in this case marked with the traces of calcined skeletons from thermonuclear explosions, next to the printed statement concerning the event; the traces remind one that if the bodies have disappeared into dust, there is little chance that they followed that of Christ.

Morris argues that all the present tendencies of American art can be brought back to four main inspirations: Duchamp, of whom he claims to be a disciple, and whose art he identifies as an art of absence, indirect and cynical; Hopper, whose realistic painting portrays an individual alienated from hostile surrounding (for Morris representation is but the reactivation of ancient magical practices motivated by the fear of annihilation and death); the Rothko-Pollock, Still, Newman trend, nonfigurative painting, which erects abstractions and is an art of presence, an expression of Eros, a substitute for transcendence, mirroring the American imperialism which becomes authoritative or gigantic when the power of the state crumbles; and, finally, an art closer to Thanatos, decorative art, mechanical and repetitive, which Morris opposes to the transcendency of the abstract icon. This art, whose ancestor, according to Morris, is Cornell, is mechanical, nostalgic of sameness and of a lost real; it avoids all decisions and a threatening future, seeking refuge in the ultimate escape of filling up space to avoid facing the void and death. It is unfortunately this art form that prevails when other modes are abandoned by the artists, who have grown weary and numb "in the face of a gigantic failure of imagination."[35] Hyper-realism and decorative art were briefly touched upon in the discussion of Baudrillard and re-producibility, but since I have borrowed from Morris his four cardinal points, I should discuss a few examples of what he calls abstract icons, "all-over or holistic, non-decorative, touch."

For him Robert Smithson's earthworks is an art which is "essentially a continuation of Abstract Expressionism's emblematic forms. Smithson's invocation of the void is but the obverse of Newman's '*sublime*' carried back to nature."[36] Smithson himself described the origin of his gigantic jetty built on the great Salt Lake: "As I looked at the site, it reverberated out to the horizons only to suggest an *immobile cyclone* while flickering light made the entire landscape appear to quake. A dormant earthquake spread into an immense roundness. From the *gyrating space* emerged the possibility of the spiral jetty. No idea, no concepts, no systems, no structure, no abstractions could hold themselves together in the actuality of that phenomenological evidence."[37]

The work proposes a special relation to earth, to the cosmos, and to time. Inspired by the whirlpool at the site of this "non-site," as he called it, and by the old myth which saw in the whirl an underground connection between the lake and the Pacific, Smithson felt attracted by the oceanic too. For him, the artist who is not a slave of time and who does not fly from it (because as all artists know, he says, time conceals the principle of death), this artist who faces temporality with all awareness will annihilate the object she looks at; the object will cease to be while its existence will "become luminous," "become art," for the artist especially. Society, by valorizing the art object, dispossesses the artist of this mental process and its relation to time. Timelessness or the ecstatic experience is that which through the exploration of the pre- and post-historical times introduces the artist "into these sites where far distant futures meet far distant pasts."[38] This activity, Smithson explains elsewhere, quoting Jean Dubuffet, is a "static gyration," a "derviche-like revolving of a being on his own axis," an "inverted version of the solution of despair."

Painters of monochromatic, two-dimensional "ideal surfaces" claim adhesion to a modernist or postmodernist stand. The 1980 all-black paintings exhibit at the Bronx Museum of the Arts was described in the catalog as "pivotal": black paintings such as Rothko's or the apocalyptic canvasses of Ad Reinhardt, attempts at "oneness," "irreducibility," "not collectable, salable, graspable," were described as the end of Modernism, whereas Marcia Hafif's, Richard Serra's, and others' black monochrome paintings were said to be "the point of emergence" of postmodernism.[39] Whatever the label one will choose for the latecomers, their painting expresses the desire to suppress the self and representation.

Marcia Hafif, in her discussion of her own monochrome paintings, argues that careful, deliberate strokes in monochromatic paintings are liberated from the servile function they fulfill in representational art, either figurative or abstract; they tend to be repetitive and linear in the making of the surface, thus bringing about a meaning from the completely arbitrary painting process: "It is at bottom purposeless and egoless," she says, applying to her own work a Zen statement on the art of archery.[40] Thus romantic self-expression is rejected, while the painting "becomes part of the painter's identity." Because line is accepted by Hafif provided it does not divide or establish position in space (distance, light, direction, or movement) all reference to temporality is avoided to allow for a "synchronic" experience. Directness and immediacy provide the painter with a "possible" action, a therapeutic and ethical salvation from this "impossible thing we know as life," and the viewer can share an experience of "wholeness," of "center," of "oneness." Hafif looks upon the artist and art as the only remedy for the "discontent" of an ill society, and further, as if painting were to function as a control over desire, she establishes parallels between her orderly method of brush-stroking and "minute description of sexual experience—clarity of a recording method to clarify the process of desire."

Although action and brushstrokes (or roller strokes) in Sam Francis's canvasses could hardly be called orderly and systematic, there is a similarity of intent in his work. Hot, brilliant colors sparkle everywhere, and white, negative spaces, born from the criss-crossing of the strokes, explode the frame, suggesting endlessness. Further, holes in the center, such as the one in a 1977 untitled painting, are intentionally left for the spectator's imagination to fill. Thus Francis's paintings satisfy a yearning for both presence (the size, all-overness, supremacy of color, spontaneity) and absence (evocation of spacelessness, going beyond the frame, the infinite, the hole in the center). They could possibly be accepted as conceptual or even as representational, since premeditated composition leads to a center in the painting in conformity to a geometry, though a two-dimensional one, inspired by the Tibetan mandala. The painting might then function as a means to some religious or areligious ecstatic end, perhaps a relation to ubiquitous timelessness or eternal presence. In his paintings from 1977 on, however, these colored and white spaces create in a free interplay a brilliant world of many mandalas where dialogue or separation between subject and object becomes meaningless, as if mind and painting became one.

If Francis's images are powerful explosives, the clumsy, delicate smearings and graffitis of Cy Twombly, while they suggest failure, can be apprehended, as Barthes notes in his 1979 preface to Yvon Lambert's catalogue raisonné, as equally powerful and subversively corrosive in their expression of oriental detachment and Zen humor. Twombly's surfaces function as sophisticated physical entities whose understatement and sparseness paradoxically suggest compactness and density. Yet the titles, the names scribbled in the canvas—Virgil, Dionysos, Pan—and the collages of famous painters or of odd plants, such as the leaves of a Chilean peppertree, establish with the classical or neoclassical world an ambiguous dialogue. The spectator experiences his own position as one of nostalgic decadence, emptiness, and hopelessness, the end of the road, or perhaps the void.

For Lacan also, finally, everything is circles and curves. He takes a mystifying pleasure in defining as a "poet" his "psychic reality," a borromean knot made of three interlocking circles; when one is cut, he says, the whole chain is undone.[41] These three circles refer to the three orders, Imaginary, Symbolic, and Real. To the Imaginary corresponds the sphericity of the body as a receptacle, a bag; to the Symbolic "the use of language as specifying itself in the logics of discourse," which is tautological and thus circular; finally, the Real, of which he says the earliest representation is the celestial dome. This Real is that which is "exterior to man." What reappears in the order of the Real is abolished, pushed away from symbolization. This foreclosure complements primary symbolization and is applied to the exclusion of the phallus as signifier of the castration complex, as was discussed earlier concerning fetishism. For Lacan, the Real is neither the "heart of the being" nor the "other of reality," but it is this unconscious "impossible to tell."[42] The Real is unspeakable also because the borromean knot "when flattened on the page" mirrors the manner in which the Imaginary informs it with meaning. "All meaning is just that flattening," it is a lie. The "only true is the hole in the circle."[43]

Whence the necessity to admit with Freud that the only real scientific claim that psychoanalysis can make is as "a science of the impossible," and if "this *id* which speaks reveals a language which knows—but without any subject being able to assume such knowledge—" it will then be necessary to posit not "a subject who is supposed to know," as Western culture would have it, a myth, "God himself" dictating from without a discourse representing the truth (of the law), but a subject which will assume itself as "knowledge-supposed-subject."[44] This writing "written as-not-to-be-read" is that of fiction. The latter does not imitate the effects of the structure of the real but exists only in the very curve of the structure. And, about this sort of writing, psychoanalysis can say nothing, says Lacan. This perspective on the unconscious finds its justification in its very defeat and accords art a privileged position in relation to knowledge.

For Philippe Sollers also, art, "irreducible to a meta-language," is the only discourse capable of transcending the limitations of knowledge. Art has for him not only an aesthetic, but also an ethical and even epistemological value which condescending Marxism and psychoanalysis have denied it. In an article "Marxism Sodomized by Psychoanalysis Itself Raped by We Don't Know What,"[45] he gives examples of the paucity of the contribution of Marxism and psychoanalysis to literary or artistic creation. These two institutions have, he says, only one unavowed and fundamental phantasy, that of replacing the Catholic Church. Except when it considers itself symptomatic, psychoanalysis becomes a "disguised religious edifice."[46] A consumer product whose value goes up or down like stock,[47] it occupies the strategic place of a body of knowledge which provides a context for knowledge, a sort of peg on which to hang all contemporary ideologies, and it is, as Deleuze and Guattari with Nietzschean overtones called it, "scientific knowledge which as disbelief is the last stronghold of belief."[48] Like the Catholic religion, it maintains a horizon where the Law refuses the subject autonomy in discourse: "Is not this church edified upon the impossibility of admitting a history of the Word-made-man, which has, as a consequence, the impossibility of admitting a history of man-made-Word?"[49] The result is the perpetuation, in the heart of discourse, of castration, of law, and of repression. This message, circular, means to be apocalyptic, in both senses of the term, that is, prophetic and unveiling: "Something catastrophic is going to happen. ... All this repression will cause you to explode. ... I try to present an apocalyptic horizon in the form of 'anyway, it was already here.' "[50] This repression is the obsession with the father alive who says "I say" and who causes language to be received like a punishing blow. In the Bible, explains Sollers, the word of the Father, his Law, is expressed from without in relation to the subject to whom he dictates his discourse: "God spoke, saying 'speak.' " In the New Testament, Christ as a subject assumes his place in the Word, and this is why he is for Sollers the "first serious atheist."[51] As the incarnation of the Word, he solves with no violence the violence exerted on the subject until then. This atheistic Christ is the model, for Sollers, to be imitated areligiously.

Sollers's recently published work, *Paradis,* constitutes an attempt to lift the "prohibition without suppressing it." This work written "as-not-to-be-read," to use the Lacanian expression, is written for the Word. Read aloud, biblically, it has rhythm and is intelligible, despite the absence of narrative and punctuation. The work is printed in italics, adopted by him as a symbol of freedom from the written law.[52] Catastrophe, he claims, will come from within; his readers have, "atomically speaking," one chance in a billion to still be here, with him. "I wonder," he says, "how this world will be, which will be in the end as if it had never been."[53] In a passage describing New York, he says that the end of the world has in fact already taken place, in the thirties or the fifties, "even if everything seems to continue, even if the slaughter house has been washed, we saw the skin of the mass grave."[54] In *Vision à New York,* published simultaneously, he explains his tightrope-walking as a blind venture justified by this very blindness, with its "voice-words" which jolt, support, or destroy one another, as so many "flames of laughter in motion."[55] For instance, he will juxtapose *névrose* and *nécrose.* It is the locus of a free circulation of the subject; sometimes it is the author's voice, sometimes he steps outside to allow the words to speak or those whom he calls the *autreurs,* the "others-as-authors." Opposing the fetishist·and archaic cult of the Great Mother, he would like to reinvent a writing which in a "vocal revelation" could become a "law in the language of the outlaws." It is also an attempt to reach some depth, to touch with words the "stuff we are made of," but also to be carried away by writing in order to *not be,* for "the fact of being is but a castration of the non-being." He describes his work as a perpetual rotation. The sounds repeat unceasingly and differently the same message, emanating from the same fiber: Hell is all around, while paradise could already be here. Like *Finnegans Wake,* held by Sollers in high esteem because he sees in it an aesthetic point of view similar to his own,[56] he would like his book to be "not like a book . . . a rectangle . . . but a circle, a curvature, a curve which therefore implies neither beginning nor end, and which, at any rate, turns."[57]

Bensimon

The temporality of the work is, therefore, inscribed in a circular space, a sacred space, hierophantic since it interrupts linear duration by what could be called an "eschatological punctuation"[58] of this duration.

Duchamp observes that "Art is the only form of activity by means of which man as such manifests himself as a real individual. By this activity he can go beyond the animal stage and into regions where neither time nor space rule. To live is to believe. At least that is what I believe."[59] Today, this belief, obtained through a difficult struggle in which the artist assumes knowledge and defends liberties, is held by Sollers as well as some of the artists discussed above. Facing the dark horizons all around, is it not the only and ultimate wisdom to assume this responsibility in a discourse, a sacred place of the present and of the word, since, as Sollers puts it, God, who is, *will be* what he is, *is* what he is, and *will be* what he will be? The artist apprehends both himself and the "Real" in the circular instant, eternal return of a same, identical and different, where past and future meet in a jolt, where the sacred, the natural, the material, the real, folds back onto itself but also is raised in the noon sun, winged Word.

Notes

1. *Holocaust* formerly meant, one will recall, sacrifice by total consumption in fire. *Apocalypse* signifies revelation, uncovering of the past and future mysteries of heaven, as well as the end of the world.

2. Gilles Deleuze and Félix Guattari, *Capitalisme et schizophrénie: L'Anti-Oedipe* (Paris: Editions de Minuit, 1972), trans. R. Huntley (New York: Viking, 1977).

3. See Jacques Donzelot, "Une Anti-Sociologie," *Esprit* (Dec. 1972): 835ff.

4. Deleuze and Guattari, *L'Anti-Oedipe*, 64.

5. *Capital,* (Paris: Pléiade, 1968), 3: 1435.

6. Deleuze and Guattari, *L'Anti-Oedipe,* 28; see also Pierre Klossowski, *Nietzsche et le cercle vicieux* (Paris: Mercure de France, 1969), 94ff. about the "höhe stimmung" and about the place of the subject in his relation to others, to the self, to God, and to the circle.

7. *Capital,* 3: 274.

8. Deleuze and Guattari, *L'Anti-Oedipe,* 363.

9. See his seminar on "The Purloined Letter," *Écrits* (Paris: Editions du Seuil, 1966), 11, about the filling of the hole and the whole question of truth; see Jacques Derrida's interesting "Facteur de vérité," *Poétique* 21 (1975): 130ff. on the transcendental topology of the letter and the "adequation de la parole pleine à elle-même," which could supply an additional understanding to Sollers's writing approach in *Paradis*.

10. This primary repression, which raised for Freud so many problems (geneticism, anticathexis, repression as neurotic defense), is reduced to a mere "production." See J. Laplanche and S. Leclaire, *Les Temps modernes* 17 (July, 1961) and J. Laplanche and J.-B. Pontalis, "Fantasme originaire, fantasme des origines et origines du fantasme," *Les Temps modernes* 19 (Apr. 1964). It is against their conclusions that Deleuze and Guattari focused their attacks; see *L'Anti-Oedipe,* 62–63.

11. Sigmund Freud, "Das Ich und das Es," in *Gesammelte Werke* (Frankfurt-am-Main: S. Fischer Verlag, 1963), 13:224.

12. See J. Laplanche, *Vie et mort en psychanalyse* (Paris: Flammarion, 1970), 210–11. Freud reaffirms a sort of "anti-life as sexuality." Thus conceived the death instinct has no energy of its own or rather its energy is the libido, i.e., "the death instinct is the very soul, the constituting principle of libidinal circulation."

13. Lacan minimizes the paradox, seeking support in the homeostatic explanation which he reinforces with ontological Heideggerian considerations (Being-for-death) and with remarks on repetition (past reversed in the specular image of the "dead" partner). See Robert Georgin, *Lacan* (Lausanne: L'age d'homme, 1977).

14. René Girard, "Système du délire," *Critique* 28 (Nov. 1972): 957ff. See also his *Des choses cachées depuis la fondation du monde* (Paris: Grasset, 1978).

15. Girard, "Système," 994.

16. The modern world has "*for ever* been oriented towards madness and death," Girard, *Des choses cachées,* 437; my emphasis. It is the refusal to accept this that brings Freud to formulate his new theory about the death instinct. For Girard the obsession with death comes from the refusal to recognize the mimetic mechanism in us.

17. René Girard, "Quand ces choses commenceront . . . ," *Tel Quel,* no. 79 (Spring 1979): 32ff.

18. Deleuze and Guattari, *L'Anti-Oedipe,* 207, 396.

19. Jean Baudrillard, *L'Échange symbolique et la mort* (Paris: Gallimard, 1976).

20. Ibid., 170.

21. Walter Benjamin, quoted in Baudrillard, 281.

22. Patrice Covo, "De quelques impasses," *Tel Quel,* no. 79 (Spring 1979): 67–71.

23. Baudrillard quotes Freud's saying that the life and death instincts are "our mythology . . . mythical beings grandiose in their mythology," *L'Échange,* 232.

24. Jean Baudrillard, *Oublier Foucault* (Paris: Galilee, 1977), 88.

25. Michel Serres, "La Thanatocratie," in *La Traduction* (Paris: Editions de Minuit, 1974), 103. Also see Jacques Derrida, "Le Retrait de la métaphore," *Poesie* 7 (1974): 116, which explains Heidegger's function of the invagination or withdrawal as an attempt to free language from the yoke of the metaphysics of the moment and of the metaphor which depends on the system. See also, more pertinently, Martin Heidegger, *Questions* (Paris: Gallimard, 1976), 4:142–57.

26. See on Serres and psychoanalysis "Le point de vue biophysique," *Critique,* no. 346 (Mar. 1976): 266–77.

27. Michel Serres, *Naissance de la physique dans le texte de Lucrèce, Fleuves et turbulence* (Paris: Editions de Minuit, 1977), 222ff. Lyotard thinks it is an atomistic Epicurean or Democritean model inspiring Deleuze and Guattari's vision of modern capitalism ("transit of objects, common concretions, exchangeable anonymous objects whose illusory existence can be maintained at the price of special energy expense"). Moreover, he remarks that this model is already present in the young Marx's writings, which use as a principle of the law of transformation the *clinamen,* which suscitates "in the heart of the atom something which can struggle and resist." Quoted in Jean-François Lyotard, "Capitalisme énergumène," in *Des Dispositifs pulsionnels* (Paris: Union Générale des Editions, 1973), 23.

28. Marguerite Duras, "Destruction and Language . . ." in *Destroy, She Said* (New York: Grove Press, 1970), 91, my emphasis. On the Durasian triangle and the Other, see M. Druon's excellent dissertation, "La scène triangulaire dans l'oeuvre romanesque de M. Duras," and C. Murphy's *Alienation and Absence in the Novels of M. Duras* (Lexington, Ky.: French Forum, 1982).

29. Marguerite Duras, *Le Ravissement de Lol V. Stein* (Paris: Gallimard, 1964), 52–54.

30. Marguerite Duras, *L'Amant anglaise* (Paris: Gallimard, 1967), 192, my emphasis.

31. M. Duras and X. Gauthier, *Les Parleuses* (Paris: Editions de Minuit, 1974), 234.

32. Ibid., 62.

33. Marguerite Duras, *India Song* (New York: Grove Press, 1976), 146.

34. Robert Morris, "American Quartet," *Art in America,* no. 10 (Dec. 1981), 104.

35. Ibid.

36. Ibid., 96.

37. Quoted in Rosalind Krauss, *Passages in Modern Sculpture* (Cambridge: MIT Press, 1981), 282.

38. Robert Smithson, *Art Présent,* no. 9 (Summer-Fall 1981): 43.

39. Quoted in Carter Ratcliff, "Mostly Monochrome," *Art in America,* no. 4 (Apr. 1981).

40. Marcia Hafif, "Getting on with Painting," *Art in America,* no. 4 (Apr. 1981), 134; Eugene Herrigel, *Art in the Art of Archery* (New York: Vintage, 1971), 41, quoted by Hafif, 134.

41. See Sherry Turkle, "Lacan in America, Poetry and Science," *Psychoanalytic Politics* (New York: Basic Books, 1978), 234–47, for a criticism of Lacan's 1975 visit to MIT, where, before a mystified scientific audience, Lacan spoke as a "mathematician and a poet." See also Lacan, "Ronds de ficelle," *Séminaire XX* (Paris: Editions du Seuil, 1975), 107–23.

42. This Real is indeed well hidden. One will seek in vain a definition in the *Vocabulaire de la Psychanalyse* by Laplanche and Pontalis (Paris: Presses Universitaires de France, 1967), which, however, contains articles on the Symbolic and the Imaginary. It is a protean term which can function in many contexts. For Jameson, for example, it is simply history. "It is not terribly difficult to say

what is meant by the real. . . . It is simply history itself . . . and . . . for psychoanalysis the history . . . in question here is obviously enough the history of the subject. . . . Both psychoanalysis and Marxism depend . . . on history in its other sense, as story and storytelling." "Imaginary and Symbolic in Lacan: Marxism, Psychoanalytic Criticism, and the Problem of the Subject," *Yale French Studies* 55–56 (1977): 338–95.

43. See Georgin, 38. "Il n'y a de vérité que de ce qui n'a aucun sens," *Séminaire du 11/12/73,* quoted in Shoshana Felman, "La Méprise et sa chance," *L'Arc* 58 (1974), 40.

44. Ibid., 40, 45.

45. Philippe Sollers, "Le Marxisme sodomisé par la psychanalyse elle-même violée par on ne sait quoi," *Tel Quel,* no. 75 (Spring 1978): 56.

46. Philippe Sollers, "Psychanalyse et Sémiotique," *Psychanalyse et Sémiotique* (Paris: Union Générale d'Editions, 1975), 126, my translation.

47. Philippe Sollers, "Le Cours de Freud," *Tel Quel,* no. 79 (Spring 1979): 98–101.

48. Deleuze and Guattari, 127.

49. Philippe Sollers, "Vers la notion de 'Paradis,' " *Tel Quel,* no. 75 (Spring 1978): 93, my translation.

50. Ibid., 96.

51. Philippe Sollers, "Pourquoi je suis si peu religieux," *Tel Quel,* no. 81 (Fall 1979): 7ff.

52. Philippe Sollers, *Paradis* (Paris: Seuil, 1981). "On the one side law blanks paragraphs on the other signature paraph on the one side right side from over beyond on the other reverse side always here on one side photography transcendence on the other razor immanence . . ." (100).

53. Ibid., 102, 215. See also 40, 41.

54. Ibid., 157.

55. Philippe Sollers, *Vision à New York* (Paris: Grasset, 1981).

56. See Jennifer Levine, "Rejoycings in Tel Quel," *James Joyce Quarterly* 16, no. 1/2 (1978–79). *Finnegans Wake* is especially appreciated for "its code breaking activity, and for its refusal of a center (God, Father, Author, Metalanguage) which might fix the text (or, indeed, the subject) in some privileged way."

57. Sollers, "Vers la notion," 93.

58. This remark comes from a commentary by M. Krieger in *"Murder in the Cathedral:* The Limits of Drama and Freedom of Vision," *The Classic Vision: The Retreat from Extremity* (Baltimore, Md.: Johns Hopkins Univ. Press, 1973), alluded to in his *Theory of Criticism* (Baltimore, Md.: John Hopkins Univ. Press, 1976), 21, in which he discusses Eliade's concept of sacred time.

59. Marcel Duchamp, quoted in M. Sanouillet, *Marchand de Sel* (Paris: Terrain Vague, 1959).

Ihab Hassan

The Culture of Postmodernism

As if modernism did not offer its share of queries, quandaries, and inconclusions, I bring further vexations in the name of postmodernism, a term that some have threatened to inscribe on my tombstone. Yet the term has become a current trope of tendencies in theater, dance, music, art, and architecture; in literature and criticism; in philosophy, psychoanalysis, and historiography; in cybernetic technologies; and even in the sciences, which are making "new alliances" with humanistic thought.

In the last two decades, the word postmodernism has shifted from awkward neologism to derelict cliché without ever attaining to the dignity of concept. Some want to theorize that concept now. And why should they be denied their theories? The effort to understand our historical presence, to perceive the interactions of language, knowledge, and power in our epoch, to valorize the living categories of our existence—surely that effort deserves our wakeful respect. More concretely, the central nisus of literary history in our time—namely, to problematize periodization, to apprehend history as theory, theory as literature, and literature as both history and theory—that nisus, I think, depends on our self-conceptions, to which postmodernism is crux.

Our concern, I have not forgotten, is with modernisms in all their versions, supplements, traces, and tergiversations; our concern, that is, centers on the enigmas of literary change. But literary change, like history itself, remains an engorged abstraction, another god that failed—unless grounded in some apprehension both personal and universal. That apprehension we call death, to which I now—I trust only abstractly—must briefly turn.

Death takes the measure of every change and inspires its metaphors. Suddenly, the body refuses its long intimacy with the will, giving itself to emptiness. Men lived, it seems, millennia without conscious knowledge of their deaths; nor do infants today possess such knowledge till they enter late childhood. Yet we all surrender nightly to dreamless sleep; and our civilization rests on burial mounds and cairns. As individuals of a secular society, we now refuse mythic time and religious consolation, and so feel death all the more acutely as rupture, cessation. No rebirth for us; no immortality or metempsychosis; no Heraclitean fire or Brunist transmutation, nor Hölderlin's *"aus dem Bunde der Wesen Schwindet der Tod."*

Ernest Becker believed that the human body represents the "curse of fate," and that culture stands on repression, not only of sexuality, as Freud thought, but also of mortality, "because man [is] . . . primarily an avoider of death."[1] We need not concur with this somber view to perceive that every creative act is also a small exercise in dying. For the new is an aspect of the unknown, "the undiscovered country from whose bourn / No traveler returns." Innovation/renovation, creation/recreation: such terms conspire deeply against our quotidian being.

Consider two familiar views of change, equally partial, perhaps equally true: one, surpassing even Heraclitus, asserts that "you can't step into the same stream once" (Cratylus); the other claims that "nothing is ever new under the sun" (Ecclesiastes). One favors change and difference, the other repetition and sameness. The first, disjunctive, preserves the gap between concrete phenomena; the second, conjunctive, fills gaps by its abstract narratives or metalanguages. We may need both, the first to perceive the New, the second to comprehend it. Yet each whispers to us of human mortality. For the discontinuous vision invokes perpetual rebirth, the phoenix rising from its ashes, while the vision of continuity yearns for retrospective immortality, the sphinx's anamnesis. Thus mortality may make cowards of us all, making politics the art of self-avoidance, making history a rehearsal of desires. Is there no way out of these deadly gyres?

Roland Barthes believed that "the New is not a fashion but a value" upon which we found our existence. "To escape from the alienation of present society, there is only one way: escape forward," he said.[2] But which way, in our day, is "forward"? Which "forward" evades mortality?

The questions, though communal, return us to the languages of the self. From Lacan we know that the symbolic subject, the self in language, constitutes itself in a *béance* or abysm; and so "no being is ever evoked by . . . [the subject] except among the shadows of death."[3] And from Foucault we learn that death serves as a cognitive principle in "the anonymous flow of speech," continually displacing the present; "to die" is an infinitive we can never complete.[4]

In short, more than an existential metaphor, more than an ontology of the new or a politics of innovation, death enters the very languages by which we try to understand change. It may also act, Heidegger thought, as the principle of any "authentic history," which finds its weight not in the "past" nor in the "today" but in the *Geschehen* or process of Existence, originating from the future, the "Being-toward-death."[5]

But it is time to abandon these morbid reflections and approach the problem at hand. History, I have suggested, moves in measures both continuous and discontinuous. Thus the prevalence of postmodernism today does not suggest that ideas or institutions of the past cease to shape the present. Rather, traditions develop, and even types suffer a sea-change. Certainly, the powerful cultural assumptions generated by, say, Darwin, Marx, Baudelaire, Nietzsche, Cézanne, Debussy, Freud, and Einstein, in their various fields, still pervade the Western mind. Certainly, those assumptions have been reconceived, not once but many times—else history would repeat itself, forever same. In this perspective, postmodernism may appear as a significant revision, if not an original *épistémè*, of twentieth-century *Western* societies.

Whence the term postmodernism? Its origin remains uncertain, though we know that Federico de Onís used the word *postmodernismo* in his *Antología de la poesía española e hispanoamericana* (1882–1932), published in Madrid in 1934; and Dudley Fitts picked it up again in his *Anthology of Contemporary Latin American Poetry* of 1942.[6] Both meant thus to indicate a minor reaction to modernism already latent within it, reverting to the early twentieth century. The term also appeared in Arnold Toynbee's *A Study of History* as early as D. C. Somervell's first-volume abridgement of 1947. For Toynbee, "Post-Modernism" designated a new historical cycle in Western civilization, starting around 1875, which we now scarcely begin to discern. Somewhat later, during the fifties, Charles Olson often spoke of postmodernism with more sweep than lapidary definition.

But prophets and poets enjoy an ample sense of time, which few literary scholars seem to afford. In 1959 and 1960, Irving Howe and Harry Levin wrote of postmodernism rather disconsolately as a falling-off from the great modernist movement.[7] It remained for Leslie Fiedler and myself, among others, to employ the term during the sixties with premature approbation, and even with a touch of bravado.[8] Fiedler had it in mind to challenge the elitism of the high modernist tradition in the name of popular culture; I wanted to explore that impulse of self-unmaking which is part of the literary tradition of silence. Pop and silence, or mass culture and deconstruction, or Superman and Godot—or, as I shall later argue, immanence and indeterminacy—may all be aspects of the postmodern universe. But all this must wait upon more patient analysis, longer history.

Yet the history of literary terms serves only to confirm the irrational genius of language. We come closer to the question of postmodernism itself by acknowledging the psychopolitics, if not the psychopathology, of academic life. Let us admit it: there is a will to power in nomenclature, as well as in people or texts. A new term opens for its proponents a space in language. A critical concept of system is a "poor" poem of the intellectual imagination. The battle of the books is also an ontic battle against death. That may be why Max Planck believed that one never manages to convince one's opponents—not even in theoretical physics!—one simply tries to outlive them. William James described the process with more cheer: novations, he said, are first repudiated as nonsense, then declared obvious, then appropriated by former adversaries as their own discoveries.

In an age of frantic intellectual fashions, values can be too recklessly voided, and tomorrow can quickly preempt today and yesteryear. The sense of supervention may express some cultural urgency that partakes less of hope than of fear. This much we recall: Lionel Trilling entitled one of his most thoughtful works *Beyond Culture* (1965); Kenneth Boulding argued that "postcivilization" is an essential part of *The Meaning of the Twentieth Century* (1964); and George Steiner could have subtitled his essay, *In Bluebeard's Castle* (1971), "Notes Toward the Definition of Postculture." Before them, Roderick Seidenberg had published his *Post-Historic Man* exactly in midcentury; and most recently, I have myself speculated, in *The Right Promethean Fire* (1980), about the advent of a post-humanist era. As Daniel Bell put it: "It used to be that the great literary modifier was the word *beyond*. ... But we seem to have exhausted the beyond, and today the sociological modifier is *post*."[9]

Hassan

My point here is double: in the question of postmodernism, there is a will and counter-will to intellectual power, an imperial desire of the mind, but this will and this desire are themselves caught in a historical moment of supervention, if not exactly of obsolescence. The reception or denial of postmodernism thus remains contingent on the psychopolitics of academic life—including the various dispositions of people and power in our universities, of critical factions and personal frictions, or boundaries that arbitrarily include or exclude—no less than on the imperatives of the culture at large. This much, reflexivity seems to demand from us at the start.

But reflection demands also that we address a number of conceptual problems that both conceal and constitute postmodernism itself. I shall try to isolate ten of these, commencing with the simpler, moving toward the more intractable.

1. The word postmodernism sounds not only awkward, uncouth, it evokes what it wishes to surpass or suppress, modernism itself. The term thus contains its enemy within, as the terms romanticism and classicism, baroque and rococo, do not. Moreover, it denotes temporal linearity and connotes belatedness, even decadence, to which no post-modernist would admit. But what better name have we to give this curious age? The Atomic, or Space, or Television Age? These technological tags lack theoretical definition. Or shall we call it the Age of Indetermanence (indeterminacy and immanence) as I have half-antically proposed?[10]

2. Like other categorical terms—say poststructuralism, or modernism, or romanticism, for that matter—postmodernism suffers from a certain *semantic* instability: that is, no clear consensus about its meaning exists among scholars. The general difficulty is compounded in this case by two factors, namely the relative youth, indeed brash adolescence, of the term postmodernism, and its semantic kinship with more current terms, themselves equally unstable. Thus some critics mean by postmodernism what others call avant-gardism or even neo-avant-gardism, while still others would call the same phenomenon simply modernism. This can make for inspired debates.[11]

3. A related difficulty concerns the *historical* instability of many literary concepts, their openness to change. Who, in this epoch of fierce misprisions, would dare to claim that romanticism is apprehended by Coleridge, Pater, Lovejoy, Abrams, Peckham, and Bloom in quite the same way? There is already some evidence that postmodernism, and

modernism even more, are beginning to slip and slide in time, threatening to make any diacritical distinction between them desperate.[12] But perhaps the phenomenon, akin to Hubble's "red shift" in astronomy, may someday serve to measure the historical velocity of literary concepts.

4. Modernism and postmodernism are not separated by an Iron Curtain or Chinese Wall; for history is a palimpsest, and culture is permeable in time past, time present, and time future. We are all, I suspect, a little Victorian, Modern, and Postmodern, at once. And an author may, in his or her own lifetime, easily write both a modernist and a postmodernist work. (Contrast Joyce's *Portrait of the Artist as a Young Man* with his *Finnegans Wake*.) More generally, on a certain level of narrative abstraction, modernism itself may be rightly assimilated to romanticism, romanticism related to the Enlightenment, the latter to the Renaissance, and so back, if not to the Olduvai Gorge, then certainly to ancient Greece.

5. This means that a "period," as I have already intimated, must be perceived in terms *both* of continuity *and* discontinuity, the two perspectives being complementary and partial. The Apollonian view, rangy and abstract, discerns only historical conjunctions; the Dionysian feeling, sensuous though nearly purblind, touches only the disjunctive moment. Thus postmodernism, by invoking two divinities at once, engages a double view. Sameness and difference, unity and rupture, filiation and revolt, all must be honored if we are to attend to history, apprehend (perceive, understand) change both as a spatial, mental structure and as a temporal, physical process, both as pattern and unique event.

6. Thus a "period" is generally not a period at all; it is rather both a diachronic and synchronic construct. Postmodernism is no exception; it requires *both* historical *and* theoretical definition. We cannot seriously claim an inaugural "date" for it as Virginia Woolf pertly did for modernism, which she said began "in or about December, 1910"—though we may sometimes woefully imagine that postmodernism began "in or about September, 1939." Thus we continually discover "antecedents" of post-modernism—in Sterne, Sade, Blake, Lautréamont, Rimbaud, Jarry, Tzara, Hofmannsthal, Stein, the later Joyce, the later Pound, Duchamp, Artaud, Roussel, Bataille, Broch, Queneau, and Kafka. What this really indicates is that we have created in our minds a model of postmodernism, a particular typology of culture and imagination, and have proceeded to "rediscover" the affinities of various authors and different moments with that model. We have, that is, reinvented our ancestors—and always

shall. Consequently, "older" authors can be postmodern—Kafka, Beckett, Borges, Nabokov, Gombrowicz—while "younger" authors need not be—Styron, Updike, Capote, Irving, Doctorow, Gardner.

7. As we have seen, any definition of postmodernism calls upon a fourfold vision of complementarities, embracing continuity and discontinuity, diachrony and synchrony. But a definition of the concept also requires a dialectical vision; for defining traits are often antithetical. Defining traits are dialectical and also plural; to elect a single trait as an absolute criterion of postmodern grace is to make of all other writers preterites.[13] Thus we cannot simply rest—as I have sometimes done— on the assumption that postmodernism is antiformal, anarchic, or decreative; for though it is indeed all these, and despite its fanatic will to unmaking, it also contains the need to discover a "unitary sensibility" (Sontag), to "cross the border and close the gap" (Fiedler), and to attain, as I have suggested, an immanence of discourse, an expanded noetic intervention, a "neo-gnostic im-mediacy of mind."[14]

8. All this leads to the prior problem of periodization itself, which is also that of literary history conceived as a particular apprehension of change. Indeed, the concept of postmodernism implies some theory of innovation, renovation, novation, or simple change. But which one? Heraclitean? Viconian? Darwinian? Marxist? Freudian? Kuhnian? Derridean? Eclectic?[15] Or is a "theory of change" itself an oxymoron best suited to ideologues intolerant of the ambiguities of time? Should postmodernism, then, be left—at least for the moment—unconceptualized, a kind of literary-historical "difference" or "trace"?[16]

9. Postmodernism can expand into a still larger problem: is it only an artistic tendency or also a social phenomenon, perhaps even a mutation in Western humanism? If so, how are the various aspects of this phenomenon—psychological, philosophical, economic, political—joined or disjoined? In short, can we understand postmodernism in literature without some attempt to perceive the lineaments of a postmodern society, a Toynbeean postmodernity, or future Foucauldian *épistémè,* of which the literary tendency I have been discussing is but a single, elitist strain?[17]

10. Finally, though not least vexing, is postmodernism an honorific term, used insidiously to valorize writers, however disparate, whom we otherwise esteem, to hail trends, however discordant, which we somehow approve? Or is it, on the contrary, a term of opprobrium and objurgation? In short, is postmodernism an evaluative or normative, as well as descriptive, category of literary thought? Or does it belong, as Charles

Altieri suggests, to that category of "essentially contested concepts" in philosophy which never wholly exhaust their constitutive confusions?[18]

No doubt other conceptual problems lurk in the matter of postmodernism. Such problems, however, cannot finally inhibit the desire to apprehend our historical presence in noetic constructs that reveal our being to ourselves. I move, therefore, to propose a provisional scheme that a strain in Western literature, from Sade to Beckett, seems to embody, and to do so by distinguishing, tentatively, among three modes of artistic change in the last hundred years. I call these avant-garde, modern, and postmodern, though I realize that all three have conspired together to create that "tradition of the new" which, since Baudelaire, brought "into being an art whose history, regardless of the credos of its practitioners, has consisted of leaps from vanguard to vanguard, and political mass movements whose aim has been the total renovation not only of social institutions but of man himself."[19]

By avant-garde, I mean those movements that agitated the earlier part of our century, including 'pataphysics, cubism, futurism, dadaism, surrealism, suprematism, constructivism, Merzism, de Stijl, and so on. Anarchic and disjunctive, these assaulted the bourgeoisie with their art, their manifestos, their antics. But their activism could also turn inward, becoming suicidal. Once full of brio and bravura, these movements have all but vanished now, leaving only their story, at once fugacious and exemplary.[20] Modernism, however, proved more stable, aloof, hieratic, like the French symbolism from which it derived; even its experiments now seem olympian. Enacted by such "individual talents" as Valéry, Proust, and Gide, the early Joyce, Yeats, and Lawrence, Rilke, Mann, and Musil, the early Pound, Eliot, and Faulkner, it commanded high authority, leading Delmore Schwartz to chant in *Shenandoah:* "Let us consider where the great men are / who will obsess the child when he can read."[21] But if much of modernism appears hieratic, hypotactical, and formalist, postmodernism strikes us by contrast as playful, paratactical, and deconstructionist. In this, it recalls the irreverent spirit of the avant-garde, and so carries sometimes the label of neo-avant-garde.[22] Yet postmodernism remains "cooler," in McLuhan's sense, than older vanguards—cooler, less cliquish, and far less aversive to the pop, electronic society of which postmodernism is a part, and thus hospitable to kitsch.[23]

Can we distinguish postmodernism from modernism further? Perhaps certain schematic differences will provide a start:

Hassan

MODERNISM	POSTMODERNISM
Romanticism/Symbolism	Pataphysics/Dadaism
Form (conjunctive, closed)	Antiform (disjunctive, open)
Purpose	Play
Design	Chance
Hierarchy	Anarchy
Mastery/Logos	Exhaustion/Silence
Art Object/Finished Work	Process/Performance/Happening
Distance	Participation
Creation/Totalization/Synthesis	Decreation/Deconstruction/Antithesis
Presence	Absence
Centering	Dispersal
Genre/Boundary	Text/Intertext
Semantics	Rhetoric
Paradigm	Syntagm
Hypotaxis	Parataxis
Metaphor	Metonymy
Selection	Combination
Root/Depth	Rhizome/Surface
Interpretation/Reading	Against Interpretation/Misreading
Signified	Signifier
Lisible (Readerly)	*Scriptible* (Writerly)
Narrative/*Grande Histoire*	Anti-narrative/*Petite Histoire*
Master Code	Idiolect
Symptom	Desire
Type	Mutant
Genital/Phallic	Polymorphous/Androgynous
Paranoia	Schizophrenia
Origin/Cause	Difference-Differance/Trace
God the Father	The Holy Ghost
Metaphysics	Irony
Determinacy	Indeterminacy
Transcendence	Immanence

The preceding table draws on ideas in many fields—rhetoric, linguistics, literary theory, philosophy, anthropology, psychoanalysis, political science, even theology—and draws on many authors—European and American—aligned with diverse movements, groups, and views. Yet the dichotomies this table represents remain insecure, equivocal. For differences shift, defer, even collapse; concepts in any one vertical column are not all equivalent; and inversions and exceptions, in both modernism and postmodernism, abound. Still, I would submit that rubrics in the right column point to the postmodern tendency, the tendency of indeterminence, and so may bring us closer to its historical and theoretical definition.

The time has come, however, to explain a little that neologism, "indetermanence," and to address the culture of postmodernism which the neologism attempts to describe. I commence with some views of Daniel Bell, who thinks that "we are coming to a watershed in Western society: we are witnessing the end of the bourgeois idea—that view of human action and social relations, particularly of economic change—which has molded the modern era for the last 200 years. And I believe that we have reached the end of the creative impulse and ideological sway of modernism, which, as a cultural movement, has dominated all the arts, and shaped our symbolic expressions, for the past 125 years."[24] Disjunctions between the realms of economy, polity, and culture; the crisis of the Protestant ethic, of middle-class values in general; the advent, beyond rising expectations, of a politics of entitlement or envy; syncretism and the jumbling of styles of culture; the increasing permeability of all society to novelty, without discrimination or resistance; the confusions of fact and fantasy in public as in private life; the enervation of the postmodern self, nourished on hedonism, consumption, febrile affluence—all these, Bell argues, have undermined the Western "order of things." But Bell goes on still further to identify not only technology but also culture (by which he means the entire symbolic universe, managed more and more by postmodern vanguards) as the culprit. For the "postmodernist temper demands that what was previously played out in fantasy and imagination must be acted out in life as well. . . . Anything permitted in art is permitted in life."[25] Thus cultural vanguards come to assume primacy "in the fields of manners, morals, and, ultimately, politics."[26] Bell exaggerates the triumph of these movements; and though he writes with acumen, he writes as a conservative sociologist, who finds it lamentable that the contemporary imagination should serve to disconfirm our policy. (I wonder if he has read much in classic American literature or sensed its powers of darkness.)

Jean-François Lyotard, however, rejoices in the very same evidence of disconfirmation. *La Condition postmoderne* both corroborates *The Cultural Contradictions of Capitalism* and profoundly challenges its values. Lyotard's central theme is the desuetude of the "great narratives" and "metanarratives" which once organized bourgeois society. The radical crisis, then, is one of *"légitimation"*—compare with Habermas's "legitimation crisis" in *Legitimations Probleme in Spät Kapitalismus*—in every cognitive and social endeavor where a multitude of languages now reign. I translate freely Lyotard's theme:

The postmodern condition is a stranger to disenchantment as to the blind positivity of delegitimation. Where can legitimacy reside after the dissolution of metanarratives? The criterion of functionality is merely technological; it cannot apply to judgments of truth and justice. The consensus obtained by discussion, as Habermas thinks? That criterion violates the heterogeneity of language games. And inventions are always made in dissent. Postmodern knowledge is not only the instrument of power. It refines our sensibilities, awakens them to differences, and strengthens our capacities to bear the incommensurable. It does not find its reason in the homologies of experts but in the paralogies of inventors.

The open question, then, is this: can a legitimation of social relations, can a just society, be made practicable in accordance with a paradox analogous to that of current scientific activity? And of what would such a paradox consist?[27]

Lyotard thus ushers us, somewhat utopically, into the postmodern era of *"les petites histoires"*: paratactical, paradoxical, paralogical narratives meant to open the structures of knowledge, as of politics, to language games, to imaginative reconstitutions that permit us either a new breakthrough or a change in the rules of the game itself.[28] He concludes: "A politics is taking shape in which the desires for both justice and the unknown are equally respected."[29] This ignores that "human justice," alas, can sanction bloody terror, and that "the unknown" can provoke intolerant reactions, provoke new quests for certainty or authority.

Still, it is of some interest that two thinkers, one conservative and the other radical, respond to a phenomenon that both call by the same name (though Bell protests against postmodernism by hyphenating the word, which both Lyotard and I find unnecessary). But the initial question remains: what is indetermanence? Or put another way: what useful scheme of postmodern transformations can we devise? The scheme I would propose proves to be less a scheme than a complex double tendency. The two tendencies are not dialectical; for they are not exactly antithetical, nor do they lead to any synthesis. Furthermore, each tendency generates its own contradictions, and contains as well elements of the other tendency. The two tendencies, then, interplay, their actions, ludic and deadly serious, suggesting the pattern of an ambilectic that now modulates important changes in nearly every domain of Western culture in the last half-century.

The *first* of these tendencies I have elsewhere called Indeterminacy.[30] But the tendency is really compounded of subtendencies evoked by the following words: openness, heterodoxy, pluralism, eclecticism, randomness, revolt, deformation. The latter alone subsumes a dozen current terms of unmaking: decreation, difference, discontinuity, disjunction, disappearance, decomposition, dedefinition, demystification, detotalization, delegitimation—let alone more technical and rhetorical terms, such as chiasmus, lapsus, schism, hiatus, diremption, suture, transumption, idiolect, heteromorph, and so on. Through all these signs moves a vast will to unmaking, affecting the body politic, the body cognitive, the erotic body, the psyche of each individual—affecting, in short, the entire realm of human discourse in the West. We may then call that tendency *Indeterminacies*, thus recognizing its plural character, which nonetheless reopens or revokes our familiar modes of thought and being.

I scarcely know where I might begin to document so pervasive, so perverse, a trend. In literature alone, our ideas of author, audience, reading, writing, book, genre, critical theory, and literature itself have all suddenly become questionable.[31] We now speak of intertextuality and semioclasty (Julia Kristeva), of a hermeneutics of suspicion (Paul Ricoeur), or a criticism of bliss and a pedagogy of unlearning (Roland Barthes). We propose schizo-analysis (Gilles Deleuze and Félix Guattari), a humanism of disappearance (Michel Foucault), a grammatology of differences (Jacques Derrida), a politics of delegitimation (Jean-François Lyotard). These *philosophies blanches* truly abound: ideologies of fracture, metaphysics of absence, theologies of the supplement, mystiques of the trace.[32] But Gaul is not the only home of epistemological Gaullism, Gallic *ratures*, and borrowed *unheimlichkeit*. Others near at hand speak of paracriticism and parabiography (Ihab Hassan), freaks and mutants (Leslie Fiedler), dialogy and the imagination of doubt (Matei Calinescu), surfiction and playgiarism (Raymond Federman), a third-phase psychoanalysis of intimacy and incompleteness (Norman Holland), a theater of impossibility, brought to the vanishing point (Herbert Blau).[33] In so speaking, they testify variously to the indeterminate, or decreative, or antinomian impulse of our moment, a moment that reaches back half a century to Heisenberg's Principle of Uncertainty in physics and Gödel's Proof of Incompleteness (or Undecidability) in all logical systems. (The two theories, though logically unrelated, express the same spirit of limitation or ambiguity, which leads Douglas Hofstadter to remark that "provability is a weaker notion than truth, no matter what axiomatic system is involved."[34] Yet in the end the epistemic factor proves to be only one of many. The force of the antinomian and indeterminate tendency derives from larger dispositions in society: a rising standard of living in the West, the disruption of institutional values, freed desires, liberation movements of every kind, schism and secession around the globe, terrorism rampant—in short, the Many asserting their primacy over the One.

We may now challenge the totalizing will, from Pharaoh or Moses through Louis XIV ("*L'état c'est moi!*") and Charlie Wilson ("What's good for General Motors is good for the country") to Stalin, Hitler, Mao, and Castro. But we may not overlook a *second* major tendency of the postmodern world, dispersing the will of the One. I call that tendency *Immanences,* a term I employ without religious echo, and by which I mean the capacity of mind to generalize itself in the world, to act upon both self and world, and so become more and more, immediately, its own environment. Various thinkers have reflected variously upon this tendency, speaking of etherialization (Arnold Toynbee), ephemeralization (Buckminster Fuller), conceptualization (Erwin Laszlo), dematerialization (Paolo Soleri), of nature historicized (Karl Marx) and the earth hominized (Teilhard de Chardin), and of a new technological and scientific gnosis (Ihab Hassan).[35] The tendency—evoked also by such sundry words as dispersal, diffusion, dissemination, diffraction, pulsion, integration, ecumenism, communication, interplay, interdependence, and interpenetration—depends, above all, on the emergence of man as a language animal, *homo pictor* or *homo significans,* a creature constituting himself, and increasingly his universe, by symbols of his own making. Is "this not the sign that the whole of this [classic] configuration is about to topple, and that man is in the process of perishing as the being of language continues to shine ever brighter upon our horizon?" Foucault asks.[36]

More than Foucault, however, Lyotard considers the role of media (*l'informatique*) in shaping the languages of self and society in advanced capitalist states; tomorrow's encyclopedias, he suggests, may be data banks which could become "nature" itself for postmodern man.[37] Media, of course, may derealize history even as they disseminate it around the world, often as kitsch or entertainment. But media also project mind to the edge of the universe or into the ghostly interstices of matter, and so abet another type of immanence, which scientists since Heisenberg have recognized as human participation or intervention in nature. Daniel Bell perceives this as the emergent stage of cultural development, implicating human beings in the recreation of reality, and confronting post-Kantian epistemologies with the enigma of artificial intelligence.[38] "Beyond this is a larger dream," Bell writes. "Just as Pascal sought to throw dice with God . . . so the decision theorists, and the new intellectual technology, seek their own *tableau entier*—the compass of rationality itself."[39] Yet both Lyotard's *"informatique"* and Bell's *"tableau entier"* have already created disquieting constraints in postmodern societies, constraints demanding from us stringent moral and political critiques.

Still other factors further the immanences of which I speak. The explosion of human populations increases the intellectual density of the earth, the possibilities of mental no less than physical interactions. (As everyone knows, a room holding one or two people differs radically from the same space containing seven, or again seventy, more.) Such intense interaction, Bell believes, augments both differences in the social structure (indeterminacies?) and syncretism in the culture (immanences?).[40] "In principle, much of this is not new," Bell adds. "What is distinctive is the change of scale. . . . All that we once knew played out on the scale of the Greek polis is now played out in the dimensions of the entire world. Scale creates two effects: one, it extends the range of control from a center of power. (What is Stalin, an unknown wit remarked, if not Genghis Khan with a telephone?) And two, when linear extensions reach certain thresholds, unsettling changes ensue."[41] Such immanences we may learn to rue. Still, though one immanence may become totalitarian, complex immanences of language and indeterminacies of theories or praxis diffract power, and so force us to reconceive the relation between wholes and parts.

This leads toward my didactic inconclusion. For the problem of postmodernism does finally engage crucial moral and political questions. These allude, as pre-Socratics used to say, to the play of the One and the Many: that is, to the essential unity of existence and its perceived diversity, its underlying sameness and visible difference—or, as we might nowadays say: to ecumenism and sectarianism, federalism and secession, centering and dispersal, presence and deferral. In our own divisive, diffusive, destructuring age, the tension between these terms threatens to snap. Yet we cannot afford to choose between the One and the Many, any more than we can accept *either* totalitarianism *or* terror.

The point is pertinent to teachers of the humanities, who have become inured to ambiguity, undecidability, dissemination, and deconstruction in the arts and theories they teach. Such ambiguity is liberating; it restores us to the multiplicity of creation; and it enhances our tolerance for differences of every kind. But such ambiguity must also imply some nexus of assent, some active context of value and power—in short, some Authority, the very authority which *both* limits and enables our shifting freedoms.

Truly, the question of authority is cardinal to current social, artistic, or epistemic debates. The authority can be as bland as the convention that permits me now to speak without interruptions from the audience; or it can be far more subtle and subversive, complex and coercive. In any case, authority—to which value is always attached—is what prevents human beings, if not from reverting to the state of nature, then from facing anew—every year, every hour—"the elementary problems of human living together" as Hannah Arendt put it.[42]

Who judges? why judge? how judge? when judge? whom or what judge? These are some of the renitent questions that postmodernism finally summons before us, and that authority must mediate. I cannot answer these queries myself, though I suspect that they are partially answered in the asking, and so must be asked again and again. Speaking for myself, in this time and in this place, I know that in searching for an answer I am more likely to turn to Emerson than Nietzsche, and to Nietzsche more than Marx, turn, that is, to an integrative yet dialogical faculty like Imagination, in which discord and concord coexist, rather than to an analytic, monological faculty, including Demystification, which becomes finally sterile.

In the end, I repeat, we cannot, *must* not, choose between the One and the Many, Clarity and Ambiguity, Classicism and Modernism, Community and Dissemination. We can only open such terms to constant negotiations, perpetual transactions of desire, freedom, and justice, mediated by authorities that we need as much to reestablish as to reinvent. Indeed, despite all the conflicts, all the aporias, which constitute our world, is not our discourse here itself exemplary of a hermeneutic community of provisional trust? Heterodox, heteromorph, heteroclite, and indeterminate withal, we live in one human universe and astonish each other with our assents. On this, the culture of postmodernism still depends.[43]

Notes

1. Ernest Becker, *The Denial of Death* (New York: The Free Press, 1975), 96.

2. Roland Barthes, *The Pleasure of the Text*, trans. Richard Howard (New York: Hill & Wang, 1975), 40.

3. Jacques Lacan, *The Language of the Self,* trans. Anthony Wilden (Baltimore, Md.: Johns Hopkins Univ. Press, 1968), 85.

4. Michel Foucault, *Language, Counter-Memory, Practice,* trans. Donald F. Bouchard and Sherry Simon (Ithaca, N.Y.: Cornell Univ. Press, 1977), 174f.

5. Martin Heidegger, *Existence and Being* (Chicago: Henry Regnery, 1949), 92.

6. For the best history of the term "postmodernism," see Michael Köhler, " 'Postmodernismus': Ein begriffsgeschichtlicher überblick," *Amerikastudien* 22, no. 1 (1977): 8–18. That same issue contains other excellent discussions and bibliographies of the term; see particularly Gerhard Hoffmann, Alfred Hornung, and Rüdiger Kunow, " 'Modern,' 'Postmodern,' and 'Contemporary' as Criteria for the Analysis of Twentieth-Century Literature," 19–46.

7. Irving Howe, "Mass Society and Postmodern Fiction," *Partisan Review* 26, no. 3 (Summer 1959), reprinted in his *Decline of the New* (New York: Harcourt, Brace, 1970), 190–207; Harry Levin, "What was Modernism?" *Massachusetts Review* 1, no. 4 (Aug. 1960), reprinted in *Refractions* (New York: Oxford Univ. Press, 1966), 271–95.

8. Leslie Fiedler, "The New Mutants," *Partisan Review* 32, no. 4 (Fall 1965), reprinted in his *Collected Essays* (New York: Stein & Day, 1971), 2: 379–400; and Ihab Hassan, "Frontiers of Criticism: Metaphors of Silence," *Virginia Quarterly* 46, no. 1 (Winter 1970). In earlier essays, I had also used the term "anti-literature" and "the literature of silence" in a proximate sense; see, for instance, Ihab Hassan, "The Literature of Silence," *Encounter* 28, no. 1 (Jan. 1967).

9. Daniel Bell, *The Coming of Post-Industrial Society* (New York: Basic Books, 1973), 53.

10. See Ihab Hassan, "Culture, Indeterminacy, and Immanence: Margins of the (Postmodern) Age," *Humanities in Society* 1, no. 1 (Winter 1978); reprinted in *The Right Promethean Fire: Imagination, Science, and Cultural Change* (Urbana: Univ. of Illinois Press, 1980), ch. 3.

11. Matei Calinescu, for instance, tends to assimilate "postmodern" to "neo-avant-garde" and sometimes to "avant-garde," in *Faces of Modernity: Avant-Garde, Decadence, Kitsch* (Bloomington: Indiana Univ. Press, 1977), though later he discriminates among these terms thoughtfully, in "Avant-Garde, Neo-Avant-Garde, and Postmodernism," in *Perspectives on the Avant-Garde,* ed. Rudolf Kuenzli and Stephen Foster (Iowa City: Univ. of Iowa Press, forthcoming). Miklos Szabolcsi would identify "modern" with "avant-garde" and call "postmodern" the "neo-avant-garde," in "Avant-Garde, Neo-Avant-Garde, Modernism: Questions and Suggestions," *New Literary History* 3, no. 1 (Autumn 1971): 49–70, while Paul de Man would call "modern" the innovative element, the perpetual "moment of crisis" in the literature of every period, in "Literary History and Literary Modernity," in *Blindness and Insight* (New York: Oxford Univ. Press, 1971), ch. 8; in a similar vein, William V. Spanos employs the term "postmodernism" to indicate "not fundamentally a chronological event, but rather a permanent mode of human understanding," in "Destruction and the Question of Postmodern Literature: Towards a Definition," *Par Rapport* 2, no.

2 (Summer 1979): 107. And even John Barth, as inward as any writer with postmodernism, now argues that postmodernism is a synthesis yet to come, and that what we had assumed to be postmodernism all along was only later modernism, in "The Literature of Replenishment: Postmodernist Fiction," *Atlantic Monthly* 245, no. 1 (Jan. 1980): 65–70.

12. In my own earlier and later essays on the subject I can discern such a slight shift; see "POSTmodernISM: A Paracritical Bibliography," *New Literary History* 3, no. 1 (Autumn 1971), reprinted in my *Paracriticisms: Seven Speculations of the Times* (Urbana: Univ. of Illinois Press, 1975), ch. 2; "Joyce, Beckett, and the Postmodern Imagination," *Triquarterly* 34 (Fall 1975): 179–200; and "Culture, Indeterminacy, and Immanence."

13. Though some critics have argued that postmodernism is primarily "temporal," and others that it is mainly "spatial," it is in the particular relation between these single categories that postmodernism probably reveals itself. See the two seemingly contradictory views of William V. Spanos, "The Detective at the Boundary," in *Existentialism 2,* ed. William V. Spanos (New York: Thomas Y. Crowell, 1976), 163–89; and Jürgen Peper, "Postmodernismus: Unitary Sensibility," *Amerikastudien* 22, no. 1 (1977): 65–89.

14. Susan Sontag, "One Culture and the New Sensibility," in *Against Interpretation* (New York: Farrar, Straus & Giroux, 1967), 293–304; Leslie Fiedler, "Cross the Border—Close the Gap," in *Collected Essays,* 2: 461–85; and Ihab Hassan, "The New Gnosticism," *Paracriticisms,* ch. 6.

15. For some views of this, see Ihab and Sally Hassan, eds., *Innovation/Renovation: New Perspectives on the Humanities* (Madison: Univ. of Wisconsin Press, 1983).

16. At stake here is the idea of literary periodicity, challenged by current French thought. For other views of literary and historical change, including "hierarchic organization" of time, see Leonard Meyer, *Music, the Arts, and Ideas* (Chicago: Univ. of Chicago Press, 1967), 93, 102; Calinescu, *Faces of Modernity,* 147ff.; Ralph Cohen, "Innovation and Variation: Literary Change and Georgic Poetry," in *Literature and History,* ed. Ralph Cohen and Murray Krieger, (Berkeley and Los Angeles: Univ. of California Press, 1974); and my *Paracriticisms,* ch. 7. A harder question is one Geoffrey Hartman asks: "With so much historical knowledge, how can we avoid historicism, or the staging of history as a drama in which epiphanic raptures are replaced by epistemic ruptures?" Or, again, how can we "formulate a theory of reading that would be historical rather than historicist"? *Saving the Text: Literature/Derrida/Philosophy* (Baltimore, Md.: Johns Hopkins Univ. Press, 1981), xx.

17. Writers as different as Marshall McLuhan and Leslie Fiedler have explored the media and pop aspects of postmodernism for two decades, though their efforts are now out of fashion in some critical circles. The difference between postmodernism, as a contemporary artistic tendency, and postmodernity, as a cultural phenomenon, perhaps even an era of history, is discussed by Richard E. Palmer in "Postmodernity and Hermeneutics," *Boundary 2,* vol. 5, no. 2 (Winter 1977).

18. Charles Altieri, "Postmodernism: A Question of Definition," *Par Rapport* 2, no. 2 (Summer 1979): 90. This leads Altieri to conclude that "the best one

can do who believes himself post-modern . . . is to articulate spaces of mind in which the confusions can not paralyze because one enjoys the energies and glimpses of our condition which they produce" (99).

19. Harold Rosenberg, *The Tradition of the New* (New York: Grove Press, 1961), 9. See also Ihab Hassan, *The Dismemberment of Orpheus,* 2d rev. ed. (Madison: Univ. of Wisconsin Press, 1982), for further elaboration of these modes.

20. See especially Roger Shattuck, *The Banquet Years* (New York: Vintage, 1968); Renato Poggioli, *Theory of the Avant-Garde,* trans. Gerald Fitzgerald (Cambridge: Harvard Univ. Press, 1968); Peter Bürger, *Theorie der Avant-Garde* (Frankfurt am Main: Suhrkamp Verlag, 1974); Calinescu, *Faces of Modernity; and Les Avant-gardes littéraires au XXᵉ siècle,* ed. Jean Weisgerber, 2 vols. (Paris: Didier, 1980). The last two works contain useful bibliographies of the avant-gardes.

21. Delmore Schwartz, *Shenandoah* (Norfolk, Conn.: New Directions, 1941), 20. Works that address modernism include Edmund Wilson, *Axel's Castle* (New York: Charles Scribner's Sons, 1931); José Ortega y Gasset, *The Modern Theme,* trans. James Cleugh (New York: Norton, 1933) and *The Dehumanization of Art,* trans. Helene Weyl (Princeton, N.J.: Princeton Univ. Press, 1948); Lionel Trilling, *Beyond Culture* (New York: Viking, 1965); Ihab Hassan, *The Dismemberment of Orpheus;* Hugh Kenner, *The Pound Era* (Berkeley and Los Angeles: Univ. of California Press, 1971); Malcolm Bradbury and James McFarlane, eds., *Modernism* (New York: Penguin, 1976); and Calinescu, *Faces of Modernity.* The last two works contain extensive bibliographies of modernism as well as postmodernism.

22. For a discussion of postmodernism, in addition to the works of Bradbury, Calinescu, and Hassan cited above, see John Barth, "The Literature of Exhaustion," *Atlantic Monthly,* Aug. 1967, and, less persuasive, "The Literature of Replenishment"; Hassan, "Joyce, Beckett, and the Postmodern Imagination," and *Paracriticisms,* esp. pp. 45f. (which refers to relevant works by Leslie Fiedler, Richard Poirier, Susan Sontag, and George Steiner); Raymond Federman, ed., *Surfiction* (Chicago: Swallow Press, 1975); Charles Russell, ed., *The Avant-Garde Today* (Urbana: Univ. of Illinois Press, 1981); Mas'ud Zavarzadeh, *The Mythopoeic Reality* (Urbana: Univ. of Illinois Press, 1976); and *Amerikastudien* 22, no. 1 (1977). Again, the last two works offer lengthy bibliographies.

23. This is a point that Hans Magnus Enzensberger mistakes in his otherwise witty and perceptive essay, "The Aporias of the Avant-Garde," *The Consciousness Industry* (New York: Seabury, 1974). I believe Daniel Bell comes here nearer the mark: "What is most striking about postmodernism is that what was once maintained as esoteric is now proclaimed as ideology, and what was once the property of an aristocracy of the spirit is now turned into the democratic property of the mass." *The Cultural Contradictions of Capitalism* (New York; Basic Books, 1976), 52.

24. Bell, 7.

25. Ibid., 53f. Carl Friedrich von Weizsäcker makes the more serious point about the predominance of pleasure in any society: "Und dann sage ich schon in diesem ganz einfachen Sinne von Glück—Erreichen von Angenehmem oder

322

Hassan

Erwünschtem, Vermeiden von Unangehenmem oder unerwünschtem Schmerz-haftem: die Orientierung an diesem Kriterium als Fundamentalorientierung einer Gesellschaft ist die Garantie des untergangs dieser Gesellschaft." *Wachstum und Lebenssinn—Alternative Rationalitäten?* Bergedorfer Gesprachskreis, Protokoll-Nr. 61 (1978): 8.

26. Ibid., 34.

27. Jean-François Lyotard, *La Condition postmoderne* (Paris: Editions de Minuit, 1979), 8f.

28. Ibid., 85f., 97f., 107.

29. Ibid., 108. Unlike Jürgen Habermas, Lyotard doubts the final value of *Diskurs,* consensus. For a critique of Habermas based on a confrontation between the latter and French thought, especially Derrida, see Dominick LaCapra, "Habermas and the Grounding of Critical Theory," *History and Theory* 16, no. 3 (Oct. 1977).

30. Ihab Hassan, "Culture, Indeterminacy, and Immanence," in *The Right Promethean Fire.* This chapter, as well as another entitled "The Re-Vision of Literature," contains material relevant to this discussion.

31. Ibid., 49–52; but see also pp. 109–14.

32. For good introductions to current French literary thought, see Jonathan Culler, *Structuralist Poetics* (Ithaca, N.Y.: Cornell Univ. Press, 1975) and *The Pursuit of Signs* (Ithaca, N.Y.: Cornell Univ. Press, 1981); Edward Said, *Beginnings* (New York: Basic Books, 1975); and Josué V. Harari, ed., *Textual Strategies* (Ithaca, N.Y.: Cornell Univ. Press, 1979); and for a thoughtful assessment of their impact, see Geoffrey H. Hartman, *Criticism in the Wilderness* (New Haven, Conn.: Yale Univ. Press, 1980). Note also that though postmodernism and poststructuralism cannot be identified, they clearly reveal many affinities. Thus in the course of one brief essay, for instance, Julia Kristeva comments on both immanence and indeterminacy in terms of her own: "Postmodernism is that literature which writes itself with the more or less conscious intention of expanding the signifiable, and thus human, realm"; and again: "At this degree of singularity, we are faced with idiolects, proliferating uncontrollably." See Julia Kristeva, "Postmodernism?" in Harry R. Garvin, ed., *Romanticism, Modernism, Post-modernism* (Lewisburg, Penn.: Bucknell Univ. Press, 1980), 137–41.

33. In addition, see such recent attempts to reconceive various disciplines as Norman O. Brown, *Closing Time* (New York: Random House, 1973); David L. Miller, *The New Polytheism* (New York: Harper & Row, 1975); Paul Fey-erabend, *Against Method* (London: NLB, 1975); Charles Jencks, *The Language of Post-Modern Architecture* (New York: Rizzoli, 1977); Hayden White, *Tropics of Discourse* (Baltimore, Md.: John Hopkins Univ. Press, 1978); and Harold Bloom, et al., *Deconstruction and Criticism* (New York: Seabury Press, 1979).

34. See Jeremy Bernstein, *Experiencing Science* (New York: Basic Books, 1978) and Douglas R. Hofstadter, *Gödel, Escher, Bach: An Eternal Golden Braid* (New York: Basic Books, 1979), 19. Both authors explain abstruse problems in such lucid and joyful prose as might put some literary critics to shame.

35. See Hassan, "The New Gnosticism," *Paracriticisms,* and "The Gnosis of Science," *The Right Promethean Fire,* for discussions of this trend.

36. Michel Foucault, *The Order of Things* (New York: Pantheon, 1970), 386.

37. *La Condition postmoderne,* 84f.; see also 16, 30f., and 63.

38. Daniel Bell, "Technology, Nature, and Society," in *Technology and the Frontiers of Knowledge* (Garden City, N.Y.: Doubleday, 1975), 34–42.

39. Ibid., 52f. But see also Hubert L. Dreyfus, *What Computers Can't Do* (New York: Harper & Row, 1979), for a skeptical counterstatement, which challenges Bell and possibly Lyotard (see n. 60). Dreyfus insists that the human mind proceeds by quantum leaps and tropes, creating whole configurations that no digital computer can simulate. The issue of Artificial Intelligence, however, remains far from settled.

40. Ibid., 54f.

41. Ibid., 56.

42. Hannah Arendt, *Between Past and Future* (New York: Viking, 1968), 141.

43. Portions of this text have appeared in Ihab Hassan, *The Dismemberment of Orpheus: Toward a Postmodern Literature,* 2d rev. ed. (Madison: Univ. of Wisconsin Press, 1982), and in *Innovation/Renovation: New Perspectives on the Humanities,* ed. Ihab Hassan and Sally Hassan (Madison: Univ. of Wisconsin Press, 1983).

Selected Bibliography

Instead of a compilation of all works informing the essays contained in this volume this selected bibliography is presented as a supplementary document. It does not duplicate the information contained in the notes to the preceding essays, nor does it constitute a complete inventory of all other available publications to date on modernism. It primarily concentrates on works of particular interest for further studies selected from those published after the imposing bibliography compiled by Malcolm Bradbury and James McFarlane for their 1976 Pelican guide, or published previously but not featured in their selection. Titles entered in the Pelican guide are given again here only when a more recent edition has appeared. Although the following selection focuses particularly on aspects of modernism discussed in these pages, attention is also given to some movements or nations which could not possibly be included in one single volume but which we consider equally central to an understanding of modernism.

ACKROYD, PETER. *Notes for a New Culture: An Essay on Modernism.* New York: Barnes & Noble, 1976.

ADORNO, THEODOR. *The Philosophy of Modern Music.* 1948. Trans. Anne G. Mitchell and Wesley V. Blomster. New York: Seabury, 1973.

ALBÉRES, R. M. *Littérature horizon 2000.* Paris: Albin Michel, 1974.

AMARAL, ARACY A., *Artes plásticas na semana de São Paulo.* São Paulo: Editoria Perspectiva, 1976.

———, et al. *Arte y architectura del Modernismo Brasileño.* Caracas: Biblioteca Ayacucho, 1978.

ANDERSON, ROBERT. *Spanish American Modernism.* Tucson: Univ. of Arizona Press, 1970.

ANTIN, DAVID. *Talking at the Boundaries.* New York: New Directions, 1976.

ARNOLD, ALBERT JAMES. *Modernism and Negritude: The Poetry and Poetics of Aimé Césaire.* Cambridge: Harvard Univ. Press, 1981.

ASHTON, DORE. *A Fable of Modern Art.* London: Thames & Hudson, 1980.

AVILA, ALFONSO, ed. *O modernismo.* São Paulo: Editora Perspectiva, 1975.

BALAKIAN, ANNA. *Surrealism, the Road to the Absolute.* Rev. and enlarged. New York: Dutton, 1970.

———, ed. *The Symbolist Movement in the Literature of European Languages.*

Vol. 2 of *A Comparative History of Literatures in European Languages.* Budapest: Akademiai Kiado, 1982.

BARON, FRANK, ed. *Rilke and the Visual Arts.* Lawrence, Kans.: Coronado Press, 1982.

BARRETT, WILLIAM. *Time of Need: Forms of Imagination in the Twentieth Century.* New York: Harper & Row, 1972.

BASSEGODA, JUAN, et al., *autores,* JOSÉ M. INFIESTA, coordinator. *Modernismo en Cataluña.* Barcelona: Ediciones de Nuevo Arte Thor, 1976.

BATISTA, MARTA ROSSETI, et al. *Brasil: 1° Tempo modernista—1917–29 Documentação.* São Paulo: Instituto des Estudos Brasileiros, 1972.

BENDER, TODD K. *Modernism in Literature.* New York: Holt, Rinehart & Winston, 1977.

BERGMANN, PAR. *Modernolatria et Simultaneita.* Upsala: Studia Litterarum Upsaliensia no. 2, 1962.

BERMAN, MARSHALL. *All That Is Solid Melts Into Air: The Experience of Modernity.* New York: Simon & Schuster, 1982.

BORNSTEIN, GEORGE. *Transformations of Romanticism in Yeats, Eliot, and Stevens.* Chicago: Univ. of Chicago Press, 1976.

BRADBURY, MALCOLM, and JAMES McFARLANE, eds. *Modernism: 1890–1930.* New York: Penguin, 1976.

BRASIL, ASSIS. *O Modernismo.* Rio de Janeiro: Pallas, 1976.

BRION-GUERRY, LILIANE, ed. *L'année 1913. Les formes esthétiques de l'oeuvre d'art à la veille de la première guerre mondiale.* Paris: Klincksieck, 1977.

BÜRGER, PETER. *Theorie der Avantgarde.* Frankfurt am Main: Suhrkamp, 1974.

CALINESCU, MATEI. *Faces of Modernity: Avant-garde, Decadence, Kitsch.* Bloomington: Indiana Univ. Press, 1977.

CARDWELL, RICHARD ANDREW. *Juan R. Jiménez: The Modernist Apprenticeship 1895–1900.* Berlin: Colloquium Verlag, 1977.

CAWS, MARY ANN. *The Eye in the Text: Essays on Perception, Mannerist to Modern.* Princeton, N.J.: Princeton Univ. Press, 1981.

————. *The Inner Theatre of Recent French Poetry (Cendrars, Tzara, Péret, Artaud, Bonnefoy).* Princeton, N.J.: Princeton Univ. Press, 1972.

————. *The Metapoetics of the Passage: Architextures in Surrealism and After.* Hanover: University Press of New England, 1981.

CHIARI, JOSEPH. *The Aesthetics of Modernism.* New York: Humanities, 1970.

CONNOLLY, CYRIL. *The Modern Movement: One Hundred Key Books from England, France, and America 1880–1950.* New York: Atheneum, 1966.

DAVIDSON, ABRAHAM A. *Early American Modernist Painting, 1910–1935.* New York: Harper & Row, 1981.

DÉCAUDIN, MICHEL, AND GEORGES RAILLARD, eds. *La Modernité, Cahiers du 20ᵉ siècle* special issue no. 5. Paris: Klincksieck, 1975. Essays by Margaret Davies, Frieda Weissmann, Henri Béhar, José Guilherme Merquior, and Marie Claire Bancquart; interview of Michel Butor by Georges Raillard.

DEL CASAL, JULIÁN, and JOSÉ ASUNCIÓN SILVA. *El Modernismo, precursores.* Monterey: Ediciones Sierra Madre, 1960.

DEL VALLE-INCLÁN, RAMON, et al. *El Modernismo, edición de Lily Litvak.* Madrid: Taurus, 1975.

DIJKSTRA, BRAM. *Cubism, Stieglitz and the Early Poetry of William Carlos Williams.* Princeton, N.J.: Princeton Univ. Press, 1978.

DNEPROV, VLADIMIR. "What Is Meant by 'Modernism.' " *Soviet Literature* 325 (1975): 157–63.

FAUCHEREAU, SERGE. *Expressionisme, Dada, Surréalisme et autres ismes.* Paris: Denoël, 1976.

FAULKNER, PETER. *Modernism.* London: Methuen, 1977.

FEIN, JOHN M. *Modernismo in Chilean Literature.* Durham, N.C.: Duke Univ. Press, 1965.

FELDMAN, MORTON. "After Modernism." *Art in America* 59 (1971): 68–77.

FERRERES, RAFAEL. *Verlaine y los modernistas españoles.* Madrid: Gredos, 1975.

FITCH, BRIAN, ed. *Au jour le siècle, I: Ecrivains de la modernité: Roussel, Blanchot, Bataille, Beckett, Simon.* Paris: Minard, 1981.

FOSTER, JOHN BURT. *Heirs to Dionysus: A Nietzschean Current in Literary Modernism.* Princeton, N.J.: Princeton Univ. Press, 1981.

FOSTER, STEPHEN, and RUDOLF KUENZLI, eds. *Dada Spectrum: The Dialectics of Revolt.* Madison, Wis.: Coda Press, 1979.

FRASCINA, FRANCIS, and CHARLES HARRISON, eds. *Modern Art and Modernism: A Critical Anthology.* New York: Harper & Row, 1982.

Les Futurismes I et II, Europe, nos. 551 (Mar. 1975) and 552 (Apr. 1975). I: Italy, France, Portugal, Brazil, Argentine, Mexico, Chile, ed. Charles Dobzynski. II: USSR, Russia, Poland, Germany, England, ed. Leon Robel.

GABLIK, SUZI. *Progress in Art.* New York: Rizzoli, 1976.

GARVIN, HARRY T. "Romanticism, Modernism, Postmodernism." In *Bucknell Review Annual 25.* Lewisburg, Pa.: Bucknell Univ. Press, 1980.

GIBIAN, GEORGE, and H. W. TJALSMA, eds. *Russian Modernism: Culture and the Avant-garde, 1900–1930.* Ithaca, N.Y.: Cornell Univ. Press, 1976.

GRAFF, GERALD. "The Myth of the Postmodernist Breakthrough." *TriQuarterly* 26 (1973): 383–417.

GREENBERG, CLEMENT. *Art and Culture: Critical Essays.* Boston: Beacon Press, 1961.

HABERMAS, JÜRGEN. "La modernité: un projet inachevé." *Critique* 413 (Oct. 1981): 950–67.

———. "Modernity versus Postmodernity." *New German Critique* 22 (1981): 4.

HARRISON, CHARLES. *English Art and Modernism, 1900–1939.* London: Allen Lane; Bloomington: Indiana Univ. Press, 1981.

HASSAN, IHAB. *The Dismemberment of Orpheus: Towards a Postmodern Literature,* rev. ed. Madison: Univ. of Wisconsin Press, 1982.

———. *The Right Promethean Fire.* Urbana: Univ. of Illinois Press, 1980.

HASSAN, IHAB, and SALLY HASSAN, eds. *Innovation/Renovation: New Perspectives on the Humanities.* Madison: Univ. of Wisconsin Press, 1983.

HELLER, ERICH. *The Disinherited Mind: Essays in Modern German Literature and Thought,* 4th ed. London: Bowes & Bowes, 1975.

HODIN, JOSEF PAUL. *The Dilemma of Being Modern: Essays on Art and Literature.* London: Routledge & Kegan Paul, 1956.

Selected Bibliography

HOUSTON, JOHN PORTER. *French Symbolism and the Modernist Movement: A Study of Poetic Structures*. Baton Rouge: Louisiana State Univ. Press, 1979.

HOWE, IRVING. *Modernism: Addresses, Essays, Lectures*. New York: Horizon Press, 1968.

JITRIK, NOÉ. *Las contradicciones del modernismo: productividad poetica y situacion sociologica*. Mexico, D.F.: El Colegio de Mexico, 1978.

JOSIPOVICI, GABRIEL. *The Lessons of Modernism and Other Essays*. Totowa, N.J.: Rowmann & Littlefield, 1977.

KÖHLER, MICHAEL. " 'Postmodernismus': Ein begriffsgeschictlicher überblick," *Amerikastudien* 22, no. 1 (1977): 8–18.

KOSTELANETZ, RICHARD. *The End of Intelligent Writing*. New York: Sheed & Ward, 1974.

————, ed. *Esthetics Contemporary*. Buffalo, N.Y.: Prometheus Books, 1978.

KUBAL, DAVID L. *The Consoling Intelligence: Responses to Literary Modernism*. Baton Rouge: Louisiana State Univ. Press, 1982.

KUENZLI, RUDOLF, AND STEPHEN FOSTER, eds. *Perspectives on the Avant-Garde*. Iowa City: Univ. of Iowa Press, 1985.

LANGBAUM, ROBERT. *The Modern Spirit: Essays on the Continuity of Nineteenth and Twentieth Century Literature*. New York: Oxford Univ. Press, 1970.

LA ROCCA, INÉS, ed. *El Modernismo hispanoamericano: antología*. Buenos Aires: Colihue/Hachette, 1979.

LEFEBVRE, HENRI. *Introduction à la Modernité: Preludes*. Paris: Editions de Minuit, 1962.

LEVIN, HARRY. *Memories of the Moderns*. New York: New Directions, 1980.

LODGE, DAVID. *The Modes of Modern Writing: Metaphor, Metonymy and the Typology of Modern Literature*. London: E. Arnold, 1977.

LUKACS, JOHN. *The Passing of the Modern Age*. New York: Harper & Row, 1970.

MAINER, JOSÉ-CARLOS. *Modernismo y 98*. Barcelona: Editorial Critica, 1980.

MARTINEZ, DAVID, ed. *El Modernismo en España: antología de poesiá española*. Buenos Aires: Librería del Colegio, 1966.

MARTINS, WILSON. *The Modernist Idea*. New York: New York Univ. Press, 1970.

MATLOWSKY, BERNICE. *The Modernist Trend in Spanish-American Poetry*. Washington, D.C.: Department of Cultural Affairs, Pan American Union, c. 1952.

MCCULLY, MARILYN. *Els Quatre gats: Art in Barcelona Around 1900*. Princeton, N.J.: The Art Museum, Princeton Univ., 1978.

MERQUIOR, JOSÉ GUILHERME. "Modernisme et après-modernisme dans la littérature brésilienne." In *Littérature latino-ámericaine d'aujourd-hui: Colloque de Cerisy*, ed. Jacques Leenhardt, pp. 189–200. Paris: Union Générale d'Editions, 1980.

MEYER, LEONARD B. *Music, the Arts and Ideas: Patterns and Predictions in Twentieth-Century Culture*. Chicago: Univ. of Chicago Press, 1967.

Modernism and Postmodernism: Inquiries, Reflections, and Speculations, special issue. *New Literary History* 3, no. 1 (Autumn, 1971). Articles by Ihab

Hassan, Jacques Ehrmann, Miklos Szabolci, George Rochberg, George Kateb, Michael T. Ghiselin, Michael Holquist, Louis Kampf, and Clement Greenberg.

MOURIER, PASCALINE. "Art nouveau et esprit nouveau: De la permanence de quelques thèmes modern style dans le surréalisme." In *Poésie et peinture du symbolisme au surréalisme en France et en Pologne,* ed. Elzbieta Grabska, pp. 12–138. Warsaw: Centre de Civilisation de l'Université de Varsovie, 1978.

NÄGELE, RAINER. "Modernism and Postmodernism: The Margins of Articulation." *Studies in Twentieth Century Literature* 5, no. 1 (Fall 1980): 5–25.

NIST, JOHN. *The Modernist Movement in Brazil: A Literary Study.* Austin: Univ. of Texas Press, 1967.

PACHMUSS, TEMIRA, trans. and ed. *Woman Writers in Russian Modernism: An Anthology.* Urbana: Univ. of Illinois Press, 1978.

PAINE, SYLVIA. *Beckett, Nabokov, Nin: Motives and Modernism.* Port Washington, N.Y.: Kennikat Press, 1981.

PALMIER, JEAN MICHEL. *Berliner requiem.* Paris: Editions Galilée, 1976.

————. *L'Expressionisme comme révolte.* Paris: Payot, 1978.

PARET, PETER. *The Berlin Secession.* Cambridge: Belknap Press of Harvard Univ. Press, 1980.

PAZ, OCTAVIO. *Children of the Mire.* Cambridge: Harvard Univ. Press, 1974.

PERKINS, DAVID. *A History of Modern Poetry: From the 1890's to Pound, Eliot and Yeats.* Cambridge: Harvard Univ. Press, 1976.

PERLOFF, MARJORIE. *Poetics of Indeterminacy: From Rimbaud to Cage.* Princeton, N.J.: Princeton Univ. Press, 1981.

PLEYNET, MARCELIN. *Art et littérature.* Paris: Editions du Seuil, 1977.

POIRIER, RICHARD. "The Difficulties of Modernism and the Modernism of Difficulty." In *Images and Ideas in American Culture: The Function of Criticism,* ed. Arthur Edelstein. Hanover, N.H.: Brandeis Univ. Press, 1979.

PONDROM, CYRENA N. *The Road from Paris: French Influence on English Poetry 1900–1920.* Cambridge: Cambridge Univ. Press, 1974.

PRADO, YAN DE ALMEIDA. *A grande Semana de Arte Moderna.* São Paulo: Livraria Editora Ltda. Edart, 1976.

READ, HERBERT. *The Philosophy of Modern Arts.* London: Faber & Faber, 1952.

REMBERT, VIRGINIA, ROBERT R. WRIGHT, RALPH EBERLY, VIRGIL JAMES, BLANCHE THEBORN, and BETTYE CALDWELL. *The Here and Now: Distinguished Professor Lecture Series.* Little Rock: Univ. of Arkansas, 1980.

RIVAS, PIERRE, ed. *Le Modernisme Brésilien,* special issue. *Europe* no. 599 (Mar. 1979). Articles by Pierre Rivas, Frederic Mauro, Mario da Silva Brito, Wilson Martins, Haroldo de Campos, Pierre Hourcade, Serge Fauchereau, Gilberto Mendonça Teles, José Alderado Castello, Teles Porto Ancona Lopez, Jean Duvignaud, Aracy Amaral, and L. H. Correa de Azevedo, and translated texts by Brazilian Modernist writers Oswald de Andrade, Mario de Andrade, Manuel Bandeira, and Jorge de Lima.

ROSEMONT, FRANKLIN, ed. *André Breton, What is Surrealism? Selected Writings.* Monad Press, 1978; dist. by Pathfinder Press, New York.

Selected Bibliography

RUSSELL, JOHN. *The Meanings of Modern Art.* New York: Harper & Row, 1981.

SCHORSKE, CARL E. *Fin de siècle Vienna.* New York: Knopf, 1980.

SCHULMANN, IVAN. *Genesis del Modernismo.* St. Louis, Mo.: Washington Univ. Press, 1968.

SHATTUCK, ROGER. "After the Avant-Garde." *New York Review of Books,* 12 Mar. 1970, pp. 41–47.

————. *The Banquet Years: The Arts in France 1855–1918: Alfred Jarry, Henri Rousseau, Eric Satie, Guillaume Apollinaire.* New York: Harcourt, Brace, 1958.

SOMVILLE, LÉON. *Devanciers du Surréalisme.* Genève: Droz, 1971.

SPENDER, STEPHEN. *The Struggle of the Modern.* Berkeley and Los Angeles: Univ. of California Press, 1963.

SULTAN, STANLEY. *Ulysses, the Waste Land, and Modernism: A Jubilee Study.* Port Washington, N.Y.: Kennikat Press, 1977.

WASSON, RICHARD. "From Priest to Prometheus: Culture and Criticism in the Post-Modern Period." *Journal of Modern Literature* 3 (1974): 1188–1202.

WEINZVERL, ERIKA. Modernismus—Seminar (Salzburg, 1974). *Der Modernismus. Beitrage zu seiner Erforschung.* Graz, Wein, Köln: Verlag Styria, 1974.

WEISBERGER, JEAN, ed. *Les Avant-gardes littéraires au XXe siècle. I. Histoire. II. Théorie.* Vols. 4 and 5 of *A Comparative History of Literatures in European Languages.* Sponsored by the International Comparative Literature Association, 1984.

WHITE, ERDMUNTE WENZEL. *Les années vingt au Brésil: Le Modernisme et l'avant-garde internationale.* Paris: Editions Hispaniques, 1977.

WOHL, ROBERT. *The Generation of 1914.* Cambridge: Harvard Univ. Press, 1979.

YOUNG, ALAN. *Dada and After: Extremist Modernism and English Literature.* Manchester: Manchester Univ. Press, 1981.

YURKIEVICH, SAÚL. *Celebración del modernismo.* Barcelona: Tusquets, 1976.

Contributors

ANNA BALAKIAN   Professor of French and Comparative Literature, New York University, Chairman, Department of Comparative Literature. Past President, American Comparative Literature Association, currently Vice-President, International Comparative Literature Association. Author of *Literary Origins of Surrealism; Surrealism: The Road to the Absolute; The Symbolist Movement: A Critical Appraisal;* and *André Breton: Magus of Surrealism;* editor and chief contributor to collaborative writing of *The Symbolist Movement in the Literature of European Languages,* published 1982 by the Academiai Kiado, Budapest, Anna Balakian has also published many articles on comparative poetics, most recently "Relativism in the Arts and the Road to the Absolute" in *Relativism in the Arts,* ed. Betty Jean Craige (Athens: Univ. of Georgia Press, 1983), articles and reviews of French poetry, the modern novel, and comparative literature theory in scholarly journals, and numerous entries in encyclopedias.

CHARLES BAXTER   Associate Professor of English, Wayne State University. Poet and short-story writer, received his Ph.D. from SUNY, Buffalo, in 1974. Charles Baxter has published two volumes of poetry (*Chameleon,* 1970, and *The South Dakota Guidebook,* 1974), critical essays in *Journal of Modern Literature, West Coast Review, Novel, Boundary, The Georgia Review,* and *The Centennial Review,* as well as fiction and poetry in *The Antioch Review, The Atlantic Monthly, Epoch, The Iowa Review, Kayak, The Minnesota Review, The Michigan Quarterly Review, New England Review, Northwest Review, Poetry, Poetry Northwest, Prairie Schooner,* and *Shenandoah,* among many others.

MARC J. BENSIMON   Professor of French, University of California, Los Angeles. A scholar of the Renaissance and the twentieth century, as well as a postmodern painter, Marc Bensimon combines his practice of the visual arts with his research interests to reflect upon the notion of modernity and postmodernity in the arts and literature. His publications, which include three books, twenty-three research articles, and twenty-nine review articles, range from Jean Vauquelin de la Fresnaie and Ronsard to Sartre and Marcel Duchamp.

RUSSELL A. BERMAN   Assistant Professor, Department of German Studies, Stanford University. Russell Berman's book *Between Fontane*

Contributors

and Tucholsky: Literary Criticism and the Public Sphere in Imperial Germany appears in the New York University Ottendorfer Series. His current research interests include literary criticism in the Weimar Republic and the sociology of the modern novel.

JAY BOCHNER   Professor of English, Department of English, Université de Montréal. Educated in France and New York, he received his Ph.D. from Columbia University in 1969. Author of *Blaise Cendrars: Discovery and Re-creation* (1978); coeditor of special issues of *Studies in Twentieth Century Literature* (1979). Articles in *Points de Vue, Revue de Littérature Comparée, Texas Studies in Literature and Language, Calamus, Exploration, Revue des Lettres Modernes, Studies in Twentieth-Century Literature, Canadian Review of American Studies, Feuille de Routes,* and *Blaise Cendrars, vingt ans après.* Jay Bochner is presently preparing work on the early foundations of Modernism in New York.

MATEI CALINESCU   Professor of Comparative Literature and West European Studies at Indiana University, Bloomington. His book *Faces of Modernity: Avant-Garde, Decadence, Kitsch* (Indiana University Press) appeared in 1977. He is at work on a larger study of postmodernism, chapters of which have appeared in such books as *Innovation/Renovation,* ed. Ihab and Sally Hassan (Madison: University of Wisconsin Press, 1983) and *The End of the World,* ed. Saul Friedländer et al. (New York: Holmes and Meier, 1984). He has also published several articles on Mircea Eliade and plans to assimilate them into a book on the relationship between Eliade's theory of myth and his fictional work.

MARY ANN CAWS   Distinguished Professor of French and Comparative Literature, Hunter College and Graduate School, City University of New York, 1983 President of the Modern Language Association, a Guggenheim Fellow, Fulbright Traveling Fellow, N.E.H. Fellow, editor of *Le Siècle éclaté* (Paris, Minard) since 1974 and coeditor of *Dada/Surrealism,* Professor Caws is a renowned specialist in twentieth-century poetry. She has published translations of poems of André Breton, Pierre Reverdy, and René Char, edited *Poems and Prose of Stephane Mallarmé, Poems of St.-John Perse, Poetry from Dada to Tel Quel,* and *The Prose Poem in France,* as well as a collection of essays on French thought. The list of her major books includes: *Surrealism and the Literary Imagination; The Poetry of Dada and Surrealism; The Surrealist Voice of Robert Desnos; The Presence of René Char; André Breton; La Main de Pierre Reverdy; "L'Oeuvre filante" de René Char; The Eye in the Text: Essays on Perception, Mannerist to Modern; The Metapoetics of the Passage; Architextures from Surrealism to the Present; Yves Bonnefoy.*

MARGARET C. DAVIES   Personal Professor, Department of French Studies, University of Reading, England. A graduate of Somerville College, Oxford, and Docteur de L'Université de Paris, Professor Davies was a lecturer at Westfield College, University of London, until 1965 and since then has been at the University of Reading, where she became Personal Professor in 1975. Her publications include: *Apollinaire,* a critical biography; *Colette,* a critical biography; *Une Saison en Enfer, analyse du texte;* and a novel, *Two Gold Rings.* She has also published numerous articles on French literature of the nineteenth and twentieth centuries, with particular reference to Rimbaud, Apollinaire, Valéry, Baudelaire, and Gracq, and to topics of general aesthetic interest such as the poetic imagination, the concept of modernity, and painting and the poetic image.

MICHEL DÉCAUDIN   Docteur dès lettres, Doctor Honoris Causa of the University of Gand, Professor of Literature, University of the "Sorbonne Nouvelle," Paris. From his first major publication, *La crise des valeurs symbolistes* (1960), to the latest, *Anthologie de la poésie française du XXe siècle: De Claudel à Char* (Gallimard, 1983), Michel Décaudin has centered his scholarly activity on various expressions of "modernité" in French literature. The editor of the works of Apollinaire (the two volumes of the Pléiade are particularly noteworthy among a number of others), Verlaine, and Rimbaud, he has authored, coauthored, and edited over twenty volumes of critical studies on Apollinaire and directed several series on twentieth-century literature in the *Revue des Lettres Modernes* (Paris: Minard) and the *Cahiers du XXe siècle*, of which issue number 5 was devoted to "la modernité."

MARTIN ESSLIN   Professor of Drama, Stanford University. Born in Budapest, Hungary, educated in Vienna, he studied English and philosophy at Vienna University and is a graduate of the Max Reinhardt Academy of Drama, Vienna. Left Austria after the invasion by Hitler, settled in England. Worked for the British Broadcasting Corporation (BBC) from 1940 to 1977, during the last fourteen years as Head of the Radio Drama Department. Since 1977 professor of drama at Stanford, where he spends winter and spring quarters of each year, he also acts as dramaturg of the Magic Theater, San Francisco. Publications include: *Brecht: The Man and His Work* (1959); *The Theatre of the Absurd* (1961); *Pinter: The Playwright* (4th ed. 1982); *Antonin Artaud* (1977); *An Anatomy of Drama* (1977); *Mediations* (1980); *The Age of Television* (1982).

CLEMENT GREENBERG   Clement Greenberg is America's most eminent critic of modern art. His career as editor, writer, critic, and cultural theorist spans forty years. During the early 1940s, he was an editor of *Partisan Review* and, from later in that decade until the mid-fifties, an editor of *Commentary.* The bulk of his art criticism between 1941 and 1954 appeared in *The Nation* and *Partisan Review.* At the same time, he has been a frequent contributor to numerous periodicals, including *Art Digest, Art in America, Art International, Art and Literature, Art News, Arts Magazine* and *Studio International.* He has written monographs on Joan Miró (1948) and Hans Hofmann (1961). Many of his critical essays were collected and published under the title *Art and Culture* in 1961, in a volume which has been acclaimed the most influential work of art criticism ever published in America. Presently Clement Greenberg lives in Norwich, New York, and remains active as a critic, panelist, and speaker.

HARVEY GROSS   Professor of comparative literature and English, State University of New York at Stony Brook. A 1981–82 Fellow of the National Humanities Center in Research Triangle Park, North Carolina, he

Contributors

also has been the recipient of a Fulbright Fellowship to Austria, and fellowships and grants from the American Council of Learned Societies, the Rockefeller Foundation, and the National Endowment for the Humanities to direct a summer seminar entitled "Toward a Theory of Modernism." Among his books related to Modernism are *The Contrived Corridor: History and Fatality in Modern Literature* (1971); *Sound and Form in Modern Poetry* (2d ed. 1968); *The Structure of Verse: Modern Essays on Prosody* (3d rev. ed. 1980). He is also the author of a volume of poems, *Plans for an Orderly Apocalypse.*

IHAB HASSAN   Vilas Research Professor of English and comparative literature, University of Wisconsin, Milwaukee. Twice a Guggenheim fellow and three times a Fulbright lecturer in France and Japan, Professor Hassan has been a visiting scholar at the Woodrow Wilson International Center for Scholars and the Rockefeller Bellagio Study Center. He has given over 250 lectures on modern culture and literature throughout the United States, Asia, and Europe. From his first publication, *Radical Innocence* (1961), on the contemporary American novel, to his most recent reflections on cultural change, Ihab Hassan has worked toward establishing distinctions between modernism and postmodernism and developing a paracritical discourse that affirms a larger role for the critical imagination as it attempts to capture the shifting modes of the postmodern consciousness. In addition to over two hundred articles and reviews, some of his major books are: *The Dismemberment of Orpheus: Towards a Postmodern Literature* (1971, rev. 1982), *Paracriticisms: Seven Speculations of the Times* (1975), and *The Right Promethean Fire: Imagination, Science and Cultural Change* (1980). His most recent work, coedited with Sally Hassan, is *Innovation/Renovation: New Perspectives on the Humanities* (1983).

RENÉE RIESE HUBERT   Professor of French and comparative literature, University of California, Irvine. Professor Hubert has received grants from the American Association of University Women, the Guggenheim Foundation, the American Philosophical Society, the National Endowment for the Humanities, and the Creative Arts Institute of the University of California. Her poetical works published in France include *Le Berceau d'Eve* (1957), *Plumes et Pinceaux* (1960), and *Chants Funèbres* (1964). She has published numerous articles on Apollinaire, Breton, Masson, Giacometti, Ernst, Éluard, Jacob, Miró, Magritte, Michaux, Klee, Malraux, and Picasso, among many other writers and painters, in journals such as *Comparative Literature Studies, Revue d'esthétique, Lettres modernes, Sub-stance, Contemporary Literature, New York Literary Forum,* and *Dada/Surrealism.*

JO-ANNA ISAAK   Currently a member of the Department of English at the University of California, Santa Barbara, Jo-Anna Isaak recently completed a Ph.D. thesis at the University of Toronto entitled "Avant-garde Art and the Avant-garde Texts of James Joyce, Gertrude Stein and the English Vorticists." The thesis is an investigation into the semiotics of literature and the visual arts. Her research into the Russian avant-garde took her to the Soviet Union in 1981 and her accounts of the *Moscow-Paris 1900–1930* appeared in *Art Monthly* and *Artforum.* Her most recent publications include "Joyce's *Ulysses* and the Cubist Esthetic," in *Mosaic;* "Our Mother Tongue," in *The Post-Partum*

Document (London: Routledge & Kegan Paul, 1983) and a review article on the French Canadian artist Paul Emile Borduas in *RACAR: Revue d'art canadienne/Canadian Art Review*.

CLAUDE LEROY   Maître-assistant, University of Paris X-Nanterre. "Agrégé de lettres modernes," Claude Leroy has published over thirty articles, particularly on Blaise Cendrars and avant-garde movements, in journals such as *Europe, Littérature, Revue des Sciences Humaines,* and *Cahiers du MNAM*. Director of special issues for *Europe* ("Blaise Cendrars," 1976, and "Cubisme et littérature," 1982) and the *Cahiers du XXᵉ Siècle* ("La parodie," 1979), editor of *Blaise Cendrars, vingt ans après* (1983) (the proceedings of the 1981 international colloquium he organized at the University of Paris X), he is currently preparing a Doctorat d'Etat thesis on *"Ecriture* and Pseudonymity in Blaise Cendrars."

ROBERT P. MORGAN   Professor of music, University of Chicago. Noted composer and musicologist, Robert P. Morgan has had numerous works performed throughout the country, among which are Symphony for Orchestra and *Convergence* (1966); three pieces as varied as *Interplay* for flute, oboe and bass, *Momentum* for orchestra, and *Study for Computer* (1972); *Repercussions* (1976), *Correspondences* for cello and percussion (1977), and Concerto for Flute, Oboe, and String Orchestra (1981). Equally active in the field of musicology, he is the recipient of a 1983–84 grant from the National Endowment for the Humanities to study formal structure in large-scale instrumental music of the nineteenth century. He is also working on a book on transformations in formal structure in nineteenth-century music, has written a book on twentieth-century music, and has published a large number of articles, monographs, and chapters in books on contemporary composers such as Stravinsky, Varese, Ives, Mahler, Stockhausen, Carter, and Schoenberg, as well as on musical theory. Among his most recent articles we note "The Theory and Analysis of Tonal Rhythm," *Musical Quarterly* (October 1978), "On the Analysis of Recent Music" *Critical Inquiry* (Autumn 1977), and "Musical Time/Musical Space" *Critical Inquiry* (Spring 1980). "The Implications of Post-Tonality: Music in a New Age," is to appear soon in a volume of essays on Postmodernism.

ROBERT WOHL   Professor of history, University of California, Los Angeles. A historian of modern European culture and politics, Robert Wohl is the author of *French Communism in the Making, 1914–1924* (1955) and *The Generation of 1914* (1979), which won the 1982 American Book Award for history in paperback. He is presently working on a cultural history of European and American aviation during the first half of the twentieth century.

Notes on the Editors

MONIQUE CHEFDOR Professor of French and comparative literature at Scripps College, principal organizer of the Claremont Colleges Comparative Literature Conference on Modernism, and editorial committee coordinator for this volume. Her major publications include *In Search of Marcel Proust* (ed., 1973), *Complete Post-Cards from the Americas* (tr. and intro., 1976), *Blaise Cendrars* (1980), articles in *Europe, Studies in Twentieth-Century Literature, Le Magazine Littéraire,* the proceedings of the Tenth Triennial ICLA Congress and *Blaise Cendrars, vingt ans après* (1983).

RICARDO QUINONES Professor of comparative and English literature at Claremont McKenna College, co-organizer of the Conference on Modernism. He is the author of *The Renaissance Discovery of Time* (1972), *Dante Alighieri* (1979; reprint, 1985), which was nominated for the MLA Marraro prize, and *Mapping Literary Modernism: Time and Development* (Princeton, N.J.: Princeton Univ. Press, 1985), a sequel to the earlier Renaissance volume.

ALBERT WACHTEL Professor of English literature at Pitzer College, NDEA and Creative Arts Institute Fellow, and Danforth Associate. His fiction and criticism have appeared in the *Journal of Aesthetics and Art Criticism, Moment Magazine, Modern Fiction Studies, Review of Contemporary Fiction, The Southern Review,* and *Spectrum,* among others.

Index

Aalto, Alvar, 71
Abbaye de Créteil (Groupe de l'), 149
Abrams, M. H., 308
Abstractionism, 37, 107, 161
Action Française, 84
Adams, Henry, 208
Adorno, Theodor W., 82, 83, 129, 131, 139, 146
—*Philosophy of Modern Music*, 129
Aesop, 25
Alain (alias Emile Chartier), 85
Alexandrine, 60
Allais, Alphonse, 31
Almanach, Vermot, 31
Altieri, Charles, 311
Amerikastudien, 3
Apollinaire, Guillaume, 27, 28, 62, 70, 75, 107, 114, 146, 148, 149, 151, 155, 157, 158, 212, 219, 250
—*Alcools*, 152, 155; "Aubade," 147; *Le Brasier*, 148; *La Chanson du Mal Aimé*, 146; *La Chirurgie Esthétique*, 157; *Les Fenêtres*, 152; *Les Fiançailles*, 148, 149; "Lettre-Ocean," 154; *Les Mammelles de Tiresias*, 62, 147; *La Mandoline, l'Oeillet et le Bambou*, 156; *La Montre*, 155; *Lundi Rue Christine*, 153; *Le Poète Assassiné*, 157; *Rhineland Poems*, 147; *Traitement Thyroïdien*, 157; *Les Trois Vertus Plastiques*, 148; *Le Voyageur*, 150; *Zaporogue Cossacks*, 147; *Zone*, 151
Apollinairean sounds, 242

Apollonian, 8, 262, 309
Aragon, Louis, 76, 80, 251
—*Anicet*, 251
Archer, The, 163, 165
Arenas, Braulio, 118
Arendt, Hannah, 318
Aristotelian rules, 82
Armory Show, 183, 200
Art and Production, 165
Art for art's sake, 18, 79
Artaud, Antonin, 59, 109, 242, 309
Arvator, Boris, 165, 168
Ash-can school, 192
Aurier, Albert, 4, 31
—*Le Moderniste Illustré*, 4, 31
Avant-garde(s), 1, 4, 27, 54, 67, 72, 80, 84, 106, 111, 118, 168, 169, 311; movement, 70, 95
Avant-gardism, 308
Avant-gardist, 81, 266

Babel, 1, 25
Babylone, 3
Bach, John Sebastian, 46
Bakhtin, Mikhail, 15, 79, 90, 91
—*Problems of Dostoevsky's Poetics*, 90
Balakian, Anna, 4, 106, 108, 111
Ball, Hugo, 106, 111, 112, 113, 114, 116, 121, 122, 123, 125
—*Das Flug auf der Zeit*, 113; Karawane, 106; *Mallarmés Blumen*, 123; "Orpheus," 124
Ballets Russes, 164
Balzac, Honoré de, 90
Bang, Hermann, 70